CONTRIBUTION TO ECONOMETRICS:

JOHN DENIS SARGAN

Volume 1

CONTRIBUTIONS
TO ECONOMETRICS:

JOHN DENIS SARGAN
London School of Economics

———— · ————

EDITED WITH AN INTRODUCTION BY
ESFANDIAR MAASOUMI
*Indiana University,
Bloomington and the University of California,
Santa Barbara, USA*

Volume 1

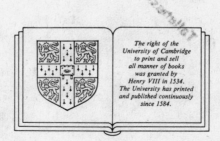

The right of the
University of Cambridge
to print and sell
all manner of books
was granted by
Henry VIII in 1534.
The University has printed
and published continuously
since 1584.

CAMBRIDGE UNIVERSITY PRESS

*Cambridge
New York   New Rochelle
Melbourne   Sydney*

Published by the Press Syndicate of the University of Cambridge
The Pitt Building, Trumpington Street, Cambridge CB2 1RP
32 East 57th Street, New York, NY 10022, USA
10 Stamford Road, Oakleigh, Melbourne 3166, Australia

First published 1988

Printed in Great Britain at the University Press, Cambridge

British Library cataloguing in publicaton data
Sargan, John Denis
  Contributions to econometrics.
  Vol. 1
  1. Econometrics
  I. Title II. Maasoumi, Esfandiar
  330'.028   HB139

Library of Congress cataloguing-in-publication data
Sargan, John Denis.
  Contributions to econometrics.
  1. Econometrics. I. Maasoumi, Esfandiar, 1950–
II. Title.
HB139.S37 1987   330'.028   87-6328

ISBN 0 521 32570 6

MC

CONTENTS

FOREWORD

Esfandiar Maasoumi has done a great service for the econometrics profession by making twenty of Denis Sargan's seminal and penetrating contributions to economic theory and econometrics available to a wide audience. Even more valuable to the profession is to put into print an additional six research papers that have hitherto gone unpublished. The contents of these two volumes represent the accomplishments of one of the most distinguished econometricians of our generation.

Denis has ranged quite widely in econometrics, statistics, and economic theory, but his greatest concentration of work has been devoted to the understanding of simultaneous equation models and the problems of statistical inference. Although systems of simultaneous equations have been studied for more than forty years, it is only more recently, with the availability of plentiful data and efficient computational facilities, that such schemes have been used substantively for modelling, analyzing, and forecasting macro-economic processes. These applications have called for deeper understanding of the econometric models and methodology. While he has investigated various aspects, Denis has focused particularly on asymptotic expansions of the distributions of estimators and test criteria, pursuing this interest from the early 1960s to the present.

Some theorems, such as the existence of specified moments of certain estimators, are genuinely finite sample results. However, in general the exact finite sample distributions derived by various authors as indicated in the introductions have been intractable and have not shed enough light on the properties of estimators and test procedures. On the other hand, the standard asymptotic normal and chi-square distributions are too crude to distinguish among many methods. More information is yielded by asymptotic expansions, which, although derived in terms of limit theorems, serve as approximations to the exact distributions. As such, they can be used for evaluating sampling variability, approximating significance levels, and comparing alternative procedures. In fact, they help to analyze each finite sample distributions, both mathematical and numerical.

Among other aspects of simultaneous equations models that have been treated by Denis are estimation procedures, identification questions, and dynamic specifications and properties. The last has brought Denis into the study of time series procedures, including spectral methods and serial correlation analysis. The editor has summarized many of these investigations in the introduction to the second volume. It is interesting to note that in spite of the fact that many of the topics studied are statistical in nature, virtually all of the papers have appeared in econometric journals.

The quantity of Denis's published professional output has been relatively small as measured in terms of number of papers (less than 50), or in terms of pages or weight of reprints. In part, this limitation is due to his way of conducting research. He investigates his problems in depth and thoroughly; he mulls over them instead of rushing into print. Years may pass between his solution of problems, as indicated by the dates of abstracts and addresses, and the printed work; in fact, some papers might not have seen the light of day if the editor had not pried them loose.

Many of the papers, in particular the ones reprinted here, contain an abundance of ideas and treat different aspects of the problems. Because many propositions are given in considerable generality and hence intricate notation and complicated proofs are involved, some of the papers may be difficult to read; the author does not shirk algebraic details. However, as penetrating studies, full of insight and suggestions, they bear careful and detailed study.

Denis has been very generous with his ideas and thoughts. Not all of them come out in his own publications; many of them appear in the writings of his students and colleagues. The list of the 34 Ph D dissertations sponsored by Denis over the nineteen years 1966 to 1985 is impressive in number, variety of topics, and caliber of students. (What a loss to British education is his early retirement!) During the academic year 1974–75, I visited the London School of Economics and participated in the weekly Econometrics Workshop that Denis sponsored. The assemblage of students and colleagues, in my opinion, constituted the most active and productive group of econometricians at that time. Denis contributed frequent original, provocative, and insightful comments.

These two volumes will preserve permanently many of his contributions to our field. I look forward to their appearance.

Theodore W. Anderson

Professor of Economics and
Statistics, Stanford University
December 5, 1986

ESFANDIAR MAASOUMI

———— · ————

1 DENIS SARGAN AND HIS SEMINAL CONTRIBUTIONS TO ECONOMIC AND ECONOMETRIC THEORY

This is the first volume of selections from John Denis Sargan's contributions to econometrics and economics. The papers are intended more as examples than any normative ordering of his many pathbreaking and seminal contributions. The collection is also a tribute to him on the occasion of his retirement at the London School of Economics and Political Science which he joined in 1963. It is intended to make some of his previously published and several important unpublished papers better known and more accessible to all econometricians, statisticians, economists and their students.

Since Sargan's is an early retirement taken by him at a most productive phase of his distinguished career, the present chapter and another in Volume 2 will necessarily be somewhat tentative and not a definitive or final statement on a lifetime of contributions. As was put very aptly by Werner Hildenbrand on a similar occasion: 'The opening address on the occasion of an important retrospective of a great artist is not expected to include a detailed analysis of all exhibits. Rather, the artist and his work are set in their context in the history of art; those features that characterise his work are highlighted and related to earlier and contemporary contributions [1].' While I too will try to do this, the lack of a well-developed, well-researched and documented history of *this* art is currently a serious handicap in the development of econometrics. Indeed, this volume itself may be regarded as containing several of the building blocks for and a contribution toward a history of econometrics. In view of this I have also tried to bring out the breadth of Sargan's contributions to economics by including (i) a bibliographical appendix of about 40 Ph.D. theses directed by him at the LSE, (ii) a more or less chronological list of *all* papers published by Denis Sargan, and (iii) reprints of three of his early contributions among several in the area of 'economic theory'.

All of Sargan's selected contributions to the theory of finite sample distributions are included in Volume 2, as are several other 'miscellaneous' papers on such topics as spectral estimation, missing observations and continuous time models. The present volume is intended to cover a wide range of contributions to both economic and econometric theories. In view of this, the papers on economic theory are followed by a collection of contributions in empirical and theoretical econometrics which address (i) general problems of estimation and testing in dynamic and simultaneous equations models, and (ii) issues of modelling for wages and prices and inference in particular specifications of the corresponding models. The first volume ends with a collection of seminal papers on the definition and characterization of the 'identification problem' in dynamic and simultaneous equation models.

It is fair and helpful to say that many people find Sargan's papers mathematically demanding. The analytical sophistication is, however, a direct consequence of the generality of the models and the results of these papers. An almost total lack of 'salesmanship' in these papers (partly reflecting his self-effacing modesty) puts the *casual* reader at a disadvantage, and means that the benefit to a reader is at least proportional to the extent of his (her) synthesis and command of the subject area. In time the typical reader can discover the depth of the author's appreciation for the practically important considerations and conditions, and for the degree of generality that explains the enduring relevance of Sargan's results to empirical and theoretical econometrics. Mathematics, then, is a necessary tool in these papers, with a role that is intentionally secondary but consequential, both in resolving the immediate problem and in opening the way for consideration of many related or deeper problems. For this reason we find that many of these papers were well ahead of their time, and continue to be very important not just for the currency of their subject matter, but also for the wealth of technical tools which will be valuable to the reader in his/her own research.

Making sense of problems, concepts and tools, and communicating the findings and the general solutions to economists and econometricians is thus a distinct feature of Sargan's work. This is prominent and easily detectable in his first nine or so published papers, chiefly on economic theory and its basic concepts and tools. In this period (up to 1958) Sargan can be seen as a mathematician serving economics with a firm grasp of the concepts in both fields. He had earlier (1944) passed the Cambridge mathematics tripos with first class honours. After his service as a junior scientific officer with the RAF coastal command (1943–46), he returned to St John's College, Cambridge, this time receiving the MA (1947) and a BA in Economics (1948). In the first period at Leeds University (1948–58) he published many of his economic theory papers such as, 'A new approach to the general distribution problem', 'An illustration of duopoly', 'Subjective probability and the economist', 'The period of production', 'The distribution of wealth', and, 'The instability of the Leontief dynamic model [2].' Sargan spent the years 1958–59 and 1959–60 in the USA at Minnesota and Chicago, respectively, at which time two of his papers (reprinted here) appeared on instrumental variables estimation. While not his first papers in 'econometrics', these publications revealed Sargan as an outstanding econometrician with rare skills and a grasp of what is relevant in statistical analysis of economic models. At least from this point on it is misleading to regard dates of publication as reliable indications of what Sargan was working on during a given period of time. Those who have been close observers, students and associates, know how deliberate, thorough and comprehensive his investigations can be. Time seems to offer no threat, with the timeliness of his contributions evidently arising from his recognition of important problems and the generality of his results. Every paper reports on a research program of several years involving and nourishing many students and colleagues. As an example, while his first full paper on finite sample distribution theory appeared in print in 1971, the abstract of a paper on this topic in a 1964 issue of *Econometrica* reveals his already well-developed concern for the practically important finite sample properties of econometric methods in the late 1950s and the early 1960s; see Sargan (1958b and 1964c). In the meantime such pathbreaking and seminal papers as Sargan (1961 and 1964a) appeared in print and introduced significant advances in the treatment of dynamic econometric models [3].

A categorisation of each of Sargan's papers into different areas is difficult and perhaps even unnecessary. Frequently each paper is a comprehensive account of a problem, the corresponding estimation methods and their properties, tests of hypotheses and other related issues, thus often involving several areas in a single paper. Broadly speaking, the areas to which he has contributed are economic theory, estimation theory in general and in simultaneous and/or dynamic models with serially correlated errors in particular, empirical studies of wage–price inflation and consumption functions, identification problems, finite sample distribution theory, and a whole host of important 'miscellaneous' contributions to (e.g.) continuous time models, spectral estimation methods, and missing data problems. The remainder of this chapter summarises his contributions to each of these areas, excluding the last two which are described in Volume 2.

Three papers in economic theory are reproduced here: two on the period of production, and one on the distribution of wealth. The period of production had played an important role in economics since Ricardo. A careful definition of this concept is required in analysing such issues as the relation between the 'capital' input and the output, or the adjustment time taken by a producer facing changes in production or demand relationships.

In most real-life situations where inputs and outputs are spread over time, definition of period of production must be based on a 'mean time'. Sargan (1955), Chapter 2 of this volume, addresses these important questions. In calculating these weighted time means, Sargan's choice of the required weights is the discounted value of the production at any point in time. (These were also used in Hicks' definition of the 'average period of payments' in his *Value and Capital*, 2nd edn, p. 186.) Sargan's definition of the period of production is useful for the analysis of the effect on the long-run equilibrium prices of interest rate fluctuations, as he demonstrates for both the single and multiproduct firms. Unlike Hicks' 'average', Sargan's mean time has the usual properties of averages (responding to a criticism of Samuelson) and is not indeterminate in the case of a marginal stream [4]. Several special production processes are analysed in the same contribution. The discussion of the difficulties arising from monopolistic and oligopolistic markets is characteristically forthright and explicit.

In a later note, Sargan (1956) introduces a set of discounted time measures which include his earlier measure of production period and are the discounted versions of Blyth's time measures which are computed from the cumulants of the frequency distribution function of the (undiscounted) expected value of output at time t. He also gives a subtle conceptual condition under which his time measures for a *marginal firm* would be the same as Blyth's measures for a production 'process'.

In 'The distribution of wealth' (reprinted here in Chapter 3), Sargan establishes the conditions under which the distribution of economic variables will be approximately log-normal. To do this he significantly expands and extends the pioneering work of Champernowne [5] on income distribution. Sargan considers a dynamic mechanism for the generation (over time) of the wealth distribution. This dynamic relationship is not an arbitrary random process and is made up of four plausible causes of change in the wealth distribution: the setting up of new households, the disappearance of existing households with some wealth passing to others, transfers (gifts) between households, and saving and capital gains. Sargan's study of this type of generating mechanism is also more general than Champernowne's in that he considers wealth (and other variables) as *continuously* distributed. This greater realism opens the way for a deeper discussion of solutions to integro-differential equations using Fourier transforms, and brings out the rather restrictive homogeneity and independence assumptions which are required for log-normal solutions. Sargan (1957a) shows that under a somewhat weaker condition of 'almost-homogeneity' the wealth distribution is approximately log-normal. This confirmed the earlier informal results of Gibrat, Kalecki and Rutherford, and some later observations for the UK data [6]. This analysis also clarified how a lack of 'almost-homogeneity' in Champernowne's linear dynamic mechanism was responsible for his conclusion that the (income) distribution will be approximately Paretian. While this method of generating and estimating income or wealth distributions is no longer *the* standard method, it continues to be popular, particularly in discussions of mobility. For instance, see Shorrocks (1976) [7]. Also a log-normal income (or welath) distribution with 'Paretian tails' is an enduring part of the folklore of the 'inequality' literature. The aforementioned papers by Sargan consistently demonstrate a concern for and a mastery of dynamic processes of interest in economics, features which are also evident in his paper and discussion on 'The instability of Leontief dynamic model' (1958*a*). Sargan's interest in formal economic theory during this early period would have a decidedly profound effect on his work in econometrics. The *relevance* of this work to empirical economics, in my opinion its most important and consistently manifested feature, owes much to this early experience. Specifically, Sargan continued the aforementioned work on dynamic models by considering the statistical evaluation of such models and by developing empirical models which are also contributions to the economic debate on wages and prices, and the role played by the 'Phillips Curve' and its variants in that debate (see the discussion below). The interest in systems of simultaneous equations and the corresponding statistical problems also reflects the influence of this period of Sargan's work, a period marked by almost universal optimism regarding the role of estimated economic models in the assessment and development of economic policy. Sargan's interest in economic theory has continued informally to the present. It has found unmistakable expression in some publications to be discussed below and in a majority of about 40 Ph.D. theses completed under his supervision on such topics as systems of demand equations, inventory decision models in the UK, consumption and production functions. But Sargan's own published works since 1957 are more conveniently and properly regarded as contributions to econometrics, and it is generally in the choice of the underlying questions and models of these papers that one can see the clear influence of his earlier interest in formal economic theory.

ECONOMETRIC THEORY

A significant group of Sargan's papers deals with numerous problems of estimation and testing in models where the explanatory variables are correlated with the random errors (shocks), including errors-in-variables, linear simultaneous equations, and particularly linear dynamic systems with serially correlated errors. In the event, the techniques proposed by Sargan and the tools he introduced have proved their general applicability in 'other' models and provided very suggestive interpretations for different techniques.

Sargan (1958*b*) on the method of instrumental variables (IV) is an acknowledged classic. The origins of 'the IV method' can be traced back to H. Working and Wright in work that precedes the better-known contributions by Reiersöl, Geary and Durbin. It is no exaggeration to say, however, that the IV method as we know it today and its properties begin with Sargan's paper. He demonstrates the general applicability of the IV method whenever 'explanatory' variables are correlated with random errors or shocks. The consistency of the method is demonstrated and, perhaps more importantly, the question of efficient estimation is resolved by deriving and minimising the asymptotic variance of the IV estimator when there are more IV's than are needed. Sargan's treatment also includes an IV interpretation of the maximum likelihood estimator (for LIML), later given for FIML in Hausman (1976) [8], a test of significance and its relation to the ML-based test, and some insightful remarks (based on work not included in the paper) concerning the small sample biases arising from the use of large numbers of IVs. The extensive finite sample work of T. W. Anderson, Sawa, Morimune, Kunitomo and others in the late 1970s and early 1980s confirmed the contrasts drawn by Sargan (1958*b*) between 2SLS (the efficient IV) and LIML. Indeed, combined with Sargan (1959*a* and 1964*a*), Sargan (1958*b*) provides the basis for more recent work, including the application to non-linear systems and some weakening of the restrictions on the underlying stochastic processes (e.g., in works by L. P. Hansen, Jorgenson and Laffont, Gallant and Amemiya [9], and the derivations of the exact and approximate finite sample distributions and properties of the IV estimators (e.g., by Mariano, Sargan, Phillips, and several other writers).

Sargan (1959*a*) is a further study of IV estimation in linear dynamic models with serially correlated errors. The treatment is very general as it considers the estimation of coefficients which are (possibly non-linear) functions of a set of underlying parameters. Asymptotic tests and confidence intervals are derived. This paper also represents a pioneering treatment of estimation and inference in econometric models which contain several 'problems' simultaneously. This latter characteristic is again present in Sargan (1961) which derives and establishes the properties of the ML estimator in linear simultaneous equations models (SEM) with serially correlated errors. This paper (section 3) also contains an interesting early discussion of the dynamic systems which have recently come to be known as VAR (Vector Autoregressive) models advocated by C. Sims (1980) [10]. This paper's results and methods of practical implementation were the subject of several important studies by D. F. Hendry [11].

The by now well-known asymptotic equivalence of FIML and the efficient system IV method (3SLS) in linear SEMs was proved in Sargan (1964*b*), published concurrently with Madansky (1964) [12]. The result holds unless *a priori* restrictions are available on the error covariance matrix. This result and the efficiency of 2SLS in its own class (which follows from Sargan (1958*b*)) have much to do with the popularity of the computationally simpler non-iterative estimators.

1964 witnessed the publication of Sargan's (1964*a*) paper on 'wages and prices', arguably one of his three or four most influential papers. It is an immense empirical study of several econometric methods, some briefly described above and some fully developed for the models of this paper. By setting new standards in the conduct of empirical econometrics this paper shaped a tradition of excellence in econometric research, particularly in Britain. Among the many pathbreaking results in this paper its 'convergence results' are probably the best known. Sargan derived the conditions under which the popular iterative estimation techniques applied in dynamic models with serially correlated errors converge to a limit [13]. The all-important problem of initialisation of such iterations with a consistent estimator is resolved with the IV method developed earlier by Durbin and in Sargan (1958*b*, 1959*a*). Aside from the 'convergence result', Sargan (1964*a*) contains other significant contributions to (1) estimation, (2) testing for higher order autoregressive (AR) errors when an AR disturbance is present, (3) comparing linear with log-linear models, (4) wages and prices modelling, and (5) construction of error-correction mechanisms. The extent of synthesis and the range of methods discussed and employed in this paper is such that Hendry and Wallis (1984) [14], a volume presented to Denis Sargan on the occasion of his retirement, is entirely devoted to studies that further explore its various issues and celebrate its tradition and standard.

Sargan has continued to explore several aspects of theoretical and empirical inference in dynamic economic systems. Several of his Ph.D. students and colleagues have also worked on these ideas and the results have been regularly reported in influential unpublished working papers and in his published papers. Some of these results appeared in print in Sargan (1980*a*), Sargan and Mehta (1983), and in D. F. Hendry, A. Pagan and J. D. Sargan (1983). The problem of testing hypotheses in dynamic models after IV estimation is treated at a general level in an unpublished paper of Sargan's, printed as Chapter 11 of this volume. In this paper Sargan provides important corrections and extensions to section 3 of Sargan (1964*a*). He also considers general tests of misspecification based on IV residuals. These tests include tests for autoregressive structure, tests for higher order autocorrelation in the errors, tests for independence of regressors and the errors, and test for exclusion of variables (zero coefficients). This paper also extends some of the earlier results of Durbin, Box and Pierce [15]. His discussion of the relationship between the various tests and their properties is extensive. In particular, Sargan shows that the class of χ^2 tests he proposes are equivalent to the usual Wald tests for zero coefficients in cases of simple IV estimation (such as for 2SLS and 3SLS estimators). In the context of general IV estimation, however, he demonstrates that his χ^2 criteria are not asymptotically equivalent to the usual Wald tests. The results of Chapter 11 are appicable to systems of equations and simplify for the case of a single relation. Sargan (1980*a*), printed as Chapter 10 in this volume, deals extensively with tests of hypotheses in single equation models. The collection of articles on inference in dynamic models including several other papers which we were unable to reprint in this volume, represent, among other things, a definitive account of inference 'in common factor' (COMFAC) models. They clarify the decisions that must be made by practitioners faced with specification choices among the structural dynamics, on the one hand, and random error processes, on the other, and how rigorous statistical methodology may be employed to explore such decision problems.

Applications of these techniques may be found in several Ph.D. theses at the LSE. Also Sargan (1980*b*, 1980*c*) report his recent analyses of the consumer price equation in the UK and its embedding in a small model of wage–price inflation in Britain. These two papers embody the corrections and improvements that Sargan felt were necessary after the 1964 paper on 'wages and prices'. See also Sargan (1971), 'A study of wages and prices in the UK 1949–68', in Johnson, H. G. and A. R. Nobay (eds.), *The Current Inflation* (London: Macmillan). Sargan has made several other contributions in the context of dynamic models which are discussed and included in Volume 2 of his selected works.

IDENTIFICATION

The problem of identification in general and in dynamic models in particular has been analysed by Sargan with particular ingenuity and care. The attention to this fundamental property of econometric models is evident throughout Sargan's work starting with the (1958*b*) paper on IV estimation where a test of identification is proposed. Several earlier contributions by F. M. Fisher, L. Wegge, T. Rothenberg [16] and others had demonstrated the necessity of a general discussion on the problem which would apply to most models and estimation methods, clarify questions of consistency and identification, and show how one might test for identification and the underlying specification. Sargan's 1975 (November) paper entitled, 'The identification and estimation of sets of simultaneous stochastic equations', an earlier version of which was presented to a meeting of the Royal Statistical Society in 1972, responds to such questions and is printed here as Chapter 12. This paper deals with dynamic non-linear-in-parameters models and generalizes the earlier results of Rothenberg (see Note 16). Sargan considers general estimation criteria which include the likelihood function and general instrumental variables estimation criterion as special cases. His results make clear that the assumption of the existence of sufficient statistics, while quite satisfactory for some linear as well as the binomial and poisson models, is not essential in a general treatment of consistency and identification. In this paper Sargan gives a set of (first order) conditions for identifiability, consistency of estimators and (equivalently) for a set of instrumental variables to be sufficient for identifying the parameters of a model.

Sargan's (1983a) presidential address at the 4th World Congress of the Econometric Society and Sargan (1983b) go further in developing such notions as asymptotic identification, almost (approximate) lack of identifiability and local unidentifiability. Sargan (1983a) deals with linear dynamic models that may be non-linear in parameters with non-linear parameter restrictions. In this paper Sargan further elaborates on the meaning of the first order conditions of identifiability as discussed by (e.g.) Fisher and Rothenberg. One of the significant results in this paper is that the *first order* conditions for lack of identifiability are far from sufficient and are smaller as a set than those ordinarily required for lack of identifiability. Sargan clarifies the nature of the additional requirements for unidentification, subscribing to the view that identification is a property of approximate econometric models rather than a putative property of the 'real world'. He therefore defines an almost lack of identifiability in models and shows that the usual estimators are generally consistent even when a model fails the traditional first order conditions of identifiability. In such cases, however, the estimators do not have asymptotically normal distributions and, as he shows in a leading case, the asymptotic distribution may have no integral moments and is a Cauchy distribution. In the same paper Sargan provides some interesting experimental evidence suggesting that, under these latter conditions, asymptotic approaches are slower and approximations to the actual distributions are poorer.

Sargan (1983b) is an important account of identifiability in models with autoregressive errors, generalizing the discussions in his unpublished 1975 paper (Chapter 12 of this volume) as well as those in Fisher (1967) on rank conditions, Hannan (1971) on systems with moving average errors, Rothenberg (1971), Hatanaka (1975) on simple counting conditions, and Deistler (1976) [17]. In particular, Sargan (1983b) gives a full analysis of the 'singularity' problem in dynamic models and its connection with the 'lesser' problem (as Sargan argues) of unidentifiability. Once again methods of detection of both problems are discussed, with a test for identification requiring the modification (the three-part division) proposed earlier in Sargan and Mehta (1983) when multiple solutions are encountered.

These articles have contributed substantially to our ability to think rigorously and clearly about a fundamental property of econometric models which are more complicated than the static (classical) linear simultaneous equations model or the multiple regression with multicollinearity.

CONCLUSION

I am tempted to mention the debt owed Denis Sargan for his intellectual leadership in the development of suitable control variates and antithetic variate methods in the conduct of simulation experiments in econometrics. But it would be almost unfair to single out one among the many 'quiet contributions' made by Sargan to topics other than mentioned in this discussion. It would be unfair both because of the inevitable exclusions and because this writer has neither the space nor the mastery to cover such a wide domain as is represented by the writings of many of Sargan's friends, associates, and numerous Ph.D. theses supervised by him at the LSE since 1963. In Volume 2 Sargan's extensive contributions to finite sample theory are discussed, as are several of his important publications in other areas.

A summary biographical account of Denis is given at the beginning of Appendix A. A point of some personal interest to me which is not clear from this account is that, while at Cambridge, Denis Sargan was one of the few students who were both qualified and 'willing' to take Sir Harold Jeffreys' course which was also taken by such notable Bayesian statisticians as Denis Lindley and Huzurbazar. While studying under Sargan (1973–77) I always found him rather forthcoming and deeply knowledgeable about the Bayesian concepts and technqiues that were increasingly relevant to my own work. It was during my interviews with him in the summer of 1983 in connection with the present project that I discovered the above fact and one of Sargan's earliest contributions on 'subjective probability'. Our discussions revealed that there are deep reasons which explain why he has generally been a 'classical' statistician in his own work while retaining the 'good' statistician's informed sympathy with all practicable methods, be they Bayesian or frequentist.

Our profession is fortunate to have Denis Sargan as a fellow traveller. It would be wonderful to aspire to the standards set by such a rare blend of elegance, craftsmanship and modesty. It is pleasing to witness his active and continuing work in econometrics, currently on estimation and testing in 'rational expectations' models as well as other problems.

Persians, like most 'easterners', generally regard their teachers in such high esteem that is difficult for others to fully comprehend. When they come across a truly great teacher–scholar it should not be surprising to find them wanting or even speechless. And it is no consolation to find that, in the case of Sargan, this inadequacy has so far transcended all cultural boundaries! As a partial remedy I finish this introduction by borrowing heavily from Hildenbrand (see Note 1).

The edifice of statistical and econometric theory may be compared to the great mosques of Isphahan, with their many colourful menarets and domes. These constructions were designed by inspired architects and constructed, extended and improved upon by great master builders. Anderson, Wald, Pearson, Fisher, Jeffreys, Neyman, Koopmans and Frisch are among the principal architects of statistics and econometrics in this century. Sargan's contributions clearly establish him as a prominent master builder of that edifice with inspired designs of his own.

ACKNOWLEDGEMENTS

I would like to thank Denis Sargan, for without his generosity this volume could not have been prepared. He provided several corrections to published papers and some revisions to previously unpublished papers. He was both forthcoming and expansive on background material which I needed, and provided such material in several meetings during the months of July and August of 1983. The selection of the papers in these volumes and my description of them benefited greatly from the above material and discussions for which I thank Denis Sargan without implicating him in any way. Much of this background information appears in the first issue of *Econometric Theory* (1985, July) which contains the transcript of an interview with Sargan conducted in 1984.

Special thanks are due Neil Ericsson at the Board of Governors, Federal Reserve System (Washington, DC). Appendix B was researched and compiled by him, and he provided extensive editorial comments and advice at several stages. I am grateful to several other people for their help and encouragement, especially Grayham Mizon and David Hendry for their timely comments and constructive suggestions, to Peter Phillips for a correction and criticisms of an earlier draft, to Ted Anderson for the Foreword to these volumes and several other suggestions and to Francis Brooke and Colin Day of the Cambridge University Press for their support. As the editor in charge, Francis Brooke's encouragement and help was essential and generously offered at every stage.

I am grateful to the editors and publishers of the following journals and publications for permission to reprint Sargan's previously published papers: *Econometrica, Review of Economic Studies, International Economic Review, The Journal of the Royal Statistical Society*, Butterworths and the Academic Press.

My thanks and appreciation go to Ms. Linda Steinwachs for her skill in typing several drafts of the manuscript.

NOTES

[1] W. Hildenbrand, 'Introduction' to *Twenty Papers of Gerard Debreu* (1982), Cambridge University Press, Econometric Society Monograph 4.

[2] Please refer to Appendix A. All references to Sargan's papers are as in Appendix A.

[3] In its usual proportions this phenomenon is a well understood consequence of publication delays. I am merely alerting the interested historian that there are other more important elements in this case.

[4] Paul A. Samuelson (1948), *Foundations of Economic Analysis*, 1st edn, p. 188, Harvard University Press.

[5] D. G. Champernowne (1953), 'Model of income distribution', *Economic Journal*, **63**, 318–51.

[6] R. Gibrat (1931), *Les inegalites economiques*, Paris; Kalecki, M. (1945), 'On the Gibrat distribution', *Econometrica*, **13**, 161–70; R. S. Rutherford (1955), 'Income distributions: a new model', *Econometrica*, **23**, 277–94.

[7] A. Shorrocks (1976), 'Income mobility and the Markov assumption', *Economic Journal*, **86**, 566–78.

[8] Hausman, J. A. (1975), 'An instrumental variable approach to full information estimators for linear and certain non-linear econometric models', *Econometrica*, **43**, 727–38.

[9] Lars Peter Hanson (1982), 'Large sample properties of the generalized method of moments estimators', *Econometrica*, **50**, 1029–54; Jorgenson, D. W. and J. Laffont (1974), 'Efficient estimation of non-linear simultaneous equations with additive disturbances', *Annals of Economic and Social Measurement*, **3**, 615–40; T. Amemiya (1977), 'The maximum likelihood and non-linear three stage least squares estimator in the general non-linear simultaneous equations model', *Econometrica*, **45**, 955–68; Gallant, A. R. (1977), 'Three stage least squares estimation for a system of simultaneous non-linear implicit equations', *Journal of Econometrics*, pp. 71–88.

[10] C. Sims (1980), 'Macroeconomics and Reality', *Econometrica*, **48**, 1–45.

[11] D. F. Hendry (1971), 'Maximum likelihood estimation of systems of simultaneous regression equations with errors generated by a vector autoregressive process', *International Economic Review*, **12**, 257–72.

[12] Madansky, A. (1964), 'On the efficiency of three-stage least squares estimation', *Econometrica*, **32**, 52–6.

[13] Care must be taken in analysing the conditions for the convergence of the iterative estimators since a multiple fixed point problem may arise when lagged endogenous variables are present, as was recently pointed out by R. Betancourt and H. Kelejian (1981, *Econometrica*).

[14] D. F. Hendry and K. Wallis (eds.), *Econometrics and Quantitative Economics* (1984), Basil Blackwell, Oxford.

[15] Box, G. E. P. and D. A. Pierce (1970), 'Distribution of residual autocorrelation in autoregressive-integrated moving average time series models', *Journal of the American Statistical Association*, **65**, 1509–26; Durbin, J. (1970), 'Testing for serial correlation in least squares regression when some of the regressors are lagged dependent variables', *Econometrica*, **38**, 410–21; Pierce, D. A. (1972), 'Residual correlation and diagnostic checking in dynamic-disturbance time series models', *Journal of the American Statistical Association*, **67**, 636–40.

[16] F. M. Fisher (1967), *The Identification Problem in Econometrics*. McGraw-Hill, NY; Leon Wegge (1965), 'Identifiability criteria for a system of equations as a whole', *Australian Journal of Statistics*, **3**, 67–77; T. J. Rothenberg (1971), 'Identification in parametric models', *Econometrica*, **39**, 577–92.

[17] E. J. Hannan (1971), 'The identification problem for multiple equation systems with moving average errors', *Econometrica*, **39**, 751–66; M. Hatanaka (1975), 'On the Global Identification of the Dynamic Simultaneous Equations model with stationary disturbances', *International Economic Review*, **16**, 545–54; M. Diestler (1976), 'The identifiability of linear econometric models with autocorrelated errors', *International Economic Review*, **17**, 26–45.

APPENDIX A: A BRIEF BIOGRAPHY OF DENIS SARGAN AND A LIST OF
HIS PUBLISHED PAPERS

Born August 23, 1924, at Doncaster, Yorkshire

1935–41	Doncaster Grammar School
1941–43	St John's College, Cambridge
1943–46	Junior Scientific Officer attached to RAF Coastal Command
1946–48	St John's College, Cambridge
1948–58	Lecturer in Economics at Leeds University
1958–59	Visiting Professor at University of Minnesota
1959–60	Assistant Professor at University of Chicago
1960–63	Reader in Econometrics at University of Leeds
1963–64	Reader in Econometrics at London School of Economics (Tooke Chair)
1964–84	Professor of Econometrics at London School of Economics
1974	Visiting Professor at Yale University
1978–79	Vice-President of the Econometric Society
1980	President of the Econometric Society
	On the editorial boards of several journals including *Econometrica* and *Econometric Theory*

Degrees

BA, Mathematics (1st Class Honours), 1944
BA, Economics (2nd Class Honours), 1948
MA, 1947

Publications

Metroeconomica (1951), 'A new approach to the general distribution problem', **3**, 108–16.

Yorkshire Bulletin of Economic and Social Research (1952), 'An illustration of duopoly', **4**, 133–45.

Yorkshire Bulletin (1953a), 'Subjective probability and the economist', **5**, 53–64.

Journal of the Royal Statistical Society (1953b), 'An approximate treatment of the properties of correlogram and periodogram', **8**, (15), 140–52.

Econometrica (1955), 'The period of production', **23**, 151–65 (printed here).

Econometrica (1956), 'A note on Mr. Blyth's article', **24**, 480–1 (printed here).

Econometrica (1957a), 'The distribution of wealth', **25**, 568–90 (printed here).

Bulletin of Oxford Institute of Statistics (1957b), 'The dangers of over-simplification', **19**, 171–8.

Econometrica (1958a), 'The instability of the Leontief dynamic model', **26**, 381–92.

Econometrica (1958b), 'The estimation of economic relationships using instrumental variables', **26**, 393–415 (printed here).

Yorkshire Bulletin (1958c), 'Mrs Robinson's warranted rate of growth', **10**, 35–40.

JRSS (1959a), 'The estimation of relationships with autocorrelated residuals by the use of instrumental variables', **B**, **21**, 91–105 (printed here).

Econometrica (1959b), 'Linear models for the frequency distributions of economic variables', *Abstract*, **27**, 315–16.

Econometrica (1961a), 'The maximum likelihood estimation of economic relationships with autoregressive residuals', **29**, 414–26 (printed here).

Econometrica (1961b), 'Lags and the stability of dynamic systems: a reply', **29**, 670–3.

Econometrica (1964a), '3SLS and FIML estimates', **32**, 77–81 (printed here).

Colston Paper (1964b), 'Wages and prices in the UK: a study in econometric methodology', in *Econometric Analysis for National Economic Planning*, P. E. Hart, G. Mills, and J. K. Whitaker (eds.), pp. 25–54, London: Butterworth Co., Ltd. Reprinted in Hendry and Wallis (eds.), *Econometrics and Quantitative Economics*, 1984, Basil Blackwell, Oxford (printed here).

Econometrica (1964c), 'An approximate distribution of the two-stage least squares estimators', Abstract, **32**, 660.

P. R. G. Layard, J. D. Sargan, M. E. Ager and D. J. Jones (1971a), 'Production functions', Part V, in *Qualified Manpower and Economic Performance* part 5, London: *An Inter-plant Study in the Electrical Engineering Industry*. London: Allen Lane, the Penguin Press, pp. 143–204.

Econometrica (1971), 'A general approximation to the distribution of instrumental variable estimates', with W. M. Mikhail, **39**, 131–69 (printed here).

(1971b), 'A study of wages and prices in the UK, 1949–1968', Chapter 4 in *The Current Inflation*, H. G. Johnson and A. R. Nobay (eds.), London: Macmillan, pp. 52–71.

Econometrica (1974a), 'The validity of Nagar's expansion for the moments of econometric estimates', **42**, 169–76.

Journal of the Royal Statistical Society (1974b), 'Some discrete approximations to continuous time stochastic models', **B**, **36**, 74–90 (printed here).

International Economic Review (1974), 'Missing data in an autoregressive model', with E. G. Drettakis, **15**, 39–58 (printed here).

International Economic Review (1975a), 'Asymptotic theory and large models', **16**, 75–91.

Econometrica (1975b), 'Gram–Charlier approximations applied to *t-ratios of k*-class estimators', **43**, 327–46.

Econometrica (1976a), 'Econometric estimators and the Edgeworth approximation', **44**, 421–48 (printed here).

A chapter in *Statistical Inference in Continuous Time Economic Models* (1976b), edited by A. R. Bergstrom. This is an expanded version of Sargan (1974b) with the same title. Amsterdam: North-Holland.

International Economic Review (1977), 'The spectral estimation of sets of simultaneous equations with lagged endogenous variables', with A. Espasa, **18**, 583–605 (printed here).

Econometrica (1978), 'The existence of moments of 3SLS estimators', **46**, 1329–50.

Review of Economic Studies (1980a), 'The consumer price equation in the post war British economy: an exercise in equation specification testing', **47**, 113–35.

Review of Economic Studies (1980b), '*A model of wage–price inflation*', **47**, 97–112 (printed here).

Econometrica (1980c), 'Some tests of dynamic specification for a single equation', **48**, 879–97 (printed here).

Econometrica (1980*d*), 'Some approximations to the distributions of econometric criteria which are asymptotically distributed as chi-squared', **48**, 1107–38.

(1981), A chapter in *Proceedings of the 1979 European Society Meetings*, edited by E. G. Charatsis, 'Edgeworth approximations to the distributions of various test statistics', with Y. K. Tse (pp. 281–95), Amsterdam: North-Holland.

Advances in Econometrics (1982), 'On Monte Carlo estimate of moments that are infinite', **1**, 267–99, edited by R. L. Basmann and G. F. Rhodes (Jr), JAI Press, Greenwich, CT.

Econometrica (1983*a*), 'Identification and lack of identification', **51**, 1605–33 (printed here).

(1983*b*), A chapter in *Studies in Econometrics, Time Series, and Multivariate Statistics* in honor of T. W. Anderson, edited by S. Karlin, T. Amemiya and L. A. Goodman, entitled 'Identification in models with autoregressive errors', New York: Academic Press, pp. 169–205 (printed here).

A chapter in the *Handbook of Econometrics Vol. II* (1983), edited by Z. Griliches and M. Intriligator, 'Dynamic specification' (with D. F. Hendry and A. R.' Pagan), Amsterdam: North-Holland.

Econometrica (1983), 'A generalization of the Durbin significance test and its application to dynamic specification', (with F. Mehta), **51**, 1551–67.

Econometrica (1983*a*), 'Testing residuals from least squares regression for being generated by the Gaussian random walk' (with A. Bhargava), **51**, 153–74.

Econometrica (1983*b*), 'Maximum likelihood estimation of regression models with first order moving average errors when the root lies on the unit circle' (with A. Bhargava), **51**, 799–820 (printed here).

Econometrica (1983), 'Estimating dynamic random effect models from panel data covering short time periods' (with A. Bhargava), **51**, 1635–59 (printed here).

(1984), A chapter in the *Handbook of Econometrics Vol. II*, edited by Z. Griliches and M. Intriligator, 'Dynamic specification' (with D. F. Hendry and A. R. Pagan), Amsterdam: North-Holland.

Econometrica (1986), 'A theory of validity for Edgeworth expansions' (with S. E. Satchell), **54**, 189–213.

APPENDIX B†: A BIBLIOGRAPHY OF Ph.D. THESES SUPERVISED BY
J. D. SARGAN

1 Chronological listing

1957   El Imam, M. M., 'The consumption function for the UK, 1929–1938' (at Leeds University).

1966   Hortala-Arau, Juan, 'Capital needs in a developing economy: Spain as a case study'.

1968   Byron, Raymond Peter, 'The estimation of systems of demand equations using prior information'.

† This Appendix was prepared by Dr Neil Ericsson of the Federal Reserve Board, Washington, DC. The research involved was supported in part by grant HR8789 from the Social Science Research Council to the project 'The Modelling and Evaluation of Dynamic Econometric Systems' while he was at Nuffield College, Oxford. Views expressed herein do not necessarily reflect those of the Board of Governors of the Federal Reserve System.

Handa, Madan Lal, 'Econometrics of import planning in India (1947–65): a case study of selected commodities'.

1969 Mikhail, William Messiha, 'A study of the finite-sample properties of some econometric estimators'.

Rowley, John Christopher Robin, 'An econometric study of fixed capital formation in the British economy, 1956–1965'.

Trivedi, Pravinchandra Kantilal, 'An econometric study of inventory behaviour in the UK manufacturing sector, 1956–67'.

Williams, Ross Allan, 'An econometric study of post-war demand for consumer durables in the United Kingdom'.

1970 Charatsis, Eleftherios G., 'Statistical methods for estimation of production functions: a cross-section and time-series analysis of the Greek manufacturing industry'.

Feiner, Michale Peter, 'An econometric study of disaggregated UK imports, 1958–66'.

Hendry, David Forbes, 'The estimation of economic models with autoregressive errors'.

Vernon, Keith, 'An econometric study of wage and price inflation in the United Kingdom for the post-war period'.

Wymer, Clifford Ronald, 'Econometric estimation of stochastic differential equation systems with applications to adjustment models of financial markets'.

1971 Drettakis, Emmanuel George, 'Missing data in econometric estimation'.

1972 Cheong, Kee Cheok, 'An econometric study of the world natural and synthetic rubber industry'.

Mizon, Grayham E., 'The estimation of vintage capital production relations'.

1974 Hebden, Julia Jennifer, 'A complete set of dynamic consumer demand equations'.

Phillips, Peter Charles Bonest, 'Problems in the estimation of continuous time models'.

1975 Espasa, Antoni, 'A wages-earnings-prices inflation model for United Kingdom 1950–1970: its specification and estimation by classical and spectral methods'.

Sylwestrowicz, Jerzy Dowoyna, 'Numerical optimization of non-linear functions of several variables using random search techniques'.

1976 Fitzpatrick, Michael Desmond, 'Varying parameter estimation and trends in the parameters which determine the modal choice associated with long distance international travel'.

Hall, Antony David, 'The relative efficiency of estimators of seemingly unrelated regressions'.

1977 Maasoumi, Esfandiar, 'A study of improved methods of estimating reduced form coefficients based upon 3SLS estimators'.

Pesaran, Bahram, 'Estimation of dynamic economic models when variables are subject to measurement errors'.

Ray, Ranjan, 'Utility maximization and consumer demand with an application to the United Kingdom, 1900–1970'.

1979 Mehta, Kirtikumar Bharusharker Jatasharker, 'Maximum likelihood estimation of economic relationships involving unobservable indicators'.

1981 Satchell, Stephen E., 'Edgeworth approximations in linear dynamic models'.

Tse, Yiu Kuen, 'Edgeworth approximation to the finite sample distribution of econometric estimators and test statistics'.

Bhargava, Alok, 'The theory of the Durbin–Watson statistic with special reference to the specification of models in levels as against in differences'.

1982 Campos Fernande, Julia, 'Instrumental variables estimation of dynamic economic systems with autocorrelated errors'.

Chong, Yock Yoon, 'Comparative methods of computing maximum likelihood estimates for non-linear econometric systems'.

Ericsson, Neil Reinhard, 'Testing non-tested hypotheses in systems of linear dynamic economic relationships'.

1983 Franzini-Bhargava, Luisa, 'Time varying coefficient models in econometrics'.

Mauleón Torres, Ignacio, 'Approximations to the finite sample distribution of econometric chi-squared criteria'.

1985 Arellano Gonzalez, Manuel, 'Estimation and testing of dynamic econometric models from panel data'.

2 Current affiliations

Arellano Gonzalez, M. (1958)
Bhargava, A. (1982)   DE†, Univ. of Pennsylvania, Philadelphia, PA
Byron, R. P. (1968)   Australian National Univ., Canberra, Australia

Campos Fernandez, J. (1982)   Banco Central de Venezuela, Caracas, Venezuela
Charatsis, E. G. (1970)   Athens School of Economics, Greece
Cheong, K. C. (1972)   University of Malaya, Kuala Lumpur, Malaya
Chong, Y. Y. (1982)   DAP Unit, Queen Mary College, London, UK

Drettakis, E. G. (1971)   Member of Parliament, Athens, Greece

Ericsson, N. R. (1982)   Federal Reserve Board, Washington, DC
Espasa, A. (1975)   Banco De Espana, Madrid, Spain

Feiner, M. P. (1970)   E.C.E., Paris, France
Fitzpatrick, M. D. (1976)   Treasury Dept., Canberra, Australia
Franzini-Bhargava, L. (1983)   Philadelphia, PA

Hall, A. D. (1976)   Australian National Univ., Canberra, Australia
Handa, M. L. (1968)
Hebden, J. J. (1974)   University of Sussex, UK
Hendry, D. F. (1970)   Nuffield College, Oxford, UK

† DE = Department of Economics.

Hortala-Arau, J. (1966)   Banco de Espana, Madrid

Maasoumi, E. (1977)   DE, Indiana Univ., Bloomington, IN
Mauleon Torres, I. (1983)   Banco de Espana, Madrid, Spain
Mehta, K. B. J. (1979)   EEC, Brussels, Belgium
Mikhail, W. M. (1969)   Cairo University, Egypt
Mizon, G. E. (1972)   DE, The University, Southampton, UK

Pesaran, B. (1977)   London, UK
Phillips, P. C. B. (1974)   DE, Yale University, New Haven, CT

Ray, R. (1977)   University of Manchester, Manchester, UK
Rowley, J. C. R. (1969)   DE, Magill University, Canada

Satchell, S. E. (1981)   DE, Univ. of Essex, Colchester, UK
Sylwestrowicz, J. D. (1975)   DAP Unit, Queen Mary College, London, UK

Trivedi, P. K. (1969)   DE, Indiana University, Bloomington, IN
Tse, Y. K. (1981)   National University of Singapore, Singapore

Vernon, K. (1970)

Williams, R. A. (1969)   Melbourne Univ., Melbourne, Australia
Wymer, C. R. (1970)   International Monetary Fund, Washington, DC

3 Sources

Authors, dates, and titles of the theses are listed as they appear in the British Library of Political and Economic Science, *Economic Journal* ('Thesis titles' in various March issues since 1973), *Abstracts of Theses* (published by ASLIB, the Association of Special Libraries and Information Bureaus), and various calendars of the London School of Economics. Yogesh Deshpande, P. J. Wallace, the staff of the British Library of Political and Economic Science, and numerous former students of Denis Sargan's provided invaluable assistance in compiling this bibliography.

————— · —————

2 THE PERIOD OF PRODUCTION

(First published in *Econometrica* (1955), Vol. 23, pp. 151–65.)

In the theory of the firm under perfect competition a period which measures the effect of the rate of interest on relative prices of inputs and outputs should be called the period of production. Alternatively, this period can be defined as the difference between an output period and an input period, each with respect to the plans of a marginal entrepreneur about to start a new firm. The output period is the weighted mean of times to future sales; similarly, the input period is the weighted mean of times to future purchases.

The value of the period of production is considered here for certain simple cases where it can be simply related to the average periods of the capital goods being used. These results provide approximations for more realistic cases where the average period of a capital good is less easily defined.

Subsequently we examine the variatons in this period of production when the rate of interest changes.

If the results are applied to an economy in which each firm produces only one commodity, a complete period of production can then be defined for each commodity, and this determines the effect of changes in the rate of interest on the ratio of the price of this commodity to an index of prices of the primary factors of production, labour and land. Finally, some rough calculations are made to estimate the order of magnitudes of actual complete periods of production.

1 INTRODUCTION

The concept of a period of production has been used in economics since the time of Ricardo both to explain the relation between capital employed and output produced and also to explain the time required by a firm to adjust to a change in production or demand relationships. There is no problem in defining the period of production for the case in which all inputs are made at one point of time and all outputs are concentrated at another point of time (the point-input point-output case). If, however, technologically related inputs and outputs are spread out over time, then means of the times to inputs and times to outputs must be used, and the definition of the period turns upon the weights used to define the means.

The appropriate choice of weights is in fact suggested by Hicks' treatment of the average period of a payment stream which is defined by using weights proportional to the discounted values of the payments†. In symbols, Hicks' definition can be written

$$T = \sum_t t(P_t e^{-rt}) \bigg/ \sum_t (P_t e^{-rt}) \tag{1}$$

where P_t is the payment of the tth period, and r is the rate of interest.

Hicks shows that if P_t is the gross profit of a firm, or if it is the change in the gross profit due to some finite change in the firm's production plan, then

$$T = -\frac{1}{K}\frac{dK}{dr}$$

where $K = \sum_t P_t e^{-rt}$. In particular, if the change in plan is a change of one unit in the amount of some indivisible input used, then P_t can be regarded as the difference in net revenue (i.e., receipts minus payments for other factors) of time t caused by the change. K is then the difference in the capitalised value of these future net revenues and so is equal to the value of the unit change in input, which at the margin will tend to equality with the cost of the input. Thus, in discussing the effect of the rate of interest on the rate of investment, the average period of the investment good determines the change in the demand price, and the new level of investment will be determined by the output of the capital goods supplied at the new demand price.

Hicks' definition has been criticised by Samuelson‡ on the grounds that if the payments stream includes some payments which are counted negative (for example, if receipts are counted positive, and payments are counted negative), then there is no reason why the average period should have the usual properties of an average (having a value between the greatest and least of the time periods averaged), and in particular if the payments stream is a marginal stream in the sense that its capital value is zero, then the denominator of expression (1) is zero and the average period indeterminate. A second criticism, which has been particularly applied to the discussion of the effect of the rate of interest on the level of investment, is that the theory may be seriously misleading in practice in that it exaggerates the effect of the rate of interest by neglecting the effect of risk.

For simplicity we will not deal here with the problem of risk but will be

---

† J. R. Hicks, *Value and Capital*, 2nd edn, Ch. 14, p. 186. Oxford: Clarendon Press (1946).
‡ Paul A. Samuelson, *Foundations of Economic Analysis*, 1st edn, Ch. 7, p. 188. Cambridge, Mass.: Harvard Univ. Press (1947).

concerned only with applying Hicks' idea to the static theory of the firm. A definition of the period of production is suggested which is designed to avoid Samuelson's difficulty in applying Hicks' average period to the firm in long period equilibrium. Ours is a study of the effect of a change in the rate of interest on long period equilibrium price levels, a problem in comparative statics.

2 THE STATIC EQUILIBRIUM

Consider a firm which is marginal in the sense that an entrepreneur is just now considering whether to start this firm producing. The entrepreneur is assumed to have a plan for starting this firm from nothing. This plan involves the purchase of certain goods and services and the sale of other goods and services. It is assumed that if the entrepreneur takes into account the value of his own services and if there are no risks, then, for the number of firms to be in equilibrium, the capitalised value of payments must be equal to the capitalised value of receipts and so the net value of the marginal firm is non-positive. We suppose that if this were not so, the equilibrium would be disturbed by the entry of new firms or the exit of existing ones.

If C is the capitalised value of expected costs and R is the capitalised value of expected receipts, then for long period equilibrium

$$R - C = 0. \tag{2}$$

If the rate of interest can be taken as constant throughout the life of the firm and equal to r

$$R = \sum_t R_t e^{-rt}, \qquad C = \sum_t C_t e^{-rt} \tag{3}$$

where R_t and C_t are, respectively, the expected receipts and costs in period t.

It is now possible to define two periods T_R and T_C as follows:

$$T_R = \sum_t (R_t e^{-rt}) t \Big/ \sum_t (R_t e^{-rt}), \qquad T_C = \sum_t (C_t e^{-rt}) t \Big/ \sum_t (C_t e^{-rt}).$$

T_R is by definition a mean of times to future sales weighted by the capitalised value of these sales. It will be called the *output period*, being in fact the Hicksian average period for sales receipts. Similarly, T_C is the average period for future purchases and will be called the *input period*. Since all the weights are positive these periods are true averages, being positive and finite.

The average period of production is then defined as the difference between the output and input periods, so that

$$T = T_R - T_C. \tag{4}$$

T_R can normally be taken to be greater than T_C (this is necessarily true if all capital assets can be disposed of costlessly at any time), so that the period of production is normally positive.

Now taking R and C, as defined by equations (3), as functions of r and of the expected values of receipts and payments, it follows that

$$\partial R/\partial r = -\sum_t R_t e^{-rt} t = -RT_R$$

and similarly

$$\frac{\partial C}{\partial r} = -CT_C$$

where the partial derivatives are understood to be taken with expected receipts and payments constant. Thus,

$$T = -\frac{\dfrac{\partial}{\partial r}(R-C)}{R}.$$

This latter equation is indeed the reason for defining the period of production as above with weights equal to discounted values. The period of production, thus defined, determines the effect of the interest rate on the relative prices of inputs and outputs in equilibrium.

Since in equilibrium $R-C=0$ for every value of r, it follows that so long as the system stays in equilibrium, the derivative of this equation is zero, or

$$\frac{d}{dr}(R-C) = 0.$$

Using equations (3), this becomes

$$\sum_t R_t e^{-rt} t - \sum_t C_t e^{-rt} t = \sum_t \frac{dR_t}{dr} e^{-rt} - \sum_t \frac{dC_t}{dr} e^{-rt},$$

or

$$RT = \sum_t \frac{dR_t}{dr} e^{-rt} - \sum_t \frac{dC_t}{dr} e^{-rt}.$$

Now let R_{it} be the expected receipts from the sale of the ith product in period t, and similarly C_{it} be the expected cost of the purchase of the ith factor of production in period t. Then

$$RT = \sum_t \sum_i \frac{dR_{it}}{dr} e^{-rt} - \sum_t \sum_i \frac{dC_{it}}{dr} e^{-rt}.$$

Now,

$$R_{it} = p_i x_{it} \qquad \text{and} \qquad C_{it} = w_i y_{it}.$$

where x_{it} is the quantity of the ith product which will be sold in period t, and y_{it} is the quantity of the ith factor which will be bought in period t, and p_i and w_i are the constant prices of the outputs and inputs which will be maintained in the static equilibrium. Then

$$\frac{dR_{it}}{dr} = \frac{dp_i}{dr} x_{it} + p_i \frac{dx_{it}}{dr}, \qquad \frac{dC_{it}}{dr} = \frac{dw_i}{dr} y_{it} + w_i \frac{dy_{it}}{dr}.$$

If $f(x_{it}, y_{it}) = 0$ is the production function connecting the quantities bought and sold in all the different periods, the changes in the quantities of outputs and inputs resulting from a change in the rate of interest must satisfy the equation

$$\sum_t \sum_i \frac{dx_{it}}{dr} \frac{\partial f}{\partial x_{it}} + \sum_t \sum_i \frac{dy_{it}}{dr} \frac{\partial f}{\partial y_{it}} = 0$$

and from the conditions for the maximisation of the capitalised value of the firm it follows that

$$\frac{\partial f}{\partial x_{it}} = \lambda p_i e^{-rt}, \qquad \frac{\partial f}{\partial y_{it}} = -\lambda w_i e^{-rt}.$$

Thus

$$\sum_t \sum_i p_i \frac{dx_{it}}{dr} e^{-rt} - \sum_t \sum_i w_i \frac{dy_{it}}{dr} e^{-rt} = 0,$$

and so

$$\sum_t \sum_i \frac{dR_{it}}{dr} e^{-rt} - \sum_t \sum_i \frac{dC_{it}}{dr} e^{-rt}$$

$$= \sum_t \sum_i x_{it} \frac{dp_i}{dr} e^{-rt} - \sum_t \sum_i y_{it} \frac{dw_i}{dr} e^{-rt} + \sum_t \sum_i p_i \frac{dx_{it}}{dr} e^{-rt}$$

$$- \sum_t \sum_i w_i \frac{dy_{it}}{dr} e^{-rt}$$

$$= \sum_t \sum_i R_{it} \left(\frac{1}{p_i} \frac{dp_i}{dr} \right) e^{-rt} - \sum_t \sum_i C_{it} \left(\frac{1}{w_i} \frac{dw_i}{dr} \right) e^{-rt}.$$

If R_i is the expected capitalised value of the receipts from the ith product and C_i is the expected capitalised value of the purchases of the ith factor, so that

$$R_i = \sum_t R_{it} e^{-rt}, \qquad C_i = \sum_t C_{it} e^{-rt},$$

then

$$RT = \sum_i R_i \left(\frac{1}{p_i} \frac{dp_i}{dr} \right) - \sum_i C_i \left(\frac{1}{w_i} \frac{dw_i}{dr} \right).$$

Now writing $j_i = R_i/R$ and $k_i = C_i/C$,

$$T = \sum_i j_i \left(\frac{1}{p_i} \frac{dp_i}{dr} \right) - \sum_i k_i \left(\frac{1}{w_i} \frac{dw_i}{dr} \right). \tag{5}$$

This may be stated verbally as follows: *The weighted average of the logarithmic derivatives of the prices of outputs minus a similar average for the prices of inputs equals the period of production, the weights being the capitalised payments corresponding to the outputs and inputs.*

Under imperfect competition equation (5) is no longer correct. The assumption of perfect competition is made, therefore, except in Section 9 where the effects of assuming imperfect competition are discussed.

The definition of the period of production given above is a general one, relating to any kind of firm producing any number of products. Thus it cannot be regarded as the period of production of a commodity unless that commodity is the sole product of the firm producing it. In the next section particular cases are considered and an approximation is developed which applies accurately only to simplified models of firms using single-capital-good processes. These models may, however, yield useful approximations for actual firms.

3 SOME SPECIAL CASES

(1) Point-output

In the point-output case the output period is just the interval between the start of the firm and the time at which the output first appears. The difference between the output period and the input period $(T_R - T_C)$ can be more easily expressed by taking the point of time at which the output appears as a new origin and then taking the mean of the times at which an input occurs weighted by the accumulated cost of the inputs.

(2) Single-durable-asset constant-returns process

If all the productive inputs affect the outputs produced only in the same period except for one inputs corresponding to a producers' durable good, and if all production ratios are fixed, then it can be shown that the period of production is directly related to Hicks' average period for the asset.

Suppose that with a single durable good of this type it is profitable to use current inputs of value I_t to produce an output of value O_t, where t is the time since installation of the capital good. Now, the firm may install capital goods at a rate which may vary following any plan, but it may be assumed that its planned rate of installation will eventually become constant, so that it will come to have a constant stock of capital goods. The value of the capital good is

$$V = \sum_{t=0}^{\infty} e^{-rt}(O_t - I_t) \tag{6}$$

and, by Hicks' definition, its average period is

$$T' = \frac{1}{V} \sum_{t=0}^{\infty} t e^{-rt}(O_t - I_t).$$

The stream of outputs can be split into two parts, one equal in value to the contemporaneous stream of current inputs, the other equal to the difference between current outputs and current inputs; and these two separate streams of outputs can be regarded as due to current inputs and to the inputs of capital goods, respectively. In considering the first stream together with the corresponding current inputs, a period of production can be defined which in this case is zero. As for the second stream of outputs, ascribed to the inputs of capital, there corresponds to each capital good a series of outputs of value $O_t - I_t$ in the tth period after the installation of the capital good. Thus, this second stream has associated with it a period of production T'. Now it is clear from our definition of the period of production as a difference of weighted means of times to outputs and of times to inputs that the period of the sum of two streams will be equal to a weighted mean of the periods of the two separate streams, the weights being proportional to the capitalised values of the outputs in each stream. Thus,

$$T = \frac{\left(\sum_{t=0}^{\infty} e^{-rt} I_t \right) \cdot 0 + \left(\sum_{t=0}^{\infty} e^{-rt}(O_t - I_t) \right) \cdot T'}{\sum_{t=0}^{\infty} e^{-rt} O_t} = T' \frac{V}{\sum_{t=0}^{\infty} e^{-rt} O_t} = kT' \tag{7}$$

where k is the proportion of the total capitalised cost to be spent on the fixed capital.

(3) Single-durable asset with production lag

If $O_t = \lambda I_{t-u}$, so that outputs reflect current input with a lag u, then the input period will be the same as if $u = 0$, but the output period will be greater by u than when $u = 0$.

Hence $T = T'' + u$, where T'' is derived according to equation (7) from the average period of the current input stream. This displays the period of production as split into two parts, the first reflecting the life of the durable equipment and the second the lag between current inputs and the consequent outputs.

(4) *Two simple processes in succession*

If a firm can be regarded as carrying on two single-capital-good processes, one of which produces the inputs (i.e., raw materials) for the second, then the period of production is easily deduced by introducing a virtual price for the product of the first process defined so that this process just makes zero net profit. Since the process is defined here to be one of constant returns, it follows that this virtual price is also the marginal cost of the intermediate good. In static equilibrium, the second process, using this virtual price to cost its raw material input, must also make zero net profit.

In discussing the effect of changes in the rate of interest on the price of the final output, the virtual price can be eliminated from two equations of type (5). It follows that

$$T = T_2 + kT_1$$

where k is the proportion of the total capitalised costs of the final process due to the intermediate good, and T_1 and T_2 are the periods of production of the initial and final processes respectively.

This can alternatively be stated as –

$$T = k_1 T'_1 + k_2 T'_2$$

where now k_1 and k_2 are the proportions of the total capitalised cost of both processes due to the fixed capital of the first and second processes, and T'_1 and T'_2 are the average periods of the corresponding assets. This formula is easily generalised to the case of several simple processes in succession.

(5) *Two simple processes in parallel*

If a firm can be regarded as producing a product by combining costlessly in fixed proportions the outputs of two different simple processes, two virtual prices can be defined for the outputs of the two processes and it then follows that

$$p = a_1 p_1 + a_2 p_2$$

where p_1 and p_2 are the virtual prices and a_1 and a_2 are the quantities of the two outputs required to produce one unit of the final product. It then follows that

$$T = \frac{a_1 p_1 T_1 + a_2 p_2 T_2}{a_1 p_1 + a_2 p_2} = k_1 T_1 + k_2 T_2$$

where T_1 and T_2 are the periods of production of the two outputs and k_1 and k_2 are the proportions of total cost which can be allocated to the two processes. This also may be written

$$T = k_1' T_1' + k_2' T_2'$$

where T_1' and T_2' are the average periods of the fixed capital goods, and k_1' and k_2' are the proportions of the total capitalised cost due to these assets.

4 A GENERAL APPROXIMATION

These results can obviously be generalised to any combination of processes of the preceding types. Stated in general, *the period of production is equal to the proportion of the total capitalised costs due to fixed capital multiplied by the weighted mean of the average periods of the fixed assets, the weights being the capitalised costs of the assets.* This approximation gives a crude idea of the periods of production of most actual firms. It is, however, merely an approximation since it has been assumed that each process and therefore the production function of the firm are subject to constant returns, and no account has been taken of non-capital overhead.

The latter problem may be dealt with by introducing an overhead period, by imputing to each expenditure on non-capital overhead a subsequent stream of net receipts. For examples, we may consider a single-process firm whose current inputs and outputs are proportional throughout the life of the fixed capital goods. Three simple cases may then be considered:

(a) Throughout the planned life of the firm non-capital overhead is proportional to gross investment. In this case the overhead period is equal to the average period of the capital good.

(b) Throughout the planned life of the firm non-capital overhead is proportional to total costs. In this case the overhead period is equal to the period of production.

(c) Throughout the planned life of the firm non-capital overhead is proportional to the cost of current inputs. In this case the overhead period is zero.

These results are all easily proved by the method used in treating case (2) in the previous section.

5 THE EFFECT OF A CHANGE IN THE INTEREST RATE ON THE PERIOD OF PRODUCTION

In this section the method followed is closely related to that used by Hicks in his Mathematical Appendix.†

If the change in the period of production caused by a small change in the rate of interest is to be considered, one must make assumptions about the nature of the price changes which are required so that capitalised receipts should equal capitalised costs in the new static equilibrium. The actual changes in prices will depend upon the supply and demand functions for all products and factors, which will themselves be affected by the change in the interest rate. Thus the actual change in the period of production depends upon a very complex set of factors.

It seems worthwhile to carry through a simplified investigation in which it is assumed that all input prices remain constant during the change, and all output prices change proportionately. If P is a price index for all outputs (and is initially unity), it follows that $dP/dr = T$.

On these assumptions, Hicks' device can be used whereby all inputs in period t or all outputs in period t can be treated as though they were a single input or output. Thus if C_t is the total value of all inputs in period t at the original prices, and if R_t is the total value of all outputs in period t at the original prices, then both C_t and R_t can be treated as if they were physical quantities of factors or products. Now

$$T = \frac{P \sum_t R_t e^{-rt} t - \sum_t C_t e^{-rt} t}{\sum_t C_t e^{-rt}}$$

so that

$$\frac{dT}{dr} = \frac{dP}{dr} \frac{\sum_t R_t e^{-rt} t}{\sum_t C_t e^{-rt}} - \left(\frac{P \sum_t R_t e^{-rt} t^2 - \sum_t C_t e^{-rt} t^2}{\sum_t C_t e^{-rt}} \right)$$

$$+ T \frac{\sum_t C_t e^{-rt} t}{\sum_t C_t e^{-rt}} + \frac{P \sum_t \dfrac{dR_t}{dr} e^{-rt} t - \sum_t \dfrac{dC_t}{dr} e^{-rt} t}{\sum_t C_t e^{-rt}} - T \frac{\sum_t \dfrac{dC_t}{dr} e^{-rt}}{\sum_t C_t e^{-rt}}.$$

The first three terms are the change in T due directly to the changes in the discount factors and to the change in the relative prices of inputs and outputs and will be called the *valuation effect* V.

Thus

$$V = -\left(\frac{\sum_t R_t e^{-rt} t^2 - \sum_t C_t e^{-rt} t^2}{\sum_t C_t e^{-rt}} \right) + T(T_R + T_C)$$

† *Value and Capital*, Mathematical Appendix, Section 24.

$$= -\left(\frac{\sum_t R_t e^{-rt} t^2 - \sum_t C_t e^{-rt} t^2}{\sum_t C_t e^{-rt}}\right) + T_R^2 - T_C^2$$

$$= -\frac{\sum_t R_t e^{-rt}(t - T_R)^2}{\sum_t R_t e^{-rt}} + \frac{\sum_t C_t e^{-rt}(t - T_C)^2}{\sum_t C_t e^{-rt}} = V_C - V_R$$

where V_C and V_R are measures of the dispersions in the times of inputs and outputs respectively. It follows that the valuation effect can be either positive or negative. For example, in the point-input flow-output case V_C is zero and the effect is negative; conversely, in the flow-input point-output case V_R is zero and the effect is positive.

The last two terms in the formula or dT/dr give the change in T caused by real changes in the quantities of inputs and outputs and can be called the *real effect*. Thus

$$\left(\sum_t C_t e^{-rt}\right)\left(\frac{dT}{dr} - V\right) = \sum_t \frac{dR_t}{dr} e^{-rt} t - \sum_t \frac{dC_t}{dr} e^{-rt}(t + T)$$

$$= \sum_t \frac{dR_t}{dr} e^{-rt}(t - T_R) - \sum_t \frac{dC_t}{dr} e^{-rt}(t - T_C)$$

$$+ T_R\left(\sum_t \frac{dR_t}{dr} e^{-rt} - \sum_t \frac{dC_t}{dr} e^{-rt}\right)$$

and the last term is zero since the changes in the inputs and outputs satisfy the production function.

Substitution terms may now be introduced with the Hicksian convention for signs as follows: $X_{tt'}$ is the substitution term corresponding to substitution between total inputs in period t and t'; $Y_{tt'}$ is the substitution term corresponding to substitution between total inputs in period t and total outputs in period t'; $Z_{tt'}$ is the substitution term corresponding to substitution between total outputs in period t and period t'. Thus

$$dC_t/dr = -\sum_{t'} X_{tt'} e^{-rt'} t' - \sum_{t'} Y_{tt'} e^{-rt'}(t' - T),$$

$$dR_t/dr = -\sum_{t'} Y_{tt'} e^{-rt'} t' - \sum_{t'} Z_{tt'} e^{-rt'}(t' - T).$$

Also

$$\frac{dC_t}{dr} = -\sum_{t'} X_{tt'} e^{-rt'}(t' - T_C) - \sum_{t'} Y_{tt'} e^{-rt'}(t' - T_R)$$

$$- T_C\left(\sum_{t'} X_{tt'} e^{-rt'} + \sum_{t'} Y_{tt'} e^{-rt'}\right)$$

and the last term is zero from the properties of the substitution terms. Similarly

$$\frac{dR_t}{dr} = \sum_{t'} Y_{tt'} e^{-rt'}(t' - T_C) + \sum_{t'} Z_{tt'} e^{-rt'}(t' - T_R).$$

Thus

$$\left(\sum_t C_t e^{-rt}\right)\left(\frac{dT}{dr} - V\right) = \sum_t \sum_{t'} Z_{tt'} e^{-r(t+t')}(t - T_R)(t' - T_R)$$

$$+ \sum_t \sum_{t'} Y_{tt'} e^{-r(t+t')}(t - T_R)(t' - T_C) + \sum_t \sum_{t'} Y_{tt'} e^{-r(t+t')}(t - T_C)(t' - T_R)$$

$$+ \sum_t \sum_{t'} X_{tt'} e^{-r(t+t')}(t - T_C)(t' - T_C)$$

and the right hand side is negative from the second order stability conditions.

Thus, in this case where all output prices change proportionally the real effect must be negative. The valuation effect may have either sign, and so the total change may be positive or negative. The real effect will be small when the elasticities of substitution are small or where both inputs and outputs are concentrated in time and the elasticities are not large.

If we now consider the most general set of price changes that is possible a much more complicated piece of algebra results, but there is no longer any necessity for the real effect to be negative. Thus, in general, there is no reason why a fall in the rate of interest should necessarily produce an increase in the period of production.

6 THE COMPLETE PERIOD OF PRODUCTION

The results of the preceding paragraphs are completely general in the sense that they apply to multi-product firms. If, however, the model is restricted so that each firm is regarded as producing only one product, more interesting results can be obtained. The period of production as previously defined is only partial in the sense that the price of the product will be affected by the rate of interest not only directly in the costs and methods of production, but also through changes in the prices of inputs (raw materials and fixed capital goods) caused by changes in their costs of production. The changes in the prices of inputs can be deduced from equations of the type (5), derived for the firms producing them. These changes can then be substituted, in the original equation, thereby eliminating the prices of all the inputs in the original productive process, but leaving still the prices of inputs in the earlier stage of production. By the same method the changes in these prices may be eliminated and so on *ad infinitum*. This process seems to lead to an infinite regress since all firms use goods produced by other firms. This difficulty is spurious, however, because the regress will only involve a finite number of goods, some of which (e.g., machine tools) are used to produce others which in turn are used to produce the first type of good.

Thus let there be n types of goods under consideration, and m other factors of production; let p_i be the price of the ith good, and p_i' be the price of the ith factor; let T_i be the partial period of production of the ith good, K_{ij} be the proportion of the capitalised cost of the ith good due to the use of the jth good, and k_{ij}' be the proportion due to the $j$the factor. Then a set of equations of the following form is obtained:

$$T_i + \sum_{j=1}^{m} \frac{k_{ij}'}{p_j'} \frac{dp_j'}{dr} = \frac{1}{p_i} \frac{dp_i}{dr} - \sum_{j=1}^{n} \frac{k_{ij}}{p_j'} \frac{dp_j}{dr} \qquad (i = 1, \ldots, n).$$

These equations can be solved to give the $(1/p)dp/dr$'s in terms of the partial periods of production and the changes in the prices of the other factors of production.

If K_{ij} is an element of the reciprocal matrix corresponding to the matrix

$$\begin{bmatrix} 1-k_{11}, -k_{12}, -k_{13}, \ldots, & -k_{1n} \\ -k_{21}, 1-k_{22}, -k_{23}, \ldots, & -k_{2n} \\ \vdots & \\ -k_{n1}, -k_{n2}, -k_{n3}, \ldots, & 1-k_{nn} \end{bmatrix}$$

then

$$\frac{1}{p_i} \frac{dp_i}{dr} = \sum_{j=1}^{n} K_{ij} T_j + \sum_{k=1}^{m} \left(\sum_{j=1}^{n} K_{ij} k_{jk}' \right) \frac{1}{p_k'} \frac{dp_k'}{dr}.$$

The expression $\sum_{j=1}^{n} K_{ij} T_j$ can be called the complete period of production of the ith good. The discussion of the first paragraph of this section indicates that all the quantities are positive. This can be proved as well as the fact that the infinite regress discussed above converges by using the results of R. Solow.†

7 A SIMPLE EXAMPLE

Suppose a machine is produced by using only labour and a raw material which latter is produced in turn by using only labour and the machine. Then using suffixes 1 and 2 to denote the machine and raw material,

† R. Solow, 'On the structure of linear models', *Econometrica*, **20**, 29–46.

respectively, the following equations are obtained.

$$T_1 = \frac{1}{p_1}\frac{dp_1}{dp} - \frac{k_{12}}{p_2}\frac{dp_2}{dr} - \frac{k'_1}{p'}\frac{dp'}{dr},$$

$$T_2 = \frac{1}{p_2}\frac{dp_2}{dr} - \frac{k_{21}}{p_1}\frac{dp_1}{dr} - \frac{k'_2}{p'}\frac{dp'}{dr}.$$

It follows that

$$T_1 + k_{12}T_2 = (1 - k_{12}k_{21})\left(\frac{1}{p_1}\frac{dp_1}{dr} - \frac{1}{p'}\frac{dp'}{dr}\right),$$

$$T_2 + k_{21}T_1 = (1 - k_{12}k_{21})\left(\frac{1}{p_2}\frac{dp_2}{dr} - \frac{1}{p'}\frac{dp'}{dr}\right).$$

Thus the complete periods of production of the machine and raw materials are $(T_1 + k_{12}T_2)/(1 - k_{12}k_{21})$ and $(T_2 + k_{21}T_1)/(1 - k_{12}k_{21})$, respectively.

8 THE PRICES OF OTHER FACTORS

It is not possible by this sort of procedure to eliminate the effects on the price of the output of changes in the prices of the 'basic' factors of production, labour and land. The complete period of production may be regarded as representing the effect of the rate of interest on the ratio of the product·price to a suitably weighted index of the 'basic' factor prices contributing at any stage to its costs of production. If in the long period the relative wages of different kinds of labour (including managerial labour) can be taken as being in fixed ratios, there still remains unsolved the problem of the effect of changes in the rate of interest on the ratios of rents (in the widest classical sense) to wages. This problem cannot be solved by considering only the theory of the firm, for its solution must depend upon the demand for the product. Indeed, the theories in this article can be reinterpreted when natural resources are important as demonstrating how the prices of these resources are ultimately determined by the prices of labour and of consumption goods and by the rate of interest.

9 IMPERFECT COMPETITION

Abandoning the assumption of perfect competition complicates the analysis considerably. Under imperfect competition it still seems appropriate to define the period of production by equation (4). It can then be shown that the relationships proved previously are still true if the vertical shifts in the firm's sales and supply curves are substituted for the actual changes in price.

The important criterion is then whether the firm expands or contracts when the interest rate falls. The fall in costs under the assumption of free entry tends to attract new firms into the industry, and thereby to increase the elasticity of the sales and supply curves of the individual firms. At the same time the general effects of the fall in the rate of interest on all prices will be to increase real incomes and consequently to produce an increase in the total demand for the particular product under consideration which must be shared by the larger number of firms. If demand for the product of the whole industry is income elastic and price inelastic, or if demand is price elastic and the costs of the industry are affected more than the average by the change in the rate of interest, the conditions favour an expansion in the output of the individual firm. In general, however, no simple criterion determines whether output will expand or contract.

If there is a fall in a firm's output, since the magnitude of the period of production indicates the size of vertical shifts in the demand curve and the actual change in price can be regarded as made up of a shift in the curve plus a movement along the curve, it follows that price will fall less than is indicated by the period of production. If output expands when the rate of interest falls then the period of production understates the effect of the interest rate on prices. A more complete discussion is given in the Appendix.

In the case of the kinked-demand-curve type of oligopoly, where the kink is determined only by the ruling market price, the solution is simple. Only a very large change in the rate of interest will have any effect on the price level. Usually the effect will be to change the number of firms producing at the same price.

10 THE MODEL AND THE REAL WORLD

The perfect competition model considered earlier in this article is obviously unrealistic. The last paragraph shows that it is difficult to say how much the substitution of imperfect competition modifies the results. Again, the model is purely static and so can only indicate the long period tendencies of the economic system. Rough calculations of the period of production, however, will at least give an idea as to the order of magnitude of the effects on prices of changes in the interest rate.

For this purpose it is assumed that goods can be divided into four categories: consumption goods, machinery, buildings, and raw materials; and that within each category the production method is the same for every good. The estimates in Table I are intended to suggest orders of magnitude. The raw material figures are intended to apply to a mineral, the main

Table I

	Partial period of production (years)	% of total capitalised cost due to:				Complete period of production (years)
		Labour	Raw material	Machinery	Building	
Raw material	4.3	77	—	23	—	5.0
Machinery	2.0	50	30	15	5	3.2
Building	1.0	30	65	5	—	4.4
Consumption goods	1.5	40	50	5	5	4.4

contribution to the partial period of production being from the original sinking of the mine and of the pithead gear, etc. The complete period of production may not be too far out for some tree crops and timber. Consumption goods do not include food. The solutions of the resulting equations give the complete periods of production as shown in the last column of the table. The results are probably very unreliable as an indication of the relative sizes of the complete periods of production, but they do show that the effect of a small change in the rate of interest on the prices of final outputs, assuming that price of labour unchanged, is not likely to be large. A change in 1% in the rate of interest will produce less than a 5% change in the price of any final output relative to the price of labour. This conclusion is still true when the effects of changes in the prices of natural resources are considered, since these changes will work in the opposite direction to the changes in the rate of interest.

Furthermore, in the real world the businessman is not so exact in his calculations as the model pretends, and he may ignore entirely changes which have only a small effect on his costs with the result that the effect of small changes in the rate of interest on prices in the ordinary medium period may be masked entirely by short period random effects such as changes in techniques or tastes.

The practical conclusions of this article are, therefore, that although small changes in the rate of interest should have a significant although small effect on real wages, it is possible that this effect may be concealed by the effects of short period fluctuations in technique or tastes. On the other hand, it is clear that the fall of the rate of interest to zero should have a large effect on the real wage rate, but it would be extremely hazardous to guess whether the increase in the real wage would be nearer 20% to 50%.

APPENDIX: IMPERFECT COMPETITION

Under imperfect competition it still follows that

$$RT = \sum_i R_i \left(\frac{1}{p_i} \frac{dp_i}{dr} \right) - \sum_i C_i \left(\frac{1}{w_i} \frac{dw_i}{dr} \right) + \sum_i \sum_t p_i \frac{dx_{it}}{dr} e^{-rt} - \sum_i \sum_t w_i \frac{dy_{it}}{dr} e^{-rt}.$$

Now, suppose that the entrepreneur regards his sales in any period as being determined purely by his price in the same period and assumes the elasticity of demand (defined to be positive) to be constant over time and equal to e_i. Suppose, moreover, that he regards the supply of any factor as determined purely by the price in that period with an elasticity of supply equal to E_i. Then, since changes in the quantities sold must satisfy the production function and since the derivatives of the production function are proportional to the marginal revenues and marginal costs, it follows that

$$\sum_i \sum_t p_i(1-1/e_i)\frac{dx_{it}}{dr}e^{-rt} - \sum_i \sum_t w_i(1+1/E_i)\frac{dy_{it}}{dr}e^{-rt} = 0.$$

Thus,

$$\sum_i \sum_t p_i\left(\frac{dx_{it}}{dr}\right)e^{-rt} - \sum_i \sum_t w_i\frac{dy_{it}}{dr}e^{-rt} = \sum_i \sum_t \frac{p_i}{e_i}\frac{dx_{it}}{dr}e^{-rt} + \sum_i \sum_t \frac{w_i}{E_i}\frac{dy_{it}}{dr}e^{-rt}$$

and so

$$\sum_i j_i\left(\frac{1}{p_i}\frac{dp_i}{dr}\right) - \sum_i k_i\left(\frac{1}{w_i}\frac{dw_i}{dr}\right) = T - \frac{1}{R}\left(\sum_i \sum_t \frac{p_i}{e_i}\frac{dx_{it}}{dr}e^{-rt} + \sum_i \sum_t \frac{w_i}{E_i}\frac{dy_{it}}{dr}e^{-rt}\right).$$

The second term on the right hand side is a negatively weighted sum of the rates of increase of all outputs and inputs. Thus, if all these rates of increase are positive, the period of production will overstate the effect of the rate of interest on prices; similarly, if they are negative the effect will be understated.

The situation is more complicated if outputs and inputs do not all move in the same direction. For example, it is possible that all outputs and inputs may increase after a fall in the rate of interest, except for one input (e.g., labour) which falls because it is bought on a particularly imperfect market and the elasticity of supply is so low that the contribution of this factor to the second term makes it negative. Therefore, although most outputs and inputs rise with a fall in the interest rate, the period of production overstates the effects on prices. The simple criterion given in the body of this paper is, therefore, really applicable only to the case of a single output and perfect factor markets.

University of Leeds

——— · ———

A NOTE ON MR BLYTH'S ARTICLE

(First published in Econometrica (1956), Vol. 24, pp. 480–1.)

This note discusses the relation between Mr Blyth's time measures and a set of discounted time measures, the first of these latter being equal to the period of production as it was defined in my article, 'The period of production' (*Econometrica* (1955), Vol. 23, pp. 151–65).

Using Mr Blyth's notation, the expected value of output at time t is denoted by $x(t)$. One may also consider the discounted value of output at time t written as $x'(t) = x(t)e^{-rt}$, and the discounted value of input written as $i'(t) = i(t)e^{-rt}$. Mr Blyth's time measures are computed from the cumulants of the frequency distribution of $x(t)$ and $i(t)$ over time, according to (18) in his article. In the same way, one may define 'discounted time measures' from the cumulants of the frequency distribution of $x'(t)$ and $i'(t)$ over time. If $^{x}k'_q$ and $^{I}k'_q$ are the cumulants of order q, these discounted time measures will be:

$$\tau'_1 = {}^{x}k'_1 - {}^{I}k'_1,$$
$$\tau'_2 = {}^{x}k'_2 - {}^{I}k'_2, \qquad (1)$$

etc.

The first of these may also be written as:

$$\tau'_1 = \frac{\displaystyle\int_0^\lambda tx(t)e^{-rt}dt}{\displaystyle\int_0^\lambda x(t)e^{-rt}dt} - \frac{\displaystyle\int_0^\lambda ti(t)e^{-rt}dt}{\displaystyle\int_0^\lambda i(t)e^{-rt}dt}$$

which is clearly the period of production as given by equation (4) in my earlier article.

Mr Blyth's approach also differs from mine in that he defines the time measures in terms of a process whereas I referred to the receipts and payments of a marginal firm. To use the results in the way that he proposes it would be necessary to assume that new firms were being started at a constant rate. This would be difficult if in fact the life of the firm were assumed infinite. However, if the firm's receipts and payments can be explained as a number of repetitions of a process, then the time measures for the firm would be the same as that of the process.

One may also point out that an expansion similar to that of equation (19) in Mr Blyth's article may be developed in terms of the discounted time measures. Indeed, one may write:

$$X(0) = \int_0^\lambda x'(t)e^{rt}dt.$$

If $M'_x(s)$ denotes the moment generating function of the time distribution of $x'(t)$,

$$X(0) = X(r)M'_x(r)$$

and

$$K'_x(s) = \log M'_x(s) = {}^X k'_1 s + \frac{s^2}{2!} {}^X k'_2 + \cdots \cdot \tag{2}$$

From these, and similar relations with respect to the inputs, one may derive using the same procedure as Mr Blyth:

$$X(0) = I(0)e^{r'r'_1 + (r'^2/2!)r'_2 + \cdots}$$

which is the new version of (19).

Now, from the definition of the moment generating function it follows that:

$$M_x(s) = \int_0^\lambda x(t)e^{st}dt = \int_0^\lambda x'(t)e^{(s+r)t}dt = M'_x(s+r).$$

Thus, if

$$D(s) = \log M_x(s) - \log M_I(s),$$

$$D'(s) = \log M'_x(s) - \log M'_I(s),$$

then:

$$D(s) = D'(s+r'), \qquad \text{when } r = r'.$$

From equations such as (1) and (2), it follows that:

$$\tau'_i = \left[\frac{\partial^i}{\partial s^i} D'(s) \right]_{s=0}$$

where the partial differentiation means that all the inputs and outputs are assumed to remain constant.

It follows that:

$$\tau_i' = \left[\frac{\partial^i}{\partial s^i} D(s) \right]_{s=-r'} = \tau_i - r'\tau_{i+1} + \frac{r'^2}{2!} \tau_{i+2} - \cdots .$$

With the same assumption regarding partial derivatives:

$$\frac{\partial^h}{\partial' r^h} \tau_i' = (-1)^h \left[\frac{\partial^{i+h}}{\partial s^{i+h}} D(s) \right]_{s=-r'} = (-1)^h \tau_{i+h}'$$

so that for example:

$$\frac{\partial \tau_1'}{\partial r'} = -\tau_2'.$$

This particular case was considered in my article as the *valuation effect* of a change in the interest rate on the period of production.

University of Leeds

J. D. SARGAN

———— . ————

3 THE DISTRIBUTION OF WEALTH

(First published in *Econometrica* (1957a), Vol. 25, pp. 568–90.)

1 INTRODUCTION

In this paper a development of the methods used by Champernowne [1] in the study of income distributions is applied to the study of the distribution of wealth. Champernowne considers the possibility that the distribution of income may be regarded as produced by a set of dynamic linear equations relating the numbers in each income group in one discrete time period to the numbers in the same and adjacent income groups in the previous time period. In this paper a similar method is used to study the distribution of wealth. This has the advantage that the unexplained dynamic relationship used by Champernowne in his theory of income distribution, is, in the case of the wealth distribution, replaced by a relationship representing the total effect of four separate causes of change in the wealth distribution. These are: (1) the setting up of new households, (2) gifts between households, (3) saving and capital gains, and (4) the disappearance of existing households with part of their wealth passing to other households.

The methods used also differ from Champernowne's in that he uses discrete time periods and discrete income groups, whereas in this paper the frequency distribution function of the continuous variable, wealth, is studied, and time is assumed to vary continuously. The advantages of this are, first, that an integro-differential equation of a reasonably simple type is obtained for the frequency distribution function, and, secondly, that in certain special cases which are of some practical interest the theory is most easily developed by the use of the characteristic function (the Fourier transform).

The results in these special cases are that the distribution of wealth tends to be approximately log-normal. Gilbrat [3] first showed empirically that a wide range of distributions of economic variables approximate the log-normal form, and proposed as an explanation that in each period the distribution is derived from that of the previous period in the following way. The variable corresponding to each member of the distribution is affected by a small proportionate change, and the proportions differ for different members of the distribution and are determined in a random manner from a given frequency distribution. This type of explanation has been elaborated with particular reference to income distributions by Kalecki [5] and Rutherford [7]. An alternative explanation of this general tendency for the distribution of economic variables to be log-normal is possibly that they can be regarded as generated by dynamic linear equations of the almost-homogeneous type as defined in Section 10 of this paper. However, since separate discussions of the generating mechanism would be required for each type of economic variable, this paper is confined to a discussion of the distribution of wealth.

2 THE BASIC ASSUMPTIONS

It will be assumed that the distribution of wealth in an economy can be defined by a distribution function $f(w)$, where $f(w)dw$ is the number of separate wealth owners in the economy whose wealth is between w and $w+dw$. For theoretical purposes it does not matter whether wealth is defined to exclude or include psychic assets. The first treatment is more suitable for practical applications. The second is perhaps theoretically preferable in that it should give a more accurate picture of how the wealth and income distributions of an economy develop. The differences between the two treatments do not affect the mathematical formulations, but affect only the interpretation to be given to the savings function and to the different distribution functions to be introduced later. Similarly, the owner of wealth may be thought of in a legal and therefore practical manner as an adult person, or, in what is probably a theoretically preferable way, as a household. The difference in definitions does not lead to any difference in the mathematical formulation, but merely in the interpretation. In this paper the verbal explanations will consider the wealth-owner as the household.

Changes in $f(w)$ can be regarded as occurring for four reasons: (1) by each household saving or making capital gains, (2) by gifts (capital transfers) between households, (3) by the founding of new households, and (4) by the disappearance of old households and the passage of all or part of their wealth to other households. This last process can be regarded as covering both the case where the household terminates by death and that part of its wealth which is not taken as taxation passes as legacies and the case where two or more households coalesce, for example, through marriage, with the combined wealth passing to the one household which remains. The effects of a general capital levy are not considered since at least the immediate effects are sufficiently obvious. Each of the four processes enumerated above will now be discussed in the most convenient order.

3 THE FOUNDING OF NEW HOUSEHOLDS

It will be assumed that any new household can be regarded as the offspring of some already existent household and that households with a given wealth have a frequency distribution per unit time of founding new households. The frequency distribution (per unit time) of new households is assumed to depend on the wealth of the founding household but to be independent of time.

Denoting this distribution function by $f_1(w, w_o)$, where w is the wealth of the new household and w_o is the wealth of the founding household, it is assumed that in any short time interval dt the number of new households founded with wealth between w and $w + dw$ by each household with wealth w_o is

$$f_1(w, w_o)dwdt.$$

Thus the contribution of this process to $\partial f/\partial t$ is $\int_0^\infty f_1(w, w_o)f(w_o)dw_o$.

In the rest of this article it is assumed that $f_1(w, w_o)$ is a function of w and w_o only, so that not only is it independent of time t, but it is also independent of $f(w)$, the wealth distribution function. This may be unrealistic.

4 GIFTS BETWEEN HOUSEHOLDS

It is assumed that each household with a given wealth has a frequency distribution per unit time of giving gifts of a given size to other households of a given wealth, which is constant over time. Denoting this function by

$$f_2(g, w, w_o),$$

where g is the value of the gift, w is the wealth of the receiving household, and w_o is the wealth of the giving households, it is assumed that each household with wealth w_o makes gifts of between g and $g + dg$ at a rate per unit of time of $f_2(g, w, w_o)dgdw$ to households with wealth between w and $w + dw$.

This assumption is obviously asymmetrical between giving and receiving, since it is assumed implicitly that $f_2(g, w, w_o)$ is independent of the form of $f(w)$, whereas it seems likely that the distribution of gifts classified by the wealth of the receiving households must depend upon the distribution function of the wealth of households, $f(w)$. Thus, for example, if $f(w) = 0$ for some particular value of w, so that there are no households with wealth w, it is clearly necessary for consistency that $f_2(g, w, w_0) = 0$ for the same value of w. If the simplifying assumption is dropped, however, the model's mathematical properties become extremely complicated. The assumption must, moreover, be retained if the linearity of the model is to be preserved. The deficiencies of this assumption do, however, lead to unsatisfactory results in some cases. This is discussed in Section 9. The assumption is to some extent justified if most gifts are made to households which are offspring of the giving household, because it was assumed in the previous paragraph that the wealth distribution of the offspring of a given household is independent of the distribution of other households.

Now the total number of households which move per unit time from the wealth range w to $w+dw$ through the receipt of gifts is

$$\int_0^\infty \left[\int_0^\infty f_2(g,w,w_o)dg\right]f(w_o)dw_o.$$

Similarly the number of households that enter the range w to $w+dw$ per unit time because of the receipt of gifts is

$$\int_0^\infty \left[\int_0^\infty f_2(g,w-g,w_o)dg\right]f(w_o)dw_o.$$

It will be convenient to ignore the effect on the giving households until the next section.

The contribution of this process to $\partial f/\partial t$ is therefore

$$\int_0^\infty \left[\int_0^\infty f_2(g,w-g,w_0)dg - \int_0^\infty f_2(g,w,w_o)dg\right]f(w_o)dw_o$$
$$= \int_0^\infty f_3(w,w_o)f(w_o)dw_o$$

where

$$f_3(w,w_o)= \int_0^\infty [f_2(g,w-g,w_o)-f_2(g,w,w_o)]dg.$$

By definition we take $f_2(g,w-g,w_o)=0$ if $w-g$ is negative.

5 SAVING

It is simplest to consider a frequency distribution function of net savings plus capital gains conditional upon the wealth of the household. Net savings are defined as net of the wealth used for founding new households and for making gifts to other households. Let this frequency distribution function be denoted by $f_4(S,w)$ where S is net saving and capital gains and w is the wealth of the saving household.

If the operation of this process is considered in isolation, the wealth distribution at a time $t + \Delta t$, for Δt small, can be deduced from that at time t since the number of households with wealth between w and $w + dw$ is equal to

$$\int_0^\infty f(w - S\Delta t)f_4(S, w - S\Delta t)dS \, dw$$

where $f(w)$ is the distribution function for w at time t. This can be expanded to the first order in Δt as

$$\int_0^\infty f(w)f_4(S, w)dS - \Delta t\left[\int_0^\infty S\frac{\partial f_4}{\partial w} f dS + \int_0^\infty S\frac{\partial f}{\partial w} f_4 dS\right]dw.$$

Now writing $\bar{S} = \int_0^\infty Sf_4 dS$ so that $\bar{S}$ is the mean net savings and capital gains of households of wealth w, this can be written

$$\left[f(w) - \Delta t\left(\bar{S}\frac{\partial f}{\partial w} + f\frac{\partial \bar{S}}{\partial w}\right)\right]dw.$$

Thus the contribution of saving to $\partial f/\partial t$ is $-(\bar{S} \, \partial f/\partial w + f \, \partial \bar{S}/\partial w)$.

If gross saving is now defined to include wealth used in founding new households and gifts to other households and if $\bar{G}$ is the mean gross savings and capital gains of households of wealth w, then

$$\bar{S} = \bar{G} - \int_0^\infty w'f_1(w', w)dw' - \int_0^\infty \int_0^\infty gf_2(g, w', w)dgdw'.$$

In the rest of this article it is assumed that gross savings and capital gains are independent of the distribution function of total wealth in the economy. This may be unrealistic.

6 THE TERMINATION OF EXISTING HOUSEHOLDS

It is assumed that there is a given proportionate rate of terminating existing households which can be written $f_5(w)$. Where the winding-up is caused by death this corresponds to the crude death rate. The direct contribution of this to $\partial f/\partial t$ is $-f_5(w)f(w)$. The passing of its wealth to other households can be treated in the same way as gifts between households. Thus a distribution function $f_6(r, w, w_o)$ per unit time can be introduced where r is the value of the transfer, w is the wealth of the receiving household, and w_o is the wealth of the terminated household.

The contribution to $\partial f/\partial t$ from this is

$$\int_0^\infty f_7(w, w_o)f_6(w_o)f(w_o)dw_o$$

where

$$f_7(w, w_o) = \int_0^\infty [f_6(r, w-r, w_o) - f_6(r, w, w_o)] dr.$$

The average wealth extracted by the government as taxation (death duties, etc.) upon the winding-up of a household with wealth w_o is

$$w_o - \int_0^\infty \int_0^\infty r f_6(r, w, w_o) dr dw.$$

In the last four paragraphs it was convenient to imagine that all households of given wealth have the same f_1 and f_2, and that all households of given wealth that are wound up have the same f_6, that is, have the same distribution functions when both founding new households and giving to other households and also when disappearing. It is clear, however, that the same results would be obtained if these distribution functions are reinterpreted as mean frequency distributions for households in a given wealth range. If, however, households are systematically heterogeneous, so that they can be classified into groups of households of different types, and if the proportions of households of each type in a given wealth range varied systematically with time, then the mean distribution functions and savings functions would also vary systematically over time. To take account of this complication it would be necessary to set up separate wealth distribution functions for each type of household, and thereby make the model slightly more complicated. For the sake of simplicity this direction has not been pursued in this paper.

7 THE COMPLETE EQUATION

The total effect of all these causes is that $f(w)$ satisfies the linear differential equation

$$\frac{\partial f}{\partial t} = -\left[\frac{\partial \bar{S}}{\partial w} - f_5(w)\right] f - \bar{S}\frac{\partial f}{\partial w}$$

$$+ \int_0^\infty [f_1(w, w_o) + f_3(w, w_o) + f_5(w_o)f_7(w, w_o)] f(w_o) dw_o. \quad (7.1)$$

A possible approach to the solution of this equation is to try to express $f(w)$ as the sum of a series of products of the form

$$f(w) = \sum_i \psi_i(t) F_i(w) \quad (7.2)$$

where each term in the series also satisfies (7.1).

Substituting $f = \psi(t)F(w)$ in (7.1) and dividing both sides by $f(w)$ it follows that

$$-\left(f_5+\frac{\partial \bar{S}}{\partial w}\right)F(w)-\bar{S}\frac{\partial F}{\partial w}$$

$$\frac{d\psi/dt}{\psi}=\frac{+\int_0^\infty [f_1(w,w_o)+f_3(w,w_o)+f_5(w_o)f_7(w,w_o)]F(w_o)dw_o}{F(w)}$$

$$=c$$

where c is a constant since the first term shows it independent of w and the second shows it is independent of t. It follows that $\psi(t)$ is of the form e^{ct}, and that $F(w)$ satisfies the equation

$$\bar{S}\frac{\partial F}{\partial w}+\left[c+f_5(w)+\frac{\partial \bar{S}}{\partial w}\right]F$$

$$=\int_0^\infty [f_1(w,w_o)+f_3(w,w_o)+f_5(w_o)f_7(w,w_o)]F(w_o)dw_o. \quad (7.3)$$

Both c and $F(w)$ may be complex. In this case if $f(w,t)$ is to remain real, the sum (7.2) must include terms which correspond to the conjugate complex quantities $\bar{c}$ and $\overline{F(w)}$. It will be convenient to use the notation

$$\lambda_1(w)=\frac{c+f_5(w)+\dfrac{\partial \bar{S}}{\partial w}}{\bar{S}},$$

and

$$\lambda_2(w,w_o)=\frac{f_1(w,w_o)+f_3(w,w_o)+f_5(w_o)f_7(w,w_o)}{\bar{S}(w)}$$

so that the (7.3) may be written

$$\frac{\partial F}{\partial w}+\lambda_1(w)F=\int_0^\infty \lambda_2(w,w_o)F(w_o)dw_o. \quad (7.4)$$

This equation can now be transformed to an integral equation of the second type. Writing

$$\mu(w)=\exp\left[\int_0^w \lambda_1(w')dw'\right],$$

$$A(w)=F(w)\mu(w),$$

it follows that

$$\frac{\partial A}{\partial w}=\mu(w)\left[\frac{\partial F}{\partial w}+\lambda_1(w)F\right]$$

$$=\int_0^\infty \exp\left[\int_{w_o}^w \lambda_1(w')dw'\right]\lambda_2(w,w_o)A(w_o)dw_o,$$

and this can be integrated to

$$A(w) = A_o + \int_0^w \int_0^\infty \exp\left[\int_{w_o}^w \lambda_1(w')dw'\right]\lambda_2(w_1, w_o)A(w_o)dw_odw_1$$

where $A_o = A(0) = F(0)$. Assuming that the order of integration can be reversed, this can be stated more simply by writing

$$K(w, w_o) = \int_0^w \exp\left[\int_{w_o}^{w_1} \lambda_1(w')dw'\right]\lambda_2(w_1, w_o)dw$$

in the form

$$A(w) = A_o + \int_0^\infty K(w, w_o)A(w_o)dw_o.$$

This is the required integral equation of the second type. The usual methods of solution may not be possible because of the infinite range of integration. In order to discuss this question it is usual to transform the variables so that the new variables have a finite range of variation. If the kernel function is non-singular after the transformation or has a sufficiently small index of singularity, then a solution may be obtained by Fredholm's method. If the conditions that make Fredholm's method possible are fulfilled, then the following general conclusions can be stated. For most values of c if $p_o = 0$ then the only solution of the equation is $p(w) = 0$. Thus for these values of c, p_o can be taken equal to unity and then there will be a unique solution $p(w)$ leading to a unique solution $F(w, c)$ of (7.3). However, for a denumerable set of c there is no solution unless p_o equals zero and then the solution $F(w, c)$ is no longer unique.

This general solution can now be written formally as a two-dimensional Stieltjes integral in the form

$$f(w) = \int F(w, c)e^{+ct}dP$$

where the domain of integration is the two-dimensional space determined by the real and imaginary parts of c. This solution is so general and vague that it does not reveal anything of the nature of the behaviour of the distribution function over time, and it is necessary to specialise the model before useful results can be obtained. In the next sections, therefore, a specialisation which seems likely on a priori grounds to give an approximation to the actual development of the distribution of wealth is examined. Furthermore, it seems likely that in practice the conditions which allow Fredholm's method of solution to be used are not fulfilled. This is certainly true of the special case considered in the next section. If this is so then no general method of solution is known, and the conclusions set out above may not be correct. This gives further reasons for considering in detail a special case where a solution is available.

8 THE HOMOGENEOUS CASE

We consider the case in which the function $K(w, w_o)$ is homogeneous of order minus one in w and w_o. The simplest case in which this is true is when $w_o f_1(w, w_o)$; $w_o^2 f_2(g, w, w_o)$; and $w_o^2 f_6(r, w, w_o)$ all have the property of being homogeneous functions of zero order, or alternatively that

$$f_1(w, w_o) = \frac{1}{w_o} f_1\left(\frac{w}{w_o}\right),$$

$$f_3(w, w_o) = \frac{1}{w_o} f_3\left(\frac{w}{w_o}\right),$$

$$f_7(w, w_o) = \frac{1}{w_o} f_7\left(\frac{w}{w_o}\right).$$

This corresponds to the case where all the distribution functions for different distributing households differ only by scale factors which are proportional to the wealth of the distributing household. It will then follow that the total number of households founded by the average household with wealth w_o is

$$\int_0^\infty f_1(w, w_o) dw = \int_0^\infty \frac{1}{w_o} f_1\left(\frac{w}{w_o}\right) dw = \int_0^\infty f(z) dz$$

where $z = w/w_o$. The result is therefore constant independent of w_o. Similarly the total number of gifts or legacies from the average household of any wealth is independent of its wealth. In the same way it can be proved that the mean size of the gift or legacy and the mean wealth of the receiving household is proportional to the wealth of the distributing household, and that the total wealth distributed in each way is proportional to the wealth of the distributing household.

It is further necessary to assume that $f_5(w) = m$, a constant, and that $\bar{S} = aw$, where a is a constant.

The basic equation (7.1) then becomes

$$\frac{\partial f}{\partial t} + (a + m)f + aw \frac{\partial f}{\partial w} = \int_0^\infty h\left(\frac{w}{w_o}\right) f(w_o) \frac{dw_o}{w_o} \qquad (8.1)$$

where

$$h\left(\frac{w}{w_o}\right) = f_1\left(\frac{w}{w_o}\right) + f_3\left(\frac{w}{w_o}\right) + m f_7\left(\frac{w}{w_o}\right). \qquad (8.2)$$

If now the general technique of the previous section is applied to (8.1), it would be appropriate to consider the possibility of a solution of the form

$$f(w) = F(w)e^{ct}.$$

In this case, however, the Fredholm method of solution is impossible but there is an obvious trial solution

$$F(w) = w^{-r}$$

and c is then found to satisfy the equation

$$c = a(r-1) - m + \int_0^\infty h(z)z^{r-1}dz.$$

This suggests an expansion of the form

$$f(w) = \int w^{-r}e^{ct}dP$$

similar to that of (7.3) of the previous section. The results of this are difficult to interpret satisfactorily, however, and a preferable but less obvious approach is through the use of characteristic functions as in the next section.

9 THE FOURIER TRANSFORM

In order to use the Fourier transform it is necessary to change to the new variables $x = \log w$, $x_o = \log w_o$, and to consider the distribution function of x which will be denoted $p(x)$.

Then

$$p(x) = e^x f(e^x)$$

so that

$$f(w) = \frac{p \log w}{w},$$

$$\frac{\partial f}{\partial w} = \frac{1}{w^2}\left(\frac{\partial p}{\partial x} - p\right),$$

and

$$\frac{\partial f}{\partial t} = \frac{1}{w}\frac{\partial p}{\partial t}.$$

Thus introducing the function

$$g(x - x_o) = \frac{e^x}{e^{x_o}} h(e^{x-x_o}),$$

the equation takes the form

$$\frac{\partial p}{\partial t} + mp + a\frac{\partial p}{\partial x} = \int_{-\infty}^{\infty} g(x - x_o)p(x_o)dx_o, \tag{9.1}$$

or, writing $x - x_o = x'$ and changing the variable of integration to x' this can be written

$$\frac{\partial p}{\partial t} + mp + a\frac{\partial p}{\partial x} = \int_{-\infty}^{\infty} g(x')p(x - x')dx'. \tag{9.2}$$

Now, since p is a distribution function so that $p(x) \geqslant 0$ for all x and

$$\int_{-\infty}^{\infty} p(x)dx$$

is convergent, it follows that there exists a characteristic function $H(s)$ such that

$$p(x) = \frac{1}{2\pi} \int_{-\infty}^{\infty} H(s)e^{-ixs}ds. \tag{9.3}$$

It then follows, assuming that differentiation under the integral sign is possible, that when (9.3) is substituted in (9.2) the equation becomes

$$\frac{1}{2\pi} \int_{-\infty}^{\infty} \left[\frac{\partial H(s)}{\partial t} + mH(s) - iasH(s) \right] e^{-ixs}ds =$$
$$\frac{1}{2\pi} \int_{-\infty}^{\infty} \cdot \int_{-\infty}^{\infty} H(s)g(x')e^{i(x'-x)s}dsdx'.$$

Now since $g(x')$ can be regarded as the difference of two distribution functions,

$$\int_{-\infty}^{\infty} g(x')e^{ix's}dx' = J(s)$$

exists, so that assuming that the order of integration in the double integral can be changed the last equation gives

$$\frac{1}{2\pi} \int_{-\infty}^{\infty} \left(\frac{\partial H}{\partial t} + H(m - ias - J(s)) \right) e^{-ixs}ds = 0$$

for all x.

This can only be true, assuming the functions involved are continuous, if

$$\frac{\partial H}{\partial t} + H[m - ias - J(s)] = 0, \tag{9.4}$$

and this immediately integrates to give

$$\log [H(t)] = \log H_o + t[J(s) + ias - m]. \tag{9.5}$$

Now, $\log H(s)$ is the cumulant generating function for the distribution defined by $p(x)$, and so the cumulant generating function is a linear function of time.

It will now be assumed temporarily that all the functions involved can be expanded as a power series in s. Let

$$\int_{-\infty}^{\infty} g(x)dx = J_o,$$

$$J(s) = J_o\left(1 + \sum_{r=1}^{\infty} \frac{\mu'r}{r!}(is)^r\right),$$

$$\log H_o = A_o + \sum_{r=1}^{\infty} \frac{K_{ro}}{r!}(is)^r,$$

and

$$\log H = A + \sum_{r=1}^{\infty} \frac{Kr}{r!}(is)^r.$$

Then it follows that

$$A = A_o + t(J_o - m),$$

$$K_1 = K_{10} + t(J_o\mu'_1 + a), \tag{9.6}$$

$$K_r = K_{ro} + tJ_o\mu'_r, r \geqslant 2.$$

Now $\exp(A)$ is the total number in the population and it follows that this grows exponentially at a rate given by $J_o - m$. This is obvious also because $J_o = \int_0^\infty f_1(w, w_o)dw$ which is the total number of new households being founded per unit time by each old household.

K_1 is the mean of the distribution, and it increases linearly at a rate equal to $a + J_o\mu'_i$. The first term reflects the effect of saving and capital gains in increasing the mean wealth per household. The second term

$$J\mu'_1 = \int_0^\infty \log\left(\frac{w}{w_o}\right)f_1(w, w_o)dw + \int_0^\infty \int_0^\infty \log\left(1 + \frac{g}{w}\right)f_2(g, w, w_o)dgdw$$

$$+ m\int_0^\infty \int_0^\infty \log\left(1 + \frac{r}{w}\right)f_6(r, w, w_o)drdw.$$

These three integrals reflect the effects on mean wealth of new families being founded, gifts, and legacies, respectively.

The variance of the distribution is K_2 and $K_2 = K_{20} + tJ_o\mu'_2$. First consider the case where μ'_2 is positive. Let a change of variable be introduced by considering $y = (x - K_1)/\sqrt{K_2}$. The cumulant function for y will be equal to

$$\frac{(is)^2}{2!} + \sum_{r=3}^{\infty} \frac{K_r}{K_2^{\frac{1}{2}r}} \frac{(is)^r}{r!}$$

and

$$\frac{K_r}{K_2^{\frac{1}{2}r}} = O(1)/t^{\frac{1}{2}(r-2)}.$$

Thus as t becomes large all the terms of the series except the first become small and ultimately the cumulant function is closely approximated by $(is)^2/2$, which is the cumulant function of the normal error function with unit standard deviation.

This discussion is very similar to that which arises in the proof of the central limit theorem, and it is therefore possible to take over Cramer's conditions for the proof of the central limit theorem unchanged [2]. Thus if $\log H(s)$ can be differentiated twice with respect to s at the origin, then for t sufficiently large the distribution function is approximated as closely as required by a normal error function in a central region covering a high proportion of households.

The condition will be fulfilled provided both the initial distribution function and the function $g(x)$ have second moments, and these conditions seem likely to be fulfilled in practice. It follows that provided μ_2' is positive the distribution of w will ultimately approximate the log-normal form.

This result can be immediately generalised to the case where m, a and $h(z)$ are functions of time. Equations (9.6) must then be replaced by

$$A = A_o + \int_0^t [J_o(t') - m(t')]dt',$$

$$K_1 = K_{10} + \int_0^t [J_o(t')\mu_1'(t') + a(t')]dt',$$

$$K_r = K_{ro} + \int_0^t J_o(t')\mu_r'(t')dt', \quad r \geq 2.$$

The ultimate normality of the distribution still holds true provided there exists a period p such that

$$\int_t^{t+p} J_o(t')\mu_2'(t')dt' \geq M_2 > 0,$$

for all t, and

$$\left| \int_t^{t+p} J_o(t')\mu_r'(t')dt' \right| \leq M_r,$$

for all t, $r \geq 3$, and providing K_{20} exists.

Although this proof suffices to demonstrate the ultimate normality of the distribution if $\mu_2' > 0$, it is possible for this model to lead to values of the K_r which are not consistent with a positive distribution function. In fact if the

K_r represents the cumulants of a positive distribution function $p(x) \geqslant 0$, it is necessary that they satisfy a set of inequalities. There are an infinite number of such inequalities, and as examples one need only cite the two of the smallest order:

$$K_2 \geqslant 0,$$

$$2K_2^2 + K_4 \geqslant 0.$$

It is clearly necessary that $\mu_2' \geqslant 0$, otherwise K_2 will become ultimately negative. The other conditions, however, will be satisfied for all t provided that the initial distribution is suitable.

Now,

$$\mu_2' = \int_0^\infty \log^2 (w/w_o) f_1(w, w_o) dw$$

$$+ \int_0^\infty \int_0^\infty \log (1 + g/w) \log (w(w+g)/w_o^2) f_2(g, w, w_o) dg dw$$

$$+ m \int_0^\infty \int_0^\infty \log (1 + r/w) \log (w(w+r)/w_o^2) f_o(r, w, w_o) dr dw.$$

The contribution of the first integral is always positive. It seems likely that the second and third integrals will be negative since $\log (w(w+g)/w_o^2)$ and $\log (w(w+r)/w_o^2)$ are usually negative whereas the other factors in the integral are positive. It follows that models of this type may be such that the inequalities are not fulfilled. If the inequalities are not fulfilled this can only be because (9.1) produces a distribution function $f(w)$ which is negative for some values of w. The possibility of this happening is not peculiar to the homogeneous model. This can happen with the general linear model discussed in the earlier sections of this article because of the limitations of the treatment of the effects of gifts and legacies. As stated in Section 4, the reason is that even if the number of households in some wealth range has fallen to zero, the model assumes that there will be a finite number of gifts and legacies received by households in this range, and that the effect of these is to move receiving households out of this range, thus reducing the number of households in it. Unless the effect of this is cancelled by the arrival of other households in this range, the model indicates that $f(w)$ becomes negative for this range of values. This is a fundamental limitation on the realism of a model based upon equations linear in the distribution function $f(w)$. The discussion of a non-linear model is much more difficult than that of a linear model, and no attempt to pursue this problem will be made here. However, if μ_2' is greater than zero and the initial distribution is appropriate, the homogeneous linear model does not lead to negative values of $f(w)$, and ultimately the distribution, being approximately log-normal, has a simple uni-modal form. Under these circumstances the linear equations may provide a good approximation so that the ultimate behaviour of the distribution may be fairly accurately represented.

10 THE ALMOST-HOMOGENEOUS CASE

This section is an exploration of the results of relaxing slightly the rigid requirements of Section 8 that are necessary to produce a homogeneous model.

It is still necessary to maintain the assumption of a constant death rate m. It will now be assumed that the mean net saving in any wealth group is only approximately proportional to the existing wealth. Assuming that $\bar{S}$ is always positive for all w it is convenient to introduce the new variable

$$y = \int_\alpha^w \frac{dw'}{\bar{S}(w')}, \qquad \alpha \text{ arbitrary.}$$

Transforming (7.1) from the variables w, t to the variables y, t, and denoting the distribution function of y by $q(y)$ so that $q = \bar{S}f(w)$, an equation analogous to (9.1) is obtained of the form

$$\frac{\partial q}{\partial t} + mq + \frac{\partial q}{\partial x} = \int_{-\infty}^{\infty} g(y - y_o, y_o) q(y_o) dy_o \tag{10.1}$$

where $g(y - y_o, y_o)$ is the transformed form of $\lambda_2(w, w_o)$ of Section 7. (10.1) differs from (9.1) primarily in that in (9.1) the function $g(x - x_o)$ is assumed to depend only on $x - x_o$ and to be independent of x_o. In this section it will be assumed that $g(y - y_o, y_o)$ is almost independent of y_o in a way that will be defined later.

It is now possible to introduce the characteristic function, but it seems best in this section to use a notation which differs slightly from that of the previous section so as to avoid the constant appearance of the imaginary i in the subsequent formulas.

Defining, for u imaginary,

$$H'(u) = \int_{-\infty}^{\infty} g(y) e^{uy} dy,$$

$$J(u, y_o) = \int_{-\infty}^{\infty} g(y, y_o) e^{uy} dy,$$

it follows, assuming differentiation under the integral sign is possible, that

$$\frac{\partial H'}{\partial t} + (m + u) H' = \int_{-\infty}^{\infty} e^{yu} dy \int_{-\infty}^{\infty} g(y - y_o) q(y_o) dy_o$$

$$= \int_{-\infty}^{\infty} e^{y_o u} J(u, y_o) q(y_o) dy_o, \tag{10.2}$$

assuming that the order of integration in the first integral may be changed.

Assuming now that all the moments of the distribution $q(y)$ are finite, it follows that

$$\frac{\partial^r H}{\partial u^r} = \int_{-\infty}^{\infty} y^r q(y) e^{uy} dy \tag{10.3}$$

exists and is finite for all r (u imaginary).

It will also be assumed that the partial derivatives of $J(u, y_o)$ with respect to y_o of all orders exist and that the MacLaurin expansion of $J(u, y_o)$ as a function of y_o is possible for at least some values of u, in the form

$$J(u, y_o) = \sum_{r=0}^{\infty} \frac{J_r}{r!} y_o^r \tag{10.4}$$

where

$$J_r = \left[\frac{\partial^r J}{\partial y_o^r} \right]_{y_o = 0}.$$

Substituting (10.4) in (10.2), assuming that the order of summation and integration can be reversed, and using (10.3), it follows that

$$\frac{\partial H'}{\partial t} + (m+u)H' = \int_{-\infty}^{\infty} e^{y_o u} \left(\sum_{r=0}^{\infty} \frac{J_r}{r!} y_o^r \right) p(y_o) dy_o = \sum_{r=0}^{\infty} \frac{J_r}{r!} \frac{\partial^r H'}{\partial u^r}. \tag{10.5}$$

(10.5) holds generally whatever the savings function and whatever the form of the function $J(u, y_o)$, providing the appropriate differentiability and convergency conditions are satisfied. In the rest of this section an approximation to (10.5) will be developed for the particular case of almost-homogeneity. This condition of almost-homogeneity is defined as the case where, if $J(u, y_o)$ is considered as a function of u and y_o, and y_o is varied while u remains constant, only a large change of order k (k large) in y_o produces any appreciable effect on $J(u, y_o)$.

Alternatively, the assumption can be defined more explicitly by introducing a new variable $Y = y_o/k$ and a new function $L(u, Y)$ so that

$$J(u, y_o) = L(u, y_o/k) = L(u, Y)$$

and then assuming that all the derivatives of L with respect to Y are of finite order as k becomes large. This can be crudely expressed by saying that y_o is divided by the scale factor k.

It is at the same time useful to introduce a new function U by the equations

$$U = \frac{\log H'}{k},$$

$$H' = \exp (kU).$$

From these it follows that

$$\frac{1}{H'}\frac{\partial H'}{\partial u}=k\frac{\partial U}{\partial u},$$

$$\frac{1}{H'}\frac{\partial^2 H'}{\partial u^2}=k^2\left(\frac{\partial U}{\partial u}\right)^2+k\frac{\partial^2 U}{\partial u^2},$$

$$\frac{1}{H'}\frac{\partial^3 H'}{\partial u^3}=k^3\left(\frac{\partial U}{\partial u}\right)^3+3k^2\frac{\partial^2 U}{\partial u^2}\frac{\partial U}{\partial u}+k\frac{\partial^3 U}{\partial u^3}$$

$$\frac{1}{H'}\frac{\partial^4 H'}{\partial u^4}=k^4\left(\frac{\partial U}{\partial u}\right)^4+4k^3\frac{\partial^2 U}{\partial u^2}\left(\frac{\partial U}{\partial u}\right)^2$$

$$+3k^2\left(\frac{\partial^2 U}{\partial u^2}\right)^2+4k^2\left(\frac{\partial^3 U}{\partial u^3}\right)\left(\frac{\partial U}{\partial u}\right)+k\frac{\partial^4 U}{\partial u^4},$$

or in general

$$\frac{1}{H'}\frac{\partial^r H'}{\partial u^r}=k^r\left(\frac{\partial U}{\partial u}\right)^r+rk^{r-1}\left(\frac{\partial^2 U}{\partial u^2}\right)\left(\frac{\partial U}{\partial u}\right)^{r-2}+O(k^{r-2}). \qquad (10.6)$$

Substituting (10.6) in (10.5) and summing the terms specified in (10.6) it follows that

$$k\frac{\partial U}{\partial t}+m+u=L\left(u,\frac{\partial U}{\partial u}\right)+\frac{1}{k}\left(\frac{\partial^2 U}{\partial u^2}\bigg/\frac{\partial U}{\partial u}\right)\cdot\left[\frac{\partial L}{\partial Y}\right]_{Y=(\partial U/\partial u)}+O(1/k^2). \qquad (10.7)$$

This equation considered as an equation for determining U is not very useful since it is non-linear. When k is very large it seems reasonable to assume that a process of successive approximations might be used by first neglecting all terms on the right hand side except the first. The resulting first approximation can then be substituted in the other terms on the right hand side to obtain a second approximation, and so on. The conditions under which this process of successive approximation will converge to a solution of (10.3) would require a rather complicated mathematical investigation which will not be attempted here. The assumption that the process does converge, and that for large k the solution is close to the solution of the equation obtained from (10.7) by omitting all terms on the right hand side except the first, is the basis of the approximations used in later sections of this paper.

In this way it is possible to discuss the general behaviour of the distribution function of wealth assuming that initially the variance of the distribution is fairly small (of order unity compared with k which is large). In the case U is of order $1/k$ initially so that for large k a first approximation to the initial behaviour of the distribution will be obtained by taking

$\partial U/\partial u = 0$ and so obtaining the approximate equation

$$k\frac{\partial U}{\partial t} + m + u = L(u, 0).$$

This simply means that initially the distribution behaves as though the model were completely homogeneous to a good approximation. The approximation remains good until $\partial U/\partial u$ becomes of order unity and so ceases to be good after a time of order k. It is clear that from this time onwards U is at least of order unity, provided the basic assumption made above holds true and that U, satisfying the equation

$$k\frac{\partial U}{\partial t} + m + u = L\left(u, \frac{\partial U}{\partial u}\right),$$

does not tend to zero for all imaginary values of u. If then $H' = \exp(kU)$ is finite at any subsequent time, it will correspond to an approximately normal distribution of the variable x with variance of order k. The larger k is, the better will be the approximation. The proof of this is again similar to that of the central limit theorem; and the proof that as k tends to infinity the distribution tends to the normal form requires only that U should have a second derivative with respect to u at the origin. Furthermore, it follows that the rate of change of U is of order $1/k$, and the proportionate rate of change of the variance is of order $1/k$.

Ultimately the form of the distribution could become constant. To discuss this question, and to obtain further insight into the behaviour of the distribution, the following method may be used. It is clear from the form of (10.5) that its solution may be expressed as a sum of a series of terms of the form $H'_c(u)e^{ct}$ and that the corresponding U_c then satisfies the equation

$$c + m + u = L\left(u, \frac{\partial U_c}{\partial u}\right) + \frac{1}{k}\left(\frac{\partial^2 U_c/\partial u^2}{\partial u_c/\partial u}\right)\cdot\left[\frac{\partial L}{\partial Y}\right]_{Y = (\partial U_c/\partial u)} + O(1/k^2). \qquad (10.8)$$

Considering only the first approximation and writing

$$\phi = \partial U_c/\partial u,$$

it follows that ϕ can be obtained by solving the equation

$$c + m + u = L(u, \phi), \qquad (10.9)$$

and U_c can then be obtained by integrating ϕ with respect to u.

There are then two possibilities. There may be some upper limit c such that for values of c above the limit the corresponding H'_c has a singularity on the imaginary axis, or else that its behaviour at $\pm i\infty$ is unsuitable. In this case it may be possible to expand any H' in terms of the H'_c corresponding to values of c below the limit. It then follows that ultimately the distribution function will tend to a form corresponding to the limiting c. Alternatively, there may be no such limiting value for c. In the first case the form of the distribution ultimately becomes constant; the numbers in each range of wealth ultimately grow at the same constant proportionate rate. The form of the distribution function and the ultimate rate of growth are independent of the initial distribution. In the second case this is not so; the ultimate form of the distribution is not constant and depends on the initial distribution.

As an example of the first possibility the case may be considered where

$$L(u, Y) = M(u, uY).$$

The critical point is then the behaviour of H' at the origin, and this can be discussed by taking a Taylor expansion of $M(u, uY)$ at the origin of the form

$$M(u, uY) = M(0, uY) + \left[\frac{\partial M}{\partial u}\right]_{u=0} u + R,$$

and if f satisfies the equation

$$c + m = M(0, f),$$

it is clear that ϕ at the origin behaves like f/u. Thus U behaves like $f \cdot \log(u)$ and H' behaves like $(u)^f$. If f is negative, H' has a singularity at the origin and the behaviour of H' at the origin is unsatisfactory. On the other hand if f is positive, the behaviour of H at the origin will be satisfactory considered as one out of a set of functions in terms of which an arbitrary characteristic function is to be expanded. In particular if a set of functions is considered which correspond to f being zero or a positive integer this will provide a satisfactory set provided that they behave satisfactorily elsewhere. Ultimately, however, the solution will only tend to a constant form if $M(0, 0) > M(0, \alpha)$ for all positive a, and in particular this condition is satisfied if $M(0, a)$ is a monotonically decreasing function of a for positive values. In this case the ultimate rate of change c is given by the equation

$$c + m = M(0, 0).$$

11 A PARTICULAR CASE

If we consider the particular case where

$$g(y - y_o, y_o) = e^{\mu y_o/k} g'(y - y_o + y_o/k), \tag{11.1}$$

an accurate solution is possible even when k is not assumed large. Assuming $\bar{S} = aw$, this corresponds to the case where the scale of the distribution functions f_1, f_2 and f_7 of the early sections of this paper are all proportional to some power of the wealth of the distributing household and where the total number of new households, gifts, and legacies are all proportionate to $w_o^{\mu/k}$, where w_o is the wealth of the distributing household.

If the characteristic function is introduced in the usual way, a differential equation is obtained which can be solved by introducing the assumption $H' = H'_c e^{ct}$, and this solution does tend as k tends to ∞ to the form developed in the previous section.

In this case

$$L(u, Y) = J(u)e^{Y(\mu - u)}$$

so that (10.9) takes the form

$$c + m + u = J(u)e^{\phi(\mu - \mu)} \tag{11.2}$$

so that

$$U_c = \int_0^u \frac{(\log J(u') - \log (c + m + u'))}{u' - \mu} \, du'. \tag{11.3}$$

If μ is non-zero this equation gives a suitable form of U for any value of c and the ultimate behaviour of the distribution depends on the initial distribution. This is clear also from commonsense considerations, since the rate of increase of the number of households will depend on whether the average wealth is large or small.

If, however, $\mu = 0$, then the solution is only suitable if $J(0) \geqslant c + m$, and for the limiting case where $c = J(0) - m$

$$U_c = \int_0^u \frac{\log J(u') - \log (J_o + u')}{u'} \, du'.$$

In the foregoing it has been assumed that k is positive. If k is taken to be negative in (11.1) this would merely change the sign of U_c in (11.3), and in the special case where $\mu = 0$ the solution is only suitable if $J(0) \leqslant c + m$. This shows that in this case the ultimate form of the wealth distribution is not constant and independent of the initial distribution.

It follows that the ultimate form of the distribution is constant and independent of the initial distribution only if $\mu = 0$ and $k > 0$. This is the case where the total number of households, gifts, and legacies due to any household is independent of its wealth, and where the scale of the distribution functions f_1, f_3 and f_7 is proportional to a power of the wealth of the distributing households which is less than one.

12 A COMPARISON WITH CHAMPERNOWNE'S RESULTS

The methods of this paper are very similar to those used by Champernowne [1] in that the distribution function in both cases is generated by a linear

Table I. *British wealth distributions*

£	1911–13	1924–30	1933–38	1946–47
100	11.7%	21.4%	24.75%	39.38%
1000	3.0%	5.8%	6.92%	11.58%
5000	0.9%	1.6%	1.84%	2.72%
10000	0.4%	0.8%	0.94%	1.34%
25000	0.2%	0.2%	0.33%	0.44%
100000	0.03%	0.04%	0.05%	0.06%

dynamic equation and in that Champernowne's basic assumptions as to its form are equivalent to the homogeneity assumption of Section 8. Champernowne, however, deduces that the ultimate form of the distribution will be approximately Paretian, in contrast to the conclusion reached here that the distribution will be approximately log-normal.

The reason for this is that Champernowne's models are not almost-homogeneous in the sense defined in this article. Even his simplest model [1, p. 322] is not completely homogeneous, in that the number in the lowest income group is determined by an equation which is different from that for the other income groups. This would correspond to a sharp discontinuity in the form of the distribution functions in the model of this paper. Even the introduction of this fairly unrealistic assumption would not suffice to reproduce the Champernowne results. In order to do this, it would be necessary to specialise the distribution functions so that households below the limit were only distributing to other households below the limit, and that households above the limit were only distributing to households above the limit except for a small region of overlap. This kind of assumption is in fact very difficult to make when using a continuous model, and since Champernowne's distribution between discrete income groups must surely be regarded as only an approximation to a continuous frequency distribution, this is to some extent a defect in the discrete approach. Champernowne's results do, however, provide an example where a model which is far from homogeneous leads to a steady distribution which is far from log-normal.

13 AN EXAMINATION OF BRITISH DATA

Gibrat [3] gives a distribution of wealth which is approximately log-normal. The data that will be considered here are the estimates by Langley [7] of the British distributions of wealth in 1911–13, 1924–30, 1936–38 and 1946–47. They are of particular interest in that they allow comparison of the variation of the distribution of wealth in the British economy over time. The basic data are summarised in Table I. In each case the cumulative percentage of total adult persons with wealth greater than the given limit is recorded.

These data cannot be directly interpreted in terms of the households model developed in the previous sections of this paper since the wealth owners are defined as adult persons. As stated in Section 2, however, it is possible to develop the model either in terms of adult persons or of households without introducing any change in the mathematical formulation so that the general conclusions of the previous sections about the form and behaviour of the distributions remain unchanged.

To illustrate these data Figure 1 has been obtained by plotting horizontlly the logarithm of the class limits, and vertically the normal variate value corresponding to the percentage frequency above each class limit. The results are in each case a series of points which lie close to straight lines. Even the slight upward concavity of the points may be explicable by the presence of differential mortality rates producing slight inaccuracies in Langley's estimates. Thus the data, over the ranges of wealth that they cover, indicate a fairly good approximation to a log-normal distribution. If a similar graphical method is used to test the approximation to a Pareto distribution, the graphs show systematic deviations from linearity.

From the figure estimates of the means and standard deviations of the normal distributions of the logarithm of wealth can be made, and these are presented in Table II.

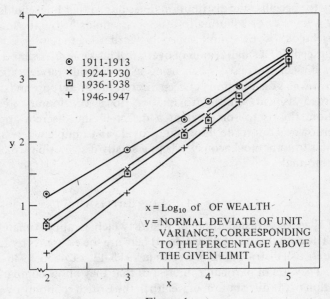

Figure 1

Table II. *Means and standard deviations of British wealth distributions*

Year	Mean	Standard deviation
1911–13	0.48	1.33
1924–30	1.13	1.16
1936–38	1.27	1.14
1946–47	1.77	1.00

Table III. *Positional statistics for British wealth distributions*

Year	Modal wealth	Median wealth	Geometric mean	Arithmetic mean	Lower quartile	Upper quartile
1911–13	£0.05	£3	£3	£23	£0.4	£24
1924–30	£0.6	£13	£13	£63	£2.2	£81
1936–38	£0.9	£19	£19	£83	£3.2	£100
1946–47	£0.9	£59	£59	£186	£12.6	£275

The change in the mean is not very interesting in itself since it is probably due primarily to changes in the general price level. The fall in the standard deviation is more significant (although the fall between 1924–30 and 1936–38 may be explicable by errors in the estimates). The major declines in any case occurred in the periods 1913–24 and 1938–46, and it is perhaps significant that each of these periods contains a major war.

During normal periods it is possible that average saving in any wealth group is approximately proportional to wealth since the well-known tendency for saving to increase more than proportionately to net income may be cancelled by the tendency, due to progressive taxation, of income net of tax to increase less than proportionately to total wealth. A second factor here is that gross income is not proportional to wealth since most of the income of the poor is derived from work and not property. During wars, however, forced savings raises the savings of the poor and increased income and profits taxes affect the savings of the wealthy. Capital gains are different for different types of assets, being largest on some real assets (particularly houses) and relatively small on government bonds and land.

Similarly, the homogeneity assumption seems reasonable for the founding of new households and for gifts between households. For legacies, however, which are probably the most important type of capital transfer, the homogeneity may be spoiled by progressive taxation. Again the effect of this increased during the two World Wars. For these war periods the model must be modified to a less homogeneous form, with a greater tendency towards the equality of wealth distribution. In fact the lack of homogeneity does not seem to have affected the log-normality of the wealth distribution over the ranges of wealth that can be estimated. To be sure, the data for the distribution of wealth above the £100 limit give a very slender basis for estimates of the distribution below this limit. However, it seems worthwhile to examine some of the consequences of assuming that the log-normal distribution does hold below the limit. The figures in Table III have been calculated on that basis.

University of Leeds

REFERENCES

[1] Champernowne, D. G., 'Model of income distribution', *Economic Journal*, 1953, **63**, 318–51.
[2] Cramer, H., *Random Variables and Probability Distributions*. Cambridge, 1937.
[3] Gibrat, R., *Les inégalites économiques*. Paris, 1931.
[4] Hellinger, E. and O. Toeplitz, *Enzyklopadie der mathematischen Wissenschaften*, Part 11, 3, Book 9, 1340–1596.
[5] Kalecki, M., 'On the Gibrat distribution', *Econometrica*, 1945, **13**, 161–70.
[6] Langley, K. M., 'The distribution of capital in private hands in 1936–38 and 1946–47', *Bulletin of the Oxford University Institute of Statistics*, 1950, **12**, 339–59.
[7] Rutherford, R. S. G., 'Income distributions: a new model', *Econometrica*, 1955, **23**, 277–94.

———— · ————

4 THE ESTIMATION OF ECONOMIC RELATIONSHIPS USING INSTRUMENTAL VARIABLES

(First published in *Econometrica* (1958), Vol. 26, pp. 393–415.)

1 INTRODUCTION

The use of instrumental variables was first suggested by Reiersøl [13, 14] for the case in which economic variables subject to exact relationships are affected by random disturbances or measurements errors. It has since been discussed for the same purpose by several authors, notably by Geary [9] and Durbin [7]. In this article the method is applied to a more general case in which the relationships are not exact, so that a set of ideal economic variables is assumed to be generated by a set of dynamic stochastic relationships, as in Koopmans [12], and the actual economic time series are assumed to differ from the ideal economic variables because of random disturbances or measurement errors. The asymptotic error variance matrix for the coefficients of one of the relationships is obtained in the case in which these relationships are estimated using instrumental variables. With this variance matrix we are able to discuss the problem of choice that arises when there are more instrumental variables available than the minimum number required to enable the method to be used. A method of estimation is derived which involves a characteristic equation already considered by Hotelling in defining the canonical correlation [10]. This method was previously suggested by Durbin [7].

The same estimates would be obtained by the maximum-likelihood limited-information method if all the predetermined variables which are assumed subject to disturbances or errors were treated as if they were jointly determined, and the instrumental variables treated as if they were predetermined variables. Such a procedure was suggested by Chernoff and Rubin [5]. It is possible to use the smallest roots of the characteristic equation for significance tests in exactly the same way as when using the maximum-likelihood method, and similar confidence regions can be defined.

All the results listed so far depend on the use of asymptotic approximations. A few calculations were made by the author on the order of magnitude of the errors involved in this approximation. They were found to be proportional to the number of instrumental variables, so that, if the asymptotic approximations are to be used, this number must be small.

2 THE STRUCTURE OF RANDOM SHOCKS AND DISTURBANCES

This article is concerned with a model in which there exist both disturbances with properties first outlined by Frisch [8] and random shocks as in the models used by Koopmans and others [12]. The only problem which will be considered is that of determining the coefficients of a single relationship.

The actual time series with which the economist is concerned are represented by x_{it}, $i = 1, \ldots, n$, $t = 1, \ldots, T$, and are assumed to be of the form

$$x_{it} = x'_{it} + x''_{it} \tag{2.1}$$

where x'_{it} is the systematic part of the variable and x''_{it} accounts for the measurement error and the random disturbances.

The x'_{it}, except for a few which have no measurement error (the constant term, the trend and the seasonal components), are either exogenous variables, or, if endogenous, are assumed to have been generated by a stochastic model of the kind considered by Koopmans [12]. The relationships under consideration will then be written

$$\sum_{i=1}^{n} \mathbf{a}_i x'_{it} = \varepsilon_t \tag{2.2}$$

where ε_t, the random shock, is assumed to be independent of the systematic parts of all the predetermined variables.

We now assume that there are some predetermined variables whose measurement errors are independent of the measurement errors of all the variables in the relationship, and of the random shock. This requirement excludes certain categories of predetermined variables: those in the relationship (unless they have no measurement error), lagged values of variables in the relationship (unless one makes the unrealistic assumption that measurement errors are not autocorrelated), and any predetermined variable which is estimated from the same data as one of the variables in the relationship. Thus, it is necessary that the sources of data used for estimating the instrumental variables should be largely independent of those used to estimate the variables in the relationship. The instrumental variables will be denoted by u_{jt}, $j = 1, \ldots, N$.

If

$$\sum_{i=1}^{n} \mathbf{a}_i x_{it} = E_t \tag{2.3}$$

it follows from (2.1) and (2.2) that

$$E_t = \varepsilon_t + \sum_{i=1}^{n} \mathbf{a}_i x''_{it}. \qquad (2.4)$$

E_t will be called the residual, and it follows from (2.4) and the discussion above that it is independent of all the instrumental variables. The notation used takes no account of the fact that some of the instrumental variables may be in the relationship. As noted above such variables must have zero measurement error, and this restricts them in practice mainly to the constant term or trend or seasonal factors.

In this notation, then, Reiersøl's method amounts to positing a zero sample covariance between the residual and each instrumental variable. One therefore obtains the following equations:

$$\frac{1}{T} \sum_{t=1}^{T} E_t u_{jt} = 0 \qquad (j = 1, \dots, N), \qquad (2.5)$$

or

$$\sum_{i=1}^{n} \mathbf{a}_i \left(\frac{1}{T} \sum_{t=1}^{T} x_{it} u_{jt} \right) = 0 \qquad (j = 1, \dots, N).$$

Equations (2.5) provide N equations for the $n-1$ ratios of the coefficients, so that if $N = n - 1$ they give a unique set of estimates of the coefficients $\mathbf{a}_i$.

The interpretation of the 'ideal economic variables' and of the 'disturbance' is a little difficult. Probably the simplest interpretation is to suppose that, if the data were available for sufficiently short periods, it would be possible to use a model in which each equation explains how some class of economic agents determine the value of one variable as a function of the previous values of other variables. Then it will be assumed that the 'ideal economic variables' are the actual variables to which the economic agents react. At the same time a random component or shock is used in the model equation to represent all those factors which affect the variable being determined by the relationship, including factors which are not easy to measure or to represent numerically, factors which have individually such a small effect that they are not worth attempting to measure, and a catch-all factor providing for the economist's ignorance of human relationships and other social, institutional, and technological factors. The random component is treated like a random variable and is assumed to be independent of the other variables (the lagged variables) in the relationship.

It is not necessarily true that the determined variable is also an ideal economic variable in the sense that it is exactly equal to the variable to which some other economic agent later reacts, or that if an economic variable appears as a cause in two different equations the appropriate values of the ideal economic variable are the same. It will be assumed that if there are differences they can be absorbed into the random shock, or equation error.

Owing to lack of data and the need to simplify the estimation problem this ideal model must be replaced by a simpler model in which short lags must be ignored or approximated by distributed lags. The ideal economic variables of this simpler model correspond to the ideal economic variables of the ideal model. The disturbances or non-systematic parts of the variables, being the differences between the actual times series and the ideal economic variables, can be regarded as real measurement errors perhaps partly due to differences in definition. It is not easy to justify the basic assumption concerning these errors, namely, that they are independent of the instrumental variables. It seems likely that they will vary with a trend and with the trade cycle. In so far as this is true the method discussed here will lead to biased estimates of the coefficients. Nothing can be done about this since presumably, if anything were known about this type of error, better estimates of the variables could be produced. It must be hoped that the estimates of the variables could be produced. It must be hoped that the estimates of the variables are sufficiently accurate, so that systematic errors of this kind are small.

In any case it will be noted that the method of this article uses the minimum assumption about the measurement error. There is no need to assume, for example, that the errors on the variables in the equation are independent of each other, and the estimated coefficients are still consistent even if the errors are autocorrelated.

Throughout this paper it will be assumed that the E_t are not autocorrelated.

3 THE ASYMPTOTIC COVARIANCE MATRIX

The main results of this article will be concerned with the asymptotic properties of the estimates. The following general notation will be used. The sample covariance matrix of the variables in the relationship will be denoted by M_{xx}; the sample covariance matrix of the instrumental variables will be denoted by M_{uu}; and the sample covariance matrix between a variable in the relationship and an instrumental variable will be denoted by M_{xu}.

The asymptotic limit of a sample function of variables will be denoted by placing a bar over the corresponding symbol. Thus $\bar{M}_{xu}$, representing the probability limit of M_{xu}, will be equal to the stationary limiting of $\mathscr{E}(x_t' u_t)$ providing that the model is not explosive, and similarly for the other covariance matrices.

Considering first the case in which $N = n - 1$ it is convenient to introduce the functions

$$w_j = \frac{1}{\sqrt{T}} \sum_{r=1}^{T} E_t u_{jt} \qquad (j = 1, \ldots, N).$$

For finite T, the w_j are not usually normally distributed. But their asymptotic joint distribution is normal. From a direct expansion of the w_j and w_k and the fact that E_t is independent of u'_{jt}, for $t \geq t'$ and of E'_t, for $t \neq t'$, it follows that

$$\mathcal{E}(w_j w_k) = \mathcal{E}\left(\frac{1}{T} \sum_{t=1}^{T} u_{jt} u_{kt} \right) \sigma^2 = \mathcal{E}(M_{uu})_{jk} \sigma^2$$

with

$$\sigma^2 = \mathcal{E}(E_t^2)$$

so that

$$\mathcal{E}(\bar{w}_j \bar{w}_k) = (\bar{M}_{uu})_{jk} \sigma^2.$$

We adopt the standardisation that the mth parameter (an arbitrary parameter) be equal to unity. We then denote by $\mathbf{a}_m$ the vector of the $n-1$ parameters which are not assumed equal to 1, by M_{xum} the $N \times N$ matrix M_{xu} with its mth rowing missing and by q_m the vector whose jth component is equal to

$$\frac{1}{T} \sum_{t=1}^{T} x_{mt} u_{jt}.$$

Then the estimate derived from (2.5) can be written

$$\hat{\mathbf{a}}_m = -q_m M_{xum}^{-1}$$

where the $\hat{\mathbf{a}}_m$ is obtained from the estimated vector by the omission of the unit in the mth position.

Now,

$$\sum_{i=1}^{n} \mathbf{a}_i \left(\sum_{t=1}^{T} x_{it} u_{jt} \right) = \sum_{t=1}^{T} E_t u_{jt} = w_j \sqrt{T},$$

and this can be written in terms of the previously defined vectors

$$\sqrt{T}(a_m M_{xum} + q_m) = w$$

where w is the vector with components equal to w_j.

From this it follows that

$$\sqrt{T}(\mathbf{a}_m - \hat{\mathbf{a}}_m) = w M_{xum}^{-1}.$$

Asymptotically $\sqrt{T}(\mathbf{a}_m - \hat{\mathbf{a}}_m)$ is distributed like $\bar{w}\bar{M}_{xum}^{-1}$ and its asymptotic variance-covariance matrix is given by:

$$\bar{M}_{uxm}^{-1}\mathscr{E}(\bar{w}'\bar{w})M_{xum}^{-1} = \sigma^2(\bar{M}_{uxm}^{-1}\bar{M}_{uu}\bar{M}_{xum}^{-1}).$$

4 THE REDUCED SET OF INSTRUMENTAL VARIABLES

In general there will be more instrumental variables available than the number of parameters to be determined. Then there arises a problem of choice as to which set of instrumental variables should be used. More generally, one may consider the problem of choosing $n-1$ linear transformations of the available N instrumental variables, so as to provide a reduced set of instrumental variables.

This reduced set of instrumental variables will be denoted by u_{it}^*, $i = 1, \ldots, n-1$, and it will be assumed that

$$u_{it}^* = \sum_{j=1}^{N} \theta_{ij} u_{jt}.$$

The problem is then to choose an optimum set of u_{it}^*. It is clear that if any particular set of u_{it}^* is considered any linear transformation of this set is an equivalent set in the sense that it will lead to the same estimates of the coefficients $\mathbf{a}_i$. The choice of the optimum set will be made only with reference to the asymptotic covariance matrix of the estimates of the coefficients.

From the results of the previous section it follows that the asymptotic variance matrix is given by

$$(T\bar{V}_m) = \sigma^2((\theta M_{uxm})^{-1}(\theta M_{uu}\theta')(M_{xum}\theta')^{-1})$$

where $\theta = (\theta_{ij})$. Now, if the elements of this matrix are denoted by V_{ij} it is convenient to introduce an arbitrary positive definite weighting matrix c_{ij} and to determine the θ_{ij} so as to minimise

$$\sum_{i=1}^{n-1}\sum_{j=1}^{n-1} c_{ij}V_{ij} = \mathrm{tr}(cV)$$

$$= \mathrm{tr}[c(\theta\bar{M}_{uxm})^{-1}(\theta\bar{M}_{uu}\theta')(\bar{M}_{xum}\theta')^{-1}]$$

$$= \mathrm{tr}[(\bar{M}_{xum}\theta')^{-1}c(\theta\bar{M}_{uxm})^{-1}(\theta\bar{M}_{uu}\theta')].,$$

Now, the optimum θ will be indeterminate to the extent that a linear transformation can be applied on the left. Further restrictions must, therefore, be imposed on the θ_{ij} to make the solution determinate, and the following seem the most appropriate restrictions.

$$(\theta\bar{M}_{uxm})c^{-1}(\bar{M}_{xum}\theta') = I,$$

$$\theta\bar{M}_{uu}\theta' = \text{a diagonal matrix}.$$

The problem is then to minimise $\mathrm{tr}(\theta \bar{M}_{uu} \theta')$ subject to these conditions. A conventional minimisation using Lagrange multipliers then shows that the rows of θ are characteristic vectors satisfying the equations

$$\bar{M}_{uu} v' = \lambda (\bar{M}_{uxm} c^{-1} \bar{M}_{xum}) v'.$$

Thus,

$$\bar{M}_{uu} \theta' = (\bar{M}_{uxm} c^{-1} \bar{M}_{xum}) \theta' \Delta,$$

where Δ is the diagonal matrix of characteristic roots. Thus,

$$\theta' = (\bar{M}_{uu}^{-1} \bar{M}_{uxm})(c^{-1} \bar{M}_{xum} \theta' \Delta).$$

The last pair of parentheses enclose a product matrix which is a square $n-1 \times n-1$ matrix, so that θ' is a linear transformation of $\bar{M}_{uu}^{-1} \bar{M}_{uxm}$. It follows that the optimum transformation matrix θ can be more simply taken to be

$$\theta = \bar{M}_{xum} \bar{M}_{uu}^{-1}. \tag{4.1}$$

With this value of θ the asymptotic variance matrix is

$$(T \bar{V}_m) = \sigma^2 (\bar{M}_{xum} \bar{M}_{uu}^{-1} \bar{M}_{uxm})^{-1}. \tag{4.2}$$

Since the optimum value of θ is independent of the matrix c it follows that c can be allowed to tend to a semi-definite matrix. In particular it follows that this choice of θ minimised the asymptotic variance of any linear function of the estimates.

Now of course the matrices $\bar{M}_{uu}$ and $\bar{M}_{xum}$ are unknown, but they are the asymptotic limits of M_{uu} and M_{xum}. This suggests that the transformation $\theta = M_{xum} M_{uu}^{-1}$ should be considered. The corresponding estimates are given by

$$\hat{a}_m M_{xum} M_{uu}^{-1} M_{uxm} = -q_m M_{uu}^{-1} M_{uxm}.$$

Provided $\bar{M}_{xum} \bar{M}_{uu}^{-1} \bar{M}_{uxm}$ is non-singular these estimates have indeed an asymptotic variance matrix equal to (4.2). This variance matrix is the probability limit of

$$s^2 (M_{xum} M_{uu}^{-1} M_{uxm})^{-1} \tag{4.3}$$

where

$$s^2 = \sum_{t=1}^{T} \frac{(\sum_{i=1}^{n} \hat{a}_i \times x_{it})^2}{T}.$$

From these results the advantage of adding one new instrumental variable can be discussed. It is clear that eliminating one variable from a set of instrumental variables is equivalent to obtaining the optimum subject to the condition that the coefficients of one of the instrumental variables are zero, so that eliminating that variable cannot improve the asymptotic variance matrix. It follows that the addition of a new instrumental variable will improve the variance matrix unless the partial correlation between each variable in the relationship and the new instrumental variable is zero after the effects of the other instrumental variables have been allowed for. In practice the addition of a new instrumental variable will usually improve the estimated variance matrix (4.3) unless it leads to an increase in s. However, the improvements are usually small after the first three or four instrumental variables have been added. Thus there may be no great advantage in increasing the number of instrumental variables, and from the later discussion it emerges that the estimates have large biases if the number of instrumental variables becomes too large. We return to this problem of whether there are advantages or disadvantages in using a large number of instrumental variables in our conclusions.

Now it is clear that for each m a different set of estimates is obtained, and that these can be summarised by saying that they are obtained from the set of n equations

$$(M_{xu}M_{uu}^{-1}M_{ux})\hat{a} = 0 \tag{4.4}$$

upon deleting the mth equation. In Section 7 it will be shown that in fact these estimates of $\hat{a}$ will differ asymptotically by quantities of order $1/T$ provided that $|\bar{M}_{xu}\bar{M}_{uu}^{-1}\bar{M}_{ux}|$ is of rank $n - 1$.

5 THE CANONICAL CORRELATION APPROACH

The symmetrical equations (4.4) immediately suggest the canonical correlation equations introduced by Hotelling [10]. In the latter analysis the intercorrelation between two sets of variables is considered, and it is shown that there are linear transformations of the two sets such that the transformed sets have the following property: The variance matrix for two variables both in the same set is the unit matrix, and the covariance between two variables, one from each set, is zero unless both have the same suffix when it is a canonical correlation.

This analysis can be applied to the present problem by taking the variables in the relationship as one set of variables, and the instrumental variables as the other set of variables. If there is actually a relationship between the variables whose residual is independent of the instrumental variables, then one linear transformation of the variables in the relationship will have zero correlation with all the instrumental variables. It follows that the smallest population canonical correlation is zero. This suggests that the smallest sample correlation should be small, and that the corresponding transformation provides an estimate of the relationship's coefficients. In fact the sample correlation coefficient is the square root of the characteristic root λ of the equation

$$(M_{xu}M_{uu}^{-1}M_{ux} - \lambda M_{xx})\hat{\mathbf{a}}' = 0. \tag{5.1}$$

The characteristic vector is an estimate of the coefficients of the corresponding linear transformation, and, when λ is the smallest root, this provides an estimate of the coefficients of the economic relationship.

If there are two or more small canonical correlations it is clear that the estimates of the coefficients will be rather badly determined, since any linear combination of the two characteristic vectors will be nearly independent of all the instrumental variables. There will be no way of deciding between these different possible vectors unless one has some information about the relationship other than the variables it contains and the independence between the residual and the present set of instrumental variables.

6 A MINIMAX APPROACH

The general properties of the canonical correlation suggest the following alternative derivation. If $\mathbf{a}_i$ is any possible set of coefficients, the linear combination

$$\sum_{i=1}^{N} b_i u_{it}$$

is considered which has the maximum correlation with

$$\sum_{i=1}^{n} \mathbf{a}_i x_{it}.$$

Then the $\mathbf{a}_i$ are chosen to minimise this maximum correlation.

It is clear that the correlation studied can be written vectorally as

$$\varrho^2 = \frac{(\mathbf{a}M_{xu}b')^2}{(\mathbf{a}M_{xx}\mathbf{a}')(bM_{uu}b')}.$$

If $\mathbf{a}$ is given, ϱ^2 is maximised for the values of b satisfying

$$M_{ux}\mathbf{a} = \mu M_{uu}b$$

and then

$$\varrho^2 = \frac{\mathbf{a}(M_{xu}M_{uu}^{-1}M_{ux})\mathbf{a}'}{\mathbf{a}M_{xx}\mathbf{a}'}.$$

Now, the minimum value for ϱ^2 with respect to $\mathbf{a}$, is equal to the smallest root of the characteristic equation

$$(M_{xu}M_{uu}^{-1}M_{ux} - \lambda M_{xx})\mathbf{a}' = 0.$$

This analysis suggests again that the value of λ would be a suitable criterion for the presence of a relationship of the suggested type.

This approach to the problem is similar to that of Durbin [7] who considers specifically the case in which only one of the variables in the relationship is jointly determined, all the other variables in the relationship being predetermined variables with measurement errors. He suggests that the appropriate procedure is to minimise the canonical correlation between the single variable E_t, which is the residual of the relationship, and the set of variables u_{jt}, $j=1,\ldots,N$. This canonical correlation is given in the previous notation by

$$T\rho^2 = \frac{wM_{uu}^{-1}w}{s^2}$$

or

$$\rho^2 = \frac{\mathbf{a}M_{xu}M_{uu}^{-1}M_{ux}\mathbf{a}'}{\mathbf{a}M_{xx}\mathbf{a}'}.$$

Thus Durbin's method is equivalent to the method developed here, although he has apparently only considered the restricted case in which $n-1$ of the variable x_{it} can be expressed as linear functions of the u_{jt} of the form

$$x_{it} = \sum_{j=1}^{N} \beta_{ij}u_{jt} + \eta_{it} \qquad (i=2,\ldots,n)$$

and the η_{it} are all random variables independent of all previous variables in the model and non-autocorrelated. These are clearly more restrictive assumptions than those used in this article.

7 THE ASYMPTOTIC DISTRIBUTION OF THE SMALLEST CHARACTERISTIC ROOT

In this section the distribution of the smallest root of (5.1) is considered on the assumption that $\bar{M}_{xu}$ is of rank $n-1$, so that only one population characteristic root is zero.

Now there will be a unique matrix H which will satisfy the equation $HH' = M_{uu}^{-1}$ and a suitable arbitrary set of linear restrictions of number $\frac{1}{2}N(N-1)$. It follows that $\overline{HH'} = \bar{M}_{uu}^{-1}$, and, if $t = wH/\sigma$, then $\bar{t} = \overline{wH}/\sigma$. Thus the components of t are all asymptotically independently normally distributed with unit variance. Now, if

$$\frac{\mathbf{a}M_{xu}M_{uu}^{-1}M_{ux}\mathbf{a}'}{\mathbf{a}M_{xx}\mathbf{a}'}$$

is considered as a function of **a**, the smallest characteristic root λ_1 is its minimum. Hence:

$$T\lambda_1 \leqslant \frac{TaM_{xu}M_{uu}^{-1}M_{ux}\mathbf{a}'}{\mathbf{a}M_{xx}\mathbf{a}'} = F(a)$$

and

$$T(\mathbf{a}M_{xu}M_{uu}^{-1}M_{ux}\mathbf{a}') = wM_{uu}^{-1}w'$$

and, of course,

$$\text{plim}\,(\mathbf{a}M_{xx}\mathbf{a}') = \sigma^2.$$

Thus the asymptotic distribution of $F(\mathbf{a})$ is the same as that of

$$\sum_{i=1}^{N} t_i^2$$

and, since the latter is a continuous function of the t_i, it follows that

$$\bar{F}(a) = \sum_{i=1}^{N} \bar{t}_i^2.$$

This has a χ^2 distribution of N degrees of freedom, so that λ is asymptotically of order $1/T$.

Now, if $\bar{M}_{xu}\bar{M}_{xu}^{-1}\bar{M}_{ux}$ is of rank $n-1$, there is a unique **a** satisfying

$$(\bar{M}_{xu}\bar{M}_{uu}^{-1}\bar{M}_{ux})\mathbf{a}' = 0$$

and $\text{plim}_{T\to\infty}\hat{\mathbf{a}} = \mathbf{a}$.

From the equations determining them and the previous result it follows that if $\hat{\mathbf{a}}$ is suitably standardised it differs asymptotically from $\hat{\mathbf{a}}_m$ by quantities of order $1/T$. The asymptotic error variance matrix of $\hat{\mathbf{a}}_m$ shows $\Delta a = \mathbf{a} - \hat{\mathbf{a}}$ is of order $1/\sqrt{T}$. Now

$$\mathbf{a}(M_{xu}M_{uu}^{-1}M_{ux} - \lambda_1 M_{xx})\mathbf{a}'$$
$$= (\hat{\mathbf{a}} + \Delta\mathbf{a})(M_{xu}M_{uu}^{-1}M_{ux} - \lambda_1 M_{xx})(\hat{\mathbf{a}}' + \Delta\mathbf{a}')$$
$$= (\Delta\mathbf{a}(M_{xu}M_{uu}^{-1}M_{ux} - \lambda_1 M_{xx})\Delta\mathbf{a}',$$

using

$$(M_{xu}M_{uu}^{-1}M_{ux} - \lambda_1 M_{xx})\hat{\mathbf{a}}' = 0$$

so that

$$\lambda_1 = \frac{\mathbf{a}M_{xu}M_{uu}^{-1}M_{ux}\mathbf{a}' - \Delta\mathbf{a}(M_{xu}M_{uu}^{-1}M_{ux})\Delta\mathbf{a}}{\mathbf{a}M_{xx}\mathbf{a}' - \Delta\mathbf{a}(M_{xx})\Delta\mathbf{a}'}.$$

Now, since $\Delta \mathbf{a}$ is asymptotically zero, it follows that

$$\plim_{T \to \infty} (\mathbf{a} M_{xx} \mathbf{a}' - \Delta \mathbf{a}(M_{xx})\Delta \mathbf{a}') = \sigma^2$$

so that the asymptotic distribution of $T\lambda_1$ is the same as that of

$$\frac{T(\mathbf{a} M_{xu} M_{uu}^{-1} M_{ux} \mathbf{a}')}{\sigma^2} - \frac{T(\Delta \mathbf{a}(M_{xu} M_{uu}^{-1} M_{ux})\Delta \mathbf{a}')}{\sigma^2}. \tag{7.1}$$

Now, if $\Delta \mathbf{a}$ is replaced by $\mathbf{a}_m - \hat{\mathbf{a}}_m$, the difference in (7.1) is easily seen to be of order $1/\sqrt{T}$. Hence, no difference will be produced in the asymptotic distribution of (7.1). Both $\mathbf{a}_m$ and $\hat{\mathbf{a}}_m$ are standardised so that their mth components are unity. In the second part of (7.1) will only appear those terms which do not involve these components. Further, the components of $\sqrt{T}(\mathbf{a}_m - \hat{\mathbf{a}}_m)$ can be represented as linear functions of the w_i. They are asymptotically jointly normally distributed with variance matrix equal to

$$\frac{\sigma^2}{T} (\bar{M}_{xum} \bar{M}_{uu}^{-1} \bar{M}_{uxm})^{-1}.$$

Thus, as before, a linear transformation of the w_i can be defined so that

$$\frac{T}{\sigma^2} (\mathbf{a} M_{xu} M_{uu}^{-1} M_{ux} \mathbf{a}) = \sum_{i=1}^{N} t_i^2$$

$$\frac{T}{\sigma^2} (\mathbf{a}_m - \hat{\mathbf{a}}_m)(M_{xu} M_{uu}^{-1} M_{ux})(\mathbf{a}'_m - \hat{\mathbf{a}}'_m) = \sum_{i=1}^{n-1} t_i^2$$

then

$$(\overline{T\lambda_1}) = \sum_{i=n}^{N} (\overline{t_i})^2$$

where all the t_i are normally and independently distributed with unit variance, so that $(\overline{T\lambda_1})$ is distributed as χ^2 with $N - n + 1$ degrees of freedom.

This provides a significance test for the hypothesis that there is a relationship between the suggested variables with a residual independent of all the instrumental variables.

This is a suitable test even when $\bar{M}_{xu}$ is of rank less than $n-1$ since it can be shown that in this case the probability of rejecting the hypothesis will be less than in the other case.

8 THE *A PRIORI* UNIDENTIFIED CASE

The results of the previous section depend on the assumption that $\bar{M}_{xu}$ is of rank $n-1$. If its rank is less than this, the relationship will be said to be *a priori* unidentified. At least two of the population characteristic roots are then zero and the equation

$$(\bar{M}_{xu}\bar{M}_{uu}^{-1}\bar{M}_{ux})\mathbf{a}' = 0$$

no longer has a unique solution.

Let us now assume that $\bar{M}_{xu}$ is of rank $n-2$ and that there is no serial correlation for any linear combination ax'_t which corresponds to the double-zero characteristic root. If λ_1 and λ_2 are the two smallest sample characteristic roots, one may prove, by the methods of the last section, that $T(\lambda_1 + \lambda_2)$ is asymptotically distributed as χ^2 with $2(N-n+2)$ degrees of freedom.

This result can now be used as an approximate significance test of the hypothesis that the relationship is *a priori* unidentified and that any possible relationship has a non-autocorrelated residual. This hypothesis is not very likely to be true *a priori* since even if there is a relationship between the suggested variables with a non-autocorrelated residual it is unlikely that there would be a second combination of these variables not only independent of all the instrumental variables but non-autocorrelated as well. In practice the significance test fairly often indicates that the hypothesis may be true, but this is probably because the smallest non-zero root of the population characteristic equation is small, the corresponding residual is not very highly autocorrelated and T is not large enough to make $T(\lambda_1 + \lambda_2)$ significant. The use of the test, however, provides a useful qualitative answer as to whether the estimates are reasonably well identified, although as noted in Section 12 the fact that the estimates are well identified does not necessarily mean that they have reasonably small standard errors.

9 ON THE USE OF VARIABLES IN THE RELATIONSHIP AS INSTRUMENTAL VARIABLES

It is now worthwhile to introduce a notation which explicitly recognises that some of the variables in the relationship may be used as instrumental variables. As noted in Section 2 this is only possible if they are predetermined variables with zero measurement errors. The most important variables which are of this type are those representing the constant term, the trend, and seasonal factors. It is convenient to use a notation very similar to that used by Anderson [3].

Let H and K^* be, respectively, the number of variables in the relationship which cannot and which can be used as instrumental variables $(K^* + H = n)$. Let K^{**} be the number of instrumental variables not in the relationship $(K^{**} + K^* = N)$.

Let the variables in the relationship which cannot be used as instrumental variables be denoted by $y_{it'}$, $i = 1, \ldots, H$; let the instrumental variables in the relationship be denoted by u_{it}^*, $i = 1, \ldots, K^*$; and let the other instrumental variables be denoted by u_{it}, $i = 1, \ldots, K^{**}$. Then M_{uu} can be partitioned as below

$$M_{uu} = \left(\begin{array}{c|c} M_{u^*u^*} & M_{u^*u^{**}} \\ \hline M_{u^{**}u^*} & M_{u^{**}u^{**}} \end{array} \right).$$

Similarly,

$$M_{xu} = \left(\frac{M_{yu}}{M_{u^*u}} \right) = \left(\begin{array}{c|c} M_{yu^*} & M_{yu^{**}} \\ \hline M_{u^*u^*} & M_{u^*u^{**}} \end{array} \right),$$

and

$$M_{xx} = \left(\begin{array}{c|c} M_{yy} & M_{yu^*} \\ \hline M_{u^*y} & M_{u^*u^*} \end{array} \right).$$

Now clearly

$$M_{u^*u} M_{uu}^{-1} = (I \mid 0)$$

so that

$$M_{xu} M_{uu}^{-1} = \left(\frac{M_{yu}}{M_{u^*u}} \right) M_{uu}^{-1} = \left(\frac{M_{yu} M_{uu}^{-1}}{I \mid 0} \right).$$

Thus

$$M_{xu} M_{uu}^{-1} M_{ux} = \left(\begin{array}{c|c} M_{yu} M_{uu}^{-1} M_{uy} & M_{yu} M_{uu}^{-1} M_{uu^*} \\ \hline M_{u^*y} & M_{u^*u^*} \end{array} \right)$$

$$= \left(\begin{array}{c|c} M_{yu} M_{uu}^{-1} M_{uy} & M_{yu^*} \\ \hline M_{u^*y} & M_{u^*u^*} \end{array} \right).$$

Writing $\hat{\mathbf{a}} = (\hat{b} \mid \hat{c})$, equations (5.1) take the form

$$\left(\begin{array}{c|c} M_{yu} M_{uu}^{-1} M_{uy} & M_{yu^*} \\ \hline M_{u^*y} & M_{u^*u^*} \end{array} \right) \left(\begin{array}{c} \hat{b}' \\ \hat{c}' \end{array} \right) = \lambda \left(\begin{array}{c|c} M_{yy} & M_{yu^*} \\ \hline M_{u^*y} & M_{u^*u^*} \end{array} \right) \left(\begin{array}{c} \hat{b}' \\ \hat{c}' \end{array} \right)$$

or

$$(M_{yu} M_{uu}^{-1} M_{uy} - \lambda M_{yy}) \hat{b}' + (1 - \lambda) M_{yu^*} \hat{c}' = 0 \qquad (9.1)$$

and

$$(1 - \lambda)(M_{u^*y} \hat{b}' + M_{u^*u^*} \hat{c}') = 0. \qquad (9.2)$$

It follows that in this case K^* of the canonical correlations are unity, the corresponding canonical transformations being those for which $\hat{b} = 0$. For the other canonical correlations $\lambda < 1$, and it is then possible to solve equations (9.2) for $\hat{c}$ in terms of $\hat{b}$ in the form

$$\hat{c}' = -M_{u^*u^*}^{-1}M_{u^*y}\hat{b}'.$$

Substituting in equations (9.1) and rearranging, we obtain

$$(M_{yu}M_{uu}^{-1}M_{uy} - M_{yu^*}M_{u^*u^*}^{-1}M_{u^*y})\hat{b}' = (\lambda M_{yy} - M_{yu^*}M_{u^*u^*}^{-1}M_{u^*y})\hat{b}'. \qquad (9.3)$$

This has eliminated the roots $\lambda = 1$ from the characteristic equation, and so has reduced the degree of the characteristic equation to H.

10 THE CONFIDENCE REGIONS

It is now possible to derive two confidence regions for the unknown coefficients of the relationship. We use the notation

$$F_1(\mathbf{a}) = \frac{T}{\sigma^2}(bM_{yy}b' + 2cM_{u^*y}b' + cM_{u^*u^*}c')$$

$$= \frac{T}{\sigma^2}(\mathbf{a}M_{xx}\mathbf{a}') = \sum_{t=1}^{T}\frac{E_t^2}{\sigma^2}$$

and has a χ^2 distribution with T degrees of freedom. Similarly,

$$F_2(\mathbf{a}) = \frac{T}{\sigma^2}(bM_{yu}M_{uu}^{-1}M_{uy}b' + 2cM_{u^*y}b' + cM_{u^*u^*}c')$$

$$= \frac{T}{\sigma^2}(\mathbf{a}M_{xu}M_{uu}^{-1}M_{ux}\mathbf{a}')$$

and from the argument of Section 7 it follows that asymptotically $F_2(\mathbf{a})$ is distributed as χ^2 with $K^* + K^{**}$ degrees of freedom. But the argument of Section 7 can be repeated for only the instrumental variables in the relationship, and it will then be found that

$$F_3(\mathbf{a}) = \frac{T}{\sigma^2}(bM_{yu^*}M_{u^*u^*}^{-1}M_{u^*y}b' + 2cM_{u^*y}b' + cM_{u^*u^*}c')$$

$$= \frac{T}{\sigma^2}(\mathbf{a}M_{xu^*}M_{u^*u^*}^{-1}M_{u^*x}\mathbf{a}')$$

is asymptotically distributed as χ^2 with K^* degrees of freedom. Further, it can be shown by the methods of Section 7 that $F_1 - F_2$, $F_2 - F_3$ and F_3 are all asymptotically independent of each other and are therefore all asymptotically distributed as independent χ^2s with $T - K^* - K^{**}$, K^{**} and K^* degrees of freedom, respectively.

Thus $FX_2/(F_1 - F_2)$ is asymptotically distributed as the ratio of two independent χ^2's and so

$$\varphi_1 = \frac{F_2}{F_1 - F_2}\left(\frac{T - K^* - K^{**}}{K^* + K^{**}}\right)$$

is distributed as the ratio of two independent estimates of the same variance based upon samples with degrees of freedom N and $T - N$ respectively. A confidence region can now be used representing all values of b and c which satisfy the inequality

$$\frac{bM_{yu}M_{uu}^{-1}M_{uy}b' + 2bM_{yu^*}c' + cM_{u^*u^*}c'}{b(M_{yy} - M_{yu}M_{uu}^{-1}M_{uy})b'} = \frac{F_2}{F_1 - F_2} \leqslant \varphi_{1L}\frac{N}{T - N}$$

where φ_{1L} is a limit which is likely to be exceeded with only a small probability, say 5%. Then, if we consider the possibility that the actual values of b and c correspond to a point outside the confidence region, it is clear that the probability of the sample φ_1 being greater than φ_{1L} would be less than 5%. Thus, using this criteron, it is unlikely that the data could have been produced if the relationship had coefficients corresponding to a point outside the confidence region. This type of confidence region will be referred to as a confidence region of Type I.

In the same way $(F_2 - F_3)/(F_1 - F_2)$ is distributed asymptotically as the ratio of two independent $\chi_{,s}^2$ and so

$$\varphi_2 = \frac{F_2 - F_3}{F_1 - F_2}\left(\frac{T - K^* - K^{**}}{K^{**}}\right)$$

is asymptotically distributed as the ratio of two independent variance estimates of degrees of freedom K^{**} and $T - N$ and, if φ_{2L} is an appropriate limit,

$$\left(\frac{F_2 - F_3}{F_1 - F_2} = \frac{b(M_{yu}M_{uu}^{-1}M_{yu} - M_{yu^*}M_{u^*u^*}^{-1}M_{u^*y})b'}{b(M_{yy} - M_{yu}M_{uu}^{-1}M_{uy})b'} \leqslant \frac{K^{**}\varphi_{2L}}{T - N}\right)$$

provides an appropriate confidence region for the components of b, which is usually more useful than the region of Type I since the coefficients c are usually not very interesting. For computational purposes it is often useful to rewrite the last equation in the form

$$\left(\frac{b(M_{yu}M_{uu}^{-1}M_{uy} - M_{yu^*}M_{u^*u^*}^{-1}M_{u^*y})b'}{b(M_{yy} - M_{yu^*}M_{u^*u^*}^{-1}M_{u^*y})b'} \leqslant \frac{K^{**}\varphi_{2L}}{T - N + K^{**}\varphi_{2L}}\right).$$

This type of region will be referred to as the Type II confidence region.

These confidence regions are exact for finite T provided all the instrumental variables are completely exogenous, that is, provided all the u_{it} are independent of all the E'_t for all t and t'. Otherwise, they are only accurate as $T \to \infty$. It is to be noted that they are valid even in the *a priori* unidentified case, although in this case they will usually be hyperbolic conics or hyperconics. Thus they are certainly usable in the more usual almost-unidentified case. Further, in view of the asymptotic approximation, they are equally well defined by the conditions that TF_2/F_1 and $T(F_2 - F_3)/(F_1 - F_3)$ are distributed as $\chi^2_{.s}$ with N and K^{**} degrees of freedom.

It is also noteworthy that these regions depend upon the assumption that the residuals are non-autocorrelated. If the residuals are positively autocorrelated the confidence regions (and of course the computed standard errors) will understate the indeterminacy of the coefficients.

11 THE ACCURACY OF THE ASYMPTOTIC APPROXIMATION

The previous sections have been concerned only with the purely theoretical problems of the asymptotic behaviour of the estimates. In practice T is unlikely to be greater than 100, and in some cases it may be necessary to attempt estimation where T is as small as 15, so that the usefulness of the asymptotic approximations depends upon their accuracy for finite T. It is very difficult to work out the actual distributions of the sample functions that have been used for finite T, and an obviously simpler approach is to attempt to calculate some of the important properties of these distributions (e.g., their moments).

The author has derived the expressions for the first and second moments for the case in which the variables are generated by linear stochastic models of the type considered by Koopmans *et al.* [12], distributed by measurement errors, and with all random elements normally distributed. The calculations are, however, too lengthy to be reproduced here.

The general conclusion is that the biases in the estimates $\hat{a}$ and $T\lambda$ are both of order $N/T\bar{\lambda}_2$ where $\bar{\lambda}_2$ is the square of the smallest non-zero population canonical correlation coefficient. The biases are of course large when $\bar{\lambda}_2$ is small, that is, when the relationship is almost unidentified.

Likewise, it is found that the size of the biases in the confidence regions is not, to a first approximation, dependent on $\bar{\lambda}_2$ but is still proportional to N. This means that even when T is large, of order 100, N must be limited if the asymptotic approximation is to be satisfactory. One may consider as a necessary requirement that $N \leqslant T/20$. This, indeed, limits severely the number of instrumental variables which may be used.

The approximation obtained by regarding $wM_{-1}w'/\sigma^2$ as distributed as χ^2 with N degrees of freedom gives a distribution for the variable which is biased in a positive direction. In particular, confidence regions based on it will be too large, and significance tests based indirectly on it will have too large a chance of accepting a suggested form of relationship. A simple change, which would probably reduce the bias considerably, is to assume that

$$\frac{T+4N}{\sigma^2} (\mathbf{a}M_{xu}M_{uu}^{-1}M_{ux}\mathbf{a}')$$

is distributed as χ^2 with N degrees of freedom.

12 A COMPARISON WITH ALTERNATIVE METHODS: (1) LEAST SQUARES

In discussing the use of least squares to estimate the coefficients of a relationship it is convenient to denote the dependent variable by y_t, and the remaining variables by z_{it}, $i=1,\ldots,p$. The relationship may then be written

$$y_t = \sum_{i=1}^{P} \mathbf{a}_i z_{it} + \varepsilon_t \qquad (t=1,\ldots,T). \tag{12.1}$$

and the least squares equations can be written

$$m_{yz} = \hat{\mathbf{a}} M_{zz} \tag{12.2}$$

where

$$m_{yz} = \frac{1}{T} \sum_{t=1}^{T} y_t z_{it}$$

and

$$M_{zz} = \frac{1}{T} \sum_{t=1}^{T} z_{it} z_{jt}.$$

Now, multiplying each of equations (12.1) by z_{jt} and summing, we obtain

$$\sum_{t=1}^{T} y_t z_{jt} = \sum_{i=1}^{P} \mathbf{a}_i \sum_{t=1}^{T} z_{it} z_{jt} + \sum_{t=1}^{T} \varepsilon_t z_{jt}$$

or

$$m_{yz} = \mathbf{a} M_{zz} + v$$

where

$$v = \frac{1}{T} \sum_{t=1}^{T} \varepsilon_t z_{jt}$$

so that

$$(\hat{\mathbf{a}} - \mathbf{a}) M_{zz} = v.$$

Now let

$$\mathscr{E}(M_{zz}) = A_{zz}.$$

It will be assumed that the variables are stationary so that A_{zz} is independent of T. Let $M_{zz} - A_{zz} = Z_{zz}$. Then

$$A_{zz}(\hat{\mathbf{a}}' - \mathbf{a}') = v' - Z_{zz}(\hat{\mathbf{a}}' - \mathbf{a}'). \tag{12.3}$$

Now, in the asymptotic approximation the second term has a probability limit of zero. If $\mathscr{E}(\bar{v}) = u$ is not zero, then asymptotically the biases in the estimates $\hat{\mathbf{a}}$ can be taken as

$$\mathscr{E}(\hat{\mathbf{a}}' - \mathbf{a}') = A_{zz}^{-1} u'. \tag{12.4}$$

It is now convenient to write $|A_{zz}| = \Delta$ and to denote the elements of the matrix adjugate to A_{zz} by Δ_{ij}. One may also write $u_i = \sigma_i \sigma \varrho_i$ where σ_i is the standard deviation of Z_{it}, σ the standard deviation of ε_t, and ϱ_i the correlation coefficient between Z_{it} and ε_t. Assuming that the variables are standardised so that $\sigma_i = 1$, the above equation (12.4) can be written

$$\Delta(\mathscr{E}(\hat{\mathbf{a}}_i - \mathbf{a}_i)) = \left(\sum_{j=1}^{P} \Delta_{ij} \varrho_j \right) \sigma.$$

An upper bound on the bias can be obtained by noting that $|\varrho_i| \leqslant 1$ and $\sigma^2 = 1 - R^2$, R being the multiple correlation coefficient. Also

$$\max_{i,j} \left(\frac{\Delta_{ij}^2}{\Delta^2} \right) = \max_i \left(\frac{\Delta_{ii}}{\Delta} \right)^2 = \left(\frac{1}{1 - R_m^2} \right)^2$$

where R_m is the maximum multiple correlation between any z_{it} and the other independent variables. From the properties of the multiple correlations one has $R_m \leqslant R$. Thus the bias is certainly less than

$$\frac{p\sqrt{(1 - R^2)}}{1 - R_m^2} \leqslant \frac{p}{\sqrt{(1 - R_m^2)}} \leqslant \frac{p}{\sqrt{(1 - R^2)}}.$$

The bias may become large if R_m is near unity or, in other words, if there is some Δ_{ii} which is large compared with Δ. Δ is then almost singular.

Returning to the notation of the previous sections, dropping the distinction between dependent and independent variables and denoting all the variables in the relationship by x_{it}, $i = 1, \ldots, n$, the biases will be large when the matrix $\bar{M}_{xx}$ is approximately of rank $n - 2$ or less. When this is true it is usual to say that the variables are confluent. In this case, even if the conditions are fulfilled which make the least squares estimates consistent, that is, even if $\varrho_i = 0$ for all i, the standard error of the estimates will still be large. When these conditions are not fulfilled it is clear by using equations (12.3) that the variance of the estimates is also large.

From the results of the previous sections it follows that if the instrumental variables have been correctly chosen their estimates are always consistent, in the sense that their biases tend to zero as T becomes infinite provided that the relationship is *a priori* identified. However, if the variables in the relationship are confluent so that $\bar{M}_{xx}$ is almost of rank $n-2$ or less, it can be shown that the standard errors of the estimates are still large.

To show this it is convenient to return to the notation and results of Section 4. Adopting again the normalisation of $\mathbf{a}_m = 1$ for arbitrary m, the asymptotic error variance matrix of the estimates of the instrumental variables is

$$V_m = \frac{\sigma^2}{T} (\bar{M}_{xum} \bar{M}_{uu}^{-1} \bar{M}_{uxm})^{-1}$$

and the corresponding error variance matrix, which would be obtained for the least squares estimates on the assumption that the method is usable, would be

$$V_m^* = \frac{\sigma^2}{T} (\bar{M}_{xxm}^{-1})$$

where $\bar{M}_{xxm}$ means $\bar{M}_{xx}$ with the mth row and column omitted. If γ is any vector with $n-1$ components, the function $\gamma \hat{\mathbf{a}}_m'$ will have an asymptotic variance

$$\frac{\sigma^2}{T} (\gamma (\bar{M}_{xum} \bar{M}_{uu}^{-1} \bar{M}_{uxm})^{-1} \gamma').$$

But, if instead the $\mathbf{a}_m$ are assumed to have a variance matrix equal to that appropriate to least squares estimates, $\gamma \hat{\mathbf{a}}_m'$ will have a variance

$$\frac{\sigma^2}{T} (\gamma \bar{M}_{xxm}^{-1} \gamma').$$

If a canonical correlation transformation is now introduced, and if H is the transformation matrix of $\bar{M}_{xxm}$, it follows that

$$H \bar{M}_{xxm} H' = I.$$

If then $H\gamma' = \delta$, it follows that

$$\gamma \bar{M}_{xxm}^{-1} \gamma' = \delta \delta' = \sum_{i=1}^{n-1} \delta_i^2,$$

and

$$\gamma (\bar{M}_{xum} \bar{M}_{uu}^{-1} \bar{M}_{uxm}) \gamma' = \sum_{i=1}^{n-1} \frac{\delta_i^2}{\varrho_i^2}$$

where the ϱ_i are the canonical correlations. Thus, unless $\delta_i = 0$ except when $\varrho_i = 1$, $\gamma V_m \gamma' > \gamma V_m^* \gamma'$ and in any case $\gamma V_m \gamma' \geqslant \gamma V_m^* \gamma'$. Thus, the standard error of $\gamma \hat{a}_m'$ is usually greater than would have been obtained if the least squares method could be used. And, in particular, if the variables are confluent so that the least squares standard errors are large, the standard errors using instrumental variables will be even larger.

Theoretically then, if the asymptotic properties of the two kinds of estimates are compared, the instrumental variables method (provided the relationship is *a priori* identified) is the better, since the estimates are consistent, whereas the least squares estimates are not. However, for finite T, the advantage of using the instrumental variables method is less certain, since the instrumental variables estimates may have large biases especially in the almost unidentified case and in the event the number of instrumental variables is large.

The best practical test is obtained by comparing the results yielded by the two methods in practical cases. Let us suppose that, using a minimum of instrumental variables, confidence regions are obtained (these are still reasonably good approximations even in the almost unidentified case) and that the least squares estimates lie outside the confidence regions. This is sufficient evidence to show that the least squares estimates are probably significantly biased. In practice this happens when it would be expected theoretically, i.e., when there are at least two important jointly determined variables, or when some of the variables treated as independent in applying the method of least squares have large and obvious random variations.

13 A COMPARISON WITH ALTERNATIVE METHODS: (2) THE LIMITED-INFORMATION MAXIMUM-LIKELIHOOD METHOD

It is clear from a comparison of the equations (9.3) and the similar equations of the limited-information maximum-likelihood (LIML) method as formulated by Anderson and Rubin [1, 2] that the two methods are in practice very similar. Indeed the equations (9.3) can be easily transformed to the form

$$(M_{yy} - M_{yu}M_{uu}^{-1}M_{uy})\hat{b}' = \mu(M_{yy} - M_{yux}M_{u*u*}^{-1}M_{u*y})\hat{b}'$$

where $\mu = 1/(1 - \lambda)$.

This differs from the LIML equations only by the replacement of z, representing all the predetermined variables, with u, representing the instrumental variables. Indeed the LIML method is equivalent to using the instrumental variables method with all the predetermined variables in the model used as instrumental variables. This procedure is reasonable since an essential assumption of the LIML method is that there are no measurement errors. As argued in Section 2, it is then possible to use the predetermined variables in the relationship as instrumental variables. The difference between the two methods can be summarised as below.

(*i*) The LIML method strictly interpreted requires that all predetermined and exogenous variables which occur in any relationship in the model should be used. The instrumental variables approach is wider in allowing the use of any suitable predetermined variable whether it occurs in any relationship or not.

(*ii*) The instrumental variable method, however, is narrower in not allowing the use of any predetermined variables occurring in the actual relationship being studied, unless it has no measurement error or disturbance, for the reasons discussed in Section 2. It is also suggested in Section 2 that it is probably not wise to use lagged values of a variable appearing in the relationship as instrumental variables.

With both methods practical difficulties of computation and theoretical considerations concerning the biases make it worthwhile in practice to use only a small selection of the vast number of possible predetermined variables or instrumental variables.

Alternatively, it may be said that the instrumental variables method consists in modifying the LIML method by treating those predetermined variables in the relationship which have measurement errors as if they were jointly determined variables. This method of treating variables with measurement errors has already been suggested by Chernoff and Rubin [5].

14 SOME GENERAL CONCLUSIONS

From the previous results and from quite a large amount of work carried out by the author to test the method in practice, part of which it is hoped will be published later, several tentative conclusions may be drawn:

(*i*) The use of the instrumental variables method will produce consistent estimates of coefficients even when large measurement errors are apparent.

(*ii*) Better results may appear to be obtained if an attempt is made to reduce measurement errors somewhat. One may, for example, smooth the series containing obvious random errors by use of moving averages. Such a process, however, often increases the autocorrelation of the residual.

(*iii*) The use of the limited-information maximum-likelihood method is likely to produce, and in practice has produced biased estimates when there are large measurement errors in any of the predetermined variables in the relationship. The least squares method is likely to produce large biases when there are large measurement errors, or when some of the independent variables are not predetermined variables and the relationship is confluent.

(*iv*) The use of large numbers of instrumental variables may not improve the accuracy of the estimates. In practice, the effect of increasing the number of instrumental variables has been tried by the author. It has been found that if the first few instrumental variables are well chosen, there is usually no improvement, and even a deterioration, in the confidence regions as the number of instrumental variables is increased beyond three or four. This might have been expected *a priori* from a study of the results achieved by Stone [15] and others when applying factor analysis to economic time series. It has usually been found that three general factors were obtained corresponding to a linear trend, the ten year business cycle, and the rate of change of the ten year cycle. Now, if all the variables in the relationship and all the instrumental variables together can be approximately analysed in this way, the maximum number of coefficients that can be simultaneously determined is three, and the addition of instrumental variables after the third will not improve the accuracy. If, however, there are large random effects (of the same order of magnitude as the cyclical movements) such as strikes, wars etc., and if the residual of the relationship can be regarded as independent of the random effects then this might allow the determination of further coefficients. The latter assumption is, however, very rarely realistic.

In practice, when data covering less than 20 years are used, it seems appropriate to use three instrumental variables: a linear trend, a lagged variable that leads in the trade cycle, and a lagged variable that lags with reference to the trade cycle. Analyses of single economic time series indicate that if longer periods of time were studied a factor analysis might disclose more general factors, for example, another factor corresponding to a parabolic trend, and two more factors to represent the building cycle. To some extent, this gain might be cancelled by the need to introduce more complicated trends into the relationship.

Leeds University

REFERENCES

[1] Anderson, T. W. and H. Rubin: 'Estimation of the parameters of a single equation in a complete set of stochastic equations', *Annals of Mathematical Statistics*, **20**, 1949, 46–65.

[2] Anderson and Rubin: 'The asymptotic properties of estimates of the parameters of a single equation in a complete system of stochastic equations', *Annals of Mathematical Statistics*, **21**, 1950, 570–92.

[3] Anderson, T. W.: 'Estimation of the parameters of a single equation by the limited information maximum-likelihood method', *Cowles Commission Monograph*, **10**, 1950, 311–22.

[4] ———: 'The asymptotic distribution of certain characteristic roots and vectors', *Proceedings of the Second Berkeley Symposium on Mathematical Statistics and Probability*, 1950, 103–30.

[5] Chernoff, H. and H. Rubin: 'Asymptotic properties of limited information estimates under generalised conditions', *Cowles Commission Monograph* 14, 1953, 200–12.

[6] Cramer, H.: *Mathematical Methods of Statistics*, 1946.

[7] Durbin, J.: 'Errors in variables', *Review of Institute of International Statistics*, **22**, 1954, 23–54.

[8] Frisch, R.: *Statistical Confluence Anlaysis by Means of Complete Regression Systems*, 1934.

[9] Geary, R. C.: 'Studies in relation between economics time series', *Journal of the Royal Statistical Society, Series B*, **10**, 1949, 158–72.

[10] Hotelling, H.: 'Relations between two sets of variables', *Biometrika*, **28**, 1936, 321–35.

[11] Hsu, P. L.: 'On the limiting distribution of roots of a determinantal equation', *Journal of the London Mathematical Society*, **16**, 1941, 183–94.

[12] Koopmans, T. C., H. Rubin and R. B. Leipnik: 'Measuring the equation systems of dynamic economics', *Cowles Commission Monograph*, **10**, 52–237.

[13] Reiersøl, O.: 'Confluence analysis by means of lag moments and other methods of confluence analysis', *Econometrica*, **9** (1), 1941, 1–23.

[14] ———: *Confluence Analysis by Means of Sets of Instrumental Variables*, 1945.

[15] Stone, R.: 'On the interdependence of blocks of transactions', *Journal of the Royal Statistical Society Supplement*, **8**, 1947, 1–13.

[16] Turnbull, H. W. and A. C. Aitken: *An Introduction to the Theory of Canonical Matrices*, 1938.

J. D. SARGAN

————— . —————

5 THE ESTIMATION OF RELATIONSHIPS WITH AUTOCORRELATED RESIDUALS BY THE USE OF INSTRUMENTAL VARIABLES

(First published in the *Journal of the Royal Statistical Society* (1959), Vol. B, 21, pp. 91–105.)

SUMMARY

THE INSTRUMENTAL VARIABLES METHOD OF ESTIMATING THE COEFFICIENTS OF A LINEAR RELATIONSHIP BETWEEN TIME SERIES WHICH HAVE MEASUREMENT ERRORS IS APPLIED TO THE CASE WHERE THE COEFFICIENTS ARE FUNCTIONS OF A SET OF PARAMETERS. THE ASYMPTOTIC ERROR VARIANCE MATRIX OF THE ESTIMATES IS OBTAINED, ASYMPTOTIC TESTS FOR THE EXISTENCE AND IDENTIFICATION OF THE SUGGESTED FORM OF RELATIONSHIP ARE SUGGESTED, AND ASYMPTOTIC CONFIDENCE REGIONS ARE GIVEN. THE GENERAL THEORY IS THEN APPLIED TO THE CASE OF A RELATIONSHIP WITH AN AUTOREGRESSIVE RESIDUAL, AND PRACTICAL COMPUTATIONAL METHODS ARE SUGGESTED.

1 INTRODUCTION

The method of instrumental variables was first suggested by Reiersøl (1945) and Geary (1948) as a method of estimating linear relationships between variables which are subject to measurement error. Durbin (1954) and the author (1958) have shown that the mathematical formalism involved is closely similar to that of the reduced-form method of estimation developed by Koopmans and Hood (1953). Theoretically the method is valuable in providing asymptotically consistent estimates even when there are fairly large measurement errors in the variables. The purpose of this paper is to extend the method to the case where the residuals are autocorrelated.

If, for example, the economic variables in the relationship in the usual form are denoted by ξ_{it}, $i = 1, \ldots, r$, the relationship may be written

$$\sum_{i=1}^{r} \alpha_i \xi_{it} = \eta_t \tag{1.1}$$

where η_t is the residual on the relationship. Now in general it may be autocorrelated, the simplest assumption being that there is a first order autoregressive relationship of the form

$$\eta_t = \psi \eta_{t-1} + E_t \qquad (1.2)$$

where the E_t are independently distributed for all t. But if (1.1) is substituted in (1.2) the result is

$$\sum_{i=1}^{r} \alpha_i \xi_{it} - \sum_{i=1}^{r} \psi \alpha_i \xi_{i(t-1)} = E_t. \qquad (1.3)$$

This can be regarded as a relationship between $2r$ variables, the ξ_{it} and one period lagged values of the ξ_{it}, which will be referred to subsequently as the transformed relationship. The coefficients of these $2r$ variables are functions of the $r+1$ parameters α_i and ψ. In a similar way if a more complicated autoregressive relationship is assumed, a transformed relationship can be produced which connects the current lagged values of the economic variables and in which the coefficients of these variables can be regarded as functions of a smaller set of parameters, these parameters being on the one hand the coefficients of the economic relationship stated in its normal form and on the other hand the coefficients of the autoregressive relationship. In the study of the transformed relationship E_t can be treated as a random series in which each term is independent of every other term.

This suggests the following generalisation. The relationship is considered connecting a set of economic variables which has coefficients which are functions of a set of parameters less in number than the number of variables in the relationship. The method of estimation suggested is similar to that developed in a previous paper (Sargan, 1958). It depends on the existence of certain variables, the instrumental variables, which are independent of the residual of the relationship. As explained in the previous paper these are the predetermined variables which are not subject to measurement errors, or that are not in the relationship.

2 THE GENERAL FORMULATION OF THE PROBLEM

In an attempt to keep the notation similar to that of the previous article the relationship will be written

$$\sum_{i=1}^{n} a_i x_{it} = E_t$$

where E_t is a residual made up of the random component or shock in the relationship plus the measurement errors of all the variables in the relationship. The a_i are assumed to be functions of a set of p variables θ_j, $p < n$. The method of instrumental variables depends on the use of the knowledge that there are some variables which can be assumed independent of the residual E_t. These are the instrumental variables and will be denoted by u_{jt}, $j = 1, \ldots, N$. The method used follows closely that used where the a_i were unrestricted and considers only the asymptotic behaviour of the estimates.

The simplest case to consider is that where $N = p$. A set of estimates of the θ_i may be obtained by writing down the equations stating that the sample covariances between the E_t and each of the u_{jt} are zero. These equations take the form

$$\sum_{t=1}^{T} \frac{E_t u_{jt}}{T} = 0 \qquad (2.1)$$

or

$$\sum_{i=1}^{n} a_i \left(\sum_{t=1}^{T} \frac{x_{it} u_{jt}}{T} \right) = 0.$$

Since the number of equations is equal to the number of unknown parameters there is the possibility of at least one determinate solution. It will be proved later that if the functions $a_i(\theta_j)$ are differentiable and there is a relationship of the type suggested then asymptotically there is a high probability that there will be at least one solution of the equations (2.1), although in general there may be several such solutions. It will be assumed that the functions $a_i(\theta_j)$ are such that there is a one-to-one correspondence between the a_i and the θ_j, so that if equations (2.1) considered as equations determining the θ_j, have multiple solutions, this necessarily means that there are real differences in the corresponding a_i.

It is now convenient to introduce a matrix notation similar to that of the previous article. It will be assumed that the vector of estimated coefficients can be written $\hat{\mathbf{a}}_\theta$ and that the sample covariance matrix for the variables can be written M_{xu} so that the equations (2.1) are written

$$\hat{\mathbf{a}}_\theta M_{xu} = 0. \qquad (2.2)$$

Adopting also the notation that the asymptotic limit of any sample variable or function is denoted by placing a bar over the corresponding symbol it is useful to discuss the asymptotic limit of the equations (2.2) which is written

$$\bar{\mathbf{a}}_\theta \bar{M}_{xu} = 0. \qquad (2.3)$$

Now the behaviour of the solutions of the equations (2.2) depends upon the nature of the solutions of equations (2.3). It may be that equations (2.3) have a unique solution, but in general it is more likely, when $N = p$, that there are several solutions. This latter case will be called the case of multiple solutions. Thirdly there is the possibility that the equations (2.3) have a continuous infinity of solutions so that they determine a curve or variety in θ space. This will be called the '*a priori* unidentified' case. In the first two cases, the case of the unique or multiple solution, it is also necessary to distinguish the solutions of the equations (2.3) which make the matrix $\bar{M}_{ux}\partial\mathbf{a}'/\partial\theta$ singular, where $\partial\mathbf{a}/\partial\theta$ denotes the matrix $(\partial\mathbf{a}_i/\partial\theta_j)$.

These will be a called singular solutions of the equations (2.3). It can be proved that if the solutions are *a priori* identified and non-singular, the probability that there is a solution of (2.2) near each solution of (2.3) tends to unity as $T\to\infty$. In general it seems reasonable to assume that the residual on the relationship is not autocorrelated, especially in the case of relationships of the type discussed in the introduction. It might in some cases be possible to distinguish between multiple solutions by using the conditions that the residual is non-autocorrelated. It will be assumed that this is not in fact attempted.

It is convenient in this section to use methods similar to those used in later sections, and so the solutions of equations (2.2) will not be studied directly, but instead the following theorem will be used.

THEOREM. *If θ is a vector representing a set of parameters, and $\mathbf{z}$ is a vector representing a set of random variables which tend in probability asymptotically to a constant $\bar{\mathbf{z}}$, and if $f(\theta, \mathbf{z})$ is a function of the two sets of variables, being a continuous function of the $\mathbf{z}$ and having finite derivatives with respect to θ for values of θ within some region of θ space and for a small finite region of $\mathbf{z}$ space surrounding $\bar{\mathbf{z}}$, then if $f(\theta, \bar{\mathbf{z}})$ has a local minimum at $\bar{\theta}$ within the region in θ space specified above, asymptotically the probability that there is a local minimum of $f(\theta, \mathbf{z})$ inside a small region of θ space surrounding $\bar{\theta}$ tends to unity. Also if $\hat{\theta}$ is defined as the minimum of $f(\theta, \mathbf{z})$ in or on the boundary of this region of θ space, $\mathrm{plim}_{T\to\infty} \hat{\theta} = \bar{\theta}$.*

This general theorem can be used in this case by considering the minimum of the sample function $X = \mathbf{a}_\theta M_{xu} M_{uu}^{-1} M_{ux} \mathbf{a}'_\theta$ with respect to θ.

If $\bar{M}_{xu}$ is non-singular, and if $\mathbf{a}_\theta$ is a function of θ with finite derivatives for all values of θ under consideration, then each minimum of $\mathbf{a}_\theta \bar{M}_{xu} \bar{M}_{uu}^{-1} \bar{M}_{ux} \mathbf{a}'_\theta$ can be surrounded by a small region, and then there is a probability tending to unity as $T\to\infty$ that there is a minimum of $X = \mathbf{a}_\theta M_{xu} M_{uu}^{-1} M_{ux} \mathbf{a}'_\theta$ inside this region.

The condition for a minimum of X is

$$\mathbf{a}_\theta M_{xu} M_{uu}^{-1} M_{ux} \frac{\partial \mathbf{a}'}{\partial\theta} = 0 \qquad (2.4)$$

and the theorem shows that asymptotically it is almost certain that there is a solution of these equations near each solution of the equations $\mathbf{a}_\theta \bar{M}_{xu} \bar{M}_{uu}^{-1} \bar{M}_{ux} \partial\mathbf{a}'/\partial\theta = 0$ that corresponds to a minimum of $\mathbf{a}_\theta \bar{M}_{xu} \bar{M}_{uu}^{-1} \bar{M}_{ux} \mathbf{a}'_\theta$. In fact the only minima that need be considered are those which satisfy the equations $\mathbf{a}_\theta \bar{M}_{xu} = 0$ and it is assume that the solution under consideration is non-singular. Then since from the theorem the minimum of X tends to $\bar{\theta}$, assuming that the derivatives are continuous it follows from the general properties of asymptotic limits that $M_{ux} \, \partial \mathbf{a}'/\partial\theta$ taken at the minimum tends in probability to $\bar{M}_{ux} \, \partial \mathbf{a}'/\partial\theta$, so that the probability that $M_{ux} \, \partial \mathbf{a}'/\partial\theta$ is singular at the minimum of X tends asymptotically to zero. Whenever $M_{ux} \, \partial \mathbf{a}'/\partial\theta$ is non-singular the equations (2.4) can be solved to give $\mathbf{a}_\theta M_{xu}=0$ and this shows that the probability that there is a solution of (2.2) near each solution of (2.3) tends to unity as $T \to \infty$, provided that the solution is non-singular. It follows also from the theorem of the Appendix that $\hat{\theta}$ is a consistent estimate of $\bar{\theta}$.

3 THE ASYMPTOTIC ERROR VARIANCE MATRIX OF $\hat{\theta}$

We define $\hat{\theta}$ as in the last paragraph as the minimum of X within or on the boundary of a small region in θ space surounding a solution of the equations (2.3). There are then three possibilities to distinguish. The first is that the minimum $\hat{\theta}$ is a solution of the equations (2.2). The second possibility is that the minimum is within the region but does not satisfy equations (2.2). The third possibility is that the minimum lies on the boundary of the region. The probability of the second or third possibility occurring tends to zero as $T \to \infty$. Defining as in the previous article the quantities $w_i = \sum_{t=1}^T E_t u_{it}/\sqrt{T}$ where $E_t = \mathbf{a}_\theta \mathbf{x}_t'$ it follows that $\mathbf{w} = \sqrt{T} \, \bar{\mathbf{a}}_\theta M_{xu}$.

Now when the first alternative occurs $\hat{\mathbf{a}}_\theta M_{xu} = 0$, so that $\sqrt{T}(\bar{\mathbf{a}}_\theta - \hat{\mathbf{a}}_\theta) M_{xu} = \mathbf{w}$. Now it is convenient to define a vector $\mathbf{v}$ by the equations,

$$\mathbf{v} = \sqrt{T}(\bar{\mathbf{a}}_\theta - \hat{\mathbf{a}}_\theta) M_{xu}, \tag{3.1}$$

whichever alternative occurs. From the definition it follows that $\mathbf{v} = \mathbf{w}$ when the first possibility occurs, so that the probability that $\mathbf{v}$ is not equal to $\mathbf{w}$ tends to zero asymptotically, and the asymptotic distribution of v is the same as that of $\mathbf{w}$. In the previous paper it was found that the joint asymptotic distribution of the components of w is normal with zero mean and variance matrix $\sigma^2(\bar{M}_{uu})$ where $\sigma^2 = \mathscr{E}(E_t^2)$.

From the assumption that $\mathbf{a}(\theta)$ has finite derivatives within the region under consideration it follows that

$$\bar{\mathbf{a}}_\theta - \hat{\mathbf{a}}_\theta = (\bar{\theta} - \hat{\theta})\left(\frac{\partial \mathbf{a}}{\partial\theta}\right)_{\theta=\bar{\theta}} + O((\bar{\theta} - \hat{\theta})(\bar{\theta} - \hat{\theta})')$$

so that

$$\mathbf{v} = \sqrt{T}(\bar{\theta} - \hat{\theta})\left(\frac{\partial \mathbf{a}}{\partial\theta}\right) M_{xu} + O((\bar{\theta} - \hat{\theta})(\bar{\theta} - \hat{\theta})'). \tag{3.2}$$

Now the second term on the right hand side is asymptotically of order zero.

For suppose on the contrary that it were at least of order unity asymptotically. Then $\bar{\theta} - \hat{\theta}$ must be at least of order $T^{-1/4}$, and then the first term would be at least of order $T^{1/4}$, so that the right hand side would be of the same order. Cancellation between the first and second terms is not possible, since they are of different orders asymptotically unless $\bar{\theta} - \hat{\theta}$ is of order unity, and this is not so since $\hat{\theta}$ is a consistent estimate of $\bar{\theta}$. But the left hand side of (3.2) is of order unity so that the right hand side cannot be of order $T^{1/4}$. It follows that the second term of (3.2) must have probability limit zero, and from the general asymptotic convergence theorem for linear functions it follows that the asymptotic distribution of $\sqrt{T}(\hat{\theta} - \bar{\theta})$ is the same as that of $-H^{-1}\bar{\mathbf{v}}$, where $H = (\partial\mathbf{a}/\partial\theta)_{\theta=\bar{\theta}}\bar{M}_{xu}$ and so $\sqrt{T}(\hat{\theta} - \bar{\theta})$ is asymptotically distributed normally with mean zero and variance matrix

$$\sigma^2\left(\left(\frac{\partial\mathbf{a}}{\partial\theta}\right)\bar{M}_{xu}\bar{M}_{uu}^{-1}\bar{M}_{ux}\left(\frac{\partial\mathbf{a}}{\partial\theta}\right)'\right)^{-1}.$$

4 THE REDUCED SET OF INSTRUMENTAL VARIABLES

It is now possible as in the previous paper to treat the case where the number of instrumental variables N is greater than the number of parameters θ, p, by considering the possibility of using linear transforms of the u_{jt}

$$u_{jt}^* = \sum_{k=1}^{N} \pi_{jk} u_{kt}, \qquad j = 1, \ldots, p.$$

The choice of the transformation π is then made so as to obtain the optimum asymptotic variance matrix for the estimates $\hat{\theta}$. If the method of the previous article is used it is found that the optimum π is given by

$$\pi = \bar{M}_{uu}^{-1}\bar{M}_{ux}\left(\frac{\partial\mathbf{a}}{\partial\theta}\right)'_{\theta=\bar{\theta}}$$

so that the corresponding estimates are given by

$$\left(\frac{\partial\mathbf{a}}{\partial\theta}\right)\bar{M}_{xu}\bar{M}_{uu}^{-1}M_{ux}\mathbf{a}'_{\theta} = 0$$

and the variance matrix is

$$\frac{\sigma^2}{T}\left(\left(\frac{\partial\mathbf{a}}{\partial\theta}\right)_{\theta=\bar{\theta}}\bar{M}_{xu}\bar{M}_{uu}^{-1}\bar{M}_{ux}\left(\frac{\partial\mathbf{a}}{\partial\theta}\right)'_{\theta=\bar{\theta}}\right)^{-1}.$$

The values of the asymptotic limits $\bar{M}_{xu}$ and $\bar{M}_{uu}$ are not in fact known, but this suggests that the equations

$$\left(\frac{\partial\mathbf{a}}{\partial\theta}\right)M_{xu}M_{uu}^{-1}M_{ux}\mathbf{a}'_{\theta} = 0$$

are considered. These are equivalent to

$$\frac{\partial}{\partial\theta}(\mathbf{a}_\theta M_{xu} M_{uu}^{-1} M_{ux} \mathbf{a}_\theta')=0 \tag{4.2}$$

Now if there is a relationship of the type suggested the relationship's coefficients must satisfy the equations

$$\mathbf{a}_\theta \bar{M}_{xu}=0. \tag{4.3}$$

If these equations can be satisfied by only one vector then the function

$$\mathbf{a}_\theta \bar{M}_{xu} \bar{M}_{uu}^{-1} \bar{M}_{ux} \mathbf{a}_\theta' \tag{4.4}$$

has a unique minimum for which the function is zero, and it follows from the theorem that asymptotically there is almost always a minimum of

$$\mathbf{a}_\theta M_{xu} M_{uu}^{-1} M_{ux} \mathbf{a}_\theta' \tag{4.5}$$

near $\bar{\theta}$, and that this minimum is a consistent estimate of $\bar{\theta}$.

If on the other hand equations (4.3) have several solutions, the basic theorem can be used to show that there will almost always be a minimum of (4.5) near to each solution of (4.3), which provides a consistent estimate. This case of multiple solutions must be distinguished from the case where the solution is quite unidentified, this latter case being that where the equations (4.3) only suffice to determine a curve or variety in θ space. If equations (4.3) are to have any solution the matrix $\bar{M}_{xu}$ must be of rank less than n. Multiple solutions are only possible if the rank is less than $n-1$. If the rank is p, and the functions $\mathbf{a}_\theta$ non-linear, multiple solutions, not necessarily real, generally occur. If, however, the rank is less than p, the solutions of equations (4.3) usually become indeterminate, and these equations determine a curve or variety in θ space, and so in $\mathbf{a}$ space. This case is the *a priori* unidentified case.

5 THE ASYMPTOTIC VARIANCE MATRIX

It now remains to prove that when the relationship is identified and the solution non-singular the estimates given by the minimum of (4.5) have an asymptotic variance matrix equal to (4.1). Defining the estimates as before as determined by the minimum of (4.5) inside or on the boundary of a small region surrounding a solution of (4.3) it follows that again there are two cases. The first case is that where the minimum is inside the region, the second is where it is on the boundary of the region, and the probability of the second case tends to zero asymptotically. Defining $\mathbf{w}$ as before it follows that $\mathbf{w}=\sqrt{T}\bar{\mathbf{a}}_\theta M_{xu}$ so that

$$\mathbf{w} M_{uu}^{-1} M_{ux} \left(\frac{\partial \mathbf{a}}{\partial\theta}\right)_{\theta=\theta} = \sqrt{T}\bar{\mathbf{a}}_\theta M_{xu} M_{uu}^{-1} M_{ux} \left(\frac{\partial \mathbf{a}}{\partial\theta}\right)'_{\theta=\theta}$$

and in the first case

$$0 = \hat{\mathbf{a}}_\theta M_{xu} M_{uu}^{-1} M_{ux} \left(\frac{\partial \mathbf{a}}{\partial \theta}\right)'_{\theta=\hat{\theta}}, \tag{5.1}$$

so that subtracting

$$\mathbf{w} M_{uu}^{-1} M_{ux} \left(\frac{\partial \mathbf{a}}{\partial \theta}\right)_{\theta=\hat{\theta}} = \sqrt{T}(\bar{\mathbf{a}}_\theta - \hat{\mathbf{a}}_\theta) M_{xu} M_{uu}^{-1} M_{ux} \left(\frac{\partial \mathbf{a}}{\partial \theta}\right)_{\theta=\hat{\theta}}$$

in the first case. It is now convenient to define

$$V = \sqrt{T}(\bar{\mathbf{a}}_\theta - \hat{\mathbf{a}}_\theta) M_{xu} M_{uu}^{-1} M_{ux} \left(\frac{\partial \mathbf{a}}{\partial \theta}\right)'_{\theta=\hat{\theta}} \tag{5.2}$$

and it follows that the difference between V and $\mathbf{w} M_{uu}^{-1} M_{ux}(\partial \mathbf{a}/\partial \theta)'_{\theta=\hat{\theta}}$ is asymptotically zero. On using the general theorem on the asymptotic behaviour of linear functions, it follows that V is asymptotically distributed like $\bar{\mathbf{w}} \bar{M}_{uu}^{-1} \bar{M}_{ux}(\partial \mathbf{a}/\partial h)'_{\theta=\bar{\theta}}$ and so is normally distributed with zero mean and variance matrix

$$\sigma^2 \left(\left(\frac{\partial \mathbf{a}}{\partial \theta}\right)_{\theta=\bar{\theta}} \bar{M}_{xu} \bar{M}_{uu}^{-1} \bar{M}_{ux} \left(\frac{\partial \mathbf{a}}{\partial \theta}\right)'_{\theta=\bar{\theta}} \right). \tag{5.3}$$

From this point the proof follows the same lines as that of Section 3. From (5.2) it can be deduced that

$$V = \sqrt{T}(\bar{\theta} - \hat{\theta}) \left(\frac{\partial \mathbf{a}}{\partial \theta}\right)_{\theta=\bar{\theta}} M_{xu} M_{uu}^{-1} M_{ux} \left(\frac{\partial \mathbf{a}}{\partial \theta}\right)'_{\theta=\hat{\theta}} + O\left(\frac{1}{\sqrt{T}}\right) \tag{5.4}$$

and it follows that if matrix (5.3) is non-singular $\sqrt{T}(\hat{\theta} - \bar{\theta})$ is asymptotically distributed normally with mean zero and variance matrix

$$\sigma^2 \left(\left(\frac{\partial \mathbf{a}}{\partial \theta}\right)_{\theta=\bar{\theta}} \bar{M}_{xu} \bar{M}_{uu}^{-1} \bar{M}_{ux} \left(\frac{\partial \mathbf{a}}{\partial \theta}\right)'_{\theta=\bar{\theta}} \right)^{-1}.$$

6 THE SINGULAR CASE

In the singular case where the matrix $\bar{M}_{ux}(\partial \mathbf{a}/\partial \theta)'$ is of rank $p-1$ or less, a discussion similar to that of the previous section can be carried through, to show that there is asymptotically a finite probability of multiple minima occurring near the singular solution and that these multiple minima will have errors which in the simplest cases are of order $T^{-1/4}$. In the simplest case when the rank of the matrix is $p-1$, there is asymptotically a probability of $\frac{1}{2}$ that there is a single minimum with error of order $T^{-1/2}$ and, a probability of $\frac{1}{2}$ of two minima with errors of order $T^{-1/4}$. However this case has a mainly academic interest since it is *a priori* unlikely that $\bar{M}_{xu}$

will take just those values which makes the solution singular, and if the solution is only almost singular the errors will be large but as in the previous section.

7 THE MINIMAX APPROACH

An alternative approach suggested by the previous article is as follows. If the θ_j, $j = 1$ to p, are any suggested set of θ and

$$U_t = \sum_{i=1}^{N} b_i u_{it}$$

is a linear combination of the instrumental variables, then the b_i are chosen so that the correlation coefficient between U_t and the residual of the equation

$$\sum_{i=1}^{n} a_i(\theta_j) x_{it} = E_t$$

is as large as possible. Then the θ_j are chosen to minimise this correlation.

Expressed vectorally the correlation coefficient is given by

$$\rho^2 = \frac{(\mathbf{a}_\theta M_{xu} \mathbf{b}')^2}{(\mathbf{a}_\theta M_{xx} \mathbf{a}'_\theta)(\mathbf{b} M_{uu} \mathbf{b}')}$$

and maximising with respect to **b** it follows that

$$\rho^2_{\max} = \phi(\theta) = \frac{\mathbf{a}_\theta M_{xu} M_{uu}^{-1} M_{ux} \mathbf{a}'_\theta}{\mathbf{a}_\theta M_{xx} \mathbf{a}'_\theta}. \tag{7.1}$$

The function to be minimised is then (7.1) and differentiation gives the first order conditions

$$\left(\frac{\partial \mathbf{a}}{\partial \theta}\right)_{\theta = \hat{\theta}} (M_{xu} M_{uu}^{-1} M_{ux} - \lambda M_{xx}) \hat{\mathbf{a}}'_\theta = 0 \tag{7.2}$$

where

$$\lambda = \frac{\hat{\mathbf{a}}_\theta M_{xu} M_{uu}^{-1} M_{ux} \hat{\mathbf{a}}'_\theta}{\hat{\mathbf{a}}_\theta M_{xx} \hat{\mathbf{a}}'_\theta}.$$

Now from the fundamental theorem it follows that if $\bar{\theta}$ is a minimum of

$$\mathbf{a}_\theta \bar{M}_{xu} \bar{M}_{uu}^{-1} \bar{M}_{ux} \mathbf{a}'_\theta / (\mathbf{a}_\theta \bar{M}_{xx} \mathbf{a}'_\theta)$$

there is asymptotically almost always a minimum of $\phi(\theta)$ in the neighbourhood of $\bar{\theta}$, and this minimum provides a consistent estimator of

$\bar{\theta}$. Now since $\hat{\theta}$ is a minimum of $\phi(\theta)$ it follows that $\phi(\hat{\theta}) \leqslant \phi(\bar{\theta})$ or

$$T\lambda \leqslant \frac{T(\bar{\mathbf{a}}_\theta M_{xu} M_{uu}^{-1} M_{ux} \bar{\mathbf{a}}_\theta')}{\mathbf{a}_\theta M_{xx} \mathbf{a}_\theta'}$$

or writing as before $\mathbf{w} = \sqrt{T} \bar{\mathbf{a}}_\theta M_{xu}$,

$$T\lambda \leqslant \frac{\mathbf{w} M_{uu}^{-1} \mathbf{w}'}{\bar{\mathbf{a}}_\theta M_{xx} \bar{\mathbf{a}}_\theta'}.$$

As in the previous paper it follows that asymptotically the last expression is distributed like a χ^2 with N degrees of freedom. It follows that λ is of order T^{-1}.

The proof of the previous Sections 5 and 6 can now be repeated, the only changes being that equation (5.1) must be replaced by the equation

$$0 = \hat{\mathbf{a}}_\theta M_{xu} M_{uu}^{-1} M_{ux} \left(\frac{\partial \mathbf{a}}{\partial \theta}\right)'_{\theta = \hat{\theta}} - \lambda \hat{\mathbf{a}}_\theta M_{xx} \left(\frac{\partial \mathbf{a}}{\partial \theta}\right)'_{\theta = \hat{\theta}} \tag{7.3}$$

that equation (5.2) has an extra term containing the factor $\sqrt{T}(\lambda)$, and therefore asymptotically zero, but that (5.4) can be repeated unchanged. Thus finally the same conclusions can be drawn, that is, that $\sqrt{T}(\hat{\theta} - \bar{\theta})$ is asymptotically distributed normally with mean zero and variance matrix

$$\sigma^2 \left(\left(\frac{\partial \mathbf{a}}{\partial \theta}\right)_{\theta = \bar{\theta}} \bar{M}_{xu} \bar{M}_{uu}^{-1} \bar{M}_{ux} \left(\frac{\partial \mathbf{a}}{\partial \theta}\right)'_{\theta = \bar{\theta}} \right)^{-1}$$

where

$$\sigma^2 = \bar{\mathbf{a}}_\theta \bar{M}_{xx} \bar{\mathbf{a}}_\theta'.$$

8 THE ASYMPTOTIC DISTRIBUTION OF $T\lambda$

The approach of the previous section has two advantages over that of the earlier sections of this paper. First in the application to the study of autoregressive residuals it gives a set of estimates symmetric between the different variables in the relationship. But more importantly the λ obtained provides the basis for a significance test for the existence of a relationship of the proposed type. For writing

$$\phi(\theta) = \frac{\mathbf{a}_\theta M_{xu} M_{uu}^{-1} M_{ux} \mathbf{a}_\theta'}{\mathbf{a}_\theta M_{xx} \mathbf{a}_\theta'}$$

and

$$\Delta\theta = \hat{\theta} - \bar{\theta}$$

then

$$\phi(\bar{\theta}) = \phi(\hat{\theta} - \Delta\theta)$$

$$= \phi(\hat{\theta}) - \Delta\theta\left(\frac{\partial\phi}{\partial\theta}\right)_{\theta=\hat{\theta}} + \tfrac{1}{2}\Delta\theta\left(\frac{\partial^2\phi}{\partial\theta\partial\theta}\right)_{\theta=\hat{\theta}}\Delta\theta' + O(\Delta\theta^3)$$

and from the definition of $\hat{\theta}$, $(\partial\phi/\partial\theta)_{\theta=\hat{\theta}}=0$, so that

$$T\lambda = T\phi(\bar{\theta}) = T\phi\hat{\theta} - \bar{\theta}\frac{T}{2}\,\Delta\theta\left(\frac{\partial^2\phi}{\partial\theta\partial\theta}\right)_{\theta\sim\theta}\Delta\theta' + TO(\Delta\theta^{-3}). \qquad (8.1)$$

The last term has probability limit zero and can be neglected in considering the asymptotic distribution of $T\lambda$. Now as in the previous section it follows that $T\phi(\theta)$ is distributed as a χ^2 with N degrees of freedom. Also

$$\tfrac{1}{2}(\mathbf{a}_\theta M_{xx}\mathbf{a}'_\theta)\frac{\partial^2\phi}{\partial\theta\partial\theta} = \left(\frac{\partial\mathbf{a}}{\partial\theta}\right)M_{xu}M_{uu}^{-1}M_{ux}\left(\frac{\partial\mathbf{a}}{\partial\theta}\right)' - \phi(\hat{\theta})\left(\frac{\partial\mathbf{a}}{\partial\theta}M_{xx}\frac{\partial\mathbf{a}'}{\partial\theta}\right)$$

$$- \phi(\hat{\theta})\left(\mathbf{a}_\theta M_{xx}\left(\frac{\partial^2\mathbf{a}'}{\partial\theta\partial\theta}\right) + \mathbf{a}_\theta M_{xu}M_{uu}^{-1}M_{ux}\left(\frac{\partial^2\mathbf{a}'}{\partial\theta\partial\theta}\right),$$

where all derivatives are understood to be taken at $\hat{\theta}$. Terms which cancel at $\theta=\hat{\theta}$ are omitted. Now since $\phi(\hat{\theta})$ is of order T^{-1} it follows that the second and third terms of (8.2) are symptotically of order T^{-1}. Also since

$$\operatorname*{plim}_{T\to\infty}(\hat{\mathbf{a}}_\theta M_{xu}) = \bar{\mathbf{a}}_\theta \bar{M}_{xu} = 0$$

the fourth term also is asymptotically zero. Thus the only term of (8.2) that is not asymptotically zero is the first, so that the second term of (8.1) is asymptotically distributed like

$$-T\frac{\left(\Delta\theta\left(\frac{\partial\mathbf{a}}{\partial\theta}\right)_{\theta=\hat{\theta}}M_{xu}M_{uu}^{-1}M_{ux}\left(\frac{\partial\mathbf{a}}{\partial\theta}\right)'_{\theta=\hat{\theta}}\Delta\theta'\right)}{\hat{\mathbf{a}}_\theta M_{xx}\hat{\mathbf{a}}'_\theta}. \qquad \textbf{(8.3)}$$

As in the previous article it can be shown that expression (8.3) is asymptotically distributed as a χ^2 with p degrees of freedom, in such a way that $T\lambda$ is asymptotically distributed as a χ^2 with $N-p$ degrees of freedom.

9 THE PROBLEM OF UNIDENTIFIABILITY

In considering this problem one possible approach is to take θ as defined by the intersection of the linear space $\mathbf{a}\bar{M}_{xu}=0$ and the variety $\mathbf{a}=\mathbf{a}(\theta)$ in $\mathbf{a}$ space. If the intersection is a curve the solution is unidentified, and this possibility depends upon the dimensions of the linear space. It is a natural development of the previous article when considering this dimension to take the roots of the characteristic equations

$$\mathbf{a}(M_{xu}M_{uu}^{-1}M_{ux} - \lambda M_{xx}) = 0$$

or equivalently the stationary values of $\mathbf{a}M_{xu}M_{uu}^{-1}M_{ux}\mathbf{a}'/(\mathbf{a}M_{xx}\mathbf{a}')$ for unrestricted values of $\mathbf{a}$. If the rank of $\bar{M}_{xu}$ is k, $n-k$ of the characteristic roots are either zero or not significantly different from zero, and the corresponding characteristic vectors can be taken as defining the linear space. As a significance test it is possible to use Anderson's (1950) distribution for the sum of the $n-k$ smallest roots and this is valid if the corresponding linear combinations of the x_{it} are not serially correlated. In practice the serial correlations are likely to be positive, and the use of Anderson's distribution is likely to be biased in the direction of giving too large a chance that the relationship appears identified, so that a rather arbitrary allowance must be made for this. The intersection of the space defined by the characteristic vectors and $\mathbf{a} = \mathbf{a}(\theta)$ then gives a first indication of the identifiability of the solution.

However this procedure does not give a test criterion for unidentifiability directly. The criterion used in the previous paper suggests that the other stationary values of $\phi(\theta) = \mathbf{a}_\theta M_{xu}M_{uu}^{-1}M_{ux}\mathbf{a}_\theta'/(\mathbf{a}_\theta M_{xx}\mathbf{a}_\theta')$ might be used. If the relationship is unidentified it may be possible to choose one of the components of the vector θ arbitrarily, say θ_1, so that $\theta_1 = \theta_{10}$ and $\mathbf{a}_\theta \bar{M}_{xu} = 0$. This will be true in particular if the latter equations can be satisfied for all values of θ_1. If the minimum of $\phi(\theta)$, λ_1 is found subject to the condition $\theta_1 = \theta_{10}$, then $T\lambda$, is distributed asymptotically as a χ^2 of $N - p + 1$ degrees of freedom. If now a second conditional minimum of $\phi(\theta)$, λ_2, is sought satisfying the condition $\mathbf{a}_\theta^* M_{xx}\mathbf{a}_\theta' = 0$, where $\mathbf{a}_\theta$ corresponds to the first minimum and $\mathbf{a}_\theta^*$ corresponds to the second minimum, it may be shown by an extension of the methods of Sections 7 and 8 that $T\lambda_2$ is asymptotically distributed independently of $T\lambda_1$ in a χ^2 of $N - p + 1$ degrees of freedom, so that $T(\lambda_1 + \lambda_2)$ is distributed as a χ^2 with $2(N - p + 1)$ degrees of freedom.

This test is likely to be biased in the direction of rejection of the hypothesis that the relationship is unidentifiable, since again it is being assumed that the two linear combinations of the x_{it} are serially independent, whereas they are likely to be positively autocorrelated, so that again an arbitrary allowance must be made for this fact. By analogy with the case of the previous paper it might seem useful to assume that θ_{10} is initially chosen so as to make λ_1 an unrestricted minimum of $\phi(\theta)$, but it seems that in this case this would bias the test seriously in the direction of accepting the assumption of unidentifiability. The suggested form of test seems particularly appropriate in the case of the relationship with first order autoregressive residuals as will appear in Section 14.

10 THE CONFIDENCE REGIONS

The method of developing the confidence regions follows closely that of the previous article. As before the sample functions

$$F_1 = \frac{\mathbf{a}_\theta M_{xx} \mathbf{a}'_\theta}{\sigma^2},$$

$$F_2 = \frac{\mathbf{a}_\theta M_{xu} M_{uu}^{-1} M_{ux} \mathbf{a}'_\theta}{\sigma^2},$$

$$F_3 = \frac{\mathbf{a}_\theta M_{xu^*} M_{u^*u^*}^{-1} M_{u^*x} \mathbf{a}'_\theta}{\sigma^2}$$

are considered, where u^* represent any selection from the instrumental variables u_{jt} of number m. Then it can be shown as in the previous article that F_1, F_2, F_3 are asymptotically distributed as χ^2 with T, N and m degrees of freedom respectively, in such a way that F_3, $F_2 - F_3$, $F_1 - F_2$ are all asymptotically independent χ^2s with m, $N - m$, $T - N$ degrees of freedom respectively. The distributions are exact if all the instrumental variables are completely exogenous variables, but are otherwise only asymptotically valid.

Thus for example $F_2(T - N)/[(F_1 - F_2)N]$ is distributed as a variance ratio asymptotically with degrees of freedom N and $T - N$. Similarly

$$[(F_2 - F_3)(T - N)]/[(F_1 - F_2)(N - m)]$$

is distributed asymptotically as a variance ratio with degrees of freedom $N - m$ and $T - N$. This gives two confidence regions of the form

$$\frac{\mathbf{a}_\theta M_{xu} M_{uu}^{-1} M_{ux} \mathbf{a}'_\theta}{\mathbf{a}_\theta (M_{xx} - M_{xu} M_{uu}^{-1} M_{ux}) \mathbf{a}'_\theta} \leqslant \frac{N \phi_{1L}}{T - N},$$

$$\frac{\mathbf{a}_\theta (M_{xu} M_{uu}^{-1} M_{ux} - M_{xu^*} M_{u^*u^*}^{-1} M_{u^*x}) \mathbf{a}'_\theta}{\mathbf{a}_\theta (M_{xx} - M_{xu} M_{uu}^{-1} M'_{ux}) \mathbf{a}'_\theta} \leqslant \frac{(N - m) \phi_{2L}}{T - N}.$$

11 THE LINEAR EQUATION WITH AUTOREGRESSIVE RESIDUALS

In the previous paper the estimation of the coefficients of the relationship was carried out on the assumption that the residual on the relationship was not autocorrelated. Since the residual is the sum of the random component on the relationship plus a linear function of the measurement errors of the variables, the assumption can only be interpreted in general as meaning that all the measurement errors and the random component are not autocorrelated. If this assumption is dropped it would appear logical to assume that each measurement error, and the random component, are being determined by a different mechanism, for example, by an autoregressive equation. However the problem of estimation which this assumption involves is very complicated, and indeed the only treatment which appears promising is that which assumes that the whole residual is determined by an autoregressive equation. This may be regarded as equivalent to assuming that all these random variables satisfy much the same autoregressive equation.

Let the original economic relationship be written

$$\sum_{i=1}^{r} \alpha_i \xi_{it} = \eta_t, \qquad i = 1, \ldots, r \tag{12.1}$$

where the ξ_{it} are the economic variables and the α_i are the coefficients in the economic relationship. It is then assumed that the η_t satisfy an autoregressive relationship of the form

$$\sum_{i=0}^{s-1} \psi_i \eta_{t-i} = E_t. \tag{12.2}$$

On substituting (12.1) in (12.2), it follows that

$$\sum_{i=1}^{r} \sum_{j=0}^{s-1} \alpha_i \psi_j \xi_{i(t-j)} = E_t$$

and writing

$$x_{(jr+i)t} = \xi_{i(t-j)}, \qquad a_{(jr+i)} = \alpha_i \psi_j, \qquad n = rs,$$

it follows that this can be written

$$\sum_{i=1}^{n} a_i x_{it} = E_t. \tag{12.3}$$

This will be called the transformed relationship. It will be assumed for simplicity that none of the variables in the economic relationship are the lagged values of other variables in the relationship. The case where this assumption is not fulfilled is only slightly more complicated but will not be considered here. Equation (12.3) is of the type that have been studied in the previous section. The variables x_{it} are the economic variables lagged up to $s-1$ times, and the coefficients a_i are functions of the α_i, the coefficients of the economic relationship, and the ψ_i, the coefficients of the autoregressive equation.

Thus the previous general theory can be applied and the instrumental variable estimates are obtained by minimising

$$\phi(\theta) = \frac{\mathbf{a}_\theta M_{xu} M_{uu}^{-1} M_{ux} \mathbf{a}_\theta}{\mathbf{a}_\theta M_{xx} \mathbf{a}_\theta'}$$

where the variables have the above meanings. It is now convenient to introduce a special suffix notation as follows. The elements of the matrix $M_{xu} M_{uu}^{-1} M_{ux}$ are denoted by B_{ij} and then D_{ijkm} is used to denote

$B_{(kr+i)(mr+j)}$. Similarly writing the elements of the matrix M_{xx} as A_{ij} it is convenient to write $C_{ijkm} = A_{(kr+i)(mr+j)}$, so that

$$\phi(\theta) = \frac{\sum_{ijkm} (D_{ijkm}\alpha_i\alpha_j\psi_k\psi_m)}{\sum_{ijkm} (C_{ijkm}\alpha_i\alpha_j\psi_k\psi_m)}. \tag{12.4}$$

Now it is difficult to minimise this directly but a process of successive approximations may be used as follows. Stage 1: Starting from arbitrary values of the ψ_i (12.4) is minimised with respect to the α_i. This involves the solution of the characteristic equations

$$\sum_j \left(\sum_{km} D_{ijkm}\psi_k\psi_m - \lambda \sum_{km} C_{ijkm}\psi_k\psi_m \right)\alpha_j = 0.$$

Stage 2: Maintaining the α_i constant at the values derived from the stage 1, (12.4) is minimised with respect to the ψ_i. This involves the solution of the characteristic equations

$$\sum_m \left(\sum_{ij} D_{ijkm}\alpha_i\alpha_j - \lambda \sum_{ij} C_{ijkm}\alpha_i\alpha_j \right)\psi_m = 0.$$

Stage 1 is now repeated with the ψ_i retained constant at the values given by the solution of stage 2, and so on.

At each stage the value of $\phi(\theta)$ is decreased, and since $\phi(\theta)$ has a minimum greater than zero the process must converge to a limit which is uniquely determined by the starting values of the ψ_i. The only complication that may arise is in the unlikely contingency that at some stage the characteristic equations have a double root at the minimum. This contingency is so unlikely to arise that it will not be considered further. The limit of the process is necessarily a stationary value of (12.4), but not necessarily a minimum. It may be a saddle point. If the direction derivatives are examined and indicate a saddle-point a small movement in the direction of decreasing ϕ will provide a new set of ψ_i with which to start a new process of successive minimisation. Thus the process leads ultimately to a local minimum of (12.4). Whether this local minimum is a suitable solution then depends upon whether $T\lambda$ satisfies the χ^2 test of Section 8.

It is obvious that the choice of the initial ψ_i is crucial, both to the ultimate solution obtained, and the speed with which it is obtained. It has been found in practice that there is usually only one suitable minimum of (12.4), especially where the number of instrumental variables used is more than adequate to give a determinate solution, and in this case the choice of the initial ψ_i can be arbitrary. However a more satisfactory initial choice is assured if the technique of Section 9 is used. This involves considering

$$\frac{\sum_{ij} a_i B_{ij} a_j}{\sum_{ij} a_i A_{ij} a_j} \tag{12.5}$$

where the a_i are not restricted. As suggested in Section 9 tests based on the stationary values of (12.5) can be used to consider whether they are significantly different from zero, and the characteristic vectors that correspond to roots which are not significantly different from zero define a linear space. The intersections or points of close approach of this linear space and the variety defined by $a_{(jr+i)} = \alpha_i \psi_j$ are obtained. Such a point of intersection or close approach provides a reasonable starting point for the process of successive approximation.

12 A COMPARISON WITH MAXIMUM LIKELIHOOD ESTIMATES

If the measurement errors are assumed zero the method of maximum likelihood can be applied to devise estimates. The simplest method is that used by Koopmans and Hood (1953). It is assumed that all the relationships in the stochastic model are stated in their transformed form, and that only the one relationship being studied is restricted to be of a given autoregressive type. Since the lagged variables in this relationship must be treated as predetermined variables, it must be assumed that they may also occur as predetermined variables in the other relationships. On these assumptions the methods of Koopmans and Hood (1953) can be used to show that the logarithm of the maximum-likelihood can be reduced to the form

$$-\tfrac{1}{2}T \log (\mathbf{a}_\theta M_{xx} \mathbf{a}'_\theta) + \tfrac{1}{2}T \log \left[\mathbf{a}_\theta (M_{xx} - M_{xz} M_{zz}^{-1} M_{zx}) \mathbf{a}'_\theta \right]$$
$$= \tfrac{1}{2}T \log (1 - \lambda).$$

Thus maximising the likelihood is equivalent to minimising λ, when all the predetermined variables in the model, including the lagged values of variables in the relationship, are used as instrumental variables. A full treatment of these maximum likelihood estimates is given by El Imam (1957).

13 THE AUTOREGRESSIVE CONFIDENCE REGIONS

The confidence region of type I in this case is

$$\frac{\sum_{ijkm} D_{ijkm} \alpha_i \alpha_j \psi_k \psi_m}{\sum_{ijkm} (C_{ijkm} \alpha_i \alpha_j \psi_k \psi_m - D_{ijkm} \alpha_i \alpha_j \psi_k \psi_m)} \leqslant \frac{N}{T-N} \phi_{1L}.$$

The confidence region of type 2 can be obtained in analogous fashion, its exact form depending on the selection of instrumental variables used to define it. It can be shown that if all the variables are free of measurement errors, confidence regions can be obtained which involve only the α_i, or only the coefficients of the jointly determined variables or any combination of these and the ψ_j. A further confidence region can be obtained by considering the von Neumann ratio of the residuals as a function of the α_i and ψ_i. This has the advantage that it is asymptotically independent of the variance ratios used to define the previous confidence regions and so can be used to give confidence regions, whose boundaries are such that the probability that both criteria are less than assigned limits is equal to 5 or 1 per cent.

14 THE FIRST ORDER AUTOREGRESSIVE RESIDUAL

If the residual is assumed to be determined by a first order autoregressive equation it seems worthwhile to introduce an alternative vector notation. In this case the transformed equation can be written

$$\sum_{i=1}^{r} \alpha_i \xi_{it} - \psi \sum_{i=1}^{r} \alpha_i \xi_{i(t-1)} = E_t.$$

The notation suggested is to write $M_{\xi\xi}$ for the variance matrix of the ξ_{it}, $_1M_{\xi\xi}$ for the covariance matrix between ξ_{it} and $\xi_{i(t-1)}$, and $_2M_{\xi\xi}$ for the variance matrix of the $\xi_{i(t-1)}$. (It is of course true that $_2M_{\xi\xi} = \bar{M}_{\xi\xi}$.) Similarly M_{xu} can be split into

$$\begin{pmatrix} M_{\xi u} \\ _1M_{\xi u} \end{pmatrix}.$$

The instrumental variables estimates are obtained by minimising

$$\phi(\theta) = \frac{\alpha(M_{\xi u}M_{uu}^{-1}M'_{u\xi} - 2\psi_1 M_{\xi u}M_{uu}^{-1}M_{u\xi} + \psi^2_1 M_{\xi u}M_{uu}^{-1}_1 M_{u\xi})\alpha'}{\alpha(M_{\xi\xi} - 2\psi_1 M_{\xi\xi} + \psi^2_2 M_{\xi\xi})\alpha'} \quad (14.1)$$

This can be done by using the method of successive minimisation described in Section 12. Since only solutions in the range $-1 \leqslant \psi \leqslant 1$ are of any interest it is perhaps simplest to locate a suitable starting value of ψ by minimising $\phi(\theta)$ for several ψ in this range. The subsequent process is first to minimise (14.1) with respect to α keeping ψ constant, and then to minimise it with respect to ψ keeping the α constant. The latter process is simplified by noting that to order T^{-1} the minimum is given by

$$\psi = \alpha_1 M_{\xi u}M_{uu}^{-1}M_{u\xi}\alpha'/(\alpha_1 M_{\xi u}M_{uu}^{-1}_1 M_{u\xi}\alpha').$$

This approximation is only useful if the minimum is well defined.

In the just identified case the solution is given by

$$\alpha\bar{M}_{\xi u} - \psi\alpha_1\bar{M}_{\xi u} = 0 \quad (14.2)$$

and assuming $\bar{M}_{\xi u}$ and $_1\bar{M}_{\xi u}$ are of rank r they can be replaced by square matrices, so that (14.2) are characteristic equations with in general r

solutions (not necessarily real). If the solution is just unidentified the matrices are of rank $r-1$, and the equations (14.2) can be solved for the α, which can be expressed as the ratio of two determinants, each polynomials of degree $r-1$ in ψ, so that in α space they define an $(r-1)$ tic curve.

Since there is a point on this curve for all values of ψ it is always possible to apply the test of Section 9 for unidentifiability. To do this it is convenient to take $\psi = 0$ in minimising $\phi(\theta)$ initially. Having obtained λ_1 in this way the second minimum can be obtained by successive approximations, using a process similar to that of Section 11.

Leeds University

REFERENCES

Anderson, T. W. (1950), 'The asymptotic distribution of certain characteristic roots and vectors', *Proc. 2nd Berkeley Symposium*, pp. 103–30.

Champernowne, D. G. (1948), 'Sampling theory applied to autoregressive sequences', *J. R. Statist. Soc.*, **B**, **10**, 204–31.

Durbin, J. (1954), 'Errors in variables', *Rev. Int. Inst. Stat.*, **22**, 23–54.

———— and Watson, G. S. (1950), 'Testing for serial correlation in least squares regression', *Biometrika*, **37**, 409–28.

El Imam, M. M. (1957), 'The consumption function of the U.K. 1929–1938', Ph.D. thesis, University of Leeds.

Geary, R. C. (1948), 'Studies in the relations between economic time series', *J. R. Statist. Soc.*, **B**, **10**, 140–58.

Klein, L. R. (1953), *A Textbook of Econometrics*. Evanston: Row Peterson.

Koopmans, T. C. and Hood, W. C. (1953), 'Estimation of simultaneous linear economic relationships', *Cowles Commission Monograph*, **14**, 112–99.

Moran, P. A. P. (1950), 'A test for the serial independence of residuals', *Biometrika*, **37**, 178–81.

Reiersøl, O. (1945), *Confluence Analysis by Means of Instrumental Sets of Variables*. Uppsala: Almquist and Wiksell.

Sargan, J. D. (1958), 'On the estimation of economic relationships by means of instrumental variables', *Econometrica*, **26**, 393–415.

J. D. SARGAN

——— . ———

6 THE MAXIMUM LIKELIHOOD ESTIMATION OF ECONOMIC RELATIONSHIPS WITH AUTOREGRESSIVE RESIDUALS

(First published in *Econometrica* (July 1961), Vol. 29, No. 3.)

1 INTRODUCTION

Since the development of the reduced form method of estimating economic relationships in the late 1940s (Koopmans [3,4]) and the renewed discussion of an autoregressive scheme for the random errors in a stochastic model, it has seemed natural that there should be a marriage of the two theories. The offspring, it was to be hoped, would be a method of estimating a complete stochastic model, or one equation from such a model, in which the random errors satisfy serial regression equations. The author here attempts a partial survey of the problems of estimation for this type of model, concentrating attention on some particular models or estimation problems where the computational difficulties are least.†

2 THE MODEL AND THE REDUCED FORM

The following notation is used: x_t is a vector with m components which are the variables in the economic relations at time t, A is an $n \times m$ matrix of the coefficients of the relations, and u_t is a vector with n components equal to the random errors in the relations at time t. The equations in the system can be written

$$Ax'_t = u'_t \qquad (t = 0, \ldots, T), \tag{2.1}$$

with the prime indicating a column vector. The u_t satisfy first order serial regression equations which can be written

$$u'_t = Ru'_{t-1} + e'_t \qquad (t = 1, \ldots, T), \tag{2.2}$$

---

† The author is very indebted to some as yet unpublished results by M. M. El Imam to which he has had access.

where e_t is a random vector of n components, the e_t for any two different time periods being independent of each other, normally distributed with zero mean and a constant variance–covariance matrix. R is an $n \times n$ constant matrix. Since the components of e_t will not be assumed independent of each other there is very little point in assuming any *a priori* restrictions on the form of R. The condition that R is diagonal, however, will be considered later.

Combining (2.1) and (2.2) we obtain

$$Ax'_t - RAx'_{t-1} = e'_t. \tag{2.3}$$

If the variance–covariance matrix of e_t is Σ the log-likelihood function is

$$L/T = k_1 + \log \det B - \tfrac{1}{2} \log \det \Sigma - \tfrac{1}{2} \operatorname{tr} (A' \Sigma^{-1} A M_{xx}$$
$$+ \operatorname{tr} (A' \Sigma^{-1} RA M_{x_1 x}) - \tfrac{1}{2} \operatorname{tr} (A' R' \Sigma^{-1} RA M_{x_1 x_1}) \tag{2.4}$$

where B is the $n \times n$ matrix of the coefficients of the current endogenous variables, and where

$$M_{xx} = \sum_{t=1}^{T} \frac{x'_t x_t}{T},$$

$$M_{x_1 x} = \sum_{t=1}^{T} \frac{x'_{t-1} x_t}{T},$$

and

$$M_{x_1 x_1} = \sum_{t=1}^{T} \frac{x'_{t-1} x_{t-1}}{T}.$$

To throw this into its reduced form, we must partition the variables x_t into current endogenous variables y_t and predetermined variables z_t, at the same time partitioning A into B, defined above, and C, which is an $n \times (m-n)$ matrix made up of the coefficients of the predetermined variables. So $A = (B \ C)$, and if we define $f'_t = B^{-1} e'_t$

$$f'_t = y'_t + B^{-1} C z'_t - B^{-1} RB y'_{t-1} - (B^{-1} RB) B^{-1} C z'_{t-1}$$
$$= y'_t - P z'_t - S y'_{t-1} + SP z'_{t-1} \tag{2.5}$$

where $P = B^{-1} C$ and $S = B^{-1} RB$.

If $\Omega = B^{-1} \Sigma B'^{-1}$ the log-likelihood function can be written as

$$L/T = k_2 - \tfrac{1}{2} \log \det \Omega - \tfrac{1}{2} \operatorname{tr} ((I - P)' \Omega^{-1} (I - P) M_{xx})$$
$$+ \operatorname{tr} ((I - P)' \Omega^{-1} S(I - P) M_{x_1 x}) - \tfrac{1}{2} \operatorname{tr} ((I - P)' S' \Omega^{-1} S(I - P) M_{x_1 x_1}). \tag{2.6}$$

Since the log-likelihood function depends on P, S and Ω only, it follows that the maximum of the likelihood subject to *a priori* restrictions on A, R

and Σ can never be greater than that corresponding to the unrestricted maximum of (2.6) considered as a function of P, S, Ω. Initially, we consider the possibility that (2.6) is allowed to reach its unrestricted maximum.

3 THE CLOSED SYSTEM

There is now an important special case that deserves separate treatment. This is a system in which there are no completely exogenous variables, so that all the predetermined variables are lagged endogenous variables.

Let h be the largest lag that occurs for any variable in any equation. Equations (2.5) can then be rewritten

$$f'_t = y'_t - (P_1 y'_{t-1} + P_2 y'_{t-2} + \cdots + P_h y'_{t-h})$$
$$- S(y'_{t-1} - (P_1 y'_{t-2} + P_2 y'_{t-3} + \cdots + P_h y'_{t-h-1}))$$

where P_r is an $n \times n$ square matrix made up of the components of P that apply to y'_{t-r}. These equations can be rewritten as

$$f'_t = y'_t - \Pi_1 y'_{t-1} - \Pi_2 y'_{t-2} - \cdots - \Pi_{h+1} y'_{t-h-1}, \qquad (3.1)$$

where

$$\Pi_1 = P_1 + S,$$
$$\Pi_r = P_r - SP_{r-1} \quad (r = 2, \ldots, h)$$
$$\Pi_{h+1} = -SP_h.$$

Note that if not all the variables y_t have the same maximum lag some of the columns of the P_r and corresponding Π_{r+1} may be all zero, for $r = h$, $r = h-1$, etc. The column of P_r corresponding to any component of y_t will only be non-zero if this variable has a lag of r periods in at least one of the relations. We assume that we can only specify the maximum lag, so that if a lag of order r occurs on any variable, then any lag less than r also occurs in at least one of the relations. It then follows that if the column is non-zero in Π_{r+1} it will be non-zero in Π_r generally.

We now consider the possibility of maximising the log-likelihood function with respect to Π unconditionally, and, having located the maximum $\hat{\Pi}$, of solving the equations

$$\hat{\Pi}_1 = \hat{P}_1 + \hat{S},$$
$$\hat{\Pi}_r = \hat{P}_r - \hat{S}\hat{P}_{r-1} \quad (r = 2, \ldots, h)$$
$$\hat{\Pi}_{h+1} = -\hat{S}\hat{P}_h. \qquad (3.2)$$

If these equations are soluble, the unconditional maximum with respect to Π is the required maximum of the likelihood function. This unconditional maximum is given by the normal regression of y_t on the lagged values of y_t occurring in the relation, as in the normal reduced form method, so that the $\hat{\Pi}_r$ are obtained by normal least squares calculations. The problem that remains is whether the equations (3.2) are soluble for arbitrary matrices $\hat{\Pi}$.

The equations (3.2) can be reduced to a single equation in S of the form

$$\hat{\Pi}_{h+1} + \hat{S}\hat{\Pi}_h + \hat{S}^2\hat{\Pi}_{h-1} + \cdots + \hat{S}^h\hat{\Pi}_1 = \hat{S}^{h+1}. \tag{3.3}$$

The method of solution of this type of matrix equation is well known and is discussed by MacDuffee [5] and Zurmühl [7].

The characteristic roots of the matrix $\hat{S}$ must satisfy the equation

$$\det (\lambda^{h+1}I - \lambda^h\hat{\Pi}_1 - \lambda^{h-1}\hat{\Pi}_2 - \cdots - \hat{\Pi}_{h+1}) = 0. \tag{3.4}$$

This is, in general, an algebraic equation of order equal to n plus the sum of the number of lags in every variable.† If we call the order of the equation p, any n of these p roots can be taken in as many ways as the number of combinations of p objects taken n at a time, and these roots can be arranged as a diagonal matrix Δ.‡ Then a solution $\hat{S}$ takes the form

$$\hat{S} = H^{-1}\Delta H \tag{3.5}$$

where any row h_r of H satisfies

$$h_r(\lambda_r^{h+1}I - \lambda_r^h\hat{\Pi}_1 - \cdots - \hat{\Pi}_{h+1}) = 0 \tag{3.6}$$

and where λ_r is a root of equation (3.4). Equations (3.6) can be solved using Hotelling's method since this is equivalent to solving

$$(\lambda I - K)x' = 0$$

where

$$K = \begin{pmatrix} L & \\ I & 0 \end{pmatrix}$$

and

$$L = (\hat{\Pi}_1', \hat{\Pi}_2', \ldots, \hat{\Pi}_{h+1}').$$

If the equation has complex roots they can be obtained by the method of Collar and Duncan [2] or Zurmühl [7].

The resulting $\hat{S}$ will be a real matrix provided that if any complex root λ_r is included in Δ so is its conjugate complex, $\bar{\lambda}_r$. The only case where a real solution is impossible is where p is even, n is odd, and all the roots of (3.4)

---

† If there are three variables in the model, two with only a single period lag, and the third with both a one and two period lag, the order of the equation is seven.

‡ In the case of the above footnote this gives 35 different choices. We do not consider the case of multiple roots since this will occur with probability zero.

are complex. If $\hat{S}$ is to be suitable as an estimate of a serial regression coefficient matrix, all its characteritic roots should have modulus less than one. Since, however, if the model is to be stationary, all the roots of (3.4) should be of modulus less than one this may be no real restriction. Usually there will be a choice of the roots to be included in the Δ, so that there are multiple solutions to the maximisation problem, and, even for small values of p and n, as illustrated in footnote $\ddagger$, there may be a rather large number of alternatives. Taking any one of these alternative $\hat{S}$ equations, (3.2) enables us to determine $\hat{P}_1$, $\hat{P}_2$ and $\hat{P}_h$ in turn. Each of these estimates corresponds to the same value for the maximum likelihood so that all give equally satisfactory estimates of P and S.

To each of these estimates of P and S there corresponds a unique A and R provided that there are just enough *a priori* restrictions on A and R. The determination of $\hat{A}$ requires the determination of $\hat{B}$ so that

$$\hat{B}(I - \hat{P}) = \hat{A}$$

and

$$\hat{B}\hat{S}\hat{B}^{-1} = \hat{R}$$

such that $\hat{A}$ and $\hat{R}$ satisfy the *a priori* conditions. If there are no *a priori* restrictions on $\hat{R}$ and the restrictions on $\hat{A}$ are linear, then the condition for just-identifiability is exactly the same as in the simple reduced form case where the random errors are not autocorrelated. In particular, a necessary condition, if the restrictions take the form that some of the coefficients are zero, is that the number of non-zero coefficients in each equation should be not more than $p - n + 1$. In addition to this, a rank condition which is the same as that of Koopmans [4] applies. Asymptotic standard errors for the estimates of A and R can be obtained by using the normal likelihood function and for the estimate of A alone by using the concentrated likelihood function of Section 5.

The only form of restriction on R that needs consideration is that it should be diagonal. As noted before it is somewhat illogical to apply this restriction without also assuming that Σ is diagonal. If R is diagonal it is clear from equation (3.5) that the solution is

$$\hat{B} = H; \qquad R = \Delta.$$

This will be a real solution only if all the roots in Δ are real, and this requires that equation (3.4) has at least n real roots. Since the equations are then determined, no further *a priori* restrictions on A are required. Since there is always *a priori* information on the form of the relationships, it follows that the assumption that R is diagonal leads to an overidentified model.

Finally it is to be noted that even though this just-identified model has multiple solutions, the addition of just one further restriction will usually produce a unique solution.

4 THE OPEN MODEL

If we now consider a model that contains some completely exogenous variables, the problem of estimating the reduced form equations must be approached differently. A count of the number of equations and unknowns shows that in general the log-likelihood function, considered as a function of Π, cannot take its unrestricted maximum. It is still possible, however, that the log-liklihood function considered as a function of P and S can reach its unrestricted maximum. The maximum of the reduced form (2.6) can be obtained by concentrating the likelihood function (Koopmans and Hood [3]). Writing $U = (I - P)$ and differentiating with respect to S,

$$\hat{S} = (UM_{xx_1}U')(UM_{x_1x_1}U')^{-1}. \tag{4.1}$$

Then differentiating with respect to Ω we obtain

$$\hat{\Omega} = UM_{xx}U' - (UM_{xx_1}U')(UM_{x_1x_1}U')^{-1}(UM_{x_1x}U') \tag{4.2}$$

and substituting this in the log-likelihood function we get

$$L/T = k_2 - \tfrac{1}{2}\log\begin{vmatrix} UM_{xx}U' & UM_{x_1x}U' \\ UM_{xx_1}U' & UM_{x_1x_1}U' \end{vmatrix} + \tfrac{1}{2}\log\left|UM_{x_1x_1}U'\right|. \tag{4.3}$$

At this stage one can solve for the maximum with respect to U by a process of successive approximation similar to that of Koopmans, Rubin and Leipnik [4]. Alternatively, there is a conceptually and often computationally simpler procedure: the method of successive maximisation. Starting with an initial arbitrary matrix U_0, equations (4.1) and (4.2) are used to determine first round estimates of S and Ω. Then (2.6) is maximised with respect to P, keeping S and Ω constant. The equations to determine P can be written

$$UM_{xz} + \hat{S}UM_{x_1z} + (\hat{\Omega}\hat{S}'\hat{\Omega}^{-1})UM_{xz_1} + (\hat{\Omega}\hat{S}'\hat{\Omega}^{-1}\hat{S})UM_{x_1z_1} = 0. \tag{4.4}$$

These equations are linear in the elements of P and so are easily solved. From this estimate of U, new estimates of S and Ω are obtained using equations (4.1) and (4.2), and these enable new estimates of U to be made from (4.4), and so on. The process must converge to a stationary value of the log-likelihood function, and a check of the behaviour of (4.3) near the stationary value will confirm a local maximum or else suggest new starting values for a further process of successive maximisation.

If there are several local maxima, which of these is reached will depend upon the initial values of U_0 used. In theory, it might be possible to obtain unbiased initial estimates for starting the process of successive approximation using the methods of Section 3 and simply treating the exogenous variables as endogenous. If it is possible to select from the resulting multiple solutions a solution in which the reduced form equations explaining exogenous variables have zero coefficients for all the endogenous variables, this would be a suitable estimate of the reduced form of the model. Such a procedure would, however, increase considerably the amount of calculation, and a simpler procedure would be to use reduced form estimates derived on the assumption that $R=0$ as starting values. This might tend to bias the estimation procedure towards zero autoregression, but it would be appropriate to test the hypothesis that $R=0$ in any case.

When estimates of P and S have been obtained, the matrix B can be obtained from the *a priori* restrictions in the usual way. The conditions for a just-identified solution are as in the previous section. If the solution of this section is compared with that of the previous one the principal difference is that the use of exogenous variables usually provides a unique reduced form, so that if the model satisfies the condition for just identifiability there will be a unique maximum likelihood estimate.

5 THE OVERIDENTIFIED CASE

If there are more restrictions than the number required for just identifiability, then the solution is usually overidentified and must be determined by maximising the log-likelihood function (2.4) with respect to A, R and Σ so as to take account directly of the *a priori* restrictions. If R and Σ are unrestricted we may use the concentrated likelihood function

$$L/T = k_3 + \log|B| - \tfrac{1}{2}\log\begin{vmatrix} AM_{xx}A' & AM_{xx_1}A' \\ AM_{x_1x}A' & AM_{x_1x_1}A' \end{vmatrix} + \tfrac{1}{2}\log|AM_{x_1x_1}A'|.$$

$$(5.1)$$

Maximisation of this subject to the *a priori* restrictions on A requires a technique similar to, and not conceptually more difficult than, those used by Chernoff and Divinsky [1], or Koopmans, Rubin and Leipnik [4].

It may also be useful from the point of view of identifiability and reduction of error variance to consider the possibility that both R and Σ are diagonal. These two assumptions are logically consistent with each other, and a successive approximation procedure can be used directly maximising (2.4) with R and Σ diagonal, which is not very much more complicated than maximising (5.1) with respect to A.

6 SINGLE EQUATION METHODS

The rest of this article considers the possibility of developing estimates for one of the equations in a stochastic model neglecting some of the *a priori* information about the form of the model. It is possible to generalise the results by considering the estimation in the same way of any subset of the equations in the model, but only the case in which the subset is a single equation will be considered here. If the first equation in the model is being studied it can be written as

$$a_1 x'_t - r_1 A x'_{t-1} = e_{1t}. \tag{6.1}$$

It would be in line with the previous sections of this paper to take r_1 as unrestricted, and this case will be considered in the next section. In the present section, however, a somewhat simpler special case is considered as an introduction to the general case. The specialisation is that R is of the form $\begin{pmatrix} r_{11} & 0 \\ r'_{21} & R_{22} \end{pmatrix}$ were R_{22} is an $n-1 \times n-1$ matrix and r_{21} is an $n-1$ vector.

The equations can then be written as

$$\left. \begin{array}{l} a_1 x'_t - r_{11} a_1 x'_{t-1} = e_{1t}, \\ A_2 x'_t - (R_{22} A_2 + r'_{21} a_1) x'_{t-1} = e'_{2t}. \end{array} \right\} \tag{6.2}$$

We could now procede to concentrate the likelihood function (Koopmans and Hood [3]) eliminating Σ_2, and then maximise in turn with respect to r_{21} and R_{22}, leaving the likelihood as a function of A_2, a_1 and r_{11}. The resulting likelihood function could then be maximised by a process of successive approximation to obtain estimates of a_1 and r_{11}. The resulting estimates are, however, still very complicated to compute.

This procedure might be simplified in two ways. Either further restrictions on the form of R could be used (e.g., $R_{22} = 0$) or some of the information about the form of the equations can be ignored. The first possibility will lead to inconsistent estimates, if the assumptions are not in fact true. The second method cuts still further the amount of *a priori* information on the form of the model that is actually being used, but the resulting estimates are consistent and the error variance matrix computed from the concentrated likelihood function is correct.

The simplest application of the second possibility is to replace equations (6.2) by

$$\left. \begin{array}{l} a_1 x'_t - r_{11} a_1 x'_{t-1} = e_{1t}, \\ A_2 x'_t - D x'_{t-1} = e'_{2t}. \end{array} \right\} \tag{6.3}$$

The information ignored is that

$$D = R_{22} A_2 + r'_{21} a_1.$$

If now the log-likelihood function is written as a function of r_{11}, a_1, A_2, D and Σ it can be maximised with respect to A_2, D and Σ, and the resulting concentrated likelihood function takes the form

$$L(a_1, r_{11}) = k_4 + \tfrac{1}{2}\log (bWb') - \tfrac{1}{2}\log (a_1(M_{xx} - 2r_{11}M_{x_1x} + r_{11}^2 M_{x_1x_1})a_1')$$

where

$$W = M_{yy} - (M_{yz}, M_{yx_1})\begin{pmatrix} M_{zz} & M_{zx_1} \\ M_{x_1z} & M_{x_1x_1} \end{pmatrix}^{-1}\begin{pmatrix} M_{zy} \\ M_{x_1y} \end{pmatrix}.$$

If we write

$$M(r_{11}) = M_{xx} - r_{11}(M_{xx_1} + M_{x_1x}) + r_{11}^2 M_{x_1x_1}$$

we can split M up into submatrices

$$\begin{pmatrix}
M_{y^*y^*}(r_{11}) & M_{y^*z^*}(r_{11}) & M_{y^*y^{**}}(r_{11}) & M_{y^*z^{**}}(r_{11}) \\
M_{z^*y^*}(r_{11}) & M_{z^*z^*}(r_{11}) & M_{z^*y^{**}}(r_{11}) & M_{z^*z^{**}}(r_{11}) \\
M_{y^{**}y^*}(r_{11}) & M_{y^{**}z^*}(r_{11}) & M_{y^{**}y^{**}}(r_{11}) & M_{y^{**}z^{**}}(r_{11}) \\
M_{z^{**}y^*}(r_{11}) & M_{z^{**}z^*}(r_{11}) & M_{z^{**}y^{**}}(r_{11}) & M_{z^{**}z^{**}}(r_{11})
\end{pmatrix}$$

where y^* represents the jointly determined variables with non-zero coefficients in the first equation, y^{**} represents the other jointly determined variables, z^* represents the predetermined variables with non-zero coefficients in the first equation, and z^{**} represents the other predetermined variables.

The log-likelihood function can be written as

$$L/T = k_4 + \tfrac{1}{2}\log (b_1 W b_1') - \tfrac{1}{2}\log (b_1 M_{y^*y^*}(r_{11})b_1' + 2b_1 M_{y^*z^*}(r_{11})c_1'$$

$$+ c_1 M_{z^*z^*}(r_{11})c_1').$$

Differentiating with respect to c_1 and b_1 subject to the normalisation $b_1 W b_1' = 1$ yields

$$\hat{c}_1' = - M_{z^*z^*}^{-1}(r_{11})M_{z^*y^*}(r_{11})\hat{b}_1',$$

$$[M_{y^*y^*}(r_{11}) - M_{y^*z^*}(r_{11})M_{z^*z^*}^{-1}(r_{11})M_{z^*y^*}(r_{11})]b_1' = \mu W b_1'. \tag{6.6}$$

Differentiating with respect to r_{11} gives

$$r_{11} = \frac{\hat{a}_1 M_{xx_1}\hat{a}_1'}{\hat{a}_1 M_{x_1x_1}\hat{a}_1'}. \tag{6.7}$$

The maximum can be obtained by a process of successive maximisations similar to that of Section 4. With arbitrary r_{11}, equations (6.6) are used to estimate a_1, just as in the simple limited information, maximum likelihood case. These estimates of a_1 are then used in equation (6.7) to derive a revised r_{11}. This in turn is used to derive new estimates of a_1, and so on.

As pointed out in Sargan [6], this is just a special case of the method of instrumental variables where all the predetermined and lagged variables in the model are used as instrumental variables. Writing $u = (z \quad x_1)$ it can be shown that the maximum likelihood estimates which are obtained by maximising

$$\mu(a_1) = \frac{b_1 W b_1'}{a_1(M_{xx} - Zr_{11}M_{xx_1} + r_{11}^2 M_{x_1x_1})a_1'}$$

can also be regarded as obtained by minimising

$$\lambda(a_1) = \frac{a_1(M_{xu} - r_{11}M_{x_1u})M_{uu}^{-1}(M_{ux} - r_{11}M_{ux_1})a_1'}{a_1(M_{xx} - Zr_{11}M_{xx_1} + r_{11}^2 M_{x_1x_1})a_1'}$$

where $\lambda = 1 - \mu$. This minimisation procedure is equivalent to the instrumental variable method.

From the properties of the maximum likelihood function or from the results of [6], it follows that $T \log \mu$ is asymptotically distributed like χ^2 with $N - n^*$ degrees of freedom, where n^* is the number of variables in the first equation and N is the number of instrumental variables, u.

The conditions for identifiability are discussed in [6]. A necessary condition for identifiability is that $N \geqslant n^*$. A discussion of the non-identifiable case and a significance test is given in [6]. In the identified case, the asymptotic error variance matrix can be estimated from the concentrated log-likelihood function in the usual way. This can then be used to give an asymptotic test of significance for the estimate of r_{11}.

7 THE GENERAL CASE

If now R is such that at least one of the elements $r_{1i} \neq 1$ is non-zero, and if there is no *a priori* information on the form of all except the first equation, then a linear transformation may be applied to the last $n - 1$ equations so that the first two equations take the form

$$\left.\begin{array}{l} a_1 x_t' + r_{12}a_2 x_{t-1}' = e_{1t}, \\ a_2 x_t' + d x_{t-1}' = e_{2t}. \end{array}\right\} \tag{7.1}$$

In writing the second equation in this form some information is already being ignored, since it is ignored that d is a linear combination of the a_i. As in the last section, the likelihood function can now be concentrated so as to leave it as a function only of a_1, a_2, d and r_{12}, in the form

$$L/T = k_5 + \tfrac{1}{2}\log\begin{vmatrix} b_1 W b_1' & b_1 W b_2' \\ b_2 W b_1' & b_2 W b_2' \end{vmatrix} - \tfrac{1}{2}\log\begin{vmatrix} a_1 M_{xx}a_1' + 2r_{12}a_1 M_{xx_1}a_2' + \\ a_1 M_{xx}a_2' + a_1 M_{xx_1}d' + \end{vmatrix}$$

$$\left.\begin{array}{cc} r_{12}'a_2 M_{x_1x_1}a_2', & a_2 M_{xx}a_1' + dM_{x_1x}a_1 + r_{12}(a_2 M_{xx_1 2} + dM_{x_1x_1}a_2') \\ r_{12}(a_2 M_{x_1x}a_2' + aM_{x_1x_1}d'), & a_2 M_{xx}a_2' + 2a_2 M_{xx_1}d' + dM_{x_1x_1}d' \end{array}\right\|. \tag{7.2}$$

Maximising first with respect to d and then with respect to r_{12}, the concentrated log-likelihood function now takes the form

$$L/T = k_5 + \tfrac{1}{2}\log \begin{vmatrix} b_1 Wb_1' & b_1 Wb_2' \\ b_2 Wb_1' & b_2 Wb_2' \end{vmatrix} - \tfrac{1}{2}\log \begin{vmatrix} a_1 Q_{xx} a_1' & a_1 Q_{xx} a_2' \\ a_2 Q_{xx} a_1' & a_2 Q_{xx} a_2' \end{vmatrix}$$
$$+ \tfrac{1}{2}\log(a_1 Q_{xx} a_1') + \tfrac{1}{2}\log(a_2 M_{x_1 x_1} a_2')$$
$$- \tfrac{1}{2}\log \begin{vmatrix} a_1 M_{xx} a_1' & a_1 M_{xx} a_2' \\ a_2 M_{x_1 x} a_1' & a_2 M_{x_1 x_1} a_2' \end{vmatrix} = k_5 + \phi(a_1, a_2), \tag{7.3}$$

where $Q_{xx} = M_{xx} - M_{xx_1} M_{x_1 x_1}^{-1} M_{x_1 x}$.

From the form of this it is clear that the likelihood function is now the ratio of two polynomials each of the fourth order in the elements of a_1 and the elements of a_2. The function is so complicated, however, that only a process of successive approximation can be used to determine its maximum.

It is, of course, impossible to identify the solution without *a priori* restrictions on a_1. To discuss this it is simplest to note that

$$\begin{vmatrix} a_1 Q_{xx} a_1' & a_1 Q_{xx} a_2' \\ a_2 Q_{xx} a_1' & a_2 Q_{xx} a_2' \end{vmatrix} \geq \begin{vmatrix} b_1 Wb_1' & b_1 Wb_2' \\ b_2 Wb_1' & b_2 Wb_2' \end{vmatrix} \tag{7.4}$$

and

$$\begin{vmatrix} a_1 M_{xx} a_1' & a_1 M_{xx_1} a_2' \\ a_2 M_{x_1 x} a_1' & a_2 M_{x_1 x_1} a_2' \end{vmatrix} \geq (a_2 M_{xx} a_2')(a_1 Q_{xx} a_1'). \tag{7.5}$$

If both inequalities can be made equalities the likelihood function can attain its greatest possible value. If the vector is split up into $(y \quad u \quad v)$, u being the completely exogenous variables, v being the lagged endogenous variables, and similarly if a_1 and a_2 are split up into (b_1, g_1, h_1) and (b_2, g_2, h_2), then the conditions for (7.4) to be an equality are

$$\left. \begin{array}{c} Q_{uy} b_1' + Q_{uu} g_1' = 0, \\ Q_{uy} b_2' + Q_{uu} g_2' = 0, \end{array} \right\} \tag{7.6}$$

and the condition for (7.5) to be an equality is

$$M_{x_1 x} a_1' = M_{x_1 x_1} a_2'. \tag{7.7}$$

Thus, a necessary condition for the solution to be identified is that, with the *a priori* restrictions on a_1, there should be at least as many equations here as unknowns. Assuming the restrictions on a_1 to be that some of its elements are zero, then the condition is that, if the number of exogenous variables in the model is p, the number of non-zero coefficients in a_1, n^*, should not be more than $2p + 1$. If $n^* = 2p + 1$ the solution will be said to be just identified, if $n^* < 2p + 1$ it will be said to be overidentified.

To obtain a necessary and sufficient condition for identification we use a theorem of Sargan [6]. Using a bar to represent 'the asymptotic limit of', it is easy to prove that the actual vectors a_1 and a_2 must satisfy equations analogous to (7.6) and (7.7):

$$\bar{Q}_{uy}b'_1 + \bar{Q}_{uu}g'_1 = 0, \qquad \bar{Q}_{uy}b'_2 + \bar{Q}_{uu}g'_2 = 0, \tag{7.8}$$

$$\bar{M}_{x_1 x}a'_1 = \bar{M}_{x_1 x_1}a'_2. \tag{7.9}$$

(The latter equation assumes $r_{12} = 1$. This is no restriction since equations (7.1) are not fundamentally changed by replacing a_2 by $r_{12}a_2$).

Then it follows that if these equations, together with the *a priori* restrictions on a_1, uniquely determine the a_1 and a_2, the expression

$$\tfrac{1}{2}\log \begin{vmatrix} b_1\bar{W}b'_1 & b_1\bar{W}b'_2 \\ b_2\bar{W}b'_1 & b_2\bar{W}b'_2 \end{vmatrix} - \tfrac{1}{2}\log \begin{vmatrix} a_1\bar{Q}_{xx}a'_1 & a_1\bar{Q}_{xx}a'_2 \\ a_2\bar{Q}_{xx}a'_1 & a_2\bar{Q}_{xx}a'_2 \end{vmatrix}$$

$$+ \tfrac{1}{2}\log(a_1\bar{Q}_{xx}a'_1) + \tfrac{1}{2}\log(a_2\bar{M}_{x_1 x_1}a'_2) - \tfrac{1}{2}\log \begin{vmatrix} a_1\bar{M}_{xx}a'_1 & a_1 M_{xx}a'_2 \\ a_2\bar{M}_{x_1 x}a'_1 & a_2\bar{M}_{x_1 x_1}a'_2 \end{vmatrix}$$

has a unique maximum for which the expression is zero. It follows from the theorem of [7] that there is a maximum of (7.3) which is a consistent estimator of a_1, a_2. Thus the solution is identified provided the linear equations (7.8) and (7.9), together with the *a priori* restrictions on a_1, determine a unique solution. This requires that the matrix which can be written

$$\begin{pmatrix} \bar{Q}_{uy^*} & | & \bar{Q}_{uu^*} & | & 0 & | & 0 \\ \hline 0 & & | & \bar{Q}_{uy} & | & \bar{Q}_{uu} & | & 0 \\ \hline \bar{M}_{x_1 x^*} & & | & & \bar{M}_{x_1 x_1} & & \end{pmatrix}$$

(where the * means that only variables which have non-zero coefficients in a_1 are retained) has rank equal to $n + n^* - 1$, where n^* is the number of non-zero elements of the vector a_1.

However, (7.3) may have multiple maxima, but it is to be noted that only a maximum for which (7.3) is near zero need be considered. It follows from the usual properties of the maximum likelihood procedure that $-T + \phi(a_1, a_2)$ is distributed asymptotically like χ^2 with $2p + 1 - n^*$ degrees of freedom. This allows the correct maximum to be located and also provides a significance test for the *a priori* restrictions which have been imposed on a_1.

When the solution is overidentified a process of successive approximation must be used to maximise ϕ. A suitable starting estimate of a_1 and a_2 can be obtained by ignoring some of the exogenous variables, so reducing the number of exogenous variables to make the solution just identified.

8 GENERAL CONCLUSIONS

Results of this general type can be extended to the case where a subset of the equations is to be estimated. However, the results of the last two sections are sufficiently difficult to use without further complication. The method of Section 6 is definitely easier to apply than that of Section 7 especially when the problem of identification is under consideration. The assumptions of Section 6 are narrower than those of Section 7, although this may not be important if a set of preliminary estimates is required to start off the estimation of a complete system using the methods of Section 5. The methods of Section 5 can be recommended as the minimum that can be done to take account of autocorrelation when only one equation is under consideration.

REFERENCES

[1] Chernoff, H. and N. Divinsky: 'The computation of maximum-likelihood estimates of linear structural equations', in W. H. Hood and T. C. Koopmans, eds., *Studies in Econometric Method*, Cowles Commission Monograph 14, New York, 1953.

[2] Collar, A. R. and W. J. Duncan: 'Matrices applied to the motions of damped systems', *Philosophical Magazine* (7), **19**, pp. 197–219, 1935.

[3] Koopmans, T. C. and W. C. Hood: 'Estimation of linear relationships', in T. C. Koopmans, ed., *Statistical Inference in Dynamic Economic Models*, Cowles Commission Monograph 10, New York: John Wiley, 1950.

[4] Koopmans, T. C., H. Rubin and R. B. Leipnik: 'Measuring the equation systems of dynamic economics), in Koopmans (see [3]).

[5] Macduffee, C. C.: *The Theory of Matrices*, New York, 1946.

[6] Sargan, J. D.: 'The estimation of relationships with auto-correlated residuals by means of instrumental variables', *Journal of the Royal Statistical Society*, **Series B**, 1959.

[7] Zurmühl, R.: *Matrizen*, Berlin, 1950.

———— · ————

7 THREE-STAGE LEAST-SQUARES AND FULL MAXIMUM LIKELIHOOD ESTIMATES

(First published in *Econometrica* (January–April 1964),
Vol. 32,. Nos. 1–2.)

This paper proves in the context of maximum likelihood estimation of linear stochastic models of the Cowles Commission type [2], that if the model is fully identified and stable and the error variance matrix unrestricted, three-stage least-squares estimates differ asymptotically from full maximum likelihood estimates by order $1/T$, where T is the number of time periods. When the full maximum likelihood estimates are best asymptotic normal so are the three-stage least-squares estimates.

1 THE LIKELIHOOD FUNCTION

The stochastic model can be written in matrix form [2] as $Ax'_t = u'_t$, where A is a matrix of coefficients, x_t is a vector of the observed variables in period t, and u_t is a vector of random variables in period t; u_t is independent of $u_{t'}$, $t \neq t'$; each u_t is distributed normally with mean zero and variance matrix Σ. Σ is assumed to be positive definite.

The log-likelihood function is given by

$$1/T \log L = k_1 + \log \det B - \tfrac{1}{2} \log \det \Sigma - \tfrac{1}{2} \operatorname{tr}(\Sigma^{-1} A M_{xx} A')$$

where B is the square non-singular matrix of the coefficients of the jointly determined variables, and M_{xx} is the sample variance matrix.

The likelihood function can be maximised with respect to Σ, assuming that there are no *a priori* restrictions on it, yielding a concentrated log-likelihood function

$$k_2 + \log \det B - \tfrac{1}{2} \log \det (A M_{xx} A').$$

Now partitioning M_{xx} into $\begin{pmatrix} M_{yy} & M_{yz} \\ M_{zy} & M_{zz} \end{pmatrix}$ where M_{yy} and M_{zz} are the second moment matrices of the jointly determined and the predetermined variables respectively, and M_{yz} is their joint second moment matrix,

$$M_{xz}M_{zz}^{-1}M_{zx} = \begin{pmatrix} M_{yz}M_{zz}^{-1}M_{zy} & M_{yz} \\ M_{zy} & M_{zz} \end{pmatrix},$$

and

$$A(M_{xx} - M_{xz}M_{zz}^{-1}M_{zx})A' = A\begin{pmatrix} M_{yy} - M_{yz}M_{zz}^{-1}M_{zy} & 0 \\ 0 & 0 \end{pmatrix}A' = BWB'$$

where $W = M_{yy} - M_{yz}M_{zz}^{-1}M_{zy}$.

Taking the logarithm of the determinmant of this equation, we obtain

$$2\log\det B + \log\det W = \log\det(A(M_{xx} - M_{xz}M_{zz}^{-1}M_{zx})A').$$

Substituting this expression for $\log\det B$ in the concentrated log-likelihood function the result is

$$1/T\log L = k_3 + \tfrac{1}{2}\log\det(A(M_{xx} - M_{xz}M_{zz}^{-1}M_{zx})A') - \tfrac{1}{2}\log\det(AM_{xx}A')$$

$$= k_3 + \tfrac{1}{2}\log\det[I - (AM_{xx}A')^{-1}(AM_{xz}M_{zz}^{-1}M_{zx}A')],$$

where I is the unit matrix.

$$(L)^{2/T} = k_4\det(I - Q) \tag{1}$$

where $Q = (AM_{xx}A')^{-1}(ARA')$ and $R = M_{xz}M_{zz}^{-1}M_{zx}$.

2 FURTHER NOTATION AND LEMMAS

It is now convenient to use A^1 to mean the two-stage least-squares estimates of A, A^2 to mean the three-stage least-squares estimate of A, A^3 to mean the full maximum likelihood estimates of A, and then $V^i = (A^iM_{xx}A^{i\prime})^{-1}$, $Q^i = V^iA^iRA^{i\prime}$, $i = 1, 2, 3$. It is assumed that the *a priori* restrictions take the form that some of the elements of A have fixed values which will usually be zero or one. The elements of A which are not fixed in this way will be called the unknown coefficients, and it will be useful to think of the unknown coefficients in all the equations arranged as a single vector, the first elements in the vector corresponding to the unknown coefficients of the first equation, and so on; the elements of the vector being in the same order as the equations. The various estimates of this vector will be denoted by α^i, $i = 1, 2, 3$.

The method of proof of the main theorem uses the stochastic order relationship of Mann and Wald [3]. They define the stochastic order symbol O_p by $x_T = O_p(f(T))$, if for each positive ε there exists $\theta_\varepsilon > 0$, such that $P(|x_T| \le \theta_\varepsilon f(T)) \ge 1 - \varepsilon$ for all T; and they show that this stochastic order relationship has all the properties of non-stochastic order relationships; in particular

$$O_p(f(T)) \times O_p(g(T)) = O_p(f(T)g(T)); \qquad O_p(f(T)) + O_p(f(T)) = O_p(f(T)).$$

LEMMA 1: *If $H(z)$ is a matrix whose elements are rational functions of a vector of stochastic variables z, and plim $z = \bar{z}$ and $H(\bar{z})$ exists and is non-singular, then $H(z)^{-1}$ and $\partial(H(z)^{-1})/\partial z$ are both $O_p(1)$.*

All the elements of the latter two matrix expressions are rational functions of z. Slutsky [6] proves that if $f(z)$ is a rational function and $f(\bar{z})$ is finite then $\text{plim}_{T \to \infty} f(z) = f(\bar{z})$. From the definition, a stochastic variable with a probability limit is $O_p(1)$.

LEMMA 2: *If $\text{plim}_{T \to \infty} (M_{zz})$ exists and is non-singular, and the model is fully identified and stable*

(i) $Q^i = O_p(1/T), \qquad (i = 1, 2, 3)$

(ii) $\dfrac{\partial Q^i}{\partial \alpha^i_k} = O_p(1/\sqrt{T}). \qquad (i = 1, 2, 3; \text{ all } k)$

Proof: For all i, $\text{plim}(A^i M_{xx} A^{i\prime}) = \Sigma$ and, since Σ is non-singular, Lemma 1 shows V^i and $\partial V^i/\partial \alpha^i_k$ to be $O_p(1)$. AM_{xz} has elements $1/T(\sum_{t=1}^{T} u_{it} z_{jt})$ which are $O_p(1/\sqrt{T})$ provided the model is stable. $A^i - A$ is $O_p(1/\sqrt{T})$ if all the equations are identified ([4; 1; 7]). So $A^i M_{xz} = AM_{xz} + (A^i - A)M_{xz} = O_p(1/\sqrt{T})$. Since $\text{plim}_{T \to \infty} M_{zz}$ is non-singular M_{zz}^{-1} is $O_p(1)$, $A^i M_{xz} M_{zz}^{-1} M_{zx} A^{i\prime}$ is $O_p(1/T)$ and $A^i M_{xz} M_{zz}^{-1} M_{zx}$ is $O_p(1/\sqrt{T})$. Equations (i) and (ii) follow.

3 A THEOREM

THEOREM: *Under the conditions of Lemma 2, $A^3 - A^2 = O_p(1/T)$.*

Proof: The likelihood function to be maximised can be taken as proportional to $\det(I - Q) = 1 - \sum_{i=1}^{n} q_{ii} + \phi(Q)$, where $\phi(Q)$ is a polynomial in the elements of Q, in which every term is at least of the second order. The equations for the full maximum likelihood estimates can be written

$$-\sum_{i=1}^{n} \frac{\partial q_{ii}^3}{\partial \alpha_k^3} + \frac{\partial \phi(Q^3)}{\partial \alpha_k^3} = 0. \tag{2}$$

The right hand expression is $O_p(1/T)^{3/2}$, since it can be expanded and every term in the expansion is a product of an element of $\partial Q^3/\partial \alpha_k^3$ and at least one element of Q^3.

Now

$$\sum_{i=1}^{n} q_{ii}^3 = \sum_{i=1}^{n} \sum_{j=1}^{n} \sum_{p=1}^{N} \sum_{q=1}^{N} v_{ij}^3 a_{jp}^3 r_{pq} a_{iq}^3,$$

where n is the number of equations in the model, and N is the total number of variables in the model. The derivative of this with respect to any a_{jp} can be expressed as a sum of terms of two types; the first, those terms which would be obtained by differentiating as though v_{ij} were constant; the second terms of the form

$$\sum_{i=1}^{n} \sum_{j=1}^{n} \sum_{p=1}^{N} \sum_{q=1}^{N} \frac{\partial v_{ij}^3}{\partial \alpha_k^3} (a_{jp}^3 r_{pq} a_{iq}^3).$$

Since $\partial v_{ij}^3 / \partial \alpha_k^3$ is $O_p(1)$ and, from Lemma 2, $\sum_{p=1}^{N} \sum_{q=1}^{N} a_{jp}^3 r_{pq} a_{iq}^3$ is $O_p(1/T)$, the sum of the terms of this type is $O_p(1/T)$. Equation (2) can then be written

$$-\sum_{j=1}^{n} \sum_{p=1}^{N} v_{rj}^3 a_{jp}^3 r_{ps} + O_p(1/T) = 0, \tag{3}$$

for all r and s corresponding to an unknown coefficient.

Considering now the three-stage least-squares estimates, the equations defining them [7] can be written in the above notation as $\sum_{j=1}^{n} \sum_{p=1}^{N} v_{rj}^1 a_{jp}^2 r_{ps} = 0$, since v_{rj}^1 are the elements of the inverse of the sample variance matrix of the residuals on the equation estimated by two-stage least-squares, and r_{ps} is the sample variance matrix of the reduced form estimates of the endogenous variables and the predetermined variables.

Adding the last two equations

$$\sum_{j=1}^{n} \sum_{p=1}^{N} v_{rj}^1 (a_{jp}^2 - a_{jp}^3) r_{ps} = \sum_{j=1}^{n} \sum_{p=1}^{N} (v_{rj}^3 - v_{rj}^1) a_{jp}^3 r_{ps} + O_p(1/T),$$

and

$$V^1 - V^3 = V^1 (A^3 M_{xx} A^{3\prime} - A^1 M_{xx} A^{1\prime}) V^3 = V^1 (A^3 M_{xx} \Delta A' + \Delta A M_{xx} A^{1\prime}) V^3$$

where $\Delta A = A^3 - A^1$. Both V^1 and V^3 are $O_p(1)$ and ΔA is $O_p(1/\sqrt{T})$ since $A^3 - A$ and $A^1 - A$ are both $O_p(1/\sqrt{T})$. So $V^3 - V^1$ is $O_p(1/\sqrt{T})$, and from Lemma 2, $\sum_{p=1}^{N} a_{jp}^3 r_{ps}$ is $O_p(1/\sqrt{T})$. The last set of equations can then be written

$$\sum_{j=1}^{n} \sum_{p=1}^{N} v_{rj}^1 (a_{jp}^2 - a_{jp}^3) r_{ps} = O_p(1/T). \tag{4}$$

As in Section 2 the elements of the matrices A^3 and A^2 can be considered as making up two vectors α^3 and α^2. The $\alpha^3 - \alpha^2$ need only contain unknown coefficients; for the *a priori* fixed coefficients $a_{rs}^3 - a_{rs}^2 = 0$.

Equations (4) can then be written as

$$K(\alpha^{2\prime} - \alpha^{3\prime}) = O_p(1/T).$$

The matrix K is a square matrix of order equal to the total number of unknown coefficients in all the equations. It can be regarded as obtained by taking the Frobenius matrix product $V^1 \odot R$, and selecting from it only those rows and columns which corresponds to unknown coefficients. K can be partitioned in the form

$$K = \begin{pmatrix} K_{11} & K_{12} & K_{13} & \cdots & K_{1n} \\ K_{21} & K_{22} & K_{23} & \cdots & K_{2n} \\ K_{31} & K_{32} & K_{33} & \cdots & K_{3n} \\ \vdots & \vdots & \vdots & & \vdots \\ K_{n1} & K_{n2} & K_{n3} & \cdots & K_{nn} \end{pmatrix}.$$

The submatrix K_{ij} is obtained by taking elements of R with rows corresponding to unknown coefficients in the ith equation and columns corresponding to unknown coefficients in the jth equation, multiplied by v_{ij}^1. K is the matrix introduced by Zellner and Theil [7]. They show that a necessary and sufficient condition for complete identification is that $\bar{K} = \text{plim}_{T \to \infty} K$ is non-singular. Therefore, if the model is identified, Lemma 1 shows that K^{-1} is $O_p(1)$, and then $\alpha^{2\prime} - \alpha^{3\prime}$ is $O_p(1/T)$.

COROLLARY: *Under the conditions of the theorem, $\sqrt{T}\alpha^3$ is asymptotically normally distributed with mean zero and variance matrix $\bar{K}^{-1}$.*

From the theorem $T(\sqrt{}\alpha^{2\prime} - \alpha^{3\prime}) = O_p(1/\sqrt{T})$, and $\sqrt{T}\alpha^2$ is asymptotically normally distributed with mean zero and variance matrix $\bar{K}^{-1}$ [7], and since the asymptotic distribution function is continuous everywhere $\sqrt{T}\alpha^3$ has the same asymptotic distribution function [3].

4 CONCLUSIONS

The preceding does not discuss directly whether three-stage least-squares estimates are best asymptotic normal. But the full maximum likelihood estimates are best asymptotic under conditions including complete identification and stability [5]. The corollary then shows that the three-stage least-squares estimates are best asymptotic normal under the same conditions.

University of Leeds

REFERENCES

[1] Basmann, R. L.: 'On the asymptotic distribution of generalised linear estimates', *Econometrica*, **28**, 97–107, 1960.

[2] Koopmans, T. C., H. Rubin and R. B. Leipnik: 'Measuring the equation systems of dynamic economics', in *Statistical Inference in Dynamic Economic Models*, Cowles Commission Monograph 10, New York, 1950.

[3] Mann, H. B. and A. Wald: 'On stochastic limit and order relationships', *Annals of Mathematical Statistics*, **14**, 217–26, 1943.

[4] Mann, H. B.: 'On the statistical treatment of linear stochastic difference equations', *Econometrica*, **11**, 173–220, 1943.

[5] Rubin, H.: 'Systems of linear stochastic equations', Ph.D. Dissertation, University of Chicago, 1948.

[6] Slutsky, E.: Über Stochastischen Asymptoten und Grenzwerte', *Metron*, **5**, 3–27, 1925.

[7] Zellner, A. and H. Theil: 'Three-stage least squares: simultaneous estimation of simultaneous equations', *Econometrica*, **30**, 54–78, 1962.

J. D. SARGAN

———— · ————

8 WAGES AND PRICES IN THE UNITED KINGDOM: A STUDY IN ECONOMETRIC METHODOLOGY

London School of Economics

(First published in *Econometric Analysis for National Economic Planning*, eds. P. E. Hart, G. Mills and J. K. Whitaker, pp. 25–54. London: Butterworth and Co. Ltd.)

The primary intention of this study was to develop methods of estimation, and to compare different methods of estimation when estimating structural relationships from economic time series when the errors in the relationships are autocorrelated. The methods used are based upon the theoretical treatment of the problem in Section 6 of my article [6], and are closely related to those given by Durbin [2].

The study was intended to consider practical problems in the use of the methods in a typical econometric investigation. It was decided to consider wages and prices in the United Kingdom since this is a subject of economic interest and substantial studies were available [1], [3], [4], [5] to form a springboard. Both wages and price determination equations were based on those used by Klein, Ball, Hazlewood and Vandome [3].

1 ALTERNATIVE METHODS OF ESTIMATION

We consider the case where a set of variables x_{it}, $i = 1 \ldots n$, $t = 1 \ldots T$, are connected by a relationship

$$\alpha_0 + \sum_{i=1}^{n} \alpha_i x_{it} = u_t. \tag{1}$$

We adopt the convention that $x_{ot} = 1$ for all t, so that the equation can be written

$$\sum_{i=0}^{n} \alpha_i x_{it} = u_t. \tag{2}$$

The u_t are determined by a first order autoregressive relation

$$u_t - k u_{t-1} = e_t \qquad (3)$$

where the e_t are independent random variables.

Combining equations (1) and (3)

$$\sum_{i=0}^{n} \alpha_i x_{it} - \sum_{i=0}^{n} k\alpha_i x_{i(t-1)} = e_t. \qquad (4)$$

This equation will be referred to as the transformed equation. Using vector notation equations (2) and (4) can be rewritten

$$\alpha \mathbf{x}'_t = u_t, \qquad \alpha \mathbf{x}'_t - k\alpha \mathbf{x}'_{t-1} = e_t.$$

It is sometimes useful to introduce vectors of length $2n+2$ by the equations

$$\mathbf{a} = (\alpha, -k\alpha), \qquad \xi_t = (\mathbf{x}_t, \mathbf{x}_{t-1})$$

and then to write the transformed equation as

$$\mathbf{a}\xi'_t = e_t. \qquad (5)$$

It is sometimes appropriate to consider the problem of estimating the coefficients $a_i, i = 0 \ldots 2n+1$, of equation (5) subject to a set of n non-linear restrictions of the form

$$a_0 a_{i+n+1} = a_{n+1} a_i, \qquad i = 1 \ldots n. \qquad (6)$$

Alternatively we may consider the problem as a special case of the more general form where the coefficients of a linear equation a_i are functions of a set of parameters forming a vector θ, so that $\mathbf{a} = \mathbf{a}(\theta)$. In this case the parameters form the vector $\theta = (\alpha, k)$ of order $n+2$. This viewpoint was adopted in my article on the estimation of such equations by the use of instrumental variables [7].

Consider first the case where all the variables x_t except one are predetermined variables and the e_t are normally and independently distributed with mean zero and variance σ^2. Then it is clear that the maximum likelihood estimates in this case are generalised least squares estimates obtained by minimising

$$\sum_{t=1}^{T} e_t^2$$

considered as a function of the α_i and k.

If we number the variables so that x_{nt} is the dependent variable it will be useful to normalise the coefficients so that $\alpha_n = -1$, so that the equation can be written

$$x_{mt} = \sum_{i=0}^{n-1} \alpha_i x_{it} + u_t.$$

Writing $M_{\xi\xi}$ for the matrix whose elements are

$$(1/T) \sum_{t=1}^{T} \xi_{it}\xi_{jt}$$

the sum of squares is

$$\sum_{t=1}^{T} e_t^2 = T\mathbf{a}(\theta)M_{\xi\xi}\mathbf{a}'(\theta)$$

and the problem is to minimise this function of the parameters θ. The function is biquadratic in the parameters k and α_i so that an explicit solution is not possible, but an iterative solution is comparatively easy. Since the second order derivatives of the likelihood function are continuous functions of the variables and parameters and have finite expectations, an estimate of the error variance matrix of the maximum likelihood estimates is obtained from the usual formula. Defining

$$s^2 = (1/T) \sum_{t=1}^{T} \hat{e}_t^2 = \hat{\mathbf{a}}(\theta)M_{\xi\xi}\hat{\mathbf{a}}'(\theta)$$

where the hat (^) indicates the estimated value, the asymptotic error variance matrix of the $\hat{\theta}$ can be estimated as

$$\frac{s^2}{T}\left[\left(\frac{\partial\hat{\mathbf{a}}}{\partial\theta}\right)M_{\xi\xi}\left(\frac{\partial\hat{\mathbf{a}}}{\partial\theta}\right)'\right]^{-1} \tag{7}$$

It is not necessary to include a term of the type

$$\frac{1}{T}\left(\hat{\mathbf{a}}(\theta)M_{\xi\xi}\frac{\partial^2\hat{\mathbf{a}}}{\partial\theta\partial\theta'}\right)$$

in expression (7) since $\mathbf{a}(\theta)M_{\xi\xi}$ is $O(1/\sqrt{T})$ except for its $(n+1)$th element, whereas the corresponding elements of $\partial^2\hat{\mathbf{a}}/\partial\theta\partial\theta'$ are zero, since $a_{n+1} = -1$, and so has second order derivatives equal to zero. It is clear that an asymptotic significance test for any coefficient is obtained by assuming that the coefficient is asymptotically normally distributed, with the given standard error.

A significance test is also available for the general formulation against the assumption that there is a relationship of the form (5) with the coefficients a_i unrestricted. In order to consider this it is necessary to take account of the fact that the matrix $M_{\xi\xi}$ is usually singular. If there is present among the set of variables x_{it} a variable which is an exact linear function of any set of $x_{j(t-1)}$ this variable will be called redundant. Examples of redundant variables are the constant term, any polynomial trend (provided all lower order powers of t are included in the equations), the seasonal shift variables, and any variable which is the lagged value of another variable in the structural equation.

For example if $x_{1t}=t$, then $x_{1t}=x_{1(t-1)}+x_{0(t-1)}$ and if we define the seasonal shift variables by $S_{1t}=1$ in the first quarter of each year but is zero in any other quarter; $S_{2t}=1$ in the second quarter of each year but is zero otherwise; and $S_{3t}=1$ in the third quarter of each year but is zero otherwise: then $S_{2t}=S_{1(t-1)}$, $S_{3t}=S_{2(t-1)}$, and $S_{1t}=x_{0(t-1)}-S_{2(t-1)}-S_{3(t-1)}$.

Although the presence of redundant variables is not the only reason why $M_{\xi\xi}$ should be singular, in practice it does appear to be the most usual cause of singularity. We use a likelihood ratio test which considers the ratio of the maximum likelihood achieved on the assumptions summarised at the start of this section, with the maximum likelihood achieved using the unrestricted equation of form (5) omitting however those variables ξ_{it} which make $M_{\xi\xi}$ singular; in particular omitting redundant variables. If m is the number of omitted variables then twice the log of the likelihood ratio is asymptotically distributed as χ^2 with $n-m-1$ degrees of freedom. If we write Q for the matrix obtained from $M_{\xi\xi}$ by omitting its $(n+1)$th row and column, q for the vector obtained by taking the $(n+1)$th row of $M_{\xi\xi}$ and omitting its $(n+1)$th element, and p for this latter element, then an equivalent asymptotic test is obtained by using the fact that, if the autoregressive assumption is correct, then the criterion

$$T[1+(1/s^2)(qQ^{-1}q'-p)]$$

is distributed asymptotically as χ^2 with $n-m-1$ degrees of freedom. If the criterion is judged significant at some conventional level of significance (for example, 5 per cent), then the autoregressive hypothesis is rejected in favour of the unrestricted equation (5). This can often be interpreted to mean that a more complicated structure of lags, or a longer lag is required in the structural equation on at least one of the variables. The modification required to the structural equation can be indicated by the coefficients of the unrestricted equation. If one of the lagged variables in the unrestricted equation has a much larger coefficient proportionally than the other lagged variables, it seems reasonable to introduce the lagged value of this variable into the structural equation, and to estimate the new form of the structural equation, assuming as before a first order autoregressive equation for the error. This process of modifying the form of the structural equation can continue until the criterion ceases to be significant. Of course at some stage in the process the autoregressive coefficient k may not be significantly different from zero, indicating that its significance in the original form of the structural equation was due to the variables in the equation having the wrong lags.

Finally a test for the first-order autoregressive equation as against a second-order autoregressive equation was made. This will be described in Section 3.

Considering now the case where the variables are subject to measurement errors or where there is more than one endogenous variable in the equation, it is necessary to consider a set of instrumental variables z_{jt}, $j = 1 \ldots N, t = 1 \ldots T$. Some of the variables ξ_{it} may be included among the instrumental variables. Introducing the matrices M_{zz} with elements

$$(1/T) \sum_{t=1}^{T} z_{it} z_{jt}$$

and $M_{z\xi}$ with elements

$$(1/T) \sum_{t=1}^{T} z_{it} \xi_{jt}$$

then the instrumental variables estimates of [7] are obtained by minimising

$$\mathbf{a}(\theta) M_{\xi z} M_{zz}^{-1} M_{z\xi} \mathbf{a}'(\theta)$$

considered as a function of the parameters θ. Mathematically the minimisation problem is exactly similar to that arising in the least squares case, the only difference being the substitution of the matrix $M_{\xi z} M_{zz}^{-1} M_{z\xi}$ in the instrumental variables case for the matrix $M_{\xi\xi}$ in the least squares case. The problem of computing the estimates will be considered in the next section.

Defining as before $s^2 = \hat{\mathbf{a}}(\theta) M_{\xi\xi} \hat{\mathbf{a}}'(\theta)$ an estimate of the asymptotic error variance matrix of θ is given by

$$(s^2/T) \left[\left(\frac{\partial \mathbf{a}}{\partial \theta} \right) M_{\xi z} M_{zz}^{-1} M_{z\xi} \left(\frac{\partial \mathbf{a}}{\partial \theta} \right)' \right]^{-1}.$$

Finally a criterion (similar to the χ^2 criterion of the least squares case) for the assumed form of the structural equation and the autoregressive equation is given by the consideration that $(T/s^2)(\hat{\mathbf{a}}(\theta) M_{\xi z} M_{zz}^{-1} M_{z\xi} \hat{\mathbf{a}}'(\theta))$ is distributed asymptotically as χ^2 with $N - n - 2$ degrees of freedom.

The method of estimation can be described by saying that it is equivalent to the method of two-stage least squares applied to the transformed equation taking account of the restrictions (6); it can be considered to be an extension of the method of two-stage least squares, in the case where all the variables are free of measurement errors and so all the pre-determined variables in the stochastic model can be used as instrumental variables. The limited information maximum likelihood estimates considered in [6] are asymptotically equivalent to these autoregressive two-stage least squares estimates but are a good deal more difficult to compute. Since there is no reason to believe that they have any advantage over the two-stage least squares estimates it was decided not to use the maximum likelihood estimates.

2 COMPUTING METHODS

The mathematical formulation of the minimisation in both cases is the same. The function to be minimised can be written

$$\alpha(A - k(B + B') + k^2 C)\alpha' \tag{8}$$

where in the least squares case

$$M_{\xi\xi} = \begin{bmatrix} A & B \\ B' & C \end{bmatrix}$$

and in the instrumental variables case

$$M_{\xi z} M_{zz}^{-1} M_{z\xi} = \begin{bmatrix} A & B \\ B' & C \end{bmatrix}$$

and A, B and C are in both cases square $n+1$ order matrices. The traditional way of minimising this function, suggested by several writers, notably Orcutt, is an iterative minimisation. Starting with some arbitrary value of k, say $k=0$, mimimise with respect to α keeping k constant. Since (8) is a quadratic in α the minimisation only requires the solution of linear equations. Now keep α constant at the new value and minimise with respect to k. Repeat the iteration starting with this new value of k, and continue until the iteration converges.

Although this process has often been discussed in the literature, its convergence has not been discussed theoretically and several writers have doubted whether it can be relied upon to converge. In Appendix A a general discussion of this type of iteration shows that the process will always lead to a stationary value of (8), moreover to a point where the function is a minimum with respect to α and k separately. There is a possibility, although a very unlikely possibility, that the point is a saddlepoint. However there is the possibility of the existence of several local minima, and in this case the iteration might converge to any one of them depending on the starting point. The discussion of [7] makes it clear that any of these local minima is an equally valid estimate provided it satisfies the appropriate criterion of the previous section. If there are several local minima satisfying the χ^2 criterion, then there are multiple solutions in the sense discussed in [7], a case where it is impossible to distinguish between several alternative and equally valid estimates. It is therefore important to find all local minima of (8). Finally there may occur the case where the equation is unidentifiable in the instrumental variables case. This is the case where for all the values of k, $-1 \leqslant k \leqslant +1$, the corresponding χ^2 criterion is not significant.

The simplest way to consider the possibility of multiple minima is to minimise (8) with respect to α for a set of values of k covering the whole range from -1 to $+1$. The actual computing routine used by the author used the set of values $k = -1, -0.9, -0.8, -0.7, -0.6, -0.5, -0.4, -0.3, -0.2, -0.1, 0, 0.1, 0.2, 0.3, 0.4, 0.5, 0.6, 0.7, 0.8, 0.9, 1.0$. When using quarterly data with seasonal variables, it was found convenient to omit $k = -1$, since this value of k makes the transformed seasonals linearly dependent; the minimum of (8) was never found in practice to be near $k = -1$ so there was no loss from the omission of this value. The calculation of this set of values of (8) not only gave material for considering whether the function had multiple minima, but also provided a suitable starting point for the iteration.

The actual computations were carried out on a Ferranti Pegasus 2 computer at the University of Leeds Computing Laboratory.† A programme was written which read the time series data, computed the matrices A, B and C, and minimised the function (8) for the above values of k. The computer chose the minimum value of the function to start the iteration. At each stage of iteration the computer printed the next value of k and the current value of the function. The iteration finished when successive values of k differed by less than a preset constant, or if the value of the function (8) increased (because of rounding errors), or the finish could be controlled by the operator. The computer then printed out the last value of $\hat{k}, \alpha$, the coefficient error variance matrix, s^2 and the χ^2 criterion.

In all the 52 cases which are reported here, and in the use of the same programme by research students at the University of Leeds, there has been no case of the occurrence of multiple minima. However an alternative defect of this procedure is the possibility of slow convergence, so that a large number of iterations are required to obtain adequate accuracy. If α and k are close to the stationary value of the function it can be approximated by a Taylor expansion quadratic in the variables. Writing ϕ for the function and ϕ_{kk} for the second derivative with respect to k, ϕ_{zk} for the vector of cross second derivatives with respect to k and any component of α and $\phi_{\alpha\alpha}$ for the matrix of derivatives with respect to two components of α we have

$$\Delta k_r \simeq \mu \Delta k_{r-1} \tag{9}$$

where Δk_r is the error in k at the rth stage of the iteration, and

---

† I am grateful to Leeds University, and to the Director and staff of the Leeds University Computing Laboratory for their help and advice.

$$\mu = \frac{1}{\phi_{kk}} (\phi_{k\alpha} \phi_{\alpha\alpha}^{-1} \phi_{\alpha k}).$$

If we assume that (9) is sufficiently accurate for all r including the initial $r = 1$, and if we assume that the initial error in k is less than 0.1, then if $\mu = 0.5$ the error is reduced to less than 10^{-6} after 17 iterations. On the Pegasus using the author's programme, one iteration took 18 seconds when $n = 10$ or 31 seconds when $n = 13$. If $\mu = 0.25$ the number of iterations is halved and if $\mu = 0.7$ the number of iterations is doubled. Even in the worst case in this set, where $\mu = 0.7$ and $n = 13$, the total time for the iteration is 16 minutes, which is relatively small compared with the time required to compute the rest of the programme (perhaps 30 minutes). The advantages of this method are the simplicity of the programme and the relative certainty of convergence, but occasionally the convergence is very slow. To assess this it would be necessary to know how frequently in practice values of μ close to one occur. It was therefore arranged that the computer calculated and printed out $(k_r - k_{r-1})/(k_{r-1} - k_{r-2})$ at each stage of the iteration since this approximates μ, and also printed out the total number of iterations. Although the author is aware that his results do not constitute in any sense a random or representative sample, in the 53 cases covered here the following distributions were obtained:

Number of iterations		Distribution and final limit of μ	
Numbers of iterations	Frequency	Final limit of μ	No. of cases
5–15	7	Less than 0.3	0
16–20	10	0.3–	7
21–24	12	0.5–	25
25–29	18	0.6–	15
30–37	5	0.7–0.8	6
Total	53	Total	53

It is clear from this that occasionally the number of iterations required was large, but even in the worst case the total time required was only 20 minutes. However more efficient iteration procedures are available. One possibility is to make use of the Aitken method of speeding the convergence. This consists in taking the values of k from two successive stages of the previous iteration, calculating $\mu_r = (k_r - k_{r-1})/(k_{r-1} - k_{r-2})$ and then obtaining an estimate of k from the equation $k = (k_r - k_{r-1})/(1 - \mu_r)$. However considering this whole process of taking two stages of the previous iteration and deriving the Aitken estimate of k, as one stage in an iteration, it was realised that it was more complex and took more time than a Newton–Raphson iteration would do. The Newton–

Raphson iteration consists of approximating the equations $\phi_\alpha = 0$, $\phi_k = 0$ which hold at the minimum by the first order Taylor series approximation to them

$$\phi_{\alpha\alpha}(\alpha_r - \alpha_{r-1}) + \phi_{\alpha k}(k_r - k_{r-1}) + \phi_\alpha = 0$$

$$\phi_{k\alpha}(\alpha_r - \alpha_{r-1}) + \phi_{kk}(k_r - k_{r-1}) + \phi_k = 0$$

and all the derivatives are worked out at α_{r-1}, k_{r-1}. This procedure, like the Aitken procedure in this case, is a second order procedure, in the sense that if the errors at any stage are of order ε then the errors at the next stage are of order ε^2. The Newton–Raphson iteration was tested by using it on 21 of the previous cases. Although in general there is the possibility of non-convergence in this procedure, since in contrast with the previous iteration it is not necessarily true that the function is reduced at each stage, with the comparatively simple function (8) in the cases that are reported here convergence was in all cases rapid. Although the stage in the iteration took slightly longer, 23 seconds for $n = 10$ and 39 seconds for $n = 13$, the reduction in the number of iterations was more than sufficient to compensate in all cases.

It was also decided to introduce a new way of selecting the starting point for the iteration, by considering the unrestricted estimate of the coefficients of equation (5). In the least squares case this is obtained by running a regression of the endogenous variable on the non-redundant variables and all the variables lagged; that is, on all the variables ξ_{it}, except those that are redundant. The coefficient of $x_{n(t-1)}$ then provides a consistent estimate of k. If we maximise (8) with respect to α for this value of k this will provide a consistent estimate of α, and this provides a starting point for the iteration. In the instrumental variables case exactly the same procedure is followed using the unrestricted instrumental variables estimate of equation (5). The method fails if $x_{n(t-1)}$ is included among the set of variables x_{it}. If for example $x_{1t} = x_{n(t-1)}$ the transformed equation takes the form

$$\alpha_0(1-k) + \sum_{i=2}^{n-1} \alpha_i x_{it} - k \sum_{i=2}^{n-1} \alpha_i x_{i(t-1)} - k\alpha_1 x_{n(t-2)} + (k+\alpha_1)x_{n(t-1)} - x_{nt} = e_t.$$

It is clear that in this case it is possible to estimate $k + \alpha_1$, and $k\alpha_1$ from the coefficients of $x_{n(t-1)}$ and $x_{n(t-2)}$, but impossible to distinguish between the estimates of k and α_1. However if there is any non-redundant variable x_{jt}, such that $x_{j(t-1)}$ does not occur among the remaining x_{it}, then it is possible to get a consistent estimate of k by taking the ratio of the coefficient of $x_{j(t-1)}$ to the coefficient of x_{jt} in the unrestricted equation. This can be used as before to obtain a starting point for the iteration.

Durbin [2] has shown that in the least squares case if all the variables except one are completely exogenous, then the initial value defined above is already an asymptotically efficient estimate of k and α. A sufficient condition for this is that u_t should be independent of x_{it} and $x_{i(t-1)}$ for all $i \neq n$. However if the x_{it} include some lagged endogenous variables, these are partly determined by the past values of e_t, which also determine u_t. Thus it is impossible to assume that u_t is independent of x_{it} and $x_{i(t-1)}$ for all $i \neq n$ unless these are all completely exogenous variables. However it is clear that these initial values have standard errors of order $1/\sqrt{T}$. Also the Newton–Raphson method has the property that if the errors at one stage are of order ε then the errors at the next stage are of order ε^2. It follows that from the given starting point after the first stage of the method the errors in the coefficients compared with the minimum values are of order $1/T$. It follows that asymptotically the values of the coefficients at this stage are equivalent to the minimum values and, in particular, if these latter are asymptotically efficient then so are the values at the end of the first stage. It was therefore decided to run a set of estimates in which the value at the first stage was compared with the initial value and the final value. This was done for ten equations each with $T = 51$. It was decided to compare only the values of k, since the values of α in the three cases were related to the values of k by almost the same relationship. The difference between the final and the initial values of k, and the final and first stage of k were divided by the sample error of the coefficient estimated from the final values of the coefficients. The resulting ratios were averaged (RMS) and the results were: for the initial value 0.77, and for the first stage value 0.34. Again the ten cases considered give a small and non-random sample but the advantage should be with the more efficient method in large enough samples.

3 AN ASYMPTOTIC TEST FOR HIGHER ORDER AUTOREGRESSION

Probably the best way of considering the possibility of higher order autoregression is to fit a second order autoregressive equation in the same way that the first order autoregressive equation was fitted and then consider the significance of the second coefficient in this equation. However since in any case only an asymptotic test was wanted, and it was intended to print out the $\hat{e}_t$ as part of a programme for computing and printing out the separate contributions of each variable x_{it} to the u_t in each period, it was decided to use the following simple and asymptotically efficient test criterion

$$r = \frac{\displaystyle\sum_{t=2}^{T} \hat{e}_t \hat{e}_{t-1}}{\displaystyle\sum_{t=1}^{T} \hat{e}_t^2}$$

where

$$\hat{e}_t = \mathbf{a}(\hat{\theta})\mathbf{x}'_t = e_t + \Delta\theta\left(\frac{\partial\mathbf{a}}{\partial\theta}\right)'\mathbf{x}'_t + O(1/T)$$

and

$$\Delta\theta = \hat{\theta} - \theta.$$

Since

$$\text{plim}\left(\frac{1}{T}\sum_{t=1}^{T}\hat{e}^2_t\right) = \sigma^2.$$

$\sqrt{T\sigma^2 r}$ is asymptotically distributed as

$$(1/\sqrt{T})\sum_{t=2}^{T}e_t e_{t-1} + \frac{\Delta\theta}{\sqrt{T}}\left(\frac{\partial\mathbf{a}}{\partial\theta}\right)'\left[\sum_{t=2}^{T}(\mathbf{x}'_t e_{t-1} + \mathbf{x}'_{t-1}e_t)\right].$$

Let

$$\text{plim}_{T\to\infty}\left(\frac{1}{T}\sum_{t=2}^{T}\mathbf{x}_t e_{t-1}\right) = \mathbf{h}$$

and assume

$$\text{plim}_{T\to\infty}\left(\frac{1}{T}\sum_{t=2}^{T}\mathbf{x}_{t-1}e_t\right) = 0.$$

In the least squares and two-stage least squares cases the $x_{i(t-1)}$ are predetermined variables and are independent of e_t, and in the instrumental variables case it seems appropriate to set up the test on the basis that the autoregressive transformation has yielded an e_t which is independent of the measurement errors on all the variables in previous periods. Cramer's theorem on asymptotic limits of linear functions shows that $\sqrt{T\sigma^2 r}$ is asymptotically distributed as

$$\frac{1}{\sqrt{T}}\sum_{t=2}^{T}e_t e_{t-1} + \sqrt{T}\Delta\theta\left(\frac{\partial\mathbf{a}}{\partial\theta}\right)'\mathbf{h}'. \tag{10}$$

Since each term of (10) is asymptotically normally distributed with mean zero and known variance a further application of Cramer's theorem shows that (10) is asymptotically normal with mean zero and variance determined by the covariance matrix for the separate terms of (10). Now in any case we can write $\sqrt{T}\Delta\theta = \mathbf{w}KH^{-1}$ where

$$\mathbf{w} = -(1/\sqrt{T})\left(\sum_{t=1}^{T}e_t\mathbf{z}_t\right)$$

and $\mathbf{z}_t$ is the vector of all the predetermined (including lagged) variables and in the least squares case includes all the current independent variables. In the least squares case

$$K = \frac{\partial \mathbf{a}}{\partial \theta} \qquad \text{and} \qquad H = \left(\frac{\partial \mathbf{a}}{\partial \theta}\right)' R \left(\frac{\partial \mathbf{a}}{\partial \theta}\right)$$

where R is the population moment matrix of the predetermined variables. In the instrumental variables case $K = R^{-1} Q \partial \mathbf{a}/\partial \theta$ and

$$H = \left(\frac{\partial \mathbf{a}}{\partial \theta}\right)' Q' R^{-1} Q \left(\frac{\partial \mathbf{a}}{\partial \theta}\right)$$

where R is the moment matrix of all the instrumental variables and Q is the moment matrix of the instrumental variables $\mathbf{z}_t$ with the variables $\mathbf{x}_t$. The equation for the instrumental variables case is given in [7], the equation in the least squares case can be regarded as derived from the instrumental case when all the independent variables are treated as instrumental variables (noting that $\partial a_n/\partial \theta = 0$ since the coefficients have been standardised by assuming $a_n = -1$).

Since the asymptotic variance matrix of $\mathbf{w}$ is $\sigma^2 R$ the asymptotic variance of the terms specified last in equation (10) is

$$\sigma^2 \mathbf{h} \left(\frac{\partial \mathbf{a}}{\partial \theta}\right) H^{-1} \left(\frac{\partial \mathbf{a}}{\partial \theta}\right)' \mathbf{h}'$$

and the variance of the first term is σ^4. It remains to compute the asymptotic covariance between the first and last terms.

The asymptotic covariance is

$$(1/\sqrt{T}) \sum_{t=2}^{T} e_t e_{t-1} \qquad \text{and} \qquad \mathbf{w} = -(1/\sqrt{T}) \sum_{t=2}^{T} e_t \mathbf{z}_t$$

is obtained by taking expectations, using

$$E(e_t e_{t-1} e_{t'} \mathbf{z}_{t'}) = \begin{cases} 0, & t \neq t' \\ \sigma^2 E(e_{t-1} \mathbf{z}_t), & t = t'. \end{cases} \tag{11}$$

Writing $v_t = \mathbf{x}_t - \mathbf{z}_t R^{-1} Q$, the v_t are random variables which are the errors on the reduced form equations. We assume that $E(v_t e_{t-1}) = 0$ which is equivalent to assuming that the first order autoregressive transformation of the original structural equation has removed all the autocorrelation and serial correlation connecting e_{t-1} with the set of variables v_t. This is certainly correct in the least squares and two-stage least squares cases where the $\mathbf{z}_t$ are taken to include all the lagged values of all the variables in the model as well as all the current predetermined variables. In the instrumental variables case the assumption is not a necessary consequence of the general assumptions of the model, i.e., this is a separate assumption, but the simplification that follows from this assumption makes it worthwhile. Then

$$E(e_{t-1}z_t)K = E(e_{t-1}x_t)\left(\frac{\partial}{a\partial\theta}\right) = h\left(\frac{\partial a}{\partial\theta}\right) + O\left(\frac{1}{\sqrt{T}}\right).$$

The covariance between

$$wKH^{-1}\left(\frac{\partial a}{\partial\theta}\right)'h' \qquad \text{and} \qquad \frac{1}{\sqrt{T}}\sum_{t=2}^{T} e_t e_{t-1}$$

is therefore

$$-\sigma^2\left\{h\left(\frac{\partial a}{\partial\theta}\right)\right\}\left[H^{-1}\left(\frac{\partial a}{\partial\theta}\right)'h'\right]$$

so that the variance of (10) is

$$\sigma^4 - 2\sigma^2 h\left(\frac{\partial a}{\partial\theta}\right)H^{-1}\left(\frac{\partial a}{\partial\theta}\right)'h' + \sigma^2 h\left(\frac{\partial a}{\partial\theta}\right)H^{-1}\left(\frac{\partial a}{\partial\theta}\right)'h'$$

and the asymptotic variance of $\sqrt{(T)}r$ is

$$1 - (1/\sigma^2)\left[h\left(\frac{\partial a}{\partial\theta}\right)H^{-1}\left(\frac{\partial a}{\partial\theta}\right)'h'\right].$$

Now $(\sigma^2/T)H^{-1}$ is the asymptotic error variance matrix of the coefficients $\hat{\theta}$ and an estimate of this has already been computed and printed out. The $\hat{h}$ can also be estimated using

$$\hat{h} = \frac{1}{T}\sum_{t=2}^{T} \hat{e}_{t-1}x_t.$$

In order to calculate this it is necessary to calculate $\hat{e}_t$, but this is done in any case, so that the results can be printed out for the scrutiny of the experimenter who will be interested in detecting any anomalous behaviour in the computed residuals. It was therefore arranged that a programme computed $\hat{e}_t$, r, $\hat{h}$, and took s^2 and V the estimated error variance matrix of the coefficients and from them computed

$$1 - \frac{T}{\sigma^4}\left[\hat{h}\left(\frac{\partial a}{\partial\theta}\right)V\left(\frac{\partial a}{\partial\theta}\right)'h'\right] \qquad (12)$$

r was then divided by the standard error derived from (12).

This was done for 30 different estimations. In only one case did the ratio exceed 2. The distribution of the 30 ratios was not significantly different from a normal distribution with mean zero and unit variance judged by a simple χ^2 test. On the whole the test gives no reason to prefer a higher order autoregressive equation to the first order equation when used with this data. (It is to be noted that the use of the χ^2 test is not strictly justified since all the equations were variants of two basic forms so that the assumption of independence between the different sample values needed to justify the use of the χ^2 is not correct.)

4 THE ECONOMETRIC MODEL

In considering a model for the determination of wages and prices a starting point was the equations used by Klein and Ball [3].

For wages they use an equation of the form

$$w_t - w_{t-4} = a_0 + a_1(p_t + p_{t-1} + p_{t-2} + p_{t-3} - p_{t-4} - p_{t-5} - p_{t-6} - p_{t-7})$$
$$+ a_2(U_t + U_{t-1} + U_{t-2} + U_{t-3}) \tag{13}$$

where the data are quarterly, and w_t is the wage rate index in quarter t, p_t is the index of retail prices in period t, and U_t is a percentage index of the number wholly unemployed (i.e. this number expressed as a percentage of the corresponding number in 1948). In the Klein–Ball case the variables are absolute values but it is convenient to use the same symbols for later equations and in some cases to use the symbols to mean the logarithms of the corresponding absolute variables. It will be convenient to refer to a version of the equation linear in the absolute values of the variables as the absolute form of the equation, and a version linear in the logarithms of the corresponding variables as the corresponding logarithmic form of the equation.

The argument for the equation above is that wage raises in any occupation are annual events, and if we consider the raises being made in any one quarter, they are assumed to be based upon the price change over the whole year and the unemployment in the same quarter. The percentage change in the wage rate over the whole year is a weighted average of the percentage raises in each quarter, and if we approximate by taking the weights to be equal we get the form (13).

However it is unnecessary to consider an equation explaining the rise in the wage index over a full year. If we consider the change in the index for one quarter only, this is due to the wage raise given to those workers whose rates change in this quarter. On the equal weights assumption the percentage change in the wage rates index will equal one quarter of the percentage raise. This leads to the equation

$$w_t - w_{t-1} = \tfrac{1}{4}a_0 + a_1(p_t - p_{t-4}) + a_2 U_t. \tag{14}$$

Klein says that he considered this form of equation but used (13) in preference because it appeared a more stable form of relation. Now if any kind of stochastic equation is considered and an unweighted moving average of the equation is taken, since the error on the average equation is the moving average of the original random error, if the original error is non-autocorrelated there will be a considerable reduction in the variance of the moving average error (it will be halved for the four quarter moving average). If there is a positive autocorrelation the reduction will be less but will still be present. So the multiple correlation will be increased by taking the moving average, although estimates of the moving average equation using least squares or two-stage least squares may be inconsistent and inefficient. To argue about the most appropriate form of equation to use, the only criterion is that the optimum form should have errors which are independent in different time periods. Since form (14) is derived most directly from the raises negotiated in successive quarters, it seems most likely to give independent errors. If anything, there may be positive autocorrelation, but in any case the moving average form will give larger autocorrelation. A study of the equation using Klein's coefficients in form (13) and then in form (14) showed nothing which could not be explained by the averaging process so that all work was done with the equation (14), and with this form the autocorrelations were low.†

The author was however not satisfied with equation (14) because it is in effect non-homogeneous in money prices. Suppose that over some time interval a large change in the price level occurs with the level of unemployment normal. According to the equation estimated by Dicks-Mireaux and Dow [1] money wages rise by a smaller percentage than prices, and real wages fall. But unions are very conscious of the effect of price rises, and it is possible that if past changes have unfavourably affected the level of real wages, they will increase their pressure so as to correct the level of real wages again. It is possible to test this possibility by introducing one extra variable into equation (14) representing real wage rates. Using a Klein linearisation, $w_{t-1} - p_{t-1}$ was used. When this was done the corresponding coefficient had the right sign and was significant with t-ratio greater than three. However, as explained in the next paragraph, it seemed likely that a linear trend was needed to explain the continuous growth in real wages over the same period. This was also found significant. Previous writers had considered it necessary to include a political factor F_t to represent the wage freeze at the end of the 1940s. Initially the Klein–Ball factor was used, defined by $F_t = (0)$ up to 4th quarter of 1951, and $F_t = 1$ thereafter. This F_t had negative non-significant coefficients. However it was then realised that to get a change in the rate of trend of wages a trend type variable was required. A new variable F_t was defined so that $F_t = 0$ up to the 4th quarter of 1951, and $F_t = t - 16$ thereafter. This can be regarded as

---

† The suggestion that the first difference of equation (13) should be used, since this gives a form with small autocorrelation, offers no advantages over the simpler (14).

obtained by cumulating the previous F_t. This variable turned out to have a positive significant coefficient in the first estimates, although in some of the later estimates it became non-significant.

The form of the wage-determination equation at this stage is

$$w_t - w_{t-1} = a_0 + a_1(p_{t-1} - p_{t-4}) + a_2 U_{t-1} + a_3(w_{t-1} - p_{t-1}) + a_4 F_t + a_5 t \quad (15)$$

It will be noted that at this stage $p_{t-1} - p_{t-4}$ has been substituted for $p_t - p_{t-4}$ of (14). This was done because it was not thought likely *a priori* that this made much difference to the theoretical interpretation of the equation, because in practice the coefficient of this variable was small and insignificant in all the many versions of the equation which the author tried; and finally because at this early stage in estimation of the equations a direct comparison of estimates using the two different forms showed no significant difference in the other coefficients. Form (15) has the advantage that all the variables on the right hand side of the equation are pre-determined so that in the absence of measurement errors autoregressive least squares estimates are consistent and unbiased. The economic interpretation of the equation can take several forms. First it is possible to consider a desired or equilibrium level of real wages w_{Et} given by the equation

$$w_{Et} = -\frac{a_0}{a_3} - \frac{a_1}{a_3}(p_t - p_{t-3}) - \frac{a_2}{a_3}U_t - \frac{a_4}{a_3}F_{t+1} - \frac{a_5}{a_3}(t+1) \quad (16)$$

and a dynamic adjustment equation

$$w_t - w_{t-1} = a_3[w_{t-1} - p_{t-1} - w_{E(t-1)}]$$

Equation (16) says that the desired level of real wages is determined by a linear trend (politically affected) and by the level of unemployment. The presence of the term $p_t - p_{t-3}$ may be regarded as an extrapolation of past price movements into the future, so that the desired level of real wages should be attained at these extrapolated prices. If the adjustment equation is to be stable $a_3 < 0$, and we then expect $a_1 > 0$, $a_2 < 0$, $a_4 > 0$, $a_5 > 0$.

If we stress that in full employment periods union pressure is the only important determinant of wages, then equation (16) can be regarded as representing the influence of unemployment on union demands. The equation can more realistically be interpreted as representing the joint nature of wage-bargaining procedure if the use of U_t as a crude measure of the excess supply of labour is stressed. If we take the actual demand for labour as strongly correlated with the number employed, this could be used as an indicator of the willingness of the employers to grant higher wages. The number unemployed is obviously also an indicator of the difficulty experienced by the employer in finding labour. Unemployment also is a good indication of the bargaining strength of the union.

Alternatively we can consider that equation (15) represents a correction to a 'Phillips' type equation [5] where the crude measure of excess supply of labour represented by U_t has been refined by introducing

$$E_t = U_t + (a_3/a_2)(w_t - p_t) + (a_4/a_2)F_{t+1} + (a_5/a_2)(t+1)$$

and taking E_t as a more exact measure of the excess supply of labour. The difference between E_t and U_t is positively related to the real wage because there is a supply of part-time and temporary labour which does not maintain its unemployment benefit or continue to seek work when the real wage is relatively low, and possibly because of labour hoarding which inflates the apparent demand for labour at times of low real wages.

The author on the whole prefers the justification in terms of union pressure, but whatever the economic justifications, the mathematical effect on the model is the same.

The dynamic adjustment equation can be solved in the form

$$w_t = -a_3 \left[\sum_{s=-\infty}^{t-1} (1+a_3)^{s+1-t}(p_s + w_{Es}) \right]$$

and this shows w_t as a weighted average of past prices and equilibrium real wages, the weights being geometrical or exponential. There is a geometrical distributed lag of money wages behind money prices and unemployment equal to $-1/a_3$. For example with $a_3 = -0.5$ the lag is two quarters or six months; with $a_3 = -0.375$ the lag is two and two thirds quarters or eight months. Since these are the extremes of the range of the estimates of a_3 found in the author's work, it follows that a fairly short lag is suggested in money wages on the equilibrium value. This will be considered later when the price equation has been estimated.

The data used were obtained by continuing the wage rates index, consumption price index, and unemployment index, of Klein, Ball, Hazlewood and Vandome [3] up to the fourth quarter of 1960. Appendix C gives the continuations used. Appendix B gives a brief summary of the various alternative forms of equations tried. The final form of the equation used was (15) and this was finally estimated by three different methods, first by autoregressive least squares, then the same equation by the single stage iteration method of Section 2 on least squares assumption, and finally using instrumental variables with complete iteration. The instrumental variables used were an index of total import prices, of export prices, the current value of total exports, consumption, and government expenditure on goods and services (all lagged one quarter, but consumption lagged two quarters, and all defined as in Klein–Ball [3]), F_t, t and three seasonals. The table below compares the results. The second line in each case contains standard errors.

Method used	$\hat{a}_1$	$\hat{a}_2$	$\hat{a}_3$	$\hat{a}_4$	$\hat{a}_5$	$\hat{k}$	s^2	χ^2
Autoregressive least squares	−0.015 (0.090)	−0.017 (0.007)	−0.497 (0.148)	+0.391 (0.161)	+0.038 (0.056)	+0.231 (0.159)	0.846	9.17 4 D.F.
L.S. single stage iteration	+0.053 (0.102)	−0.015 (0.008)	−0.438 (0.137)	+0.231 (0.148)	+0.057 (0.061)	+0.178 (0.163)	0.921	8.76 4 D.F.
Inst. variables	+0.062 (0.262)	−0.289 (0.145)	−0.388 (0.512)	+0.283 (0.456)	+0.049 (0.110)	+0.441 (0.597)	1.022	0.51 2 D.F.

Comparing first the instrumental variable estimates with the full least squares estimates, the standard errors of the instrumental variables estimates are much larger, but the coefficients are not greatly different except the coefficient of U. This difference could be a result of the presence of measurement error of a definitional kind, but it is less than twice the instrumental variables standard error. The author was prepared to take the difference as sampling error and accept the least squares estimates. As a consequence there seemed little point in trying to find a better set of instrumental variables to reduce the standard errors.

Comparing the two sets of least squares estimates the differences in coefficients are small and certainly not significant. The average distributed lag $-1/\hat{a}_3$ is approximately half a year. Doubling the 1948 level of unemployment produces a 3.5 per cent change in the equilibrium real wage [cf. (16)]. Using (16) it can be seen that the *equilibrium* real wage grows at 2.5 points a year under a Conservative government, but not significantly under a Labour government. The χ^2 criterion is quite close to the 5 per cent significance limit. This suggested that longer lags might be required in some of the variables in the equation. However at this stage it was decided to look for further data. None of the different forms of the equation considered by the author had a significant k; the use of the author's quarterly form of the wage determination equation had been only too successful in removing the autocorrelation of the residuals in the equation, so that the use of a method of estimation designed to take account of autocorrelation is unnecessary. However from previous work with pre-war data the author was aware that with the same type of equation and using the official Ministry of Labour Index of Wage Rates, the residuals of the equation have a first order autocorrelation close to one. It is also clear that the official index is a poor index; that is, it has a relatively large measurement error, so that these data could be used to give some practical experience of the relative advantages of the use of least squares and instrumental variable methods in these circumstances. Since the results are mainly of methodological interest a full description of the data and the different forms of equation considered will not be given but a brief summary is given here.

The wage rates index was taken from the *Ministry of Labour Gazette* (various dates). The consumption prices index was taken from 'The consumption function in the U.K. 1924–38', by El Imam (unpublished Ph.D. thesis at Leeds University). It differed from the official cost of living index mainly in correcting the gross overweight of food prices in the latter index. Unemployment was included as an index of the number unemployed estimated from the unemployment insurance data by correcting for changes in coverage. Initially all the data were used on a quarterly basis from the first quarter 1922 to the last quarter 1938, but it was evident from a consideration of the residuals of the fitted equations that the results for 1922 and 1923 were much worse than for the other years so that later estimates were made omitting the first two years. A political factor of the trend shift type was included defined in exactly the same way as the post-war political factor. When using the instrumental variable method, exactly the same set of instrumental variables was used as in the post-war case.

Although nine estimates of different versions of the equation were made, no very satisfactory estimates were obtained. Using least squares and the same form of equation as (15) the results were as in the table below (the second line in each case gives standard errors).

Method used	$\hat{a}_1$	$\hat{a}_2$	$\hat{a}_3$	$\hat{a}_4$	$\hat{a}_5$	$\hat{k}$	s^2	χ^2
Least squares	-0.362	$+0.004$	$+0.207$	-0.534	-0.009	$+0.807$	0.306	12.65
	(0.056)	(0.011)	(0.192)	(0.073)	(0.073)	(0.047)		4 D.F.
Inst. variables	$+0.334$	-0.006	-0.320	-0.164	$+0.219$	$+0.792$	0.449	0.92
	(0.279)	(0.029)	(0.409)	(0.508)	(0.398)	(0.565)		2 D.F.
Omitting F_t and	$+0.406$	$+0.003$	—	—	-0.008	$+0.585$	0.359	2.33
$(w_{t-1}-p_{t-1})$	(0.166)	(0.009)			(0.016)	(0.391)		4 D.F.

Notable are the facts that the coefficient $\hat{a}_1$ of the rate of change of prices is significant and negative; that the only other significant coefficient is that of the political factor which is also negative; that $\hat{k}$ is quite close to one, and that the χ^2 criterion is significant. The latter result alone gives sufficient reason for rejecting the present estimates, but the pattern of coefficients looks unsatisfactory on *a priori* grounds. The instrumental variables estimates given in the third and fourth lines of the table agree much better with *a priori* expectation, but none of them is significantly different from zero. In particular it is to be noted that $\hat{k}$ is not significant. This may be taken as an indication that the strong autocorrelation is present in the measurement errors but not in the random error in the structural equation. Because of the non-significance of the coefficients the author tried various equations in which sets of the coefficients were assumed to be zero. The form of most interest among these is given in lines five and six of the table.

Real wages and the political factor have been omitted. Since the coefficient of the price change is close enough to one third, one may interpret this to mean that money wage rates in each quarter rise at the same rate as the average increase in prices in the previous three quarters. However the results are not very satisfactory. They might be improved by the use of a wider set of instrumental variables, but a more obvious method would be to use a better index of wage rates. The author did not pursue this matter since he considered that greater value would result from a further study of the post-war data.

5 THE LOGARITHMIC MODEL

The discussion of the choice between using equations linear in the variables or alternatively of using equations linear in the logarithms of the variables has usually been carried on using *a priori* arguments only. Klein used a linear form for his equation because he was estimating a large model, and the prediction problem becomes difficult if non-linear equations are used. It is usually assumed that since any simple mathematical form for the structural relationships is only an approximation, the mathematical form of the approximation is not important. However this is incorrect. The choice of model to use should be based on the data available; the choice between a linear and log-linear form of equation should be made using the theories of statistical decisions in the same way as the choice between different values for the coefficients.

It is not difficult to embed the problem in a continuum of models in such a way that the linear and log-linear models are just two special cases out of the continuum. The consideration of this suggests that asymptotically it is efficient to use a likelihood ratio criterion. It is not difficult to develop this for a general linear model, but for reasons of relevance and simplicity only the single equation least squares case is considered here.

Suppose that the dependent variable Y_t is determined by the equation

$$Y_t = \sum_{i=0}^{n} A_i X_{it} + U_t$$

where the X_{it} are a set of variables independent of the U_t and the coefficients A_i may be subject to any *a priori* restrictions such as those of Section 1 which would make the above equation a transformed form of a structural equation with autoregressive error. Suppose now that $x_{it} = \log X_{it}$ and $y_t = \log Y_t$. The second hypothesis is that the structural equation is of the form

$$y_t = \sum_{i=0}^{n} a_i x_{it} + u_t.$$

In order to use the likelihood ratio method it is assumed that both random errors form independently normally distributed time series with constant standard deviations Σ and σ respectively.

Suppose that the likelihood function defined in the normal way for the first hypothesis is $F(A, \Sigma)$ and for the second hypothesis is $F(a, \sigma)$. These likelihood functions differ in that the first is the joint frequency density function of the Y_t while the second is the joint distribution function of the y_t. If the ratio of the likelihood functions is to be used as a criterion it is necessary to transform the variable so that both are density functions for the same set of sample variables. We can do this by changing the likelihood function for the second hypothesis so that it becomes a density function for the Y_t by introducing the factors $dy_t/dY_t = 1/Y_t$. The likelihood function for the second hypothesis is then

$$\left(\prod_{t=1}^{T} 1/Y_t \right) F(a, \sigma).$$

Now maximising both likelihoods with respect to A, Σ and a, σ respectively, and introducing $S = \hat{\Sigma}$ and $s = \hat{\sigma}$ respectively, the maxima of the two likelihood functions are $(1/S^T)e^{-1/2T}$ and

$$\left(\prod_{t=1}^{T} 1/Y_t \right) (1/s^T)e^{-\frac{1}{2}T}$$

where T is the number of time periods. Defining the geometric mean of the Y_t by

$$Y_G^T = \prod_{t=1}^{T} Y_t$$

the likelihood ratio is $(S/Y_G s)^T$. This suggests that we use $S/Y_G s$ as a criterion for deciding between the two models. A conventional discussion would now require us to obtain the distribution function of the criterion on each hypothesis; possibly to use a continuous sampling plan so that we sample until we can reject one hypothesis or the other. However the distribution of the criterion is a very complicated function of the parameters of the true model, so that the author has decided not to develop this type of solution here. Since there seems no *a priori* reason to prefer one model to the other, it seems simplest to accept the first hypothesis if $S/Y_G s$ is less than one, and *vice versa*. This corresponds to a maximum likelihood choice.

A more sophisticated argument is obtained by using decision theory. Suppose we are only interested in using the right type of model, so that our loss function is $+1$ if we have the wrong model and 0 if we have the right model. We then want to compare the total *a posteriori* probability of the first hypothesis with the second. Writing R for the ratio of the *a posteriori* probabilities it can be shown that $\log R = T \log (S/Y_G s) + f(T)$ where $f(T)$ is $O(1)$ as $T \to \infty$. $f(T)$ is a complicated function of the *a priori* distributions and data. However when T is sufficiently large the decision turns on the value of $S/Y_G s$.

Since the ratio $S/Y_G s$ for the standard form of equation was 0.987, the criterion on the whole indicated that the non-logarithmic form of equation was better. However the advantage was very slight, $(S/Y_G s)^T$ being 0.513, so that the data cannot be regarded as being strongly in favour of the linear form of equation. It was therefore decided to explore further the logarithmic form of relation. The initial form of equation considered was exactly the same as (15) except that the symbols are to be interpreted as meaning the logarithms of the corresponding variables. The estimate of this equation was

$$w_t - w_{t-1} = -\ 0.005(p_{t-1} - p_{t-4}) -\ 0.0143 U_{t-1}$$
$$(0.086) \qquad\qquad (0.0064)$$

$$-\ 0.395(w_{t-1} - p_{t-1}) +\ 0.00085 F_t +\ 0.00119 t.$$
$$(0.136) \qquad\qquad (0.00074)_{,t} \quad (0.00037)$$

The figures in brackets are standard errors. $\hat{k} = 0.189\,(0.157)$, $s^2 = 0.479 \times 10^{-4}$ and $\chi^2 = 11.88$ (4 D.F.).

It is notable here that the coefficient of F_t is not significant and that the χ^2 is significant at the 5 per cent level. The latter suggests that a more complicated structure of lags was required.

It is a rather unsatisfactory feature of the above equation that the linear trend forms an important part of explanation of wages. It was decided to experiment with new variables which might be important in explaining the trend. First of these was real profits, defined as an index of gross company profits deflated by an index of consumption goods prices. In terms of the symbols of [3] this was D/p, and the data was taken from the same sources. When this variable was put into the equation and the coefficients estimated by least squares, the corresponding coefficient was positive but small and not significant. In an effort to improve this a moving average of real profits for the previous 12 quarters was used, the three year period being chosen by analogy with the three year period used by Milton Friedman for 'permanent income'. The estimate of the corresponding coefficient was increased to 0.021 (0.013). It was decided that the profit variable did not give much promise of improving the explanation of wage determination. As an alternative it was decided to use a variable representing productivity. The simplest variable to estimate quarterly is industrial productivity which was obtained by dividing the official index of industrial production by the number of employed workers in the appropriate industries, in terms of

Klein's symbols P/E_p. When this variable was introduced into the standard equation it was found to have a positive but relatively small and non-significant coefficient. This variable was then also subject to a three year moving average, and the resulting average substituted in the standard equation. Although the estimated coefficient was increased, it was still not significant. The resulting equation was estimated as below

$$w_t - w_{t-1} = -\ 0.005(p_{t-1} - p_{t-4}) -\ 0.0129U_{t-1} +\ 0.00085F_t$$
$$(0.055) \qquad\qquad (0.0067) \qquad (0.00079)$$

$$-\ 0.386(w_{t-1} - p_{t-1}) +\ 0.00104t +\ 0.053(I_{t-1})$$
$$(0.139) \qquad\qquad (0.00049) \quad (0.072)$$

where I_t is the moving average of productivity for the three years up to and including the current quarter.

All these alternative variables were introduced into the log-linear form of equation, and all these equations gave significant χ^2 criterion. However before pursuing this matter it was decided to simplify the equation by omitting the non-significant $p_{t-1} - p_{t-4}$ and F_t. The resulting equation estimated by least squares was

$$w_t - w_{t-1} = -\ 0.0120U_{t-1} -\ 0.271(w_{t-1} - p_{t-1}) +\ 0.00133t, \quad (17)$$
$$(0.0058) \qquad (0.073) \qquad\qquad (0.00036)$$

$\hat{k} = 0.206$ (0.151), $s^2 = 0.496 \times 10^{-4}$, and $\chi^2 = 2.59$ (2 D.F.). The non-significant χ^2 compared with the previous results suggested that it might be worth considering equations with more complicated lags in prices and with lagged values of F_t. The author considered various combinations of lagged political factors plus rates of price change without finding any combination of variables which satisfied the two statistical conditions, that all the coefficients are significant, and the χ^2 criterion is not significant. However consideration of the unrestricted form of the transformed equation suggested that longer lags on the other variables were appropriate, and the author was led to consider equations involving U_{t-2}, U_{t-3}, U_{t-4}, $w_{t-2} - p_{t-2}$, $w_{t-1} - w_{t-2}$, and $w_{t-2} - w_{t-3}$. Various combinations of these variables were considered, new forms of equation being obtained by modifying previous forms, omitting variables whose coefficients were non-significant, and increasing the lag on variables when this was suggested by the coefficients of the unrestricted estimate of the transformed equation. The author does not feel it to be worthwhile to give details of all the equations tried but some information is given in Appendix B. It was found better to include a long lag on unemployment and in the later estimates unemployment was represented by U_{t-4}. The coefficient of $(w_{t-2} - w_{t-3})$ was also significant whereas the political factor was frequently insignificant and it was ultimately decided to omit this variable. The form of equation which was judged most satisfactory of those considered was the following

$$w_t - w_{t-1} = -\ 0.018U_{t-4} - \ 0.375(w_{t-1} - p_{t-1}) + \ 0.106(w_{t-1} - w_{t-2})$$
$$\phantom{w_t - w_{t-1} = }(0.008) \qquad\qquad (0.119) \qquad\qquad\qquad (0.064)$$

$$-\ 0.524(w_{t-2} - w_{t-3}) + \ 0.0019t. \qquad\qquad (18)$$
$$(0.157) \qquad\qquad (0.0008)$$

$$s^2 = 0.353 \times 10^{-4}, \qquad \hat{k} = 0.441\ (0.186), \qquad \chi^2 = 0.12\ (4\ \text{D.F.}).$$

All the coefficients are significant except that of $w_{t-1} - w_{t-2}$; it was decided to retain this variable because of the presence of $w_{t-2} - w_{t-3}$. It is to be noted that $\hat{k}$ is significant. This was true of the $\hat{k}$ of several forms of equation considered.

One possible explanation of the rather complex set of lags of w_t in this equation is got by considering what happens when all w_{t-i}, $i > 0$, are eliminated from this equation by using lagged versions of the equation. By such a procedure it is possible to express w_t as a linear function of U_{t-i} for all $i \geqslant 4$, and p_{t-i} for all $i \geqslant 1$. The result can be summarised as expressing w_t as a weighted moving average of past unemployment and prices. If we carry out this process with equation (18) not all the coefficients are positive but relatively trivial changes in the coefficients of (18) will produce two moving averages with positive weights. For example the equation

$$w_t - w_{t-1} = -0.018U_{t-4} - 0.328(w_{t-1} - p_{t-1}) + 0.128(w_{t-1} - w_{t-2})$$
$$-0.512(w_{t-2} - w_{t-3}) + 0.0019t$$

can be solved to give

$$w_t = \phi(L)(-0.055U_{t-4} + p_{t-1}) + 0.0058t$$

where $\phi(L)$ is the infinite series

$$\phi(L) = 0.328 + 0.262L + 0.134L^4 + 0.107L^5 + 0.055L^8 + 0.044L^9 \dots$$

and L is a lag operator intepreted for a general variable x_t as meaning that $L^r x_t = x_{t-r}$. The general structure of the weights in the above distributed lag operator may not be very realistic; possibly it may be interpreted as an approximation to the idea that there is an immediate impact effect, represented by the first two weights, and then a much longer-lagged distributed long term effect, but certainly if we work out the average lag corresponding to these weights we find that the lag of wages on prices is 4.02 quarters, and the lag of wages on unemployment is 7.02 quarters. These are longer than the lags associated with equation (17), which gives a lag of 3.69 quarters on both prices and unemployment. It will be noted that in the above calculations of lags the price index has been treated as an exogenous variable; we have assumed it possible to change prices to a new level and hold them there while observing the consequent change in wages. However if prices are treated as endogenous, so that the rise in wages produces a consequent change in prices, as in Section 7, the lag in the wage on unemployment and other exogenous variables is found to be much greater.

An alternative explanation of equation (18) to which the author attaches some probability, is in terms of the demonstration effect of recent wage increases. It seems reasonable to assume that if one union sees an earlier union in the sequence of yearly wage bargains obtain a large rise, then it is encouraged to increase its wage demands. This would lead to a direct relationship between the wage increases in one quarter and those in previous quarters. But a more fundamental problem with the general form of wage determination equation studied here is that the use of a general index of real wages obscures the important distinction between the wage rates of the individual union and the wage rates of other unions. If a union is relatively satisfied with its own real wage rates (i.e., if they are high compared with some normal level), then it will not press for a large increase. If on the other hand the real wage rates of workers belonging to other unions are relatively high, this will encourage the union to press for a larger raise to preserve differentials. These influences, the effect of recent raises and other wage rates, on the wage bargain are almost impossible to study with aggregate data. The author did not proceed further with the current investigation, because he became dissatisfied with its aggregative form. A study using disaggregated data is obviously needed.

6 THE PRICE DETERMINATION EQUATION

In order to discuss the policy implications of the wage determination equation, it must be considered in relation to a price determination equation. The author decided to estimate equations similar to the Klein–Ball equations 3.20, 3.22, 3.23, 3.24 of [3]. The main differences between the sets of estimates were that the data used here were quarterly from beginning 1948 to end 1961 although most of the data were defined as in Klein–Ball, that the equations were in log-linear form, and that they were made homogeneous in money prices.

Apart from this it was decided to include both wage rates and average earnings in the equations, since it is not clear which is the most appropriate in determining changes in the marginal cost or average cost of output. For example if differences between the two variables occur because of changes in overtime working, it is not clear that the entrepreneur would take overtime rates into account in fixing prices, since the extra labour costs are to some extent compensated by reduced overhead cost. If wage drift is caused by movement of labour between different occupations this is not increasing the costs of production in either industry. If the wage drift is caused by the earnings of piece workers increasing because of increased productivity with no change in the price rate, this may lead to an increase in unit costs. In fact the coefficient of the wage rate was relatively large compared with the coefficient of earnings. The latter coefficient was never significant at the 5 per cent level. The estimates were made for each equation using both the autoregressive least squares and instrumental variables programmes, the set of instrumental variables being the same as those used for the wage determination equation. It was found worthwhile to modify Klein's tax variable and to introduce productivity variables so that in all 13 separate estimates of the different equations were made.

The final estimates of the different equations were as below:

$$p_t - w_t = 0.012(w_{et} - w_t) + 0.198(p_{I(t-2)} - w_t)$$
$$\quad (0.054) \qquad\qquad (0.014)$$

$$+ 0.875T_{it} - 0.115R_t - 0.0018t, \qquad (3.20)$$
$$(0.706)_{it} \quad (0.052) \quad (0.0008)$$

$$\hat{k} = 0.587 \,(0.115), \qquad s^2 = 0.745 \times 10^{-4}, \qquad \chi^2 = 0.55 \,(4 \text{ D.F.}),$$

$$p_{ft} - w_t = 0.182(p_{if(t-2)} - w_t) - 0.027(S_{ut} - w_t) - 0.0037t + 0.016Z_t \quad (3.22)$$
$$(0.042) \qquad\qquad (0.022) \qquad\qquad (0.00075) \quad (0.008)$$

$$\hat{k} = 0.460 \,(0.147), \qquad s^2 = 0.169 \times 10^{-3}, \qquad \chi^2 = 3.44 \,(3 \text{ D.F.}),$$

$$p_{dt} - w_t = 0.890(p_t - w_t) + 0.134(p_{me(t-2)} - w_t) - 0.0029t \quad (3.23)$$
$$(0.188) \qquad\qquad (0.025) \qquad\qquad (0.0009)$$

$$\hat{k} = 0.568 \,(0.129), \qquad s^2 = 0.179 \times 10^{-3}, \qquad \chi^2 = 5.06 \,(2 \text{ D.F.}),$$

$$p_{ot} - w_t = 0.737(p_t - w_t) + 0.040(p_{im(t-2)} - w_t) - 0.0028t \quad (3.24)$$
$$(0.108) \qquad\qquad (0.020) \qquad\qquad (0.0009)$$

$$\hat{k} = 0.781 \,(0.090), \qquad s^2 = 0.660 \times 10^{-4}, \qquad \chi^2 = 4.35 \,(2 \text{ D.F.})$$

where w_e is average weekly wage earnings; p_t is index of total import prices; T_i is ratio of consumption expenditures at market prices to consumption expenditures at factor cost; R is ratio of index of industrial production to number employed in the same industries; p_f is retail price index for food, drink and tobacco; P_{if} is price index for food, drink and tobacco imports; S_u is index of subsidies on food and agricultural products; $Z = 1$ in 1954 and 1955, $= 0$ otherwise; p_d is price index of consumer durables; p_{me} is price index of imported, non-ferrous metals; p_o is price index of non-food, non-durable consumer goods; p_{im} is price index of basic material imports.

The definitions and sources are as in [3] except for the definition of T_i. This definition was used because it was realised that if the entrepreneur passed on the tax to the consumer the coefficient of T_{it} would be one. In fact the coefficient had a relatively large standard error, and the difference between it and one was small and certainly not significant. In all the estimates the k was significant. There seemed no reason to depart from the structure of lags used by Klein–Ball, and in particular no lag was introduced in the wage rate variable. Despite this the estimates using least squares and instrumental variables differed by only relatively trivial amounts, and the differences were certainly not significant.

7 ECONOMIC AND POLICY IMPLICATIONS

This section considers the economic implications of the wage and price determination equations by first looking at the moving equilibrium solution, and then considering the time lags in the movement to equilibrium.

The static implications of both equation (17) and (18) are almost identical. Those for equation (17) are

$$w - p = 0.00491t - 0.0443U.$$

The first coefficient shows that real wages in the moving equilibrium increase at a rate of roughly 2 per cent per annum. The second coefficient can be interpreted by saying that if unemployment doubles, thereby adding 0.69 to U since the units are in natural logarithms, this produces a 3 per cent fall in the real wage in equilibrium. To obtain the corresponding changes in money wages and prices account must be taken of the static equivalent of equation (3.20) of the last section. This is

$$p - w = 0.198(p_I - w) + 0.875T_i - 0.115R - 0.0018t.$$

Eliminating $p - w$ and solving for w the resulting equation is

$$w = p_I + 5T_i - 0.22U + 0.015t - 0.58R. \qquad (19)$$

Similarly for p we obtain

$$p = p_I + 0.010t - 0.58R + 5T_i - 0.18U.$$

Concentrating on the trend in money wages and prices, the equations suggest that if prices are to be stabilised, R must increase at 6.7 per cent per annum; and that if wages are to be stabilised in relation to import prices then R must increase at 10 per cent per annum. Alternatively if R is increasing at 2.7 per cent per annum as it did in the sample period, the total trend in (3.20) because of this and the linear trend, is roughly equivalent to 1 per cent per annum. If money prices are to keep in line with the prices of imports this trend must be increased to 1.6 per cent; if money wages are to keep in line with the prices of imports the trend on the price equation must be increased to 2 per cent. The objective of stabilising money wages in relation to import prices looks rather difficult, but the objective of stabilising home prices in relation to import prices looks more capable of realisation. The estimate of the required change in the range of growth in industrial productivity may be too large since it depends upon an estimate of a coefficient of R which has a large standard error, and no allowance is made for an improvement in non-industrial productivity.

Considering now the influence of unemployment on money wages and prices, doubling unemployment would ultimately reduce money wages by 15 per cent and prices by 12 per cent. It also follows that a 1 per cent change in indirect tax rates ultimately changes both prices and money wages by 5 per cent, a relatively large multiplier effect. Finally note that prices and money wages ultimately change in proportion to a change in import prices. This means that in this model devaluation has a purely temporary effect. In equilibrium internal costs are changed proportionally to the extent of the devaluation.

Considering now the dynamic behaviour of the model, eliminate $w_{t-1} - p_{t-1}$ from equation (17) using equation (3.20) and the result is

$$w_t - w_{t-1} = -0.12U_{t-1} - 0.054(w_{t-1} - p_{I(t-3)})$$
$$+0.271T_{i(t-1)} + 0.00084t - 0.031R_{t-1}. \tag{20}$$

This can be interpreted in terms of an exponentially weighted distributed lag of average length 18.5 quarters. The effect of this can be illustrated by considering a once for all change in one of the variables p_I, U, or T_i. Suppose for the sake of simplicity that all the variables except the trends have been held constant for a sufficient length of time for the model to be in its moving equilibrium, and then a change is made in U to a new constant level, which will lead to a change in the equilibrium level given by equation (19). Since the difference between w_t and the new equilibrium level is being reduced by the factor 0.946 per quarter, it will take 13 quarters before the wage rate has moved half way to its new equilibrium value, and 43 quarters before the wage rate has moved 90 per cent of the way to the equilibrium.

Applying the same type of analysis to a devaluation, and assuming that this has an immediate full impact on import prices, according to the equation it will be three quarters before money wage rates are at all affected. It will be a further 13 quarters before money wage rates have risen by half the change in import prices, and 43 quarters before they have risen by 90 per cent of the change in import prices. More crudely, half the initial impact of the devaluation has disappeared by the end of four years, and 90 per cent by the end of 11 years. In the light of these rather long lags, the force of the statement that devaluation has only a temporary impact is weakened.

Consider finally the immediate impact of government policy on the rate of change of money wages. For the first year after the change in the policy variable, the model shows that the effect of the second term on the right of the previous equation can be neglected, so that the effect of a change in U or T_i is to change the rate of change in money wage rates. It is of some interest to compare this initial impact with those obtained by previous investigators. Considering again the effect of a doubling of the level of unemployment this increases log (unemployment) by 0.69 and decreases the rate of change of money wage rates by 3.3 per cent per annum. Comparing this with Klein–Ball equation (3.18e) where the equivalent change is an increase in the unemployment index of 100, according to their equation a doubling of unemployment would reduce the rate of change of money wage rates by 9.1 per cent per annum. Our results show a much smaller effect. The difference might to some extent be explained by sampling error but not entirely. It is to be noted that in our model there is no level of unemployment which will lead to stationary wage rates. The presence of the trend in (20) ensures that the trend in money wages can only be suppressed by a change in the rate of increase of productivity.

The previous discussion has been carried on making use of wage determination equation (17). If instead equation (18) is used the equilibrium results are very little changed. In place of equation (20) the following equation is obtained for the dynamic behaviour of the model.

$$w_t - w_{t-1} = -0.018U_{t-4} - 0.075(w_{t-1} - p_{I(t-3)}) + 0.375T_{i(t-1)}$$
$$+ 0.106(w_{t-1} - w_{t-2}) - 0.524(w_{t-2} - w_{t-3}) + 0.0012t - 0.042R_{t-1}.$$
$$(21)$$

Solving this to give w_t in terms of previous values of U, p_I and T_i we get a distributed lag formula with average lag of 17.9 quarters. Considering the time taken for the wage rate to reduce the initial difference from the equilibrium value, it is necessary to consider the latent roots of equation (21). These are the roots of the equation

$$\lambda^3 - 1.031\lambda^2 + 0.630\lambda - 0.524 = 0.$$

This has one real root, 0.949, and two complex roots with a period of approximately one year and a damping factor of 0.74 per quarter. In the medium period of 10 to 40 quarters with which we are concerned the large real root dominates the solution, so that a process of approximation can be used to estimate the time period required for the solution to approach within any distance of the equilibrium value. It is found that the time for the distance to halve its initial value is 11 quarters approximately, and the time for the distance to become one tenth is 33 quarters. These are somewhat smaller lags than with equation (17), but not sufficiently so to affect general policy conclusions.

The initial impact is also increased. Doubling the level of unemployment will initially reduce the rate of increase in mone y wage rates by 5 per cent per annum. The difference between this and the Klein–Ball result is reduced, and could be due to sampling errors.

8 GENERAL CONCLUSIONS

This study has shown that it is relatively simple to take account of first order autoregression in estimating the coefficients of a structural equation if it is possible to use an electronic computer. The method could easily be generalised to take account of higher order autoregression, but in no case in the present investigation did the data warrant the fitting of a higher order autoregression.

The wage determination equation used in this paper leads to policy conclusions which differ fundamentally from those implied by previous investigators. In particular they suggest that the effect of devaluation is only temporary, and that it is impossible to restrain money wages indefinitely by maintaining unemployment at some appropriate level. An increase in unemployment has a once-for-all effect on money wages. However the lags in the model are of order several years so that the immediate short period prediction from the model is not greatly different in kind, but rather smaller quantitatively than in previous models.

APPENDIX A: THE METHOD OF ITERATIVE MAXIMISATION

CONSIDER THE GENERAL METHOD OF MAXIMISING A FUNCTION $f(\mathbf{a}, \mathbf{b})$ which is a function of two vectors $\mathbf{a}$ and $\mathbf{b}$ by the following iterative procedure. First maximise with respect to $\mathbf{b}$ keeping $\mathbf{a}$ constant, and then maximise with respect to $\mathbf{a}$ and keeping $\mathbf{b}$ constant, and iterate. Although the procedure may not be very efficient, it converges to a local maximum in a very wide class of cases.

Basic assumptions

(i) For some c the set of points $f(\mathbf{a}, \mathbf{b}) > c$ is bounded.
(ii) The function is continuous throughout this region.

Take as arbitrary starting point some point within the region, and label the successive points obtained by the iteration $(\mathbf{a}_t, \mathbf{b}_t)$ and the successive values of the function f_i, $i = 1, 2, 3 \ldots$.

Since the function cannot decrease at any stage, the points must stay within the bounded region. Since f_i is a positive monotonic sequence with an upper bound (since the function is continuous on a closed set) the sequence converges to its upper bound f^*. Also since the sequence $(\mathbf{a}_i, \mathbf{b}_i)$ is bounded it possesses limit points.

Consider any limit point $(\mathbf{a}^*, \mathbf{b}^*)$. Since there is a subsequence of points, denoted by $(\mathbf{a}_i^*, \mathbf{b}_i^*)$, which converges to the limit point and the function is continuous, $f(\mathbf{a}^*, \mathbf{b}^*) = f^*$.

There are three possibilities to be considered. Either all except a finite number of the subsequence are obtained by maximising with respect to $\mathbf{a}$, when the limit point is called of type a, or all except a finite number are obtained by maximising with respect to $\mathbf{b}$, when the limit point is of type b, or the subsequence has an infinite number of points of both types when the limit point is of type ab. We suppose that the limit point is of type a or ab; the limit point of type b can be considered by interchanging a and b in the following argument.

Suppose $f(\mathbf{a}, \mathbf{b}^*)$ had not a maximum at $\mathbf{a} = \mathbf{a}^*$. Then there exists $\mathbf{a}^{**}$ such that $f(\mathbf{a}^{**}, \mathbf{b}^*) > f(\mathbf{a}^*, \mathbf{b}^*) = f^*$. By continuity there exists δ_1 such that $f(\mathbf{a}^{**}, \mathbf{b}) > f^*$ if $|\mathbf{b} - \mathbf{b}^*| < \delta_1$. Now since the subsequence $(\mathbf{a}_i^*, \mathbf{b}_i^*)$ tends to the limit point of type a or ab there exists a point of this subsequence obtained by maximising with respect to $\mathbf{a}$, such that $|\mathbf{b}_i^* - \mathbf{b}^*| < \delta_1$. And then $f(\mathbf{a}^{**}, \mathbf{b}_i^*) > f^* \geqslant f(\mathbf{a}_i^*, \mathbf{b}_i^*)$. But $\mathbf{a}_i^*$ was obtained by maximising $f(\mathbf{a}, \mathbf{b}_i^*)$ with respect to $\mathbf{a}$. This is a contradiction showing that

$$f(\mathbf{a}^*, \mathbf{b}^*) \geqslant f(\mathbf{a}, \mathbf{b}^*)$$

for all $\mathbf{a}$.

Suppose now that $f(\mathbf{a}^*, \mathbf{b})$ had not a maximum at $\mathbf{b} = \mathbf{b}^*$, so that there exists $\mathbf{b}^{**}$ such that $f(\mathbf{a}^*, \mathbf{b}^{**}) > f^*$. There exists δ_2 such that $f(\mathbf{a}, \mathbf{b}^{**}) > f^*$ if $|\mathbf{a} - \mathbf{a}^*| < \delta_2$ from continuity. We can find a point of the subsequence obtained by maximising with respect to $\mathbf{a}$ such that $|\mathbf{a}_i^* - \mathbf{a}^*| < \delta_2$. At the next stage of the iteration we choose $\mathbf{b}$ so as to maximise $f(\mathbf{a}_i^*, \mathbf{b})$. If we take $\mathbf{b} = \mathbf{b}^{**}$ we obtain $f(\mathbf{a}_i^*, \mathbf{b}^{**}) > f^*$. This contradicts the definition of f^* as an upper bound of the sequence. Thus $f(\mathbf{a}^*, \mathbf{b}^*) \geqslant f(\mathbf{a}^*, \mathbf{b})$ for all values of $\mathbf{b}$. From these two results it follows that if $f(\mathbf{a}, \mathbf{b})$ has all first order derivatives at $(\mathbf{a}^*, \mathbf{b}^*)$ this is a stationary point of the function.

Since the presence of more than one limit point would require that the function had several stationary points of this type each with a value of the function equal to f^*, in general there will only be one limit point. Indeed it can be shown that the stationary points must satisfy further very restrictive conditions. It must be possible to link the points in a cyclic chain so that each pair in the chain differs only in the value of one of the vectors $\mathbf{a}$ or $\mathbf{b}$. In practice only the presence of a single limit point need be considered and in this case the sequence of points converges to this limit point. So the original sequence will converge to one of the stationary values in the region. Furthermore only maxima or saddle points need be considered.

However the likelihood of the limit point being a saddlepoint is low. Suppose that the limit point were a saddlepoint and that at some stage of the iteration the current point had been obtained by maximising with respect to $\mathbf{b}$. The linear space $\mathbf{b} = \mathbf{b}_i$ must not intersect the region where $f > f^*$ for then the sequence would obviously not converge to the saddlepoint. This condition is unlikely to be fulfilled for all i.

In particular if the vector $\mathbf{b}$ has only one component, as in the case considered in the body of the paper, convergence to a saddle point is extremely unlikely. If there is a direction through the saddle point (α, β) such that $f(\mathbf{a}^* + k\alpha, \mathbf{b}^* + k\beta) > f^*$ for all $|k| < \delta$, and this condition is certainly satisfied if the function has continuous second order derivatives at the saddlepoint, then we can find a point of the sequence obtained by maximising with respect to $\mathbf{b}$ which lies within a distance $\delta\beta$ of the limit point. If this point is $(\mathbf{a}_i, b_i)$ take $k = (b_i - \mathbf{b}^*)/\beta$. The corresponding point on the line defined above could be taken as the next point in the iteration, and unless $k=0$, $f_{i+1} > f^*$. This is a contradiction showing that the sequence does not converge to the saddlepoint. The only case where the sequence does converge to the saddlepoint is where for some finite, i, $b_i = b^*$. In this case the next point in the sequence is the saddlepoint, and so are all subsequent points. This case however occurs with probability zero.

APPENDIX B: SUMMARY OF EQUATIONS ESTIMATED

For each equation estimated a list of the symbols for the variables in the equation is given, using the symbols defined in the body of the paper or in [3], preceded by the method of estimation. For this L.S. means ordinary least squares, I.V. means instrumental variables, A.L.S. means autoregressive least squares, and A.I.V. means autoregressive instrumental variables. The addition of a star means that the equation was also estimated by single iteration method.

Post-war non-logarithmic wage determination equation

In all these equations $w_{t-1} - p_{t-1}$, and U_{t-1} were included, and seasonal shifts.
1. L.S. Old F_t, $p_{t-1} - p_{t-4}$.
2. A.L.S. Old F_t, $p_{t-1} - p_{t-4}$.
3. A.L.S. Old F_t, $p_{t-1} - p_{t-4}$, t.
4. A.L.S.* New F_t, $p_{t-1} - p_{t-4}$, t.
5. A.L.S. New F_t, $p_{t-1} - p_{t-4}$, t, three seasonal trend variables.
6. A.I.V. New F_t, $p_{t-1} - p_{t-4}$, t.
7. A.I.V. New F_t, $p_t - p_{t-4}$, t.
8. A.L.S. New F_t, $p_{t-1} - p_{t-5}$, t.
9. A.L.S. New F_t, F_{t-1}, $p_{t-1} - p_{t-4}$, t.

Pre-war non-logarithmic wage determination equation

In all these equations t and the seasonal shift variables were included.
10. L.S. F_t, $w_{t-1} - p_{t-1}$, $p_{t-1} - p_{t-4}$, U_{t-1}.
11. A.L.S. F_t, $w_{t-1} - p_{t-1}$, $p_{t-1} - p_{t-4}$, U_{t-1}.
12. A.I.V. F_t, $w_{t-1} - p_{t-1}$, $p_{t-1} - p_{t-4}$, U_{t-1}.
In this and all subsequent estimates the years 1922 and 1923 were omitted.
13. A.I.V. F_t, $w_{t-1} - p_{t-1}$, $p_{t-1} - p_{t-4}$, U_{t-1}.
14. A.I.V. A.I.V. $w_{t-1} - p_{t-1}$, $p_{t-1} - p_{t-4}$, U_{t-1}.
15. A.I.V. $w_{t-1} - p_{t-1}$, $p_{t-1} - p_{t-4}$, U_{t-2}.
16. A.I.V. $w_{t-1} - p_{t-1}$, U_{t-1}.
17. A.I.V. $w_{t-1} - p_{t-1}$, $p_{t-1} - p_{t-4}$.
18. A.I.V. $p_{t-1} - p_{t-4}$, U_{t-1}.

Post-war logarithmic equations

WAGE DETERMINATION

In all these equations t and the seasonal shift variables were included.

19. A.L.S. F_t, $w_{t-1} - p_{t-1}$, U_{t-1}, $p_{t-1} - p_{t-4}$.
20. A.I.V. F_t, $w_{t-1} - p_{t-1}$, U_{t-1}, $p_{t-1} - p_{t-4}$, $(D/p)_{t-1}$.
21. A.I.V. F_t, $w_{t-1} - p_{t-1}$, U_{t-1}, $p_{t-1} - p_{t-4}$.
22. A.L.S. F_t, $w_{t-1} - p_{t-1}$, U_{t-1}, $p_{t-1} - p_{t-4}$, $(D/p)_{t-1}$.
23. A.L.S. F_t, $w_{t-1} - p_{t-1}$, U_{t-1}, $p_{t-1} - p_{t-4}$, $(\bar{D}/\bar{p})_{t-1}$. This last variable was a three year average of past profits deflated.
24. A.L.S. F_t, $w_{t-1} - p_{t-1}$, U_{t-1}, $p_{t-1} - p_{t-4}$, $(P/E_p)_{t-1}$.
25. A.L.S. F_t, $w_{t-1} - p_{t-1}$, U_{t-1}, $p_{t-1} - p_{t-4}$, $(\bar{P}/\bar{E}_p)_{t-1}$. This last variable was a three year average of past labour productivity.
26. A.L.S.* $w_{t-1} - p_{t-1}$, U_{t-1}.
27. A.L.S. $w_{t-1} - p_{t-1}$, U_{t-1}, $p_{t-1} - p_{t-4}$, $p_{t-2} - p_{t-5}$, Ft.
28. A.L.S. $w_{t-1} - p_{t-1}{}^3$, U_{t-1}, $p_{t-1} - p_{t-4}$, $p_{t-1} - p_{t-2}$, F_t, $w_{t-1} - w_{t-2}$.
29. A.L.S. $w_{t-1} - p_{t-1}$, U_{t-1}, $p_{t-1} - p_{t-4}$, F_t, $w_{t-1} - w_{t-2}$.
30. A.L.S. $w_{t-1} - p_{t-1}$, U_{t-1}, U_{t-2}, $p_{t-1} - p_{t-4}$, F_t, $w_{t-1} - w_{t-2}$.
31. A.L.S. $w_{t-1} - p_{t-1}$, U_{t-1}, $p_{t-1} - p_{t-4}$, F_t, $w_{t-1} - w_{t-2}$, $w_{t-2} - w_{t-3}$.
32. A.L.S. $w_{t-1} - p_{t-1}$, U_{t-1}, U_{t-2}, U_{t-3}, $p_{t-1} - p_{t-4}$, F_t, $w_{t-1} - w_{t-2}$.
33. A.L.S. $w_{t-1} - p_{t-1}$, U_{t-3}, $p_{t-1} - p_{t-4}$, $p_{t-2} - p_{t-5}$, $p_{t-1} - p_{t-2}$, F_t, $w_{t-1} - w_{t-2}$, $w_{t-2} - w_{t-3}$.
34. A.L.S. $w_{t-1} - p_{t-1}$, U_{t-3}, $p_{t-1} - p_{t-4}$, $p_{t-2} - p_{t-5}$, $w_{t-1} - w_{t-2}$, $w_{t-2} - w_{t-3}$, $w_{t-3} - w_{t-4}$.
35. A.L.S. $w_{t-1} - p_{t-1}$, U_{t-3}, $p_{t-1} - p_{t-4}$, F_t, F_{t-1}, $w_{t-1} - w_{t-2}$, $w_{t-2} - w_{t-3}$.
36. A.L.S. $w_{t-1} - p_{t-1}$, $w_{t-2} - p_{t-2}$, U_{t-3}, $p_{t-1} - p_{t-4}$, F_t, F_{t-1}, $w_{t-1} - w_{t-2}$, $w_{t-2} - w_{t-3}$.
37. A.L.S. $w_{t-1} - p_{t-1}$, U_{t-3}, U_{t-4}, $w_{t-1} - w_{t-2}$, $w_{t-2} - w_{t-3}$.
38. A.L.S. $w_{t-1} - p_{t-1}$, U_{t-4}, F_t, F_{t-1}, $w_{t-1} - w_{t-2}$, $w_{t-2} - w_{t-3}$.
39. A.L.S. $w_{t-1} - p_{t-1}$, U_{t-4}, F_t, F_{t-1}, F_{t-2}, $w_{t-1} - w_{t-2}$, $w_{t-2} - w_{t-3}$.
40. A.L.S. $w_{t-1} - p_{t-1}$, U_{t-4}, F_{t-2}, $w_{t-1} - w_{t-2}$, $w_{t-2} - w_{t-3}$.
41. A.L.S.* $w_{t-1} - p_{t-1}$, U_{t-4}, $w_{t-1} - w_{t-2}$, $w_{t-2} - w_{t-3}$.
42. A.L.S. $w_{t-1} - p_{t-1}$, U_{t-4}, F_{t-2}, $w_{t-1} - w_{t-2}$.

Price determination equations

3.20. All these equations included $w_{et} - w_t$, $p_{I(t-2)} - w_t$, t and seasonal shifts.
43. A.L.S. Old T_i.
44. A.L.S. New T_i.
45. A.I.V. New T_i.
46. A.L.S.* New $T_i \cdot (P/E_p)_t$.
47. A.L.S.* New $T_i \cdot (\bar{P}/\bar{E}_p)_t$.
3.22. All these equations included $p_{if(t-2)} - w_t$, $S_{ut} - w_t$, Z_t, t, and seasonals.
48. A.L.S.* $w_{et} - w_t$.

49. A.I.V. $w_{et} - w_t$.
50. A.L.S.*
3.23. All these equations included $p_t - w_t$, $p_{me(t-2)} - w$, t, and seasonals.
51. A.L.S.* $w_{et} - w_t$.
52. A.I.V. $w_{et} - w_t$.
53. A.L.S.*
3.24. Both equations included $p_t - w_t$, $p_{m(t-2)} - w_t$, t, and seasonals.
54. A.L.S.* $w_{et} - w_t$.
55. A.L.S.*

APPENDIX C: DATA USED

THE DATA USED WERE A CONTINUATION OF THOSE GIVEN IN [3], TABLE VII. FOR THE WAGE EQUATION THESE WERE CONTINUED FOR THREE YEARS, FOR THE PRICE EQUATION FOUR YEARS. ONLY THE CONTINUATIONS ARE GIVEN IN THE FOLLOWING TABLE.

	p	w	U	p_f	p_d	p_0	S_u	p_{if}	p_{im}	p_{met}
1958	141.3	165.8	137.8	143.5	130.5	132.4	59.5	131.6	133.2	148.0
	143.4	166.4	146.4	146.8	129.3	130.4	59.5	135.8	133.8	144.0
	142.2	168.1	146.7	144.0	128.2	129.9	59.5	135.8	128.6	149.5
	142.5	171.0	173.7	144.3	128.0	129.9	59.5	138.8	125.5	152.8
1959	143.7	171.7	195.4	145.1	129.7	131.1	56.0	136.7	117.1	145.1
	142.7	172.1	156.6	144.2	126.1	129.6	56.0	133.9	128.6	149.0
	142.2	172.6	134.8	142.4	124.3	129.8	56.0	135.8	130.1	146.6
	142.5	173.1	139.8	144.2	125.1	129.2	56.0	140.4	125.0	150.0
1960	143.3	174.9	145.4	143.5	125.6	131.6	56.2	136.2	125.4	155.7
	143.5	176.8	114.0	145.2	126.2	129.6	56.2	132.5	121.3	150.4
	145.3	177.7	100.8	146.1	126.2	130.7	56.2	133.5	127.2	150.0
	145.6	179.1	115.6		126.2	131.7	56.2	137.6	121.2	148.1
1961	145.8	182.5	—	145.0	126.2	134.1	71.1	133.0	124.7	146.4
	146.3	183.9	—	144.8	127.0	133.2	71.1	133.5	126.0	148.5
	150.3	184.9	—	151.4	127.9	135.2	71.1	127.4	121.7	150.2
	150.6	186.3	—	151.3	127.2	135.8	71.1	128.8	116.3	152.1

I am grateful to J. E. Tozer for compiling the above data. The pre-war data are given in full in the next table.

	w	p	U		w	p	U		w	p	U
1921		145.3		1927	102.0	104.8	73.0	1933	95.0	92.1	164.8
		137.8			101.0	103.9	59.7		95.0	91.3	149.1
		131.8			101.0	103.4	60.8		95.0	91.5	138.9
	130.0	118.9	103.7		100.0	101.9	64.3		95.0	91.5	131.4
1922	118.1	117.2	112.4	1928	100.0	104.1	66.6	1934	95.0	91.3	133.4
	111.2	111.1	99.6		100.0	103.1	64.9		95.5	91.1	122.6
	106.6	111.0	84.0		100.0	103.5	74.7		95.5	92.0	122.6
	99.1	110.6	81.7		100.0	103.3	78.8		95.5	91.6	122.2
1923	98.0	108.3	81.7	1929	100.0	102.5	78.2	1935	96.0	91.6	130.6
	98.0	106.7	72.4		100.0	102.6	65.5		96.0	92.1	117.6
	98.6	107.4	73.6		99.5	102.4	66.6		97.0	92.4	113.6
	99.1	107.2	72.4		99.5	102.9	74.2		97.0	92.6	110.1
1924	99.1	106.7	68.4	1930	99.5	101.5	89.2	1936	98.5	92.7	117.1
	99.7	105.9	59.7		99.5	100.3	102.0		99.0	93.2	101.2
	100.3	105.6	64.3		99.5	100.0	118.8		99.5	93.6	94.4
	100.9	107.0	69.5		99.0	98.8	133.1		100.0	93.8	93.9
1925	101.5	107.1	71.8	1931	98.5	97.2	151.9	1937	101.0	94.3	95.0
	102.0	107.0	70.7		98.0	96.7	149.1		102.5	95.4	82.3
	101.5	106.4	74.7		97.0	95.4	158.4		103.5	96.3	79.7
	101.5	104.5	69.5		96.5	94.9	154.6		104.5	97.3	88.6
1926	101.5	105.2	66.0	1932	96.0	94.9	154.7	1938	106.5	96.7	104.8
	101.0	106.0	80.5		96.0	94.9	157.2		107.0	97.3	103.6
	101.0	106.8	91.5		95.5	93.4	164.7		107.0	97.2	103.6
	101.0	107.4	86.3		95.5	93.4	159.7		107.0	97.2	105.8

REFERENCES

[1] Dicks-Mireaux, L. A. and Dow, J. C. R. (1959), 'The determinants of wage inflation; United Kingdom 1946–1956', *Journal of the Royal Statistical Society*, A, **122**, 145–84.

[2] Durbin, J. (1960), 'The estimation of parameters in time-series regression models', *Journal of the Royal Statistical Society*, B, **22**, 139–53.

[3] Klein, L. R., Ball, R. J., Hazlewood, A. and Vandome, P. (1961), *An Econometric Model of the United Kingdom*, Oxford.

[4] Lipsey, R. G. and Steuer, M. D. (1961), 'Relations between profits and wage rates', *Economica*, **28**, 137–55.

[5] Phillips, A. W. (1958), 'The relation between unemployment and the rate of change of money wage rates in the United Kingdom, 1861–1957', *Economica*, **25**, 283–300.

[6] Sargan, J. D. (1959), 'The estimation of relationships with autocorrelated residuals by the use of instrumental variables', *Journal of the Royal Statistical Society*, B, **21**, 91–105.

[7] Sargan, J. D. (1961), 'The maximum likelihood estimation of economic relationships with autoregressive residuals', *Econometrica*, **29**, 414–26.

DISCUSSION ON THE PAPER BY J. D. SARGAN

CHAIRMAN: M. McMANUS

DURBIN   I liked Sargan's treatment of the question of the convergence of his development of the Cochrane–Orcutt procedure. Many discussions of iterative estimation procedures are bedevilled by doubts about whether the procedure can be relied on to converge. Sargan points out that with the Cochrane–Orcutt type of iteration one is minimising a quadratic function at each step. The sequence of values of the quadratic function so obtained is therefore a bounded decreasing function which necessarily converges to a limit. With the development of electronic computation, iterative procedures are bound to be increasingly employed. Convergence of many of these methods can be guaranteed by making use of an argument similar to Sargan's. In the case of maximum-likelihood estimates, for example, one would calculate the value of the likelihood function at each stage of the iteration and would only accept the step if the likelihood increased. If the likelihood decreased one could take a new trial value half-way between the previous trial value and the value at the previous stage of the iteration and one could continue searching in this kind of way, accepting only values which increase the likelihood function. In this way one obtains an increasing sequence of likelihoods bounded above at the absolute maximum which necessarily converges. Further useful elaborations of this approach are given by Hartley.[1] Of course there is no guarantee that such a process necessarily attains the overall maximum since the function may have multiple maxima. To cover this point, supplementary investigations of the kind suggested by Sargan are necessary.

Sargan contrasts the Cochrane–Orcutt method with the Newton–Raphson method. For many applications R. A. Fisher's scoring method, which is very similar to the Newton–Raphson method except that the matrix of second derivatives is replaced by an estimate of its expected value,

[1] Hartley, H. O. (1961), 'The modified Gauss–Newton method for the fitting of non-linear regression functions by least squares', *Technometrics*, **3**, 269–80.

is to be preferred. It is worth pointing out that at least when the predetermined variables are all exogenous, the Fisher scoring method turns out to be virtually equivalent to the original Cochrane–Orcutt procedure. This is another pointer towards the efficiency of the Cochrane–Orcutt method.

Furthermore, may I say that I do not accept Sargan's suggestion that because a first-round estimate in an iterative procedure is fully efficient in the asymptotic sense one might just as well accept it rather than continue the iteration until convergence is achieved. I think that the objectivity of, say, a maximum-likelihod estimate is worth the extra computing time as compared with a first-round value which necessarily depends to some extent on an arbitrarily selected starting value.

Sargan's methods are based on the assumption that the disturbances have a first- or second-order autoregressive structure. This leads to tractable procedures but there is no guarantee that the resulting estimates will be efficient if the true autocorrelation structure of the disturbances is non-autoregressive. This was shown by Watson[2] and by Watson and Hannan[3]. Ideally one would like to have methods that would enable one to inspect the autocorrelation structure and to make appropriate allowance for it. Alternatively, one would like to see developed methods which are robust over a wide variety of autocorrelation structures.

BALL: Since Durbin has dealt with the methodological aspects of Sargan's interesting paper, the following remarks are confined mainly to the economic and policy aspects.

The choice of the Klein–Ball model of wage-price behaviour as a starting point is an interesting one, for as far as we could ascertain without using a test of the kind proposed by Sargan, several of the estimated equations in this model, including the wage rate equation, suffered from the presence of autocorrelation. It was shown subsequently[4] that the wage rate equation as originally estimated was a relatively inefficient conditional predictor of the wage level over the four years that followed the end of the sample period in 1956. More satisfactory predictors were obtained by applying post-estimation transformations of a simple kind to the original structural equation, with the aim of taking advantage in prediction of the autocorrelation structure. Since, as pointed out by Dicks-Mireaux and Dow [1], some knowledge of the autocorrelation structure could have been deduced from the underlying assumptions about the distribution of wage

[2] Watson, G. S. (1955),'Serial correlation in regression analysis I', *Biometrika*, **42**, 327–41.
[3] Watson, G. S. and Hannan, E. J. (1956), 'Serial correlation in regression analysis II', *Biometrika*, **43**, 436–48.
[4] Ball, R. J. (1962), 'The prediction of wage rate changes in the United Kingdom 1957–60, *Economic Journal*, **72**, 27–44.

increases in a given year, it seems clear that use of the knowledge should have been made in the original formulation and estimation of the model, as implied by Sargan in Section 4 of his paper. The original estimates were clearly inefficient and for similar reasons the recorded standard errors of the estimates were too low.

Over the seven years since the original work was done on the Klein–Ball model, a substantial amount of work on wage rates, earnings and prices has appeared that justifies a severe re-scrutiny of the theory and assumption that underlay this model. If not everyone will agree to call this progress, at least one can point to change. However, I am not sure that Sargan's analysis has helped to disperse some of the clouds of difficulty that surrounded the original model and I find parts of the theoretical development a little puzzling.

Most of the recent statistical literature on money wages has been concerned with money wage dynamics and very little with equilibrium theories of the money and real wage levels. The majority have formulated wage adjustment equations that relate the change in money wages to some measure of excess demand on familiar market clearing principles. This rationalisation of the introduction of unemployment into the adjustment equation was used by Phillips [5], Lipsey[5] and Klein and Ball[6]. But as Lipsey has emphasised, knowledge of the adjustment functon does not, in general, tell us anything about the equilibrium market structure. Simple knowledge of the adjustment function cannot even tell us whether the market is stable unless the measure of excess demand is explicitly related to the underlying market structure, for the parameters of the original demand and supply equations will partly determine the dynamic solution of the model as a whole. To use Lipsey's illustration, the hypothesis that relates wage change to unemployment is consistent with the view that organised labour has succeeded in autonomously shifting the supply curve of labour relative to the demand curve. To say something about the long-term development of money and real wages requires a detailed specification of the market structure as a whole. It seems to me that Sargan's model, as embodied in his equations (15) and (16) and as explained in the text, confuses the characteristics of the equilibrium market structure and the dynamic adjustment function, as they are usually interpreted. He relates the equilibrium *level* of real wages to the *level* of unemployment, where conventional economic theory relates unemployment to a rate of change.

If we apply neo-classical labour market theory, a possible model is the

[5] Lipsey, R. G. (1960), 'The relation between unemployment and the rate of change of money wage rates in the United Kingdom, 1862–1957: a further analysis', *Economica*, **27**, 1–31.
[6] Klein, L. R. and Bal, R. J. (1959), 'Some econometrics of the determination of absolute prices and wages', *Economic Journal*, **69**, 465–82.

following. Let the labour demand and supply equations be given by

$$N^S = f(w/p \,|\, \mathbf{z}) \tag{1}$$

$$N^D = g(w/p \,|\, \mathbf{x}) \tag{2}$$

where $\mathbf{z}$ and $\mathbf{x}$ are vectors of variables that are regarded as exogenous to the labour market. Add the adjustment function

$$\Delta(w/p) = \lambda(N^D - N^S) = \lambda L(w/p \,|\, \mathbf{z}, \mathbf{x}). \tag{3}$$

For practical purposes consider the approximations

$$w/p \simeq \alpha_1 w - \alpha_2 p \tag{4}$$

$$U \simeq \beta_0 - \beta_1 L(w/p \,|\, \mathbf{z}, \mathbf{x}), \qquad \beta_0 > 0 \tag{5}$$

then

$$\Delta w = \frac{\alpha_2}{\alpha_1} \Delta p + \frac{\lambda \beta_0}{\beta_1 \alpha_1} - \frac{\lambda}{\alpha_1 \beta_1} U. \tag{6}$$

Due to the approximation (4) traditional theory cannot tell us anything *a priori* about the coefficient on the price variable. It is not clear, therefore, that Sargan's concern with the non-homogeneous character of the Klein–Ball equation is, in general justified. Following traditional theory the level of unemployment will itself, in part, be a function of real wages, so that, in principle, the real wage variable included in addition to unemployment in his equation (15) is redundant. The point is not that neo-classical theory is acceptable, but much of the market analysis has been conducted as though it were, and if the underlying labour market equations of neo-classical equilibrium theory are to be rejected, what are we to put in their place? If the market is rapidly stable the equilibrium solution becomes critical for long run policy. The full equilibrium solution will not require zero unemployment, but that level of unemployment that corresponds to zero excess demand for labour. Hence the proviso that $\beta_0 > 0$ in my equation (5). It is also worth noting that the equilibrium referred to is not, in general, a static one if the particular solution of the system is a function of time. It follows that conclusions such as 'the *equilibrium* real wage grows at 2.5 points a year under a Conservative Government but not significantly under a Labour Government' must be treated with great caution, for this assumes that changes in the level of real wages will have no effect on the level of excess demand for labour if this is measured by unemployment, which in deriving this conclusion is *ex hypothesi* held constant.

This formulation of the wage equation also raises the question of the relationship of the short period adjustment functions that have been estimated, and long run theories that focus not on money but on real wages and the distribution of factor incomes. Some economists may share my own sympathy with the view that the traditional theory of real factor prices and factor shares may have some validity in the long run. The relationship between the short and long run theories can only be properly set out if the equilibrium theory in the traditional sense is fully specified. This is beyond the scope of the present comments, but it is worthwhile raising the question of the influence of productivity which plays a peculiar role, not only in Sargan's model, but also in the model developed by Dicks-Mireaux.[7]

The original Klein-Ball model was criticised by Dicks-Mireaux on the ground that the net effect of productivity within the framework of the model was inflationary. This was because productivity was assumed to affect the earnings gap, but no association was found on a quantity basis between prices and productivity. In the Sargan and Dicks-Mireaux models productivity appears with a negative sign in the price equation but not elsewhere in the model. As can be seen from Sargan's 'equilibrium' equation in Section 7, the net effect of a change in productivity is apparently deflationary. But if conclusions are drawn from these reduced form equations about the longer term, which is very relevant for variants of incomes policy that are designed to meet inflation as a secular problem, the effects of money wages are distinctly peculiar. Both the Sargan and Dicks-Mireaux models tell us that the effect of a rise in productivity will be to reduce the equilibrium level of money wages at a given moment of time. This happens because the cost of living adjustment is treated as symmetrical, i.e., not only do money wages adjust upward to a rise in the cost of living, but they also adjust downwards when it falls. In models of this type where productivity has no immediate positive effect on the money wage level, real wages *ceteris paribus* will increase with productivity only if money wages fall less rapidly than prices. I would regard the implications as *a priori* highly implausible, if applied to the long run, and if this is the case grave doubts emerge about the validity and interpretation of conclusions drawn from sub-system reduced forms analysis of the kind discussed by Sargan in his Section 7.

Attempts to relate productivity directly to wages reported by Sargan (and by Dicks-Mireaux[7]) were unsuccessful, which may on the surface appear puzzling,. But if one continues to work with a modified version of the neo-classical labour market as given above, there is no reason for expecting that productivity should appear explicitly in the short period adjustment function which includes unemployment. One would expect productivity to appear as an element in the vectors of exogenous variables that appear in my equations (1) and (2). It follows that *ceteris paribus* shifts in the level of productivity will alter the equilibrium level of real wages, which in the short run equations will be reflected in changes in the level of

[7] Dicks-Mireaux, L. A. (1961), 'The interrelationship between cost and price changes, 1946–59: a study of inflation in post-war Britain', *Oxford Economic Papers*, **13**, 267–92.

unemployment. The net direct effect of a productivity shift on the labour markets cannot be determined *a priori*, and hypotheses about its effect can only be properly tested after my equations (1) and (2) have been fully specified and unemployment as a variable eliminated from the model.

I sympathise strongly with Sargan's suggestion that we require disaggregated wage and price studies, for the mechanism referred to by Sargan and described by Arthur Ross as 'coercive comparisons' is surely an essential ingredient in understanding the movement of the general wage level and explaining the inherent stickiness in the wage structure that has been documented by Phelps Brown and Browne[8] and Dicks-Mireaux and Shepherd[9]. Disaggregation may also be essential to an understanding of the influence of productivity changes, for the distribution of productivity increases may turn out to be as important as changes in its aggregate level. If the economy is to grow steadily at full employment, changes in relative productivity will not, in general, leave the appropriate relative prices unchanged. It is not difficult to make a plausible case for the view that given the institutional characteristics of our kind of economy, the likely effect of increase in productivity will be a rise in incomes rather than a complete adjustment through prices. If this is the case, an equilibrium allocation of resources will demand some inflation. This takes us somewhere near the kind of model proposed by Schultze[10] in which in an economy with sticky wages and prices in a downward direction, mild inflation is the price we must pay for efficient resource allocation.

These remarks are, of course, not intended as an implicit criticism of Sargan's approach at the aggregate level which many people have followed. They are intended only to indicate where possible future developments may lie. The time has certainly come to consider the relationship between the statistical models of wages and price determination and the body of traditional theory on real factor prices, factor shares and resource allocation, which may require a more disaggregated approach than most of us have hitherto pursued. It is clear that here is a fertile field for future study.

SARGAN   In reply to Durbin's remarks, the case for iteration is not strong if the only reason for being interested in full maximum likelihood estimates is that they are asymptotically efficient. Even if computer time is a practically free good, there is a slight waste in the iteration. He would be correct in saying that the Cochrane–Orcutt and the Newton–Raphson

[8] Phelps Brown, E. H. and Browne, M. H. (1962), 'Earnings in industries of the United Kingdom, 1948–59', *Economic Journal*, **72**, 517–49.

[9] Dicks-Mireaux, L. A. and Shepherd, J. R. (1962), 'The wages structure and some implications for incomes policy', *National Institute Economic Review*, No. 22, 38–48.

[10] Schultze, C. (1959), *Recent Inflation in the United States*, Study Paper No. 1, Study of Employment, Growth, and Price Levels, for the Joint Economic Committee, Washington.

iterations are close approximations to each other in the case which he studied previously in [2]. The essential requirement is that

$$u_t = \sum_{r=0}^{\infty} k^r e_{t-r}$$

should be independent of all the x_{it} and $x_{i(t-1)}$, $i = 1 \ldots n-1$. This is certainly satisfied if the x_{it}, $i = 1 \ldots n-1$, are exogenous variables. But if they include some lagged endogenous variables then these also will depend on lagged values of the e_t, and so be correlated with u_t. Finally, it is to be noted that the R. A. Fisher method of taking expectations of second derivatives of the log-likelihood function is not easy in this case, where lagged endogenous variables are included in the equation, since the expectations depend on the coefficients of all the equations in the dynamic model of which this is a part. The Fisher method would not be practicable unless one were estimating all the equations of the model simultaneously, and even so it would have the major disadvantage of a large additional computational burden.

On Ball's main criticism, I would agree that it is usual to think of the type of wage equation that I have been estimating as a price-adjustment equation, and also that a more complete model of this type would treat unemployment as an endogenous variable. To do this would require an equation explaining the actual number employed, and the actual number retaining their names on the employment exchange registers. But can these be considered the same as the demand and supply of labour? In the body of the paper I give reasons for doubting this. In a situation where wages are largely determined by union bargaining it may be possible to formalise in terms of supply and demand but I think this approach is a little artificial. On the point that it seems unconvincing that an increase in productivity should cause a fall in wage rates: the equation concerned has a large positive trend, and the effect of productivity increases is to slow down this trend. I would still feel that this is a correct possibility, which corresponds to the usual suggestion that a cure for inflation would be a more rapid increase in productivity.

LESER Regarding the economic and policy implications, I feel that the extrapolation of the moving equilibrium equations is a little dangerous, and non-linearities in the equations, of the kind introduced by Verdoorn and Post (cf. p. 180), might be considered, e.g., before one comes near a 10 per cent increase in industrial output per head there may be considerable stresses and strains. Similarly, a doubling of unemployment would set up resistance.

The conclusions regarding the effect of devaluation one would assume to be true in the long run, but the dynamic analysis in the paper itself qualifies them. Moreover, import prices may not be exogenous for a large country like the United Kingdom but may depend on internal demand. Also, devaluation affects exports and may through this influence production, productivity and unemployment, so that other things do not remain equal. This is not a criticism of the model, but I feel that conclusions containing policy implications should be very carefully stated.

FISHER I would like to add to Durbin's remarks about iterative procedures and the use of high speed computers.

When most statistical calculations were performed by hand, statisticians sought to reduce the computational load of iteration by concentrating on (a) increasing the speed of convergence of a process, and (b) reducing the difficulty of computation at each iteration. An example of the former is R. A. Fisher's method of scoring where the information matrix is used in place of the matrix of second-order partial derivatives in the Newton–Raphson process. An example of the latter is the modification originally suggested by Finney and later emphasised by Aitchison and Silvey, namely the use of the first approximation of the information matrix in all iterations of the method of scoring. This eliminates the need to calculate a matrix inverse at each stage. The process converges in probability to the maximum-likelihood solution, provided the initial approximation is consistent. In practice, choice of the first approximation may sometimes be considerably different from the maximum-likelihood solution, and because of this, the process may become divergent. However, with the usual method of scoring, where a new information matrix is calculated at each stage, the process is convergent probably because each iteration is based on the most recent approximation. I have recently come across a case of this kind. In addition, the use of high speed computers tends to reduce the cost of matrix inversion and, hence, much of the advantage of the Aitchison–Silvey modification. Nevertheless, used in conjunction with the method of scoring, the Aitchison–Silvey modification may reduce the overall cost of computation in a similar way to that proposed by Hartley and mentioned by Durbin. The essential idea of this further modification (which has proved useful in my own work) is to use the method of scoring until a 'satisfactory' estimate of the information matrix is obtained, and then to use this approximation in all later steps. If $\mathbf{t}$ is the vector of parameters to be estimated and $\mathbf{t}^{(k)}$ is the kth approximation to the maximum-likelihood solution, then the method of scoring can be represented by

$$\mathbf{t}^{(k+1)} = \mathbf{t}^{(k)} + I_{(k)}^{-1} D_{(k)}$$

where $I_{(k)}$ is the information matrix evaluated at $\mathbf{t}^{(k)}$ and $D_{(k)}$ is the corresponding evaluation of the column vector of first-order partial derivatives of the log-likelihood function. This process is continued until, with two successive iterations,

$$\left| \mathbf{t}^{(k)} - \mathbf{t}^{(k-1)} \right| < \left| \mathbf{t}^{(k-1)} - \mathbf{t}^{(k-2)} \right|$$

holds. Thereafter, say for $m > k$, the following is used:

$$\mathbf{t}^{(m+1)} = \mathbf{t}^{(m)} + \mathbf{I}_{(k)}^{-1} \mathbf{D}_m.$$

Looking to the future, it is apparent that computers are becoming faster and more adaptable. This being so, it seems likely that modifications to the Newton–Raphson process and the method of scoring, such as Hartley's and the one just mentioned, will lead to only marginal improvements in the computational load. Evidently the advent of modern computers has reduced the need to look for modifications of existing iterative procedures which reduce the computational load at each step. The need now is for procedures with more satisfactory convergence properties.

SMYTH   I am still not clear on one point. Does the present procedure remove the asymptotic bias caused by the combination of lagged endogenous variables and autocorrelated errors? Even if it removes the large sample bias, is not the short sample bias (which is usually in the opposite direction to the large sample bias) still present? Monte Carlo studies (that I have undertaken) suggest that with ordinary least squares such short sample bias may be very important.

SARGENT   I have not come to insist that Sargan's maximisation procedures be subjected to the constraint that wages should not rise more than $3–3\frac{1}{2}$ per cent per annum. I am puzzled by the fact that, whereas in the price determination equations account is taken of the influence of wage drift as well as wage rates, there is no mention of wage drift in the equations explaining wage rates. I suspect that the system of relationships required to explain the movement of wage rates should include the influence of drift on rates, of rates on drift, of unemployment on rates and of unemployment on drift. The part played in this system by the level of unemployment might well be different from that which it appears to play in Sargan's wage rate equation. From my own (non-econometric) work on this, it appears that the rate of increase in the difference between hourly rates of wages and hourly earnings (a slightly different measure of drift than that usually adopted) is inclined to increase sharply as unemployment falls at the beginning of the boom, and gradually falls away as increases in wage rates take over the running in the later stages of the boom and the beginning of the recession. Thus there are periods of both positive and negative correlation between unemployment and drift. It might also be that, in a system which included drift, productivity would be seen to play a more important part, since opportunities for drift are often created by the fact that the growth of productivity in certain firms outstrips that in the rest.

ROY   There is an alarming statement in Section 7 about the ultimate effect of changes in indirect tax rates on wages and prices. If a 1 per cent increase in the tax variable, T, ultimately results in a 5 per cent rise in the wage and price level, is it fair to observe that a 5 or 6 per cent increase in indirect tax rates, as conventionally defined, is required to increase T by 1 per cent?

SARGAN   That is correct. In fact my 1 per cent change is a 1 per cent change in the rate of taxation on consumption goods, not a percentage change in the tax rate. It is defined in Section 6.

On Leser's point I agree that the 10 per cent per annum effect of productivity change that I suggest in (3.20) may be regarded as being extremely doubtful simply because the coefficient involved has a large standard error (about half its magnitude) so it is only just significant. A change within the range of the confidence interval that I associate with the coefficient would make a very big difference in that 10 per cent per annum. I was in fact rather surprised to find that I obtained a significant coefficient here. I do not think that these estimates give much guidance to what percentage change in the index of productivity is required to cure inflation. I admit also to overstating the devaluation result; it seemed an interesting result to put forward for discussion. Moreover I agree that imports and many other things ought to be treated as endogenous variables rather than exogenous variables. This simply means that one should build a larger model in order to draw any conclusions.

On the points made by Fisher and Smyth, I think Smyth's points in particular are most important. That is, I am assuming all the time that asymptotic sampling methods are adequate in this field. It is a question of whether the sample size is large enough and one can assume that k is small enough, i.e., that the biases are not important. I feel myself that this is probably the case, but I agree that it would be nice to have small sampling theory or Monte Carlo results to confirm this. I do not have them but I hope Durbin will be producing some soon.

On Sargent's point, that I ought to have given more emphasis on earnings in my models. I was intending to build a three equation model, in which one first of all explained wage rates, and then explained the wage drift, and then the price level. But when I came to look at the price equation, I tested to see whether in fact earnings was the appropriate variable to include in that equation and found that the coefficients were not significant except in one place, and certainly not in the general equations for prices. So it then seemed to be a convenient simplification to omit the wage drift factor since it did not seem an important explanation in changes of price. However, it seems that I ought to have included real earnings as well as real wage rates, in the wage equation and I did not try this. This is something that perhaps ought to be done in the future.

JOHANSEN   May I put a brief question on what I consider to be the main idea of this paper? You state the philosophy that 'to argue about the most appropriate form of equation to use, the only criterion is that the optimum form should have errors which are independent in different time periods'. Should not this philosophy lead you to argue about equation (1) in economic terms, and introduce additional variables and lags etc. there, until it becomes unnecessary to introduce an equation like equation (3), which is an equation between unobservable variables and therefore less accessible to economic interpretation?

SARGAN   There does seem to be an argument for using the transformed form of the equation, that is, the equivalent of equation (4) with no restrictions on its coefficients. But it seems to me reasonable to suppose that when you state a structural equation in what you think of as being its normal economic theory form, you could get autocorrelation of the errors. It is certainly possible that this kind of transformation, using the idea of the first order autoregressive equation, has got some *a priori* probability attached to it; this is what I feel, and therefore you do not necessarily have to assume that you are going to estimate the equation which has independent errors.

J. D. SARGAN

———— . ————

9 A MODEL OF WAGE-PRICE INFLATION

London School of Economics and Political Science

(First published in Review of Economic Studies (1980b), Vol. 47,
pp. 97–112.)

1 INTRODUCTION

This paper reports the results of estimating a simple three equations model
of wage–price inflation, where the endogenous variables to be explained
have been taken to be the index of retail prices, the index of weekly wage
rates, and the official average earnings index. These three variables were
chosen to be explained together, firstly to avoid the choice as to whether the
wage rates index or the average earnings variable should represent the
labour cost variable, and secondly to allow the alternatives of using hourly
wage rates, weekly wage rates, and the appropriately adjusted average
earnings for the various exogenous variables (such as overtime working) to
be resolved empirically. The price equation has been fully discussed already
in a previous paper (1976) and will only briefly be discussed here. The wage
and earnings equations were estimated by OLS, 2SLS and FIML methods
using an eclectic approach to previous explanations of these variables.

2 THE WAGE EQUATION

The form of the model estimated here is a development of that used by
Espasa (1973), but also explores some hypotheses suggested by Johnston
and Timbrell (1973) and Parkin *et al.* (1976). In the discussion of the wage
equation by Espasa he noted that the rate of change of the wage index could
be significantly related to the real wage rate (with intepretation as in Sargan
(1964)), but also to the ratio of average earnings to the wage rate index,
with a possible interpretation that if earnings are high compared with the
wage rate then activity is high, and also workers try to consolidate their
temporary prosperity by incorporating the higher level of earnings into the
basic wage rate. Alternatively the interaction between earnings and wage

rates can perhaps be regarded as an inadequate and aggregated representation of the battle of the differentials. Previous work has attempted to build disaggregated models of the labour market in which each occupational group of workers responds to differentials between their own wage level and those of other groups of workers, for example the work by Vernon reported in Sargan (1971). Each macro-variable can be regarded as a differently weighted aggregate of the underlying micro-wage-variables, and the dynamic models which are estimated for the macro-variables represents an empirical attempt to represent the complex dynamics of the micro-model. Following the previous work by Johnston and Timbrell (1973) it was decided to explore the use of the income tax retention rate as a variable in the wage equation. It was also decided following Parkin *et al.* (1972), (1976), to explore the use of expected rates of price inflation. The equations were initially estimated using single equation estimators, but were re-estimated by simultaneous equation system estimators. All the equations in this paper are in log linear form with the symbols representing the logarithms of the economic variables.

The most general form of wage equation used can be summarised as

$$\Delta w_t = \alpha_1(L)(w-p)_t + \alpha_2(L)(e-w)_t + \alpha_3(L)S_t$$

$$+ \alpha_4(L)U_t + \alpha_5 R_t + \alpha_6 \dot{p}_{et} + \alpha_7 t + \text{seasonals}$$

where all the variables (except t) are the logarithms of economic variables. w_t is the official weekly wage rates index, p_t is the index of retail prices, e_t is the average earnings index, S_t is a moving average of the working days lost in strikes in the previous three years, U_t is percentage unemployment (wholly unemployed), R_t is the average income tax retention ratio as defined by Johnston and Timbrell (1973), (I am grateful to Rod Apps of Manchester University for supplying me with a series for this over my sample period), $\dot{p}_{et}$ is a series for the expected rate of change of prices with various alternative assumptions as to suitable surrogate variables. The $\alpha_i(L)$ are various lag operator polynomials of relatively low order. The equation is intended to allow various alternative sets of variables to be tested as explanations of the rate of change of the wage rate index. The use of $(w-p)$ and $(e-w)$ as variables was suggested by my own previous work (1964) and that carried out by Espasa (1973). There are several justifications that can be presented for the appearance of the real wage $(w-p)$ variable. A quasi neo-classical justification suggested among others by Parkin *et al.* (1976) is that excess demand for labour depends on the real wage, and that the rate of change of the money wage depends upon the excess demand. This explanation is not entirely convincing, since it assumes that both the short term demand and supply of labour depend only on the real wage. Clearly some measure of effective demand should be included. In Sargan (1964) where unemployment played a significant part in the wage equation I suggested that the real wage variable might be regarded as adjusting the admittedly rather arbitrary official unemployment index to give a better index of excess demand. However here where empirically the standard unemployment variable has little effect an alternative approach through the theory of bilateral monopoly may make more sense. Clearly both sides in a wage bargaining procedure are concerned with the real wage. To try to model optimal strategies for the participants in a single industry is so difficult, particularly in view of the great uncertainties about the short term and long term effects of actual current wage bargains, that the short term adoption of rules of thumb by either side would not be surprising, which would then be modified rather arbitrarily in response to fairly recent experience. The $(e - w)$ variable has been discussed at the beginning of this section. The conventional earnings-drift equation is clearly rather arbitrary, and can be rejected empirically. A very general approach of the Samuelson disequilibrium model type would have the rate of change of all variables related to disequilibrium measures for each variable. The approach of this paper has been rather to start with a separate equation approach which however in each equation a rather general lag structure is formulated for the basic three variables (wages, prices, and average earnings) but introducing these variables in such a way to preserve the long period zero price homogeneity of the model. In this way it was intended only to introduce additional explanatory variables where their presence was really necessary. The risk, that in this single equation approach a misspecified set of equations would be obtained, is greatly reduced by carrying out final tests of misspecification on a set of full information maximum likelihood estimates. The use of the strike variable S_t was suggested by the work of Godfrey (1971) and Knight (1972). The actual variable used was determined empirically, after the results of using two other series had been compared. The primary reason for the three year average is to smooth out the randomness in the raw data, but if this raw data is contemplated over this sample period it is clear that there has been a great increase in working days lost towards the end of the sample period, and the long moving average gives a representation of this general change in the level of strike activity without reproducing the other random quarter to quarter activity. The sign of the observed coefficients confirms that the variable may be regarded as a surrogate for a measure of worker/trade union militancy (i.e. that employers are reluctantly agreeing to wage increases after strike activity). It would of course have been better to have a direct measure of worker attitudes but the author believes that this is a satisfactory indicator of an important element in the British experience. An alternative interpretation is that, in those periods where S_t had apparently its largest effect, certain important groups of workers (not always the same group) have considered that differentially their wage rate had fallen behind and that they were willing to strike to regain their own concept of an appropriate differential, and that in a high proportion of these cases the strike was successful. In any case it might be better to include an equation explaining the behaviour of the S_t variable, in the model, but given the long moving average in its definition from the point of view of prediction and estimation it is possible to treat S_t as a predetermined variable.

A further variable which requires discussion is s_t which represents the government series for standard hours. As discussed extensively in Sargan (1976) and as was to be expected on *a priori* grounds, the price equation contains only the hourly wage rates index. However in wage bargaining it seems likely that workers are interested in both weekly and hourly wage rates. A more complete model would have contained equations to explain both variables, and it is obviously necessary to check any equation estimated against simultaneous equation bias by using instrumental variable estimates treating both variables as endogenous variables. In so far as the model is of the disequilibrium type in which the logarithmic rate of change of the hourly wage rate and the logarithmic rate of change of standard hours are both determined by variables which can be regarded as predetermined (and which represent the extent to which wage rates and standard hours differ from their equilibrium values in the previous period) the estimated equations might be regarded as reduced form equations. It would be equally valid to write down a pair of reduced form equations for $(w_t - w_{t-1})$ and $(s_t - s_{t-1})$, or a pair of reduced form equations for $h_t - h_{t-1}$ and $s_t - s_{t-1}$, where h_t is the logarithm of hourly wage rates, and $h_t = w_t - s_t$. These reduced form equations can be estimated consistently by least squares if the errors are serially independent. Provided that no constraints are applied excluding particular variables selectively from either equation the weekly wage rate equation would be estimated by OLS as the sum of the two hourly rate and the standard hours equations. In theory the decision as to standard hours depends on factors both on the supply and demand side, and in practice there may be a fairly arbitrary and artificial element here, since there is no necessary tendency for standard hours and actual hours to move together, so that a decrease in standard hours may appear in collective bargaining as likely to increase average weekly earnings through an increase in overtime payments. Intuitively from the actual path of the standard hours variable during the sample, which had periods of relatively small change with only two major changes of level, and from *a priori* considerations about the importance of real weekly wage rates, it was decided to concentrate on the weekly wage rate, but introduce s_t, the standard hour variable, into the equation, and also $(s_t - s_{t-1})$ to consider whether a recursive explanation, with hourly wage rates independent of the rate of change of standard hours, could be accepted. (This would have been the case if $(s_t - s_{t-1})$ had the coefficient one in the equation with $(w_t - w_{t-1})$

as the dependent variable.) It was in fact decided that such a recursive explanation could be rejected empirically, and that an equation explaining the rate of change of weekly wage rates, without including the rate of change of standard hours, was the most satisfactory form for inclusion in a three equation wage–price inflation model.

Initial experimentation with the model was concerned with setting up a suitable lag structure for the basic variables, before testing whether the inclusion of additional variables was required. At this stage several alternative lag structures were estimated, and it was the case (as is frequently found) that alternative models in which the basic equation has a more complicated lag structure did equally well as models where the structural equation has a simpler dynamic structure and the error is explained by an autoregressive equation. Details of these estimates are presented in the earlier version of this paper Sargan (1977). An example of this type of estimate is given in Table I, equation 1, where α_1, α_2, α_3 are estimates of the coefficient of an autoregresive equation of the form $u_t = \alpha_1 u_{t-1} + \alpha_2 u_{t-2} + \alpha_3 u_{t-3} + \varepsilon_t$, where ε_t is a white noise series. Estimates by means of instrumental variables produced very similar estimates of these equations. This set of estimates was also used to consider the impact of public pressure (price and income policies) on a wage equation of this form, making use of a set of dummy variables, similar to those of Smith (1968) and also by using a Chow test dividing up the sample period into a policy-off and a policy-on period. The dummy variable results produced significant coefficients dummies of different signs for different periods of restraint when estimated by ordinary least squares but insignificant when estimated by using instrumental variables.

As an alternative approach equations 2, 3, 4 of Table I show a Chow-test comparison, where the policy-on periods are taken to be 1965.Q.1–1969.Q.4, and 1971.Q.4–1973.Q.4, and the policy-off period is the remainder of 1952.Q.1 to 1973.Q.4 based on Bispham (1975) and Parkin *et al.* (1972). The dynamic formulation of the equation was deliberately left rather unconstrained, so that, if, as was to be expected, the dynamics differed in policy-off and policy-on periods, the specification was sufficiently flexible for this to be estimated consistently. Clearly if we ignore the problem of the presence of lagged endogenous variables we can test for heteroskedasticity and change in coefficients by using F-ratio tests. The F-ratio for heteroskedasticity is 1.952 with degrees of freedom 15 and 45, with a corresponding 5 per cent confidence limit of 1.90. The Chow-test criterion is 1.936 with degrees of freedom 14 and 60, with a corresponding 5 per cent confidence limit of 1.89. Both criteria are nominally just significant at the 5 per cent limit, but in view of the dependence on the asymptotic approximation required by the presence of lagged endogenous variables; because of the possible presence of simultaneous equation bias; and finally

Table I

Equation no.	1	2	3	4	5	6	7
Estimation method	ALS	OLS	OLS	OLS	ALS	OLS	OLS
				Sample period			
Variable	1952.Q.1 −1973.Q.4	1952.Q.1 −1973.Q.4	Policy-off	Policy-on	1952.Q.1 −1973.Q.4	1952.Q.1 −1973.Q.4	1952.Q.1 −1973.Q.4
$(w-p)_{t-1}$	−0.219(2.76)	−0.205(1.73)	−0.153(1.34)	0.388(0.84)	−0.084(0.90)	−0.068(0.80)	−0.169(2.44)
$(w-p)_{t-2}$	—	−0.034(0.28)	−0.39(0.32)	−0.454(1.37)	0.034(0.35)	—	—
$(w-p)_{t-3}$	—	—	—	—	—	0.004(0.046)	−0.057(0.63)
$(e-w)_{t-1}$	0.216(2.48)	0.399(2.45)	0.609(3.15)	−0.362(0.99)	0.356(2.45)	0.220(2.93)	0.236(3.08)
$(e-w)_{t-2}$	—	−0.165(1.10)	−0.083(0.47)	0.285(0.62)	0.131(1.20)	—	—
$w_{t-1}-w_{t-2}$	—	0.437(3.10)	0.520(3.11)	−0.794(1.71)	—	0.115(1.07)	0.213(2.17)
$w_{t-2}-w_{t-3}$	—	—	—	—	—	−0.257(2.58)	−0.208(2.11)
S_{t-1}	0.021(4.17)	0.023(2.47)	0.018(1.84)	0.007(0.30)	0.021(2.67)	0.015(3.06)	0.022(5.79)
S_{t-2}	—	−0.002(0.19)	0.002(0.19)	0.008(0.35)	−0.008(0.92)	—	—
U_{t-1}	—	0.002(0.15)	0.015(0.12)	−0.028(0.90)	0.018(2.34)	—	—
U_{t-2}	—	0.002(0.21)	−0.003(0.28)	0.036(1.39)	—	—	—
s_t-s_{t-1}	—	—	—	−1.017(2.21)	—	—	—
R_t	0.0001(0.19)	0.0000(0.02)	−0.0013(1.26)	0.0002(0.081)	−0.007(0.07)	−0.383(3.94)	−0.226(5.97)
t	—	—	—	—	−0.0017(2.07)	−0.0015(1.33)	−0.0016(1.74)
α_1	0.587(4.96)	—	—	—	—	—	—
α_2	−0.365(2.93)	—	—	—	−0.420(3.61)	—	—
α_3	0.332(3.17)	—	—	—	—	—	—
S.D.	0.0072	0.0091	0.0075	0.0105	0.0078	0.0082	0.0084
D.W.	—	2.008	1.696	2.160	—	1.896	1.770
R^2/Crit	—	0.244	0.575	0.602	8.27	0.503	0.478
D.F.	—	74	45	15	12	77	78

Note: The numbers in brackets are the asymptotic *t*-ratios. *S.D.* is the usual estimate of the standard deviation of the error on the equation and *D.W.* is the Durbin–Watson statistic for the OLS estimates. For the OLS estimate the crude R^2 (uncorrected for degrees of freedom) is given. For the ALS estimates where only a single autoregressive coefficient is estimated the GIVE programme gives a criterion which is asymptotically distributed as a χ^2, which is based on the likelihood ratio test with a less constrained equation which includes all the lagged values of the variables in the equation and estimates by OLS. This is given as Crit. in the table for equation 5, where twice lagged variables are used, since only α_2 is assumed to be non-zero in estimating the equation.

because the different income policies do not seem to have been at all uniform in their effects, it is perhaps best to assume that the evidence for a significant effect is not adequate.

It seems a little premature to assume a regular or systematic development of the impact of incomes policy over time based on one or two cases where it seems to have occurred.

The estimates including the variable R_t are presented as equations 5, 6 and 7 of Table I. Equation 5 is an example of an equation containing the variable $s_t - s_{t-1}$. It illustrates the tendency of the sign of this variable to be negative (i.e. the opposite of the expected sign) when estimated by OLS. For this reason and because its coefficients became positive and insignificant when estimated by instrumental variables, in equations 6 and 7 this variable is omitted, and also U_{t-1} which was not found significant in later equations. Equation 6 is an example of an equation in which the coefficient of R_t is significant with the expected sign. It seems natural to assume that the effect of R_t is through the concept of the net real weekly wage rate after tax. Insofar as there is not a large gap between weekly earnings and the weekly wage rate both e_t and w_t will be reduced in the same proportion by taxes and the ratio of net earnings to net standard rates will be much the same before and after tax. On the other hand one should take account of the point raised by Johnston and Timbrell (1973) that the taxes paid by the worker may contribute to the social wage.

Suppose that we write that:

Total Real Wage = Net Real Private Wage + Real Social Wage,

Net Real Private Wage = (Gross Real Private Wage) × Retention Ratio,

Net Real Direct Tax Payment

$$= (1 - \text{Retention Ratio}) \text{ Gross Real Private Wage},$$

so that

log Total Real Wage

$$= \text{log Net Real Private Wage} + \log\left(1 + \frac{\text{Real Social Wage}}{\text{Net Private Wage}}\right)$$

$$= \text{log Gross Real Private Wage} + \log \text{Retention Ratio}$$

$$+ \log(1 + (e^{-R} - 1)\theta)$$

where R is the log of the retention ratio and θ is the proportion that the worker's real social wage bears to his real direct tax payments. So denoting the log gross real private wage rate by $(w - p)$ we have

$$\text{log Total Real Wage} = w - p + \log(\theta + (1 - \theta)e^R). \tag{1}$$

Now assuming that some constant proportion of direct taxes levied on the worker contributes to his social income, and that R is small this can be approximated by $w - p + (1-\theta)R$, with θ constant. Since $0 \leq \theta \leq 1$, this indicates that the coefficient of R should be less than the real wage and if R is not small then differentiation of the formula with respect to R gives a smaller marginal effect. Of course it is true that the assumption that θ is constant is crude, and that if θ varies systematically with R a different marginal coefficient will be obtained, but for small R the effect of varying θ is relatively small as can be seen by noting that the derivative of (1) with respect to R is

$$[(1-\theta) - (e^{-R} - 1)(\partial\theta/\partial R)]/(1 + (e^{-R} - 1)\theta).$$

Since $(e^{-R} - 1)$ is relatively small, even if $\partial\theta/\partial R$ is negative, so that the social wage falls as tax rates increase, the numerator will still most likely be less than one, and the denominator greater than one. It therefore seemed unikely that the coefficient of R should be greater than the coefficient of $w - p$, and it seemed worthwhile both to test the significance of the observed difference, and to obtain estimates subject to this inequality constraint. In fact for equation 6 the difference between the coefficient of R_t and of the sum of the coefficients of $(w - p)_{t-1}$ and $(w - p)_{t-3}$ is -0.319 and the asymptotic t-ratio is 2.033, which is just significant at the 5 per cent level. However in finite samples the 5 per cent is likely to be an underestimate of the true probability of rejection, and so equation 7 was estimate by constraining the sum of the coefficients of $(w - p)_{t-1}$ and $(w - p)_{t-3}$ to be equal to the coefficient of R_t. A second Chow-test for an equation of the form of equation 6 was carried out to test for differences in policy-on and policy-off coefficients using the same division of the sample as before. The details will not be reported since they were very similar to the earlier results.

3 SHORT SAMPLE WAGE EQUATION

As reported already, when an attempt was made to include a surrogate expected rate of change of prices variable in the previous equation with the previous data by using a long Almon distributed lag of rates of change of the price index the estimated weight distribution was implausible and the total coefficient was negative and insignificant. This might however be a result of non-linearity in the underlying formation of expectations relationship, or in the impact of expected price change on the wage determination equation. It seemed worth while to make use of the independent estimate of price expectations provided by Parkin and Carlson (1975). This gives a much shorter (52 observations) sample from 1961.Q.1 to 1973.Q.4. The variable represents the expected proportionate change of prices over the next year and was introduced without logarithmic transformations into equations of a form similar to those of the previous section with a one quarter lag (the variable is the expected percentage change/100).

It was found that if equations specifications similar to that of Table I were estimated with the short sample, with or without $\dot{p}_{et}$, all the t-ratios became relatively small and insignificant. This is illustrated by equation 8 of Table II, and equation 9 of Table II, where more variables are excluded. Equation 13 shows estimates where the sum of the coefficients on real income is equated to the coefficient of R_t. In none of these estimates were the coefficients of the trend and quarterly dummies significant, so that at this stage it was decided to omit these variables and the $(e-w)$ and $w_{t-1}-w_{t-2}$ variables. Equation 10 does not constrain the coefficient of $\dot{p}_{et}$, equation 11 sets it to 0.250, which is the value corresponding to the Phelps–Friedman natural rate of unemployment theory (1970), and equation 12 sets the coefficient to zero. This experiment indicates that R_t and $\dot{p}_{et}$ are substitutes in the explanation of $w_t - w_{t-1}$. If the coefficient of $\dot{p}_{et}$ is set to 0.250, the coefficient of R_t is not significant; if it is set to zero, the coefficient of R_t is significant (but not significantly different from the coefficient of $(w-p)_{t-3}$). In all these runs the coefficient of $\dot{p}_{et}$ was estimated in the range from 0.140 to 0.160 and in no case (even when the coefficient of R_t was put equal to zero) was it significantly different from zero. On the other hand in no case was it significantly different from 0.250, and the standard deviation of equation error was smaller for this coefficient equal to 0.250 than for the coefficient equal to zero. However it is clear that it is difficult to determine this coefficient with sufficient accuracy to throw light on the ultimate behaviour of the rate of inflation using single equation estimates.

4 THE EARNINGS EQUATION

The earnings equation can be regarded as a slightly more dynamic form of a wage drift equation. An important new variable in this equation is h_{rt}, which is the logarithm of the ratio of actual hours to standard hours in manufacturing. This variable was included after estimates including this variable and a separate variable for standard hours had shown that the corresponding coefficient was small and insignificant. The variable $U_{t-1} - U_{t-2}$ was included rather than U_{t-1} and U_{t-2} separately after it had been found that in the latter case the estimated coefficient of U_{t-2} was positive and significant, and that in the presence of $U_{t-1} - U_{t-2}$, the coefficient of U_{t-1} was small and insignificant. An attempt to discriminate between policy-on and policy-off periods by the use of dummies and by use of Chow-tests proved insignificant. The second form of the equation was estimated by instrumental variables because the equation contains $w_t - w_{t-1}$ which is a current endogenous variable. Judged by Box–Pierce

Table II. Short sample wage equations

Equation no.	8	9	10	11	12	13
	OLS	OLS	OLS*	OLS*	OLS*	OLS
Variable						
$(w-p)_{t-1}$	−0.058(0.283)	—	—	—	—	0.114(1.077)
$(w-p)_{t-2}$	−0.080(0.468)	—	—	—	—	—
$(w-p)_{t-3}$	—	−0.078(0.801)	−0.036(0.600)	−0.023(0.391)	−0.052(0.880)	−0.278(0.906)
$(e-w)_{t-1}$	0.111(0.577)	0.069(0.523)	—	—	—	0.077(0.719)
$(e-w)_{t-2}$	0.071(0.341)	—	—	—	—	—
$w_{t-1}-w_{t-2}$	−0.165(0.699)	−0.249(1.540)	−0.259(1.761)	−0.267(1.813)	—	−0.309(1.905)
$w_{t-2}-w_{t-3}$	—	0.014(1.889)	0.009(2.524)	0.010(2.797)	−0.248(1.666)	−0.305(2.124)
S_{t-1}	0.019(1.463)	—	—	—	0.008(2.244)	0.013(2.750)
S_{t-2}	0.003(0.203)	—	—	—	—	—
U_{t-1}	−0.001(0.071)	—	—	—	—	—
R_t	0.075(0.342)	−0.026(0.138)	−0.128(1.428)	−0.066(0.913)	−0.209(2.856)	−0.164(1.161)
$\dot{p}_{et}$	0.160(1.458)	0.141(1.408)	0.141(1.496)	0.250(0†)	—	0.143(1.713)
t	0.0002(0.138)	—	—	0.0002(0.278)	—	0.0001(0.154)
S.D.	0.0086	0.0083	0.0080	0.008α	0.0082	0.0084
D.W.	2.161	2.512	2.550	2.573	2.419	2.516
Crit/R^2	0.609	0.597	0.575		0.533	0.615
D.F.	36	39	44	45	45	38

Note: All these equations are estimated by OLS. The remaining details are explained in the note to Table I.

* Note that these equations contain no seasonal dummies.

† Note that the coefficient of $\dot{p}_e$ has been constrained to the value 0.250, in this column.

Table III. *Earnings equations*

Variable	OLS	IV	IV
$w_t - w_{t-1}$	0.566(7.757)	0.724(3.870)	0.222(1.889)
$w_{t-2} - w_{t-3}$	0.165(2.254)	—	—
$(e-w)_{t-1}$	−0.396(5.641)	−0.526(5.880)	−0.365(6.900)
$p_{t-1} - p_{t-2}$	−0.135(1.915)	−0.136(1.702)	−0.073(1.134)
hr_{t-1}	0.378(3.788)	0.563(4.357)	0.581(5.546)
S_{t-1}	−0.007(2.685)	−0.007(2.391)	—
$U_{t-1} - U_{t-2}$	−0.014(2.259)	—	−0.016(2.692)
t	0.0012(4.897)	0.0015(5.520)	0.0007(2.031)
I_{t-4}	—	—	0.463(5.018)
S.D.	0.0063	0.0067	0.0065
D.W.	1.99	1.75	1.87
R^2/Crit	0.705	—	—
D.F.	74	—	—

diagnostics the estimated errors on the equation were not serially correlated, and attempts to estimate by autoregressive least squares gave insignificant autoregressive coefficients. In later work with FIML estimates it was discovered that I_{t-4}, where I is the log of GNP at market prices divided by GNP at factor cost prices, was significantly correlated with the error on the earnings equation. Although no very plausible reason why this should be so has been suggested it was decided to re-estimate on this basis. The estimates are given in Table II, based on the sample 1952.Q.1– 1973.Q.4.

5 LONG SAMPLE FIML ESTIMATES

Having specified a model of three equations explaining prices, and the rate of change of wage rates and earnings it was decided to estimate this using full information maximum likelihood. The equation for prices is similar to that in the fifth column of Table 7 of Sargan (1976). A combined cost variable $c_t = w_t - s_t + 0.15m_t$ is defined, where w_t is the logarithm of the weekly wage rates index, s_t is standard hours, and m_t is the logarithm of the import prices index. The variable Ac_{2t} is defined as $\sum_{r=0}^{7} (8-r)^2 c_{t-r}$, a quadratic log-tailed seven quarter maximum lag Almon distributed lag. Then apart from two sets of seasonal dummy variables the price equation takes the form

$$p_t = 0.00292 Ac_{2t} + 0.517 I_{t-4} + 0.213 p_{t-1} - 0.0079 U_{t-1} - 0.0025t.$$

Note however that in the context of the simultaneous equation model Ac_{2t} is a current endogenous variable so that in order to estimate the model

Table IV. *FIML long sample estimates*

Variable	Price equation (standardised coefficient p_t)	
$w_t - w_{t-1}$	0.332(2.403)	0.314(2.252)
p_{t-1}	0.241(2.647)	0.234(2.555)
U_{t-1}	−0.008(2.327)	−0.008(2.380)
c_t^*	0.281(8.651)	0.284(8.781)
I_{t-4}	0.441(4.340)	0.450(4.476)
SD	0.007 13	0.007 24

	Wage equation (standardised coefficient $w_t - w_{t-1}$)	
$(e-w)_{t-1}$	0.225(3.010)	0.245(3.218)
$(w-p)_{t-1}$	−0.073(0.870)	−0.169(2.467)
$(w-p)_{t-3}$	−0.013(0.102)	−0.054(1.602)
$w_{t-1} - w_{t-2}$	0.122(1.144)	0.215(2.207)
$w_{t-2} - w_{t-3}$	−0.248(2.515)	−0.204(2.085)
S_{t-1}	0.015(3.136)	0.022(5.943)
R_t	−0?78(3.613)	−0.223(5.915)
SD	0.007 01	0.007 56

	Earnings equation (standardised coefficient $e_t - e_{t-1}$)	
$w_t - w_{t-1}$	0.340(2.926)	0.322(2.569)
$(e-w)_{t-1}$	−0.363(7.152)	−0.359(7.015)
$p_{t-1} - p_{t-2}$	−0.097(1.569)	−0.091(1.443)
hr_{t-1}	0.575(5.727)	0.565(5.550)
I_{t-4}	0.403(4.724)	0.45(4.771)
$U_{t-1} - U_{t-2}$	−0.014(2.626)	−0.014(2.602)
SD	0.005 51	0.005 78

Note: SD shows the standard deviation of the structural equation error.

it was necessary to define a new variable $c_t^* = 0.01 Ac_{2t} - 0.64(w_t - w_{t-1})$, which can be considered a predetermined variable, and then to include both c_t^* and $w_t - w_{t-1}$ in the price equation. No attempt was made in FIML estimation to constrain the ratio of the coefficients of the two variables to be 0.64, but it was clear that this constraint was reconcilable with the estimated coefficients. Table IV contains FIML estimates of the structural coefficients for the long sample (1951.Q.1 to 1973.Q.4), omitting the trend, constant and seasonal coefficients.

The LSE FIML programme allows extensive comparison between the restricted reduced form and the unrestricted OLS estimates of the reduced form, both by direct comparison of the estimated coefficients, but also by a comparison of the residuals on each set of equations within and outside the sample period. On all these criteria it was judged that the model estimated in the second column of Table IV was satisfactory. An overall test of the specification of the model is provided by the likelihood ratio criterion, comparing the value of the likelihood at the constrained optimum with the corresponding unconstrained optimum. For this model the criterion was 39.424, which is asymptotically distributed as a χ^2 with 30 degrees of freedom. The corresponding 5 per cent confidence limit is 43.8. However, on *a priori* grounds I would prefer that the coefficient of R_{t-1} is the same as the sum of the coefficients of $(w-p)_{t-1}$ and $(w-p)_{t-3}$. The asymptotic *t*-ratio for this hypothesis derived from these estimates is 2.052, which is marginally significant at the 5 per cent level. The third column gives the FIML estimates subject to this constraint. Again comparing the reduced forms the differences appear relatively trivial, but the likelihood ratio criterion is now 43.382 with a 5 per cent asymptotic confidence limit of 41.33. However, given the tendency for finite sample biases to be positive for such likelihood ratio criteria, it seems reasonable to accept the constraint.

6 SHORT SAMPLE FIML AND ARFIML ESTIMATES

With the long (up to 92 observations) sample it is not possible (without rewriting the existing programme) to use the ARFIML programme which allows full information maximum likelihood estimation with a single lag vector autoregressive stochastic process generating the errors (the lag can be chosen to be any number of unit time periods). With the shorter sample (up to 52 observations) it was possible to use this programme, and in view of the results of the single equation estimation of the wage equation it seemed particularly interesting to try the two period lag, but estimates were also made with a one period and four period lag. Since the various models with different lags are not nested, a standard significance test for discrimination is not available, and the four quarter likelihood is slightly larger than for the first order case, which is larger than the likelihood for the two quarter case. The ratios are too small to be near significance so that results are quoted for both the single quarter and four quarter lagged cases in Table V, and also for the ordinary FIML estimates.

For the ARFIML 1 case the autoregressive matrix is estimated as

$$R_1 = \begin{pmatrix} 0.929 & -0.633 & 0.189 \\ 0.307 & 0.065 & -0.610 \\ 0.131 & 0.128 & -0.401 \end{pmatrix}.$$

In this case the matrix is strongly significantly non-zero, and almost equally significantly non-diagonal. The autoregressive matrix for the four quarter

Table IV. *FIML and ARFIML estimates* (*short sample*)

Variable	Method of estimation FIML	ARFIML 1	ARFIML 4
	Price equation (standardised coefficient p_t)		
$w_t - w_{t-1}$	0.038(0.161)	−0.152(0.793)	0.180(0.970)
p_{t-1}	0.227(1.656)	−0.393(2.823)	0.439(3.522)
U_{t-1}	−0.007(1.524)	−0.002(0.216)	−0.008(1.980)
c_t^*	0.301(5.863)	0.458(9.006)	0.221(4.832)
I_{t-4}	0.597(3.968)	0.205(0.911)	0.512(3.319)
SD	0.007 25	0.006 12	0.004 86
	Wage equation (standardised coefficient $w_t - w_{t-1}$)		
$(e-w)_{t-1}$	0.102(1.043)	0.347(2.713)	0.086(0.932)
$(w-p)_{t-1}$	0.154(1.657)	0.228(2.510)	0.185(2.188)
$(w-p)_{t-3}$	−0.257(2.103)	−0.155(1.625)	−0.314(2.878)
$w_{t-1} - w_{t-2}$	−0.320(2.227)	−0.176(1.197)	−0.397(2.898)
$w_{t-2} - w_{t-3}$	−0.315(2.700)	−0.355(3.204)	−0.268(2.475)
S_{t-1}	0.015(3.376)	0.021(3.807)	0.014(3.292)
R_t	−0.103(0.834)	0.073(0.571)	−0.129(1.140)
$\dot{p}_{et}$	0.167(2.353)	0.258(3.695)	0.172(2.749)
SD	0.007 13	0.006 32	0.006 89
	Earnings equation (standardised coefficient $e_t - e_{t-1}$)		
$w_t - w_{t-1}$	0.024(0.116)	−0.042(0.254)	−0.150(0.662)
$(e-w)_{t-1}$	−0.438(6.057)	−0.404(6.004)	−0.459(6.468)
$p_{t-1} - p_{t-2}$	−0.304(3.150)	−0.292(2.990)	−0.456(3.492)
hr_{t-1}	0.479(4.190)	0.514(5.174)	0.495(4.245)
$w_{t-2} - w_{t-3}$	—	—	
I_{t-4}	0.335(2.534)	0.394(3.708)	0.466(3.396)
$U_{t-1} - U_{t-2}$	−0.012(1.524)	−0.020(2.987)	−0.014(1.872)
SD	0.007 31	0.006 38	0.006 99

Note: that for the ARFIML estimates *SD* is the standard deviation of the error on the autoregressive equation.

lagged case is estimated as:

$$R_4 = \begin{pmatrix} -0.075 & 0.578 & -0.292 \\ -0.234 & -0.110 & -0.137 \\ -0.070 & 0.024 & -0.292 \end{pmatrix}.$$

Of these elements the r_{12} and r_{13} are significantly different from zero. The R_4 matrix is asymptotically significantly different from zero at the 1 per cent level, and asymptotically significantly non-diagonal at just above the 5 per cent level. It is noticeable that the most marked improvement in prediction accuracy arises in the first equation, and that on the other hand the first order lag model produces relatively lower errors on the second and third equations.

7 ECONOMIC INTERPRETATION AND GENERAL COMMENTS

The equations of this model can lead to very different inflationary behaviour for relatively small changes in the estimated parameters. During the period of the sample the change from a fixed to a floating exchange rate has also affected the behaviour of the model. The model as it is estimated has sufficiently complicated dynamics that it seems worthwhile to present a simple version. For this we ignore the difference between earnings and wage rates, and ignore the lag in the price equation. These simplifications can be expected to change the short term dynamics and perhaps the short term stability, but not to affect the paths corresponding to steady rates of growth and long term dynamics. We then have the simple three equation model

$$p = \alpha_1 w + \alpha_2 m + \delta_1$$

$$\dot{w} = \beta_1 \dot{p}_e - \beta_2)(w - p) + \delta_2$$

$$\ddot{p}_e = \gamma(\dot{p} - \dot{p}_e).$$

Here the variables are as defined in the paper, except that the variables have been taken as in continuous time, and that $\dot{p}$ and $\dot{p}_e$ are time derivatives measured in the same units. The other variables in the model are treated as predetermined and absorbed into the constant terms δ_1 and δ_2. Consider first the case where m is also treated as predetermined, $\dot{w}$ satisfies an equation of the form

$$\ddot{w} + \gamma\dot{w} = (\beta_1\gamma\alpha_1 - \beta_2(1-\alpha_1))\dot{w} - \beta_2\gamma w(1-\alpha_1)$$
$$+ \alpha_2((\beta_1\gamma + \beta_2)\dot{m}) + \gamma\beta_2\alpha_2 m + \gamma\delta_2 + \beta_2\gamma\delta_1.$$

There is no difficulty in showing that the conditions $0 \leq \alpha_1 \leq 1$, $0 \leq \beta_1 \leq 1$, $\gamma \geq 0$, ensure stability, and that if $\beta_2 > 0$, $\gamma > 0$, $\alpha_1 < 1$, we have a long period equilibrium corresponding to

$$w = \alpha_2/(1-\alpha_1)[(\beta_1/\beta_2 + 1/\gamma)\dot{m} + m + (\delta_2/\beta_2 + \delta_1)/(1-\alpha_1)].$$

Clearly if $\alpha_2 + \alpha_1 = 0$, so that the price equation is first order homogeneous w is proportional to m in the long run, so that the economy achieves equilibrium by a favourable change in the terms of trade (with of course a consequent deterioration in the balance of payments). Even if $\beta_1 = 1$ the general long run behaviour is the same.

If however the important price becomes endogenous then the situation may be more complicated if we assume speculative effects. However a simple (but perhaps optimistic assumption) is that the government can stabilise the exchange rate and chooses to keep m in line with p. Again simplifying by ignoring time lags, we can write

$$m = p + \varepsilon.$$

The special case which is of most interest is that where $\alpha_2 + \alpha_1 = 1$. From the price equation we then have

$$p = w + (\delta_1 + \alpha_2 \varepsilon)/\alpha_1,$$

and then

$$\ddot{w} + \gamma \dot{w} = \beta_1 \gamma \dot{w} + \gamma(\delta_2 + \beta_2(\delta_1 + \alpha_2 \varepsilon)/\alpha_1).$$

Now if $\beta_1 < 1$, we have a Phillips curve relationship connecting $\dot{w}$ with the exogenous variables. However if $\beta_1 = 1$, then we have the natural rate of unemployment situation discussed, for example by Lucas (1972) that there is no steady rate of inflation corresponding to given levels of the exogenous variables.

These simplified models indicate how relatively small changes in the estimated coefficients may alter their long run properties. A fuller discussion of the dynamic behaviour and economic interpretation of these models will be made in a later paper. The estimated models have been found to verge on instability so that changes in exogenous variables may produce large fluctuations in the price level and the rate of change of price level.

The dynamics of the model are critically dependent on the actual coefficients, and if we modify the model to obtain 'rationality' assuming that the estimated non-rationality is due to misspecification, estimation bias, aggregation bias, etc. the resulting dynamic behaviour may be considerably changed. Similarly long run trade-offs will be sensitive to such adjustments. On the other hand, if essentially we are interested in the existence of policies (translated into values of exogenous variables) which will lead to appropriate behaviour over time in the variables (which will be here interpreted to mean constant rates of price inflation) then it is found that our values for the trade-off between different instruments, corresponding to a given rate of inflation are relatively insensitive to such changes in the coefficients of the models. Results of this type will be the only economic characteristic of the model discussed here.

Taking first the model corresponding to the last column of Table IV the price equation was considered in two forms which can be written:

$$p_t = 0.132(w_t - w_{t-1}) + 0.00284 \sum_{j=0}^{7} (8-j)^2 c_{t-j} - 0.008 U_{t-1}$$

$$+ 0.450 I_{t-4} + 0.234 p_{t-1} - 1.7128 - 0.0024t$$

or

$$p_t = 0.132(w_t - w_{t-1}) + 0.00284 \sum_{j=0}^{7} (8-j)^2 c_{t-j} - 0.008 U_{t-1}$$

$$+ 0.666 I_{t-4} + 0.334 p_{t-1} - 3.2736 - 0.0044t,$$

where

$$c_t = w_t - s_t + 0.15 m_t.$$

The second form of the equation is homogeneous in prices, and assumes indirect taxes have a proportional impact on prices, and the constant term and trend have been adjusted so that it predicts unbiasedly over the average of the last year of the sample (1973). The wage equation was:

$$w_t - w_{t-1} = 0.245(e-w)_{t-1} - 0.169(w-p)_{t-1}$$

$$- 0.054(w-p)_{t-3} + 0.215(w_{t-1} - w_{t-2})$$

$$- 0.204(w_{t-2} - w_{t-3}) + 0.0225 S_{t-1} - 0.0565 + 0.0002t.$$

The earnings equation was

$$e_t - e_{t-1} = 0.322(w_t - w_{t-1}) - 0.359(e-w)_{t-1} - 0.091(p_{t-1} - p_{t-2})$$

$$+ 0.56 hr_{t-1} + 0.405 I_{t-4} - 0.014(U_{t-1} - U_{t-2}) - 1.8488 + 0.0007t.$$

All three equations are quoted with the average of the four seasonal constant terms. In the 'rational' form of the model since there seemed no reasonable explanations of why the level of the earnings/wage rates should depend on the level of indirect taxes it was assumed that $0.405 I_{t-1}$ was omitted from the earnings equation and the constant on the equation increased to 0.0183. It was decided to consider the values of once for all changes in the exogenous variables from standard paths which are linear trends related to the existing trends at the end of the sample period, and to attempt to track a price path which starts at a level at the end of the sample period which is close to the actual value, and which had an acceptable trend value. Rather than considering a rate of unemployment (or other exogenous variables) which corresponded to price stability it was decided to consider an 8 per cent annual price inflation. The corresponding target path was taken as

$$p_t = 5.65 + 0.02t$$

where t is measured from 0.1974.Q.1, and the standard paths for the other variables were taken as

$$s_t = -0.059 - 0.0005t,$$

$$U_t = 5.50,$$

$$I_t = 4.61,$$

$$R_t = -0.20 - 0.003t,$$

$$hr_t = 0.08.$$

The variable S_t, which is regarded as a surrogate worker or trade union aggression variable, was considered to satisfy $S_t = 6.70 + \delta t$, where δ was either zero, 0.05 or 0.08. The latter value was taken as corresponding to the rate of change of the variable over the last three years of the sample, when strike levels had been increasing. The former value was taken as corresponding to an alternative regime in which the strikes variables was stabilised. The middle value was in fact chosen to ensure that prices had the desired growth rate.

We also consider two alternative import price assumptions. In the first $m_t = 5.55 + 0.015t$, again corresponding to the trend in m_t towards the end of 1973. In the second we write $m_t = p_t - 0.10$. Here the assumption is made that the government is holding import prices in fixed ratio to consumer prices by varying the floating exchange rate. Clearly the equation is not at all realistic, but it seems quite a reasonable case to explore when what is under discussion is the level of exogenous variables which correspond to steady trend behaviour of the endogenous variables. The procedure followed was to substitute the standard values of the exogenous variables into the equations and to introduce arbitrary shift variables δ_i into the constant of the ith equation, $i = 1, 2, 3$. Now solving the price equation for $w_t = \alpha + \beta t$, given the assumed variation of p_t we find easily that if m_t follows the exogenous path and the non-homogeneous form of the price equation is used, the path of the wage variable is

$$w_t = 6.122 - 1.72\delta_1 + 0.0278t.$$

Treating the earnings equation in the same way and solving $(e - w)_t = \alpha + \beta t$ we find easily that

$$e_t = 6.416 + 2.78\delta_3 - 1.72\delta_1 + 0.0297t.$$

Now substituting this into the wage equation we obtain

$$-0.0357 = \delta_2 + 0.682\delta_3 + 0.385\delta_1$$

$$= 0.033\Delta m + 0.484\Delta I - 0.223\Delta R + 0.382\Delta hr - 0.003\Delta U.$$

The $\Delta m, \Delta I, \Delta R, \Delta hr$, represent shifts in the exogenous variables m, I, R, hr from their standard values required to ensure that the price equation follows its standard trend line. If we now consider the required shift in each exogenous variable if the other exogenous variable shifts are put to zero we obtain:

$$-\Delta m = -1.08, \qquad \Delta I = -0.074,$$
$$\Delta R = 0.160, \qquad \Delta hr = -0.093, \qquad \Delta U = 11.$$

The last coefficient is rather unrealistic since it neglects the correlation between different variables correlated with effective demand and it seemed more realistic to consider the indirect effects of unemployment on wage inflation by means of the change in the ratio of average hours worked to normal hours. This is not an easy relationship to quantify, particularly given the recognised difficulties caused by the apparent shift in the relationship between unemployment and the general level of activity in recent years, and the tendency for unemployment to lag cyclically behind the average hours variable. A suitable static form of equation, is

$$U^* = 50.77 - 0.5(Ah) - 0.0025t$$

where U^* is the percentage unemployed, Ah is average hours per operative in manufacturing industry, expressed as an index number which equals 100 for the average of 1962. Thus a proprtionate reduction in (hr) of 9.3 per cent, assuming that this occurs through a proportionate change of Ah (i.e. an absolute reduction of 9 points) would require an increase in the unemployment percentage of 4.5 per cent, i.e. to a level of 7.1 per cent. The model suggests a required fall of import prices (obtained perhaps by manipulating the exchange rate – which does not seem at all practical given the constraints on such changes imposed by the necessity to safeguard the balance of payments. The required ΔI seems a more reasonable possibility, although it should be noted that from the definition of I, the changed required is a fall of 8.5 per cent in the average *ad valorem* tax rate. Note that the apparent change in the average direct tax rate is much larger. Since the retention ratio was standing at about 0.80 towards the end of the sample period, the required change is that it should rise to 0.93. Of course a combined change in all these variables seems a more reasonable possibility, or alternatively the successful negotiation of an incomes policy, although the evidence from the sample is not encouraging on past attempts at this.

Turning now to the short sample results and considering only those generated by the four quarter lag autoregressive equation, the three equations with the average of the year constant terms can be written (where since the price equation is very close to homogeneity, its coefficients have been adjusted to give exact homogeneity):

$$p_t = 0.00225 \sum_{j=0}^{7} (8-j)^3 c_{t-j} - 0.0078 U_{t-1} + 0.5273 I_{t-4}$$

$$+ 0.439 p_{t-1} - 2.5627 - 0.0030t,$$

$$w_t - w_{t-1} = -0.397(w_{t-1} - w_{t-2}) - 0.2681(w_{t-2} - w_{t-3}) + 0.0836(e_{t-1} - w_{t-1}),$$

$$+ 0.01365 S_{t-1} + 0.1833(w_{t-1} - p_{t-1})$$

$$- 0.3142(w_{t-3} - p_{t-3}) - 0.1289 R_t + 0.172 \dot{p}_{et} - 0.1058 - 0.0004t,$$

$$e_t - e_{t-1} = -0.1501(w_t - w_{t-1}) + 0.4660 I_{t-4} + 0.4951 hr_{t-1}$$

$$- 0.4595(e_{t-1} - w_{t-1}) - 0.4556(p_{t-1} - p_{t-2})$$

$$- 0.0138(U_{t-1} - U_{t-2}) - 2.0096 + 0.0013t.$$

As before t is measured with 1974.Q.1 as origin. The necessary changes in the exogenous variables required to achieve standard trend paths was considered as before, except that corresponding to the price trend coefficient of 2 per cent per quarter it was assumed the $\dot{p}_{et}$ (which is defined as an expected annual price change) was set at 0.08.

As before from the price equation the corresponding wage trend was found to be

$$w_t = 6.125 - 2.179\delta_1 + 0.0267t.$$

The earnings equation then led to a trend on earnings of

$$e_t = 6.424 - 2.179\delta_1 + 2.176\delta_2 + 0.0295t.$$

These results are closely comparable to the corresponding results for the long sample model. However, when these are substituted into the wage equation a very different result is achieved. The equation gives:

$$0.0518 = 0.281\delta_1 + \delta_2 + 0.186\delta_3.$$

This indicates that to obtain the steady trend path some relaxation is appropriate. This results should not perhaps be taken very seriously, since sampling errors make it unreliable. Note for example that the standard error of the constant term on the wage equation is 0.033. But a comparison of the results for the long sample and the short sample shows that even for comparisons such as these, which can be expected to be relatively robust to changes in lag specification provided the chosen paths are not too far from the range of variation of the variables in the sample period, the choice of sample and exact form of model specification has a marked effect on the outcome. As our previous estimates based on policy-on/policy-off subsamples confirmed the price and earnings equations are relatively constant over time, but the wage equation is more variable and less easy to specify in a relatively unchanging form.†

REFERENCES

Bispham, J. A. (1975), 'The new Cambridge and monetarist criticisms of "conventional" economic policy making', *National Institute Economic Review No. 74*, 39–57.

Espasa, A. (1973), 'A simultaneous dynamic equation model for wages, earnings and price inflation in the United Kingdom 1949–1970' (Paper presented at the European Econometric Society Meetings, Oslo).

Godfrey, L. (1971), 'The Phillips curve: income policy and trade union effects' in Johnson, H. G. and Nobay, A. R. (eds.) *The Current Inflation* (London: Macmillan).

Johnston, J. and Timbrell, M. (1973), 'Empirical tests of a bargaining theory of wage rate determination', *Manchester School*, **41**, 141–67.

Knight, K. G. (1972), 'Strikes and wage inflation in British manufacturing industry 1950–1968', *Oxford Bulletin*, **37**, 281–94.

Lucas, R. E. (1972), 'Testing the Natural Rate Hypothesis' in Eckstein, O. (ed.), *The Econometrics of Price Determination* (Federal Reserve System, Washington).

Parkin, M., Sumner, M. T. and Jones, R. A. (1972), 'A survey of the econometric evidence on the effects of income policy on the rate of inflation', in Parkin, M. and Sumner, M. T. (eds.), *Incomes Policy and Inflation* (Manchester University Press).

Parkin, M., Sumner, M. and Ward, R. (1976), 'The effects of excess demand, generalized expectations and wage price controls on wage inflation in the UK: 1956–71', in Brunner, K. and Meltzer, A. H. (eds.), *The Economics of Price and Wage Controls* (Norht Holland).

Parkin, M. and Carlson, J. A. (1975), 'Inflation expectations', *Economica*, **42**, 123–38.

Phelps, E. S. (1970), 'Money wage dynamics and labor market equilibrium', in Phelps, E. S. (ed.), *Microeconomic Foundations of Employment and Inflation Theory* (New York: Macmillan).

Sargan, J. D. (1964), 'Wages and prices in the UK' in Hart, P. E., Mills, G. and Whittaker, J. K. (eds.), *Econometric Analysis for National Economic Planning* (London: Butterworth).

Sargan, J. D. (1976), 'The consumer price equation in the post war British economy' (LSE Econometrics Programme Discussion Paper No. A11).

Sargan, J. D. (1977), 'A model of wage price inflation' (LSE Econometrics Programme Discussion Paper No. A15).

Sargan, J. D. (1971), 'A study of wages and prices in the U.K. 1949–68', in Johnson, H. G. and Nobay, A. R. (eds.), *The Current Inflation* (London: Macmillan).

Smith, D. C. (1968), 'Incomes policy' in Caves, R. E. (ed.), *Britain's Economic Prospects* (London: George Allen and Unwin).

† The researches reported here were financed by a grant for the SSRC to the SEPDEM programme. I am grateful to J. D. Sylwestrowicz for his research and computer programming assistance and to the other participants in this programme for their comments.

J. D. SARGAN†

——— . ———

10 SOME TESTS OF DYNAMIC SPECIFICATION
FOR A SINGLE EQUATION

(First published in *Econometrica* (May, 1980), Vol. 48, No. 4.)

This paper discusses the constraints on a dynamic equation represented by the possibility of factoring out an autoregressive error specification from a general lag structure. A suitable Wald test is defined and applied to a practical case.

1 INTRODUCTION

This paper explores a problem which has not been considered very systematically in the econometric literature since the publication of [8]. An earlier version of this paper [12] discusses the simultaneous equation version of this problem. In a single equation context the problem is defined by considering a structural equation which can be written

$$\alpha'(L)x_t = u_t \qquad (1)$$

where x_t, $t = 1, \ldots, T$, is an $n \times 1$ vector of economic variables in period t, and u_t is the scalar error on the structural equation, $\alpha(L)$ is an $n \times 1$ vector of polynomials in the lag operator L, and u_t is generated by a scalar ARMA equation of the form

$$\rho(L)u_t = s(L)\varepsilon_t \qquad (2)$$

where ε_t is white noise.

Eliminating u_t we obtain a combined equation,

$$\rho(L)\alpha'(L)x_t = s(L)\varepsilon_t. \qquad (3)$$

We can alternatively write the equations in the form

$$\psi'(L)x_t = s(L)\varepsilon_t \qquad (4)$$

† I am grateful to the S.S.R.C. for providing a grant for project SEPDEM which financed this work, to J. D. Sylwestrowicz who was responsible for all computer aspects of this work, and to my colleagues, particularly D. Hendry and G. Mizon, for their advice.

where

$$\psi(L) = \rho(L)\alpha(L).$$

It may often be the case that we wish to explore the possibility that the errors on a structural equation are ARMA in form, as modelled in the equation (2). If we ignore the implicit constraints on the coefficients of $\psi(L)$ which follow from $\psi(L) = \rho(L)\alpha(L)$, we still retain a valid stochastic model, but (i) the estimates of α and ρ will be relatively inefficient, (ii) the dynamic structure of $\psi(L)$ will be unnecessarily complicated compared with $\alpha(L)$, and (iii) prior constraints on $\alpha(L)$ when applied to $\psi(L)$ may yield inconsistent estimates.

A traditional approach to estimating the model defined by (3) would be to estimate (1) with errors generated by a relatively simple stochastic process of type (2), possibly using such estimates to test various restrictions on the equation (1). Then tests would be made for the adequacy of the formulation (2), and so on. Although there is no doubt that in sufficiently large samples, by using a sufficiently general model, suitable diagnostic tests can be used to test the adequacy of the specification, e.g. those of the Box–Pierce type [6] which test for the lack of serial correlation of the estimated ε_t, and for the independence of ε_t and the exogenous variables in the system (for a general disussion of this type of test see my [9]), in finite samples it seems very possible that difficulties will arise in determining the lag structure of both the ARMA equations and the structural equations. In practice it is found that additional lags in the autoregressive specification may appear to be a substitute for additional lags in the structural equation, in the sense that models are often found to be acceptable when subject to diagnostic tests if the degree of $\rho(L)\alpha(L)$ is a certain value, and unacceptable if the degree is reduced by decreasing either the degree of $\rho(L)$ or the degree of $\alpha(L)$. This is not surprising when it is realised that the basic model that is being considered is (4), and that the decision that is required to move from (4) to a specification of the form (1) and (2), depends upon the acceptability of various implicit constraints, together with the *a priori* constraints suggested by economic considerations. It would seem appropriate to formulate the model explicitly in terms of (4) and the implicit constraints on (4) and to use a nested set of Wald tests so that a whole sequence of tests can be made of alternative forms of the model using a single set of relatively simple estimators for an unconstrained set of equations such as (4). For example, if the equation (1) contains only one endogenous variable, then it is permissible to estimate (4) using a standard ARMA with exogenous variables computing program, and if we accept the special assumption that the errors in (1) are generated by a simple autoregressive process, so that $s(L) = 1$, we can estimate (4) by OLS.

A practical limitation on this procedure is caused by the loss of degrees of freedom which follows if (4) is estimated unconstrainedly with a medium sized number of variables and a large number of lags. For example, if equation (4) contained six variables, each with lags of up to six periods, together with three seasonals and a constant term, then it would contain 40 variables (lagged and non-lagged). Given the biases that result in estimating time series models when a large number of variables are used, it would be prudent not to estimate such an equation with less than 100 observations. Indeed, Monte Carlo studies, and the use of Nagar approximations to the bias of such estimators show that the bias depends very much on the parameters of the model but the rule of thumb that the sample size should be greater than $2\frac{1}{2}$ times the number of variables leads to tolerable biases if the latent roots of the system are not too close to the unit circle.

Of course having started with a $\psi(L)$ and $s(L)$ with the maximum lags which are judged to be estimable using this type of rule of thumb, it would then be possible to reduce the degrees of $\psi(L)$ and $s(L)$ by using asymptotic significance tests of the likelihood ratio or Wald type. If this were done in the case of $\psi(L)$, it might become more difficult to accept a factorisation of the type $\psi(L) = \rho(L)\alpha(L)$, and a preferable alternative is to first factorise if possible, and then to consider reducing the maximum lags on both $\rho(L)$ and $\alpha(L)$, taking account of the economic constraints on $\alpha(L)$.

Given this general background and given the advantages of the Wald tests [11] in ease of computation, particularly in avoiding repeated maximisation of complicated non-linear likelihood functions, it seems worthwhile to try the Wald tests by writing suitable computer programs for the relevant criteria.

2 SEQUENCES OF WALD CRITERIA

An advantage of Wald criteria is that they are rather flexible, in that they can be defined in terms of any set of estimators, not merely in terms of maximum likelihood estimators as shown by Stroud [13], and the asymptotic distribution of such criteria depends only on local properties of the constraint functions. The asymptotic power of the Wald test depends on the efficiency of the estimators used, but asymptotically efficient estimators, such as maximum likelihood estimators, give tests equivalent to likelihood ratio tests. Let us suppose then that we have a model defined in terms of P parameters forming a vector θ, and that $\hat{\theta}$ is some consistent and asymptotically normally distributed estimate of θ such that $\sqrt{T}(\hat{\theta} - \theta)$ has a variance matrix which can be consistently estimated by $\hat{\Omega}_\theta$. We then consider some general set of p constraints which form a vector of functions

$$\phi(\theta) = 0. \tag{5}$$

The denoting the first derivative matrix at $\hat{\theta}$ by $\partial\phi/\partial\theta'$ and defining

$$\hat{\Omega}_\phi = \left(\frac{\partial\phi}{\partial\theta'}\right)\hat{\Omega}_\theta\left(\frac{\partial\phi}{\partial\theta'}\right)',$$

the Wald criterion for testing the complete set of restrictions is

$$w = T\phi(\hat{\theta})'(\hat{\Omega}_\phi^{-1})\phi(\hat{\theta}), \tag{6}$$

and, on the null hypothesis presented above including the assumptions that all the constraints (1) are satisfied, w is distributed asymptotically as a χ^2 with p degrees of freedom, provided that the plim $\hat{\Omega}_\phi$ is non-singular and that $\partial\phi/\partial\theta'$ is a continuous function of θ at the true population point.

Suppose we now consider some set of constraints $\phi_1(\theta) = 0$ forming the first p_1 constraints of the set (5) and the corresponding w_1 defined by taking

$$\Omega_1 = \frac{\partial\phi_1}{\partial\theta'}\hat{\Omega}_\theta\left(\frac{\partial\phi_1}{\partial\theta'}\right)'$$

and

$$w_1 = T\phi_1(\hat{\theta})'\Omega_1^{-1}\phi_1(\hat{\theta}).$$

w_1 is asymptotically distributed as a χ^2 with p_1 degrees of freedom, but by regarding $w - w_1$ as a quadratic in $\sqrt{T}\phi(\hat{\theta})$ which is asymptotically distributed $N(0, \text{plim }\hat{\Omega}_\phi)$ we can show that $w - w_1$ is asymptotically distributed as a χ^2 with $p - p_1$ degrees of freedom independent of w_1.

Now suppose that there is some natural ordering of our set of hypotheses so that we should not wish to accept the rth restriction $\phi_r(\theta) = 0$, if we had previously rejected the restriction $\phi_{r+1}(\theta) = 0$, i.e., we consider the sequential set of hypotheses of the form

$$[\phi_s(\theta) = 0, \text{ all } s \text{ such that } p \geqslant s \geqslant r] \tag{7}$$

for each r, but would not consider

$$[\phi_s(\theta) = 0, \text{ for all } s \in S],$$

for some S a general set of integers $\leqslant p$. Denote the set of restrictions of the form (7) for given r by $\phi^{(r)}(\theta) = 0$ and the corresponding w by $w(r)$. Suppose we consider two sets $r_1 > r_2$.

Then we can show that $w(r_1)$, $w(r_2) - w(r_1)$, $w - w(r_2)$ are asymptotically distributed as independent χ^2,s with degrees of freedom $p - r_1 + 1$, $r_1 - r_2$ and $r_2 - 1$, respectively. In particular if $r_1 = r$, $r_2 = r - 1$, we can write

$$\Omega_\theta^{(r_2)} = \begin{pmatrix} \Omega_\theta^{(r)} & \omega_1 \\ \omega_1' & \omega_{11} \end{pmatrix}$$

and

$$\phi^{(r_2)} = \begin{pmatrix} \phi^{(r)} \\ \phi_{r_2} \end{pmatrix},$$

and then

$$w(r-1) = \phi^{(r_2)'}(\Omega_\theta^{(r_2)})^{-1}\phi^{(r_2)}$$

$$= \phi^{(r)'}(\Omega_\phi^{(r)})^{-1}\phi^{(r)} - \frac{(\phi_{r_2} - \phi^{(r)'}(\Omega_\phi^{(r)})^{-1}\omega_1)^2}{(\omega_{11} - \omega_1(\Omega_\phi^{(r)})^{-1}\omega_1)}.$$

Thus $w(r-1) - w(r) = t_{(r-1)}^2$ where

$$t_{(r-1)} = (\phi_{r_2} - \phi^{(r)'}(\Omega_\phi^{(r)})^{-1}\omega_1)/\sqrt{[(\omega_{11} - \omega_1'(\Omega_\phi^{(r)})^{-1}\omega_1]}$$

and there is no difficulty in showing that all the t_r, $r = 1, \ldots, p$, are asymptotically identically and independently $N(0, 1)$. Also the asymptotic distribution of t depends upon the validity of $\phi_2(\theta) = 0$, $s \geq r$, but not upon the truth of the restriction for $s < r$. This is asymptotically equivalent to the multiple regression case considered in Section (3.2) of Anderson's 'Statistical analysis of time series' [1]. One can introduce a uniform t ratio limit t^*, such that if $\varepsilon = P(|t| > t^*)$ is obtained from the unit variance normal distribution then $(1 - \varepsilon)^p = 0.95$, to ensure that the probability of accepting the overall null hypothesis that $\phi(\theta) = 0$, when this is true, is held at more than 0.95 asymptotically. As discussed by Anderson, it is also possible to allow the *t ratio limit to vary with* r. It might also be appropriate in some cases, as discussed below Section 4, to consider only a restricted set of r values.

The assumption that there is a natural ordering of the constraints is somewhat limiting, but in practice we can set up Bonferroni type inequalities which ensure that we bound the probability of errors of the first kind as discussed in [3]. However, this leads to an increase in the recommended critical t ratio, and so to an increase in the probability in errors of the second type. Thus a more decision theoretic approach might be preferable.

3 THE WALD CRITERIA FOR THE SINGLE EQUATION CASE

The testing problem which is to be considered is that of choosing the order of the autoregressive equation explaining the errors on a single structural equation which itself contains lagged variables. We can consider this with a very general choice of estimators. Thus the structural equation can contain more than one endogenous variable, provided it is estimated by some consistent estimator which is asymptotically normally distributed and whose asymptotic variance matrix can be consistently estimated, e.g. by using suitable instrumental variables.

In the context of estimating equations with the form of (3) and (4), consider the following general procedure. We wish to start with as unconstrained a specification as possible, so as to apply a sequence of Wald tests for various hypotheses about the degree of the polynomials $\rho(L)$ and $\alpha(L)$. The obvious convenient method is to start from an unconstrained estimate of (4). We can use the usual technique for deciding what degree the $\psi(L)$ polynomials should have, depending on the use of t ratios or F ratios. Thus it might be decided to test each of the polynomial $\psi_j(L)$ separately where $\psi_j(L)$ is the jth component of $\psi(L)$ and allow the degree of the polynomial to be determined by separate t ratio tests. Alternatively it might be imposed that all the $\psi_j(L)$ should have the same degree, in which case the joint degree could be established by the use of F tests. Since it is proposed to discriminate between models with different degrees of the polynomials $\rho(L)$ assuming that the $\psi_j(L)$ have fixed degrees, this preliminary testing of the degree of the $\psi_j(L)$ leads to a superimposition of two sets of tests, and it may be better to simply set the degree of all the $\psi_j(L)$ equal to a level determined rather arbitrarily to ensure that the asymptotic tests do not lose validity through the loss of degrees of freedom. The author has some work in progress on approximating the finite sample distributions of this type of criterion which he hopes will throw light on this problem. But for the present a rule of thumb saying that if R is the maximum lag in $\phi(L)$ then $(R+1)n < 0.4T$ is suggested. Note that if instrumental variable estimation is used we could presumably make use of up to Rth order lagged values of some set of instrumental variables of number greater than n, subject to a similar restriction on the total number. It would certainly be of some interest to analyse and perhaps make a simulation study of the consequences of pretesting in this way, but this will not be attempted here.

If pretesting is carried out, it would be necessary to fix a lower non-zero bound for the degree of the $\psi_j(L)$, equal to the degree of the polynomial $\rho(L)$ for which we wish to be able to make appropriate tests. Thus with quarterly data and adequate sample size one would always wish to be able to test for a common factor polynomial $\rho(L)$ of degree four, to allow for an autoregressive seasonal effect. In this case only the coefficients of lag greater than four would be tested for significance in pretesting the initial estimates of the $\psi_j(L)$. If, in addition, the economic model postulated lags on particular variables in the structural equation, these extra lags should not be prevented. In any case the next set of tests, which have been named tests of dynamic specification by Mizon [6], will be carried out holding constant the set of maximum lags in the $\psi_j(L)$, and we consider the general case where the maximum lag depends upon j.

In Appendix B conditions that a set of polynomials $\psi_j(z)$ of degree f_j, $j = 1, \ldots, n$, should possess as common factor a polynomial $\rho(z)$ of degree r are proved. We assume that the polynomials are ordered so that

$f = f_1 \geqslant f_2 \geqslant \cdots \geqslant f_{n-1} \geqslant f_n$. We assume that $\rho(z) = 1 + \sum_{k=1}^{r} \rho_k z^k$, and $\psi_j(z) = \sum_{k=0}^{f_j} \psi_{jk} z^k$. Then we assume that for some j, $\psi_{j0} = 1$, corresponding to the standardised coefficient in the unconstrained equation. Now by counting the total number of parameters in (1) and (2) compared with the number of parameters in an unconstrained version of (4) we see that the number of implicit constraints must be $r(n-1)$.

The required constraints can be expressed by stating that a certain matrix whose elements are equal to the coefficients ψ_{jk} or zero should have a given rank. To make this statement operational it must be translated into equivalent conditions that a certain set of $r(n-1)$ determinants of submatrices are all zero. Equivalently we can consider an algorithm yielding a matrix all of whose elements should be zero. This has the advantage of simplicity and a considerable saving of computer time. The determinantal constraints have some advantage when analytic formulae for first derivatives are used to define the Wald criteria, but these formulae are still so complicated as to make programming difficult and the use of numerical approximations to the derivatives of Appendix A advisable. If these approximations are used, then the algorithm constraints are much preferable in terms of computing time, and simplicity of programming.

The matrix to be considered and the algorithm are generalisations of the well-known process of Euclidean elimination; see, for example, Bochner [2]. I have not found a discussion of the general case, so I give the proofs of the following statements in Appendix B. It is convenient to denote the *row* vector whose elements are ψ_{jk}, $k = 1, \ldots, f_j$, by ψ_j. We also introduce the notation O_s, to mean a row vector of s zeroes, and define $d_j = f - f_j$. Then consider the matrix

$$
\Psi_0 = \begin{pmatrix}
 & \psi_1 & \\
\psi_2 & & O_{d_2} \\
O\psi_2 & & O_{(d_2-1)} \\
O_2\psi_2 & & O_{(d_2-2)} \\
\cdots & & \cdots \\
O_{d_2} & & \psi_2 \\
\psi_3 & & O_{d_3} \\
\cdots & & \cdots \\
O_{d_3} & & \psi_3 \\
\vdots & & \vdots \\
O d_n & & \psi_n
\end{pmatrix}.
$$

Note that this matrix has $f+1$ columns and N rows, where $N = n + \sum_{j=2}^{n} d_j$; that it can be divided into n submatrices Ψ_j, where the jth submatrix has $f+1$ columns and (d_j+1) rows; and that the kth row of Ψ_j has $k-1$ zeroes before ψ_j, and d_j-k+1 zeroes after ψ_j. We now define

$$
\Psi_a = \begin{pmatrix} & \psi_1 \\ 0_{d_2} & \psi_2 \\ 0_{d_3} & \psi_3 \\ \cdots & \cdots \\ 0_{d_n} & \psi_n \end{pmatrix}
$$

as a matrix with n rows and $f+1$ columns, and

$$
\Psi_{(k)} = \begin{pmatrix} \Psi_0 & 0_{Nk} \\ 0_{n1}\Psi_a & 0_{n(k-1)} \\ 0_{n2}\Psi_a & 0_{n(k-2)} \\ \vdots & \vdots \\ 0_{nk} & \Psi_a \end{pmatrix} \tag{8}
$$

where 0_{pq} represents a zero matrix of dimension $p \times q$.

There are two types of cases.

(a) *Cases of Type 1:* These cases arise where $N < n+f-r$, where r is the degree of the common factor which is to be tested. Equivalently this is the case where

$$
\sum_{j=1}^{n} (f_j-r) > (n-1)(f-r). \tag{9}
$$

Then define k as the smallest integer satisfying

$$
(n-1)k \geqslant \sum_{j=1}^{n} (f_j-r) - (n-1)(f-r). \tag{10}
$$

Then a necessary and sufficient condition that $\psi_j(z)$ have a factor polynomial of degree r is that $\Psi_{(k)}$ be of rank $f+k+1-r$. Superficially it appears that this gives too many constraints, since if we consider all determinants of order $f+k+2-r$ containing as submatrix the upper left hand square submatrix of dimension $f+k+1-r$ we obtain $f(N-f+r-1+k(n-1))$, and the last factor by (10) is greater than $n-1$. However, we show in the Appendix that we obtain the correct number of constraints in cases of this type, if we consider only the first $f+k+n-r$ rows of $\Psi_{(k)}$, and ensure that this matrix is of rank $f+k+1-r$, and that if this matrix is of this rank then $\Psi_{(k)}$ will be of the same rank.

Note as a special case that if $f_j=f$ for all j, then condition (9) is certainly satisfied and we can write

$$\Psi_0 = \Psi_a = \begin{pmatrix} \psi_1 \\ \psi_2 \\ \vdots \\ \psi_n \end{pmatrix}.$$

(b) *Cases of Type 2:* Cases of Type 2 arise where condition (9) is not satisfied. It is then convenient to define a revised matrix Ψ_b, obtained by reordering the rows of Ψ_0. We write

$$\Psi_b = \begin{pmatrix} \Psi_{b_0} \\ \Psi_{b_1} \\ \Psi_{b_2} \\ \vdots \\ \Psi_{bd_n} \end{pmatrix},$$

defining Ψ_{bj} to contain all the rows of Ψ_0 which have $d_n - j$ zeroes after the polynomial coefficients. The rows of Ψ_{bj} are ordered so that Ψ_s occurs before Ψ_t if $s < t$. As an example if

$$\Psi_0 = \begin{pmatrix} \psi_1 & & \\ \psi_2 & & 0_2 \\ 0 & \psi_2 & 0 \\ 0_2 & & \psi_2 \\ \psi_3 & & 0_2 \\ 0 & \psi_3 & 0 \\ 0_2 & & \psi_3 \end{pmatrix}$$

so that $d_2 = 2$, $d_3 = 2$,

$$\Psi_b = \begin{pmatrix} \psi_2 & & 0_2 \\ \psi_3 & & 0_2 \\ 0 & \psi_2 & 0 \\ 0 & \psi_3 & 0 \\ & \psi_1 & \\ 0_2 & & \psi_2 \\ 0_2 & & \psi_3 \end{pmatrix}.$$

We now inductively define 'vanishing rows' as follows. We consider the kth row of Ψ_b for $k = 1, \ldots, N$. In considering row k define n_k as the number of rows up to row $k-1$ which are not vanishing, and m_k as the number of zeroes on the right hand side of the row. Then label k a vanishing row if $f-n_k-m_k<r$. Also if any row j, for $j>k$ is a right-translated version of row k where k is a vanishing row in the sense that it contains the same ψ_s, and has fewer right zeroes and more left zeroes, label it a 'surplus vanishing row'. If this procedure is carried out for all $k=1,\ldots,N$, and then a matrix Ψ_b^* is obtained from Ψ_b by eliminating all surplus vanishing rows, it will be found that Ψ_b^* has precisely $f+n-r$ rows. Then necessary and sufficient conditions for the set of polynomials to have a common polynomial factor of degree r is that Ψ_b^* be of rank $f+1-r$, and one can obtain precisely $r(n-1)$ determinants of dimension $f+2-r$ to be equated to zero, to give $r(n-1)$ constraints as explained in Appendix B.

4 AN ALTERNATIVE ALGORITHMIC APPROACH

(a) *Cases of Type 1:* The algorithm is applied by first defining $\Psi_{b(k)}$ as in equation (16) but replacing Ψ_0 on the right hand side of (16) by Ψ_b. Then define $\Psi_{b(k)}^*$ as the matrix obtained by retaining only the first $f+k+n-r$ rows of $\Psi_{b(k)}$. The algorithm is the usual procedure using elementary row operations for reducing $\Psi_{b(k)}^*$ to an upper triangular matrix. At stage j suitable multiplies of row j are subtracted from all succeeding rows so as to ensure that in these rows element j is equated to zero. If for any row $s>j$, this has altered the row s (i.e., if the element in column j of row s was initially non-zero), and if some latter row $t>s$ is a right-translated version of row s, then row t is replaced by a corresponding right-translated version of the new row s. At any stage if a new version of a row appears which contains only r non-zero elements, this is labelled a vanishing row. It can be shown that in this case vanishing rows will not appear until stage $j=k+f-r$. At this stage, unless row j if the last row of a block, there will be some vanishing rows, and will certainly be some non-vanishing rows. By operating on the remaining non-vanishing rows with the lowest indexed non-vanishing row as at the earlier stages, a final version of the matrix is obtained with $(n-1)$ vanishing rows. The $r(n-1)$ elements in these vanishing rows can be regarded as functions of the initial ψ_{jk}. And the constraints to be used in the Wald test of the null hypothesis can be taken as those obtained by setting all these $r(n-1)$ elements equal to zero.

(b) *Cases of Type 2:* The algorithm in cases of this type is precisely the same as set out above applied to the matrix Ψ_b^*, except that, defining a vanishing row as one with only r non-zero elements, we omit stage j, if j is a vanishing row. It will be found that after all rows of Ψ_b^* have been considered we have formed precisely $(n-1)$ vanishing rows and that the $r(n-1)$ elements in these rows can be taken as the required $r(n-1)$ constraint functions.

In either case we can immediately define a corresponding set of determinantal constraints by multiplying the algorithmic constraint values by the values of the pivots used in the elementary row operations to compute the constraints. These provide an appropriate set of $r(n-1)$ determinantal constraints.

5 GENERAL CONSIDERATIONS

When the general analysis of Section 2 was originally written, it was thought that an interesting application of this type of analysis would be to the special case of Sections 4 and 5 when this preconception was simply based on the nested nature of the set of hypotheses under consideration, leading to the belief that each model could be expressed as a special case of the preceding more general model by applying some additional constraints.

The nested nature of the hypotheses follows by noting that if we have two models with the same f_i, but with different values of r, $r_1 > r_2$ say, then we can write the model for $r = r_1$ in the form

$$\psi(L) = \alpha_1(L)\rho_1(L)$$

$$= \alpha_1(L)\rho_2(L)\rho_3(L)$$

where $\rho_2(L)$ is of degree r_2, and $\rho_3(L)$ is of degree $r_1 - r_2$. Thus

$$\psi(L) = \rho_2(L)\alpha_2(L)$$

where

$$\alpha_2(L) = \rho_3(L)\alpha_1(L).$$

Note that there are as many ways of formulating a model with $r = r_1$, into different models with $r = r_2$, as there are ways of factorising $\rho_1(L)$ into real factors, one of which is of degree r_2. Thus as discussed in [11] there are problems in applying appropriate likelihood ratio tests if the true $\rho(L)$ has complex roots, and in any case the likelihood function when r is specified to be too small will have multiple maxima, and this will lead to the asymptotic size (null probability) of the likelihood ratio tests being misspecified. It is partly because the Wald tests are not affected in this way (in addition to the reasons stated at the beginning of Section 2) that it seemed worthwhile to consider their properties.

A closer scrutiny of the sets of constraints shows that it is not easy to represent explicitly the set of constraints for the case where the degree of $\rho(L)$ is $(r+1)$, as made up of first the set of constraints for the case where the degree of $\rho(L)$ is r, plus a set of $(n-1)$ extra constraints. Of course in general provided an appropriate Jacobian condition was satisfied it would be possible to do this using an implicit function representation for the extra constraints. However, in this case this Jacobian condition breaks down, if the true degree is $(r+1)$. When the Jacobian condition is not satisfied the usual asymptotic χ^2 approximation gives a poor approximation to the exact distribution. The detail of the argument is given in Appendix B, but if we consider first the set of restrictions that apply to a given value of r ($\rho(L)$ of degree r), and then consider the more numerous set of constraints that correspond to $\rho(L)$ of degree $r+1$, and if we denote the two sets of constraints by $\phi^{(r)}(\theta)=0$ and $\phi^{(r+1)}(\theta)=0$ (note this is a slightly different definition of r from that of Section 2), then we consider only the case where we use the determinantal constraints of Section 4. Then if $\phi^{(r+1)}(\theta)=0$ for the true θ, not only does $\phi^{(r)}(\theta)=0$ but also $\partial\phi^{(r)}/\partial\theta=0$. Thus the conditions that plim $\hat{\Omega}_\phi^{(r)}$ is non-singular is broken and $(\hat{\Omega}_\phi)^{-1}$ is $0(T)$ and $w(r)$ is no longer asymptotically distributed as a χ^2. Indeed we have that $\text{plim}_{T\to\infty}\sqrt{T}\phi^{(r)}(\theta)=0$, so that the scaled constraint functions tend to zero rather than having non-trivial asymptotic normal distributions. The result means that the usual asymptotic distribution of $w(r)$ is not valid in this case, and the usual treatment of constraint testing is not applicable to this case. Thus if the true $r=\bar{r}$, then the Wald test is asymptotically valid to test $r=\bar{r}$ against $r=\bar{r}+1$, but is not valid to test $r=\bar{r}$ against $r=\bar{r}-1$. Practical experience seems to indicate that the Wald criterion is biased downward for $r<\bar{r}$, but further study is required of the sampling theory for this case.

In Section 7 an illustrative comparison is made with the use of the likelihood ratio tests. The use of likelihood ratio tests is not straightforward in this case since it can be shown that in estimating with $r<\bar{r}$, the likelihood function will have multiple maxima which may seriously bias the likelihood ratio tests. Reference [11] discusses this and suggests alternative tests for dynamic specification.

6 COMPUTER IMPLEMENTATION

Suitable subroutines have been written in Fortran to compute both types of constraint function (algorithmic and determinantal constraints) suitable for insertion into any program computing single equation econometric estimators. For the purpose of this application the subroutines were inserted into the D. Hendry general instrumental variable estimation program (GIVE) [5]. A general Fortran subroutine was also written for computing the approximate Wald criteria for any set of constraints as suggested in Appendix A. It was arranged that following the estimation of the coefficients of $\psi(L)$ by means of GIVE the program computed the Wald constraints individually and their asymptotic t ratios, and then the overall approximate Wald χ^2 criteria for the sets of constraints corresponding to any set of values of r called at the start of the program.

7 AN ILLUSTRATION OF THE APPLICATION OF THE WALD CRITERIA TO THE DYNAMIC SPECIFICATION OF A WAGE EQUATION

The equation tested below was part of a three equation model for wage price inflation in the UK reported in [10]. All the variables are logarithms of the corresponding economic variables as follows: w_t is the official weekly wage rates index, p_t is the consumption price deflator for the official estimates of quarterly real consumption, e_t is the corresponding official estimate of average weekly earnings, S_t is the moving average of the working days lost through strikes in the three years up to and including the current quarter. The equation also included a constant term, three quarterly seasonal dummies, and a linear trend. The coefficients of these variables will not be reported in the following tables. The sample ran from 1953.Q.1 to 1973.Q.4. The basic form of equation is illustrated by the OLS estimates

$$w_t - w_{t-1} + \alpha_1(w_{t-1} - p_{t-1}) + \alpha_2(e_{t-1} - w_{t-1}) + \alpha_3 S_{t-1} = u_t. \qquad (11)$$

Money wage rates move in reaction to real wage rates, the ratio of earning to wage rates, and a 'pushfulness' variable obtained from a strike variable.

The Wald criteria are obtained by taking this as $\alpha'(L)x_t = u_t$ and considering autoregressive equations of order up to $r = 4$. Thus $\psi(L)x_t = \varepsilon_t$ was estimated by OLS including up to 4th order lags in all the variables of (11). The Wald criteria are of determinantal type.

In Table I the Wald criteria for $r = 1, 2, 3, 4$, are given in column 2 with the appropriate degrees of freedom in column 3. In column 4 the successive differences are given of the Wald criteria. Note that if it were not for the problems raised in Section 5, it would be appropriate to assume that all of these are asymptotically distributed as independent χ^2 of 3 degrees of freedom provided $r \geq \bar{r}$ equals the true population r.

It seems at first sight that $\bar{r} = 4$ might be rejected, on the basis of the difference between $r = 3$ and $r = 4$, compared with a χ^2_3 1 per cent confidence limit of 11.35, so that this suggests that we require a structural equation form in which at least some of the variables of equation (19) have one extra

Table I. *Wald criteria*

r	Wald criteria	D.F.	Differences	D.F.
1	0.00	3	0.00	3
2	0.84	6	0.84	3
3	2.14	9	1.30	3
4	14.53	12	12.39	3

Table II. *Likelihood ratio criteria*

r	Likelihood ratio criteria	D.F.	Differences	D.F.
1	10.86	3	10.86	3
2	8.71	6	—	3
3	13.90	9	5.19	3
4	17.82	12	3.92	3

lag. However, the Wald criteria for $\bar{r}=3$ at 2.14 is relatively small considered as approximately a χ^2 of 9 degrees of freedom. If indeed $\bar{r}=4$ then the distributions of the Wald criteria for $r=1,2,3$, are no longer approximated by the χ^2's corresponding to their number of degrees of freedom and it seems from recent empirical work, from a Monte Carlo study of a simple case, and from some corresponding asymptotic theory that there would be a downward bias in the Wald criteria for these cases if $\bar{r}=4$. Thus the Wald criteria for $r=1,2,3$ confirm the hypothesis that $\bar{r}=4$. If this were so, the difference between the Wald criteria for $r=3$ and $r=4$ would not be asymptotically distributed as a χ_3^2, and so the differences column of Table I cannot be used. On the other hand the Wald criterion for $r=4$ in the second column of Table I has a valid asymptotic χ^2 distribution if $\bar{r}=4$, and this is certainly not significant with degrees of freedom 12. Thus the Wald criteria suggest that $\bar{r}=4$ can be accepted. (The Wald criteria for $r=1,2,3$ agree with the criteria for $r=4$, but of course the criteria are strongly related and so do not give independent confirmation.) As a check on this the corresponding likelihood ratio tests were carried out, involving consideration of equations of the form (14) for $r=0, 1, 2, 3, 4$. These equations were estimated by the RALS computer program. It was found (as was to be expected in view of [11]) that there were multiple maxima to the likelihood function. Table II reports likelihood ratio criteria based on the global maximum of the likelihood function for each case. Table III gives the corresponding estimates for the parameters.

The likelihood ratio criteria in the second column test the restrictions for each r with null hypothesis $r=0$. First note that the estimates for $r=1$ necessarily lead to a real $\rho_1(\rho_1=0.796)$. However the $r=2$ estimates correspond to a quadratic $\rho(L)$ with complex roots so that the $r=2$ case is not nested in the $r=1$ case. This explains why the $r=1$ case has an apparently significant likelihood ratio criterion (2 per cent χ_3^2 limit $=9.837$), but none of the other criteria on difference criteria are significant at the 5 per cent limit. Thus whether the original criteria of column 2 or the difference criteria of column 4 of Table II are considered, it appears that the hypothesis $\bar{r}=4$ can be accepted. Thus the maximum likelihood criteria agree with the Wald test; the difference between the Wald and likelihood

Table III. *Estimated equations with dependent variable: $w_t - w_{t-1}$*

Variables	$f=4, r=4$	$f=4, r=3$	$f=4, r=2$	$f=4, r=1$
$(w-p)_{t-1}$	−0.120(2.11)	−0.129(1.09)	−0.121(1.05)	−0.131(1.08)
$(e-w)_{t-1}$	0.210(1.93)	0.279(2.36)	0.216(1.70)	0.123(0.84)
S_{t-1}	0.021(3.46)	0.018(2.41)	0.019(2.43)	0.019(2.08)
$w_{t-1}-w_{t-2}$	—	0.841(8.65)	0.431(2.20)	−0.499(2.42)
$(w-p)_{t-2}$	—	0.018(0.16)	0.052(0.39)	−0.038(0.29)
$(e-w)_{t-2}$	—	−0.214(1.97)	0.044(0.25)	0.224(1.52)
S_{t-2}	—	−0.010(1.26)	−0.016(1.21)	0.010(1.00)
$w_{t-2}-w_{t-3}$	—	—	0.362(2.02)	−0.476(2.10)
$(w-p)_{t-3}$	—	—	−0.117(1.06)	−0.187(1.54)
$(e-w)_{t-3}$	—	—	−0.135(1.15)	−0.021(0.13)
S_{t-3}	—	—	0.009(1.02)	0.013(1.34)
$w_{t-3}-w_{t-4}$	—	—	—	−0.098(0.49)
$(w-p)_{t-4}$	—	—	—	0.015(0.11)
$(e-w)_{t-4}$	—	—	—	−0.076(0.49)
S_{t-4}	—	—	—	−0.012(1.27)
ρ_1	0.364(2.74)	−0.536(3.49)	−0.167(1.11)	0.796(6.44)
ρ_2	−0.139(1.15)	−0.569(3.84)	−0.576(4.49)	—
ρ_3	0.261(2.12)	−0.230(1.52)	—	—
ρ_4	0.087(0.67)	—	—	—
S.D.	0.008 66	0.008 64	0.008 57	0.008 88

ratio criteria for $r=4$ is within the range of differences between asymptotically equivalent criteria observed in other econometric tests. The low values of the Wald criteria for $r=1, 2, 3$ are to be expected if $\bar{r}=4$, as the other tests suggest.

8 GENERAL COMMENTS

The approach followed in this paper to determining dynamic specification is only one of several as suggested by Mizon [6]. The discrimination between lags in structural equations and lags in autoregressive error processes is obviously difficult to test satisfactorily. The method suggested in this paper may not be the best available but is obviously worthy of further exploration, and comparison with alternatives. Research directed to this end is continuing at London School of Economics as part of the S.S.R.C. financed program in quantitative economics.

London School of Economics

Manuscript received August, 1977; revision received March, 1979.

APPENDIX A: APPROXIMATING THE WALD CRITERION

The Wald criterion in its usual form requires the use of a subroutine specifying the derivatives of the constraints. Of course this subroutine may be available and required for the particular numerical optimisation procedures used in estimating the constrained estimates. However, this need not be the case, and the obvious alternative of using approximating first differences is likely to be comparatively accurate, since rounding-off errors are relatively small in approximating first derivatives. Since for each criterion it will only be necessary to approximate once, it is not worthwhile to devote much time to choosing an optimum step length (compared with the use of such procedures in iterative numerical optimisation where it is worthwhile to devote time to improving an initial approximating step length since the step length will be used a large number of times). However, it is also clear that the variance matrix $\hat{\Omega}_\phi$ provided a natural metric for the choice of step length. Indeed it is clear that the Wald criterion is based upon the assumption that

$$\phi_i(\hat{\theta}) - \phi_i(\theta)$$

can be closely approximated by

$$\frac{\partial \phi_1}{\partial \theta'} \Delta \theta$$

for changes $\Delta \theta$ of say up to twice the asymptotic standard error; the magnitude of the error in the approximation is determined by the effect of the remainder in the Taylor series expansion, which depends upon the magnitude of the second derivatives near the true value of θ. Considering now the errors made in replacing

$$\frac{\partial \phi_i}{\partial \theta_j}$$

by

$$(\phi_i(\hat{\theta} + \delta_j) - \phi_i(\hat{\theta} - \delta_j))/2h_j \qquad (12)$$

where δ_j is a vector which has all its elements zero, except its jth element which is equal to h_j. Note first of all that, if instead of using this symmetric difference, we had used a simple asymmetric difference, the errors would be proportional to a second derivative. And then if we take h_j proportional to the asymptotic standard error the errors in using (12) in place of the exact first derivative cannot be of a larger order of magnitude than the asymptotic approximation errors in the exact Wald criterion as $T \to \infty$. Indeed it is clear that if for example we take $h_j = \sqrt{(\omega_{jj})}/k\sqrt{T}$, where ω_{jj} is the jth diagonal element of $\hat{\Omega}$, and k is a scalar greater than one, e.g. $k = 10.00$, then we could show that asymptotically the approximate Wald criterion would have the same asymptotic distribution as the exact Wald criterion whether the set of constraints held true or not, so that the asymptotic probability and power of the test are not affected by the use of the difference approximation. An alternative which might work equally well in practice would be to take $h_j = 10^{-3}$, for all i, leading to errors of order 10^{-6} in the extracted first derivatives. This ignores however the possibility of large scaling factors which often occur in econometric estimators (e.g. where constant terms, trends and seasonals occur together with original economic variables), and does not give the same nice theoretical property of asymptotic equivalence.

APPENDIX B: THE ALGORITHM AND ITS PROPERTIES

The constraints result stated in the body of this article follow from a consideration of the Euclidean algorithm, which is the operation of obtaining the remainder after one polynomial is divided by a second of equal or lower degree. We can write the resulting equation

$$f(x) - g(x)h(x) = r(x). \tag{13}$$

$f(x)$ and $g(x)$ are the two polynomials, $h(x)$ is the divided polynomial, and $r(x)$ is the remainder. Note that if $f(x)$ and $g(x)$ have a common factor polynomial, then $r(x)$ also contains this factor. To enable the procedures of Section 5 to be represented in this form it is convenient to write $\psi_j(z) = z^{fj}g_i(x)$, where $x = 1/z$. Each row of any ψ matrix can be regarded as a polynomial of degree equal to d, if $d + 1$ is the number of elements which are known to be non-zero in the corresponding ψ vector. A row, which is similar to another row of the matrix, except that it has more right hand zeroes, and correspondingly less left hand zeroes, will be called a left hand translated version of the row and vice versa. Any elementary row operation arising in the algorithm described in Section 4 can be regarded as defining a division of type (13) above. The new version of the row represents a remainder polynomial of degree less than both $f(x)$ and $g(x)$. Note that a left hand translated version of a row can be regarded as equivalent to multiplying that row by a power of x equal to the number of shifts when applying equation (13). Thus in considering the algorithm applied to Ψ_b, if we take from a row a multiple of a row from the same sub-block Ψ_{bk}, we are subtracting a constant multiple of one polynomial from another. If on the other hand we are subtracting a multiple of a row from another row in a later sub-block, we are subtracting the corresponding polynomial multiplied by some power of x from the later polynomial.

We define $\Psi_{b(k)}^{(j)}$ recursively as follows: $\Psi_{b(k)}^{(0)} = \Psi_{b(k)}$. The jth stage of the algorithm consists first of subtracting suitable multiples of the jth non-vanishing row of $\Psi_{b(k)}^{(j-1)}$ from later rows (note that an earlier and later row is used here to mean one with smaller or larger suffix), and then modifying any later right-translated version of any row which has been changed to agree with the new version of that row. The result of this set of operations is $\Psi_{b(k)}^{(j)}$. The ith row of this matrix will now be denoted by ψ_{ij}^* (and the sth element of this row vector will be denoted by ψ_{ijs}). Each ψ_{ij}^* can be regarded as corresponding to a polynomial in x (normally regarded as having its last non-zero element multiplied by x^0, although in terms of the comparison with the basic operation (13) it may be useful to think of the last element of the row (which in fact may be zero) as the coefficient of x^0, and the last non-zero element being the coefficient of x^{m_i}, *where* m_i is the number of zeroes on the right hand side of row i. Note the m_i does not change in the course of the algorithm, since the rows of $\Psi_{b(k)}$ have been ordered so that m_i is weakly decreasing in i. On the other hand the algorithm is such that the number of left hand zeroes in ψ_{ij}^* is at least j for $i > j$. Thus as j increases, the total number of zeroes in each row is increasing, so that the degree of the corresponding polynomial in each row is decreasing with j for all $i > j$. Note that if a row contains a polynomial of degree r, when it is subtracted from other rows of the same sub-block of $\Psi_{b(k)}$ it will produce polynomials of degree $r-1$. However, if all the initial $\psi_j(z)$ have a common factor $\rho(z)$, the remainder polynomials of degree r will be a multiple of $\rho(z)$, and the remainder polynomials of degree $r-1$ will be identically zero. Conversely if a row of zeroes is produced by subtracting a multiple of one polynomial of rth degree from another, the two polynomials only differ by a constant factor. It is clear that if we denote a ψ_{ij}^* corresponding to a polynomial of degree $r-1$ as a vanishing row, then a necessary condition that the initial $\psi_j(z)$ contain a common factor of degree r is that the r elements of the vanishing row which are not automatically made zero by the elimination algorithm, should in fact be zero, or that the corresponding determinants extracted from earlier rows, omitting previous vanishing rows should all be zero.

We now consider cases of type 1. We first show that the rows of Ψ_b itself may contain vanishing rows only in its last block. We look at the last row of each block Ψ_{bj}, since it is clear that if such a block has a vanishing row, the same stage of the algorithm that makes the row vanish will make the last row of the block vanish. We call $\psi_{j(j-1)}^*$ as defined above, the final form of row j. Denote the number of non-zero elements in the final form of the last row of ψ_{bj} by g_j. Then $g_{(j-1)}-g_j$ is equal to the number of non-vanishing rows in Ψ_{bj} minus one (this last due to the extra right hand zero between the two adjacent blocks).

Then

$$g_{(d_n-1)} \geqslant f - (N - n - 1)$$

$$= f + 1 - \sum_{i=2}^{n} d_i$$

$$> 1 + r, \quad \text{from (9),}$$

so that the last but one block has all its rows non-vanishing. But now, if $g_i > 1 + r$, the ith block has all its rows non-vanishing, so that $g_{(i-1)} > g_i$ and so $g_{(i-1)} > 1 + r$. Thus by induction all earlier rows are non-vanishing.

Now labelling the blocks of $\Psi_{b(k)}$ in the same way as those of Ψ_b, let Ψ_{bj} be the first block whose last row is vanishing. It follows as before that all blocks $\Psi_{bi}, i < j$ have all non-vanishing rows. Let the earliest row of Ψ_{bj} to vanish be row q of $\Psi_{b(k)}$. Consider first the possibility that row q is in fact the second row of block Ψ_{bj}, and note that Ψ_{bj} has n rows, since $j \geqslant d_1$. Note also that it is impossible for the earliest vanishing row to be the first row of Ψ_{bj}, because the number of non-zero elements in this row is equal to the number in the previous row which by assumption is non-vanishing. Now if row q has only r non-zero elements then all later rows in this block will also have r non-zero elements at the same stage. Thus the last $n-1$ rows of the block are all vanishing.

If now the earliest vanishing row is the pth in its block, $p > 2$, we have in block $jn - p + 1$ vanishing rows, but we can make up a total of $n - 1$ vanishing rows by noting that the first row of the next block will have $r + 1$ non-zero elements at the stage at which the earlier rows have r elements, and that this first row can now be used to reduce the remaining $(p-2)$ non-vanishing rows. When $p = 2$ it is clear that at the previous stage we have a block of n polynomials all of degree r, all proportionate to each other. Equally when $p \neq 2$, looking first at block $(j+1)$ we see that at the previous stage the first $(p-1)$ polynomials are all proportionate of degree r. But now the last of these polynomials is a right-hand translated version of the last non-vanishing row in the previous block. And the rth degree remainder polynomials corresponding to the later rows of this block must be proportional to this. Thus in this case the rth degree remainder polynomials from the $(q-1)$th row onwards provide a block of $(n+1)$ consecutive proportionate rth degree polynomials. Note that the first of these is the same as the last, except for the left hand shift.

We deduce the condition (10) defining k. Suppose $p=2$, and q is the first vanishing row. There are then precisely $n-2$ further rows in the block so that

$$q + n - 2 = N + kn,$$

and in order that the number of non-zero elements be r we need that

$$f + k + 1 - (q - 1) = r.$$

From this we have easily that (10) is satisfied as an equality. On the other hand if $p > 2$, then we have that the first vanishing row occurs in the last but one block so that $f + k - (q - 1) = r$, but now there is a non-vanishing row as the first row of the last block so that we require

$$q + n - 1 < N + kn.$$

This requires that (10) be a strict inequality.

Now we work backwards through the algorithm proving that at each stage the remainder polynomials have this same factor, $\rho(z)$. Denote the form of the vector in the jth row after stage s by ψ_{js}^*; then if the next block after the one containing row s has b rows, we have the following:

$$\psi_{js}^* = \psi_{j(s-1)}^*, \qquad j \leqslant s,$$

$$\psi_{js}^* = \psi_{j(s-1)}^* - \lambda_{js}\psi_{s(s-1)}^*, \qquad j = s+1, \ldots, s+b-1, \tag{14}$$

$$\psi_{(j+b)s}^* = L^{-1}\psi_{js}^*, \qquad j \geqslant s,$$

where L is a single left hand shift operator, and λ_{js} is a scalar. From these we derive

$$\psi_{j(s-1)}^* = \psi_{js}^*, \qquad j < s,$$

$$\psi_{s(s-1)}^* = L\psi_{(s+b)s}^*, \tag{15}$$

$$\psi_{j(s-1)}^* = \psi_{js}^* + \lambda_j L\psi_{(p+s)s}^*, \qquad j = s+b-1.$$

Thus given ψ_{js}^*, $j = 1, \ldots, s+b$, one can obtain $\psi_{j(s-1)}^*$, $j = 1, \ldots, s+b-1$, and deduce that if all $\psi_{js}(z)$, $j = s+1, \ldots, (s+b)$ have a common factor $\rho(z)$, then the same is true for $\psi_{j(s-1)}^*(z)$, $j = s, \ldots, (s+b+1)$. This reverse iteration is continued until $s = 0$, at which stage $\psi_j(z)$ also contain the same common factor.

Similar argument can be applied to cases of type 2. If the inequality (9) is changed to an equality then by an extension of the argument of the previous section we see that the first vanishing row is the second row of the last block of Ψ_b, and the later rows of this block provide a further $n-2$ vanishing rows. If the inequality (9) is reversed we can see that there must be vanishing rows in the preceding blocks. For if there are no vanishing rows before row $(N-n)$, then row $N-n$ would contain $N-n-1$ left hand zeroes and one right hand zero, which by the reversal of (9) is less than r. It is easily seen that if at any stage any block contains a row with $r+1$ non-zero elements, then the succeeding rows of the block vanish, and succeeding blocks have a first row with $(r+1)$ non-zero elements and all later rows vanishing. Applying this to the last block, we see that the final form of its first row is non-vanishing, and is followed by a set of vanishing rows, which will be surplus vanishing rows, if they correspond to $\psi_i(z)$, which have already had vanishing rows in earlier blocks. Thus in the matrix obtained by omitting surplus vanishing rows, the number of non-vanishing rows must be just enough to ensure that the row corresponding to $\psi_1(z)$ has precisely $r+1$ non-zero elements in its final form. Thus the number of non-vanishing rows (including the $\psi_1(z)$ row) is $1+(f-r)$. In addition we have $(n-1)$ vanishing rows, showing that the total number of rows in Ψ_b^* is $n+f-r$. Note that when surplus vanishing rows are eliminated, we are in fact reducing the last stages of the algorithm to one involving fewer functions, so that in the reverse iteration we normally start out with less than the total number of functions, but at the stage at which another function is introduced into the set under consideration using equations of the type (15) one can deduce that the corresponding remainder function contains the common factor.

The corresponding determinantal constraints are obtained by taking for each vanishing row with index q, the $n_q \times n_q$ determinants obtained by taking the previous n_q non-vanishing rows and the first n_q-1 columns, plus one extra non-zero column. It will be found that there are precisely r such submatrices for each vanishing row.

We now consider the relationships between the constraints for two successive values of r, considering only cases of type 1. We consider first the constraints corresponding to the algorithmic approach, for $r=r^*$ and for $r=r^*+1$. Suppose for $r=r^*+1$ the first vanishing row occurs at stage $s=q-1$, so that the first vanishing row is row q, and noting as before that q is not the first row of its block. We discuss only the case $n>p>2$, but similar results can be demonstrated for the case $p=2$ and $p=n$. The vanishing rows are then the ψ_{js}^*, $j=q,\ldots,q^*$, where q^* is the last row of this block, and then ψ_{jq}, $j=q^*+2,\ldots,q^*+p-1$. (Note $q=s+1$.)

Now considering $r=r^*$, we see that ψ_{qs}^* is now non-vanishing, so that the algorithm can be carried to one more stage. We write ψ_{jki} for the ith element of ψ_{jk}^*, and $\lambda_j = \psi_{jsq}/\psi_{qsq}$, $j=q,\ldots,q^*+1$, and

$$\mu_j = \frac{\psi_{jq(q+1)}}{\psi_{(q^*+1)s(q+1)} - \lambda_{(q^*+1)}\psi_{qs(q+1)}}, \qquad j=q^*+2,\ldots,q^*+p.$$

Now writing $\tilde{\psi}_{jq}$ for the contents of the jth row, $j=q+1,\ldots,q^*+1$, after the appropriate multiple of two q has been subtracted, we have

$$\tilde{\psi}_{jqm} = \psi_{jsm} - \lambda_j \psi_{qsm}. \tag{16}$$

Also writing $\tilde{\psi}_{j(q+1)}^l$ for the contents of the jth row, $j=q^*+2,\ldots,q^*+p+1$, after μ_j times the $\tilde{\psi}_{(q^*+1)q}$ has been subtracted, we have

$$\tilde{\psi}_{j(q+1)m} = \psi_{jqm} - \mu_j \tilde{\psi}_{(q^*+1)qm}. \tag{17}$$

Note that $q^*+p=q+n$, so that $\psi_{(q^*+p+1)qm} = \psi_{(q+1)q(m-1)}$. The original algorithmic constraints for $r=r^*+1$ are

$$\psi_{jsm}=0, \qquad j=q,\ldots,q^*, \qquad m=q,\ldots,q+r^*,$$

$$\psi_{j(q+1)m}=0, \qquad j=q^*+2,\ldots,q^*+p, \qquad m=q+1,\ldots,q+r^*+1.$$

The algorithmic constraints for $r=r^*$ are

$$\tilde{\psi}_{jqm}=0, \qquad j=q+1,\ldots,q^*, \qquad m=q+1,\ldots,q+r^*,$$

$$\tilde{\psi}_{j(q+1)m}=0, \qquad j=q^*+2,\ldots,q^*+p+1, \qquad m=q+2,\ldots,q+r^*+1.$$

Now consider the equivalent determinantal constraint. Consider first the $s\times s$ square submatrix occupying the top left hand corner of $\Psi_{b(k)}$, and denote its determinant by D_0. Denote by D_{0jm} the determinant of the $q\times q$ square submatrix obtained by adjoining the qth row and the mth column of $\Psi_{b(k)}$. Then $D_{0jm}=D_0\psi_{jsm}$. Denote by D_{ijm} the determinant of the $(q+1)\times(q+1)$ submatrix obtained by adjoining the (q^*+1)th row and the $(q+1)$th column, and then the jth row and the mth column. Then $D_{1jm}=D_0\psi_{(q^*+1)s(q+1)}\psi_{jpm}$. Now define D_0^* as the determinant of $q\times q$ top left hand submatrix of $\Psi_{b(k)}$, and note that $D_0^*=D_0\psi_{qsq}$. Denote by D_{0jm}^* the determinant of the $(q+1)\times(q+1)$ square submatrix obtained by adjoining the jth row and the mth column. Then $D_{0jm}^*=D_0^*\tilde{\psi}_{jqm}$. Also denote by D_{1jm}^* the $(q+2)\times(q+2)$ submatrix obtained by adjoining to D_0^* the (q^*+1)th row and the $(q+1)$th column and then the jth row and the mth column. Then $D_{1jm}^*=D_0^*\tilde{\psi}_{(q^*+1)q(q+1)}\tilde{\psi}_{j(q+1)m}$.

For $r=r^*$ the determinantal constraints are

$$D_{0jm}=0, \qquad j=q,\ldots,q^*, \qquad m=q,\ldots,q+r^*$$

$$D_{1jm}=0, \qquad j=q^*+2,\ldots,q^*+p, \qquad m=q+1,\ldots,q+r^*+1. \tag{18}$$

For $r=r^*+1$ the determinantal constraints are

$$\left.\begin{array}{ll} D_{0jm}^*=0, \qquad j=q+1,\ldots,q^*, \qquad m=q+1,\ldots,q+r^*, \\ D_{1jm}^*=0, \qquad j=q^*+2,\ldots,q^*+p+1, \qquad m=q+2,\ldots,q+r^*+1. \end{array}\right\} \tag{19}$$

We now deduce from (16) that

$$D_{0jm}^*=D_0\psi_{qsq}\tilde{\psi}_{jqm}$$

$$=D_0(\psi_{qsq}\psi_{jsm}-\psi_{jsa}\psi_{qsm})$$

$$=\frac{1}{D_0}(D_{0qq}D_{0jm}-D_{0jq}D_{0qm}) \tag{20}$$

and from (17) that

$$D_{1jm}^*=D_0^*\tilde{\psi}_{(q^*+1)q(q+1)}\tilde{\psi}_{j(q+1)m}$$

$$=D_0^*(\tilde{\psi}_{(q^*+1)q(q+1)}\psi_{jqm}-\psi_{jq(q+1)}\tilde{\psi}_{(q^*+1)qm})$$

$$=D_0(\psi_{(q^*+1)s(q+1)}\psi_{qsq}\psi_{jqm}-\psi_{(q^*+1)sq}\psi_{qs(q+1)}\psi_{jpm}$$

$$-\psi_{jq(q+1)}\psi_{qsq}\psi_{(q^*+1)sm}+\psi_{jq(q+1)}\psi_{(q^*+1)sq}\psi_{qsm})$$

$$=\frac{1}{D_0}\left(D_{1jm}D_{0qq}-\frac{\psi_{(q^*+1)sq}}{\psi_{(q^*+1)s(q+1)}}D_{1jm}D_{0q(q+1)}\right.$$

$$\left.-\frac{\psi_{(q^*+1)sm}}{\psi_{(q^*+1)s(q+1)}}D_{1j(q+1)}D_{0qq}+D_{1j(q+1)}D_{0qm}\right). \tag{21}$$

Now note that if $r = r^* + 1$, then plim $D_0 \neq 0$, and plim $\psi_{(q^*+1)s(q+1)} \neq 0$, but that plim $D_{1jm} = 0$ and plim $D_{0qm} = 0$ for all the j and m specified in (18). Thus it follows that the first derivatives of the D^*_{0jm}, and D^*_{1jm} with respect to the D_{0jm} and D_{1jm} have probability limit zero if $r = r^* + 1$. Since it is clear that the D_{0jm} and D_{1jm} have finite derivatives with respect to the basic parameters (the coefficients of the original $\psi_j(L)$ functions), it follows that the corresponding $\partial \phi^{(r)} / \partial \theta = 0$ at $\theta = \bar{\theta}$, and so the analysis of Appendix A cannot be applied.

It might be thought possible to avoid this problem by using as constraints the ψ_{jsm}, ψ_{jqm}, $\tilde{\psi}_{jqm}$ and $\tilde{\psi}_{j(q+1)m}$. But then if $r = r^* + 1$, the $\tilde{\psi}$ are not well defined at the true parameter values and so the general Wald criteria to test $r = r^*$ are not well defined, and the usual asymptotic theory does not apply. There is no obvious way of constructing an 'ad hoc' procedure for deriving the asymptotic distribution.

REFERENCES

[1] Anderson, T. W.: *The Statistical Analysis of Time Series*. New York: John Wiley and Sons, 1971.

[2] Bochner, M.: *Higher Algebra*. London: Macmillan, 1935.

[3] Dunn, O. J.: 'Confidence intervals for the means of dependent, normally distributed variables', *Journal of the American Statistical Association*, **54** (1959), 613–21.

[4] Hannan, E. J.: 'The identification problem for multiple equation systems with moving average errors', *Econometrica*, **39** (1971), 751–65.

[5] Hendry, D. F.: 'User's manual for GIVE', Mimeo, London School of Economics, 1973.

[6] Mizon, G. E.: 'Model selection procedures', in *Studies in Modern Economic Analysis*, ed. by M. J. Artis and A. R. Nobay. Oxford: Basil Blackwell, 1977.

[7] Pierce, D. A.: 'Distribution of residual autocorrelations in the regression model with autoregressive-moving average errors', *Journal of the Royal Statistical Society, Series B*, **33** (1971), 140–6.

[8] Sargan, J. D.: 'Wages and prices in the United Kingdom: a study in econometric methodology', in *Econometric Analysis for National Economic Plannings*, ed. by P. E. Hart, G. Mills, and J. K. Whitaker. London: Butterworths, 1964.

[9] ———: 'Testing after estimation by instrumental variables', Working Paper for SEPDEM Program, London School of Economics, 1976.

[10] ———: 'A model of wage price inflation', Discussion Paper, No. A, Quantitative Economics Program, London School of Economics, 1977.

[11] ———: 'A generalisation of the Durbin significance test and its application to dynamic specification', Working Paper for Quantitative Economics Program, London School of Economics, 1977.

[12] ———: 'Some tests of dynamic specification', Discussion Paper A.16, London School of Economics Econometric Program, 1977.

[13] Stroud, T. W. F.: 'On obtaining large sample tests from asymptotically normal estimators', *Annals of Mathematical Statistics*, **42** (1971), 1412–24.

11 TESTING FOR MISSPECIFICATION AFTER ESTIMATING USING INSTRUMENTAL VARIABLES

Unpublished LSE working paper (1973)

1 INTRODUCTION

The background to this paper is as in my Colston Symposium paper; [5], in a sense this is a correction and extension of Section 3, which is unfortunately marred by an incorrect sign. The results of this paper are an extension of the results of Durbin [2] and of Box and Pierce [1], [4].

2 TESTING RESIDUALS USING ARBITRARY INSTRUMENTAL VARIABLES

Consider a single equation

$$X\mathbf{a}(\theta) = u \tag{1}$$

where X is a $T \times n$ data matrix of variables both endogenous and exogenous, and $\mathbf{a}(\theta)$ is an $n \times 1$ coefficient vector, whose elements are continuous function of a set of p parameters forming a vector θ. We also require $\partial \mathbf{a}/\partial \theta$ to be continuous in θ and of full rank at $\bar{\theta}$, the true value of θ. An example of the practical use of this formulation is in the Colston symposium paper, or in my paper in *JRSS* 1959 [6] where the u_t are the errors on a general rth order autoregressive equation

$$\eta_t - \sum_{s=1}^{r} \rho_s \eta_{t-s} = u_t \tag{2}$$

and there is an underlying structural equation of the form

$$\sum_{i=0}^{k} \beta_i' y_{t-i} + \sum_{i=0}^{j} \gamma_i' z_{t-i} = \eta_t. \tag{3}$$

The y_t are vectors of endogenous variables, and the β_i have the same dimension; at least one element of β_0 is standardised. The z_t are vectors of exogenous variables, and the γ_i are coefficient vectors. Then the X matrix consists of the y_{t-i}, $i=0,\ldots,r+k$, and z_{t-i}, $i=0,\ldots,r+j$, and the elements of $\mathbf{a}(\theta)$ are bilinear (quadratic) in the ρ_s, β_i and γ_i. However the model is quite general and can be applied to any situation of this type providing only that the errors on the resulting equations are serially independent, and the y_t can be regarded as generated by some set of stochastic difference equations as in [3].

We assume that the equation has been estimated by instrumental variables using a set of instrumental variables Z of number m, so that the estimated θ minimised $\mathbf{a}'(\theta)(X'Z)(Z'Z)^{-1}(Z'X)\mathbf{a}(\theta)$ as a function of θ and satisfies the first order conditions

$$\left(\frac{\partial \mathbf{a}}{\partial \hat{\theta}}\right)'(X'Z)(Z'Z)^{-1}(Z'X)\mathbf{a}(\hat{\theta})=0. \tag{4}$$

Here we write $\hat{\theta}$ for these estimates and $\dfrac{\partial \mathbf{a}}{\partial \hat{\theta}}=\dfrac{\partial \mathbf{a}}{\partial \theta}$ evaluated at $\hat{\theta}$, and $\Delta\theta=\hat{\theta}-\theta$, where from now on θ is used to mean the true model values of the parameters. Defining $\hat{u}=X\mathbf{a}(\hat{\theta})$, we consider a χ^2 criterion based on

$$\hat{\mathbf{w}}=\frac{W'\hat{u}}{\sqrt{T}} \tag{5}$$

where W is a set of N instrumental variables, which may or may not overlap with Z. We assume that

$$\mathrm{plim}\left(\frac{Z'Z}{T}\right)=M \text{ is non-singular and that}$$

$$\mathrm{plim}\left(\frac{W'W}{T}\right)=M^* \text{ is non-singular and that}$$

$$\mathrm{plim}\left(\frac{Z'X}{T}\right)\frac{\partial \mathbf{a}}{\partial \theta} \text{ is of rank } p.$$

Now define $W^+=(\overset{N}{W}:\overset{m}{Z})$ and consider $M^+=\mathrm{plim}\left(\dfrac{W^{+\prime}W^+}{T}\right)$. Now if W and Z have some variables in common then M^+ will not be of rank $(N+m)$. Suppose the rank of M^+ is $N+m-m_1$, then we can find an $(N+m)\times(m_1)$ matrix

$$\begin{pmatrix} C_1 \\ C_2 \end{pmatrix}\!\!\begin{matrix} N \\ m \end{matrix}$$
$$\underset{m_1}{}$$

such that

$$M^+\begin{pmatrix} C_1 \\ C_2 \end{pmatrix}=0.$$

Now writing $W^* = WC_1$, $Z^* = -ZC_2$, we have that

$$\text{plim} \frac{(W^* - Z^*)'(W^* - Z^*)}{T} = 0.$$

And we can say that W^* is asymptotically equivalent to Z^*, so that we can linearly transform the W and Z so that they have m_1 instrumental variables in common asymptotically. Now write $m_2 = m - m_1$, and we will say that there are m_2 instrumental variables in the set of Z variables which are not asymptotically equivalent to W variables.

Now considering the asymptotic distribution of $\hat{w}$, we have

$$\hat{w} = \frac{W'u}{\sqrt{T}} + \frac{W'X}{T}\left(\frac{\partial a}{\partial \theta}\right)^* (\sqrt{T}(\Delta \theta)) \tag{6}$$

where by the mean value theorem we can find suitable points in θ space between θ and $\hat{\theta}$ to evaluate the first derivatives which will be denoted $\left(\frac{\partial a}{\partial \theta}\right)^*$ so that

$$a(\hat{\theta}) - a(\theta) = \left(\frac{\partial a}{\partial \theta}\right)^* \Delta \theta$$

and then from (4) we have

$$\sqrt{T}(\Delta \theta) = -\left[\left(\frac{\partial a}{\partial \theta}\right)'\left(\frac{X'Z}{T}\right)\left(\frac{Z'Z}{T}\right)^{-1}\frac{Z'X}{T}\left(\frac{\partial a}{\partial \theta}\right)\right]^{-1}$$

$$\times \left(\frac{\partial a}{\partial \theta}\right)'\left(\frac{X'Z}{T}\right)\left(\frac{Z'Z}{T}\right)^{-1}\left(\frac{Z'u}{\partial T}\right).$$

Now write

$$H = \underset{T \to \infty}{\text{plim}}\left[\left(\frac{W'X}{T}\left(\frac{\partial a}{\partial \theta}\right)^*\right) \times \left[\left(\frac{\partial a}{\partial \hat{\theta}}\right)'\left(\frac{X'Z}{T}\right)\left(\frac{Z'Z}{T}\right)^{-1}\left(\frac{Z'X}{T}\right)\left(\frac{\partial a}{\partial \theta}\right)^*\right]^{-1}\right.$$

$$\left. \times \left(\frac{\partial a}{\partial \theta}\right)\left(\frac{X'Z}{T}\right)\left(\frac{Z'Z}{T}\right)^{-1}\right]$$

$$= K^{*\prime}\frac{\partial a}{\partial \theta}\left[\left(\frac{\partial a}{\partial \theta}\right)'KM^{-1}K'\frac{\partial a}{\partial \theta}\right]^{-1}\left(\frac{\partial a}{\partial \theta}\right)'KM^{-1}$$

where $K = \text{plim}\left(\frac{X'Z}{T}\right)$ and $K^* = \text{plim}\left(\frac{X'W}{T}\right)$ and $\left(\frac{\partial a}{\partial \theta}\right)$ is evaluated at the true θ, and $K'\frac{\partial a}{\partial \theta}$ is assumed to be of rank p.

Define

$$w^+ = \frac{W^{+\prime}u}{\sqrt{T}}.$$

Then we have that

$$\hat{\mathbf{w}} = \frac{W'\hat{u}}{\sqrt{T}} = \frac{W'u}{\sqrt{T}} - H\frac{Z'u}{\sqrt{T}} + O\left(\frac{1}{\sqrt{T}}\right) = (I, -H)\mathbf{w}^+ + O\left(\frac{1}{\sqrt{T}}\right).$$

Now $\mathbf{w}^+$ is asymptotically normally distributed $N(0, \sigma^2 M^+)$ on the usual assumptions that the W and Z are predetermined variables generated by a stable stochastic difference equation system with exogenous variables satisfying suitable conditions, e.g. all are bounded for all t as in [3]. Thus using the Cramer linear transformation theorem we deduce that $\hat{\mathbf{w}} \underset{a}{\sim} N(0, \sigma^2 \Omega_w)$ where $\Omega_w = (I, -H)M^+\begin{pmatrix} I \\ -H' \end{pmatrix}$. From this we could obtain a χ^2 criterion in the usual way. The simplest case is where Ω_w is non-singular.

We can then write

$$\hat{\Omega}_m = \frac{G'W}{T} - \frac{W'X}{T}\left(\frac{\partial \mathbf{a}}{\partial \hat{\theta}}\right)\left[\left(\frac{\partial \mathbf{a}}{\partial \hat{\theta}}\right)'\left(\frac{X'Z}{T}\right)\left(\frac{Z'Z}{T}\right)^{-1}\frac{Z'X}{T}\left(\frac{\partial \mathbf{a}}{\partial \hat{\theta}}\right)\right]^{-1}$$

$$\times \left(\frac{\partial \mathbf{a}}{\partial \hat{\theta}}\right)'\left(\frac{X'Z}{T}\right)\left(\frac{Z'Z}{T}\right)^{-1}\frac{Z'W}{T}$$

$$- \frac{W'Z}{T}\left(\frac{Z'Z}{T}\right)^{-1}\left(\frac{Z'X}{T}\right)\frac{\partial \mathbf{a}}{\partial \hat{\theta}}\left[\left(\frac{\partial \mathbf{a}}{\partial \hat{\theta}}\right)'\left(\frac{X'Z}{T}\right)\left(\frac{Z'Z}{T}\right)^{-1}\frac{Z'X}{T}\left(\frac{\partial \mathbf{a}}{\partial \hat{\theta}}\right)\right]^{-1}$$

$$+ \left(\frac{W'X}{T}\right)\left(\frac{\partial \mathbf{a}}{\partial \hat{\theta}}\right)\left[\left(\frac{\partial \mathbf{a}}{\partial \hat{\theta}}\right)'\left(\frac{X'Z}{T}\right)\left(\frac{Z'Z}{T}\right)^{-1}\frac{Z'X}{T}\left(\frac{\partial \mathbf{a}}{\partial \hat{\theta}}\right)\right]^{-1}\left(\frac{\partial \mathbf{a}}{\partial \hat{\theta}}\right)'\frac{W'X}{T} \quad (7)'$$

and easily deduce that

$$\text{plim } \hat{\Omega}_w = \Omega_w$$

Now factorizing $\hat{\Omega}_w^{-1} = LL'$ where L is upper triangular and considering $L'\hat{\mathbf{w}}/s = t$, where $\text{plim } s^2 = \sigma^2$, we have that

$$t \underset{a}{\sim} N(0, I)$$

and therefore

$$\hat{\mathbf{w}}'\hat{\Omega}_w^{-1}\hat{\mathbf{w}}/s^2 \underset{a}{\sim} \chi_N^2.$$

However we cannot assume in general that Ω_w is of rank N.

Consider first the case where the rank of $\dfrac{W^{+\prime}W^+}{T}$ is $N + m_2$, where $m_2 < m$, as would be the case if the sets of variables W and Z had precisely

$m - m_2 > 0$ variables in common. Also

$$
\begin{bmatrix}
I & \vdots & 0 \\
\cdots\cdots\cdots\cdots\cdots & \vdots & \cdots \\
-\dfrac{Z'W}{T}\left(\dfrac{W'W}{T}\right)^{-1} & \vdots & I
\end{bmatrix}
\times
\begin{bmatrix}
\dfrac{W'W}{T} & \dfrac{W'Z}{T} \\[2ex]
\dfrac{Z'W}{T} & \dfrac{Z'Z}{T}
\end{bmatrix}
$$

$$
=
\begin{bmatrix}
\dfrac{W'W}{T} & \dfrac{W'Z}{T} \\[2ex]
0 & \dfrac{Z'Z}{T} - \left(\dfrac{Z'W}{T}\right)\left(\dfrac{W'W}{T}\right)^{-1}\dfrac{W'Z}{T}
\end{bmatrix}.
$$

We have that $\dfrac{W^{+\prime}W^+}{T}$ is of rank $N + m_2$ iff

$$
\frac{Z'Z}{T} - \left(\frac{Z'W}{T}\right)\left(\frac{W'W}{T}\right)^{-1}\frac{W'Z}{T}
$$

is of rank m_2. Now write $D_1' = \dfrac{(Z'Z)^{-1/2}Z'W}{\sqrt{T}}$

$$
Q_\theta = \frac{(Z'Z)^{-1/2}(Z'X)}{T^{1/2}}\left(\frac{\partial \mathbf{a}}{\partial \hat{\theta}}\right)\left[\left(\frac{\partial \mathbf{a}}{\partial \hat{\theta}}\right)'\left(\frac{X'Z}{T}\right)\left(\frac{Z'Z}{T}\right)^{-1}\left(\frac{Z'X}{T}\right)\frac{\partial \mathbf{a}}{\partial \hat{\theta}}\right]^{-1}
$$

$$
\times \left(\frac{\partial \mathbf{a}}{\partial \hat{\theta}}\right)'\frac{(X'Z)(Z'Z)^{-1/2}}{T}
$$

where Q_θ is idempotent of rank p with probability one, and $W^* = (I - Z(Z'Z)^{-1}Z')W$, then we can write

$$
\hat{\Omega}_w = D_1(I - Q_\theta)D_1 + \frac{W^{*\prime}W^*}{T}
$$

$$
+ \frac{W^{*\prime}X}{T}\left(\frac{\partial \mathbf{a}}{\partial \hat{\theta}}\right)\left[\left(\frac{\partial \mathbf{a}}{\partial \hat{\theta}}\right)'\left(\frac{X'Z}{T}\right)\left(\frac{Z'Z}{T}\right)^{-1}\frac{Z'X}{T}\left(\frac{\partial \mathbf{a}}{\partial \theta}\right)\right]^{-1}\left(\frac{\partial \mathbf{a}}{\partial \hat{\theta}}\right)'\frac{X'W^*}{T}
$$

Note that if $\alpha'\hat{\Omega}_w\alpha = 0$ for some vector α it is necessary and sufficient if

$$
W^*\alpha = 0 \tag{8}
$$

and

$$
(I - Q_\theta)D_1'\alpha = 0. \tag{9}
$$

Now (8) gives

$$
W\alpha = Z(Z'Z)^{-1}ZW\alpha
$$

$$
= Z\gamma
$$

Testing for misspecification

where

$$\gamma = (Z'Z)^{-1}ZW\alpha.$$

Now (9) gives

$$0 = (I - Q)D_1'\alpha = \frac{(Z'Z)^{1/2}}{T}\left\{ I - \frac{(Z'Z)^{-1}}{T}\frac{(Z'X)}{T}\frac{\partial\mathbf{a}}{\partial\hat{\theta}}\left[\left(\frac{\partial\mathbf{a}}{\partial\hat{\theta}}\right)'\frac{(X'Z)}{T}\right.\right.$$

$$\left.\left. \times\left(\frac{Z'Z}{T}\right)^{-1}\left(\frac{Z'X}{T}\right)\left(\frac{\partial\mathbf{a}}{\partial\hat{\theta}}\right)\right]^{-1}\frac{\partial\mathbf{a}'}{\partial\hat{\theta}}\left(\frac{X'Z}{T}\right)\right\}\gamma$$

or

$$\gamma = \frac{(Z'Z)^{-1}}{T}\left(\frac{Z'X}{T}\right)\frac{\partial\mathbf{a}}{\partial\hat{\theta}}\delta$$

where

$$\delta = \left[\left(\frac{\partial\mathbf{a}}{\partial\hat{\theta}}\right)'\left(\frac{X'Z}{T}\right)\left(\frac{Z'Z}{T}\right)^{-1}\left(\frac{Z'X}{T}\right)\frac{\partial\mathbf{a}}{\partial\hat{\theta}}\right]^{-1}\frac{\partial\mathbf{a}'}{\partial\hat{\theta}}\left(\frac{X'Z}{T}\right)\gamma.$$

Thus

$$W\alpha = Z\left(\frac{Z'Z}{T}\right)^{-1}\left(\frac{Z'X}{T}\right)\frac{\partial\mathbf{a}}{\partial\hat{\theta}}\delta. \tag{10}$$

Multiplying (10) by W' we have

$$\alpha = \frac{(W'W)^{-1}}{T}\frac{(W'Z)}{T}\frac{(Z'Z)^{-1}}{T}\left(\frac{Z'X}{T}\right)\left(\frac{\partial\mathbf{a}}{\partial\hat{\theta}}\right)\delta \tag{11}$$

and substituting this into (10) we find

$$0 = (I - W(W'W)^{-1}W')Z\left[\frac{(Z'Z)^{-1}}{T}\frac{(Z'X)}{T}\frac{\partial\mathbf{a}}{\partial\hat{\theta}}\right]\delta = d, \text{ say.} \tag{12}$$

Now suppose we can write

$$\frac{Z'Z}{T} - \frac{Z'W}{T}\frac{(W'W)^{-1}}{T}\frac{W'Z}{T} = D_2'D_2$$

where D_2 is $m_2 \times m$ of rank m_2, and

$$D_3 = \left(\frac{Z'Z}{T}\right)^{-1}\left(\frac{Z'X}{T}\right)\frac{\partial\mathbf{a}}{\partial\hat{\theta}}.$$

Then (12) implies

$$D_2D_3\delta = 0 \tag{1)3}$$

and conversely since

$$d'd = \delta' D_3' D_2' D_2 D_3 \delta$$

(noting that $I - W(W'W)^{-1}W'$ is idempotent) if (13) is satisfied so is (12).

Now the rank of $D_2 D_3$ is certainly less than m_2. Thus if $m_2 < p$ then there is certainly one δ satisfying (10). If the rank of $D_2 D_3$ is m_3, and $m_3 < p$, then there are $p - m_3$ linearly independent solutions of (13), and for each of these (11) gives a corresponding α, so that Ω_w is of rank $N + m_3 - p$. In general we would expect $m_3 = m_2$, so that the rank of $\hat{\Omega}_w$ would be $N + m_2 - p$. Consider first the case where the rank m_3 is independent of T and rank $(\Omega_w) = N + m_3 - p$.

Now we show that,

$$\hat{\mathbf{w}}' \hat{\Omega}_w^- \hat{\mathbf{w}}/s^2 \underset{a}{\sim} \chi^2_{N+m_3-p}$$

where $\hat{\Omega}_w^-$ is the generalised inverse of $\hat{\Omega}_w$.

To discuss this note that we can write

$$\hat{\Omega}_w = L^* \Lambda L^{*\prime}$$

where Λ is a diagonal matrix containing the non-zero latent roots of $\hat{\Omega}_w$ and L^* is $N \times (N + m_3 - p)$ such that $L^{*\prime} L^* = I_{N+m_3-p}$ and then

$$\hat{\Omega}_w^- = L^* \Lambda^{-1} L^{*\prime}.$$

Now write

$$\mathbf{w}^* = \Lambda^{-1/2} L^{*\prime} \hat{\mathbf{w}}/s,$$

and note that

$$\hat{\mathbf{w}}' \hat{\Omega}_w^- \hat{\mathbf{w}}/s^2 = \hat{\mathbf{w}}' L^* \Lambda^{-1} L^{*\prime} \hat{\mathbf{w}}/s^2 = w^{*\prime} w^*.$$

Also using Cramer's General Linear Transformation theorem the $\mathbf{w}^*$ are asymptotically normally distributed with asymptotic variance matrix

$$L^+ \sigma^2 \Omega_w L^{+\prime}$$

where

$$L^+ = \text{plim}(\Lambda^{-1/2} L^{*\prime}/s)$$
$$= \text{plim}(\Lambda^{-1/2} L^* \hat{\Omega}_w L^{*\prime} \Lambda^{-1/2})$$
$$= I_{N+m_3-p}.$$

Thus the $\mathbf{w}^*$ are asymptotic t ratios and $\mathbf{w}^{*\prime} \mathbf{w}^* \underset{a}{\sim} \chi^2_{N+m_3-p}$. Suppose now that $\dfrac{W^{+\prime} W^+}{T}$ may have higher rank than plim $\hat{\Omega}_w$, but the rank of Ω_w is known to be r.

Then we write $\hat{\Omega}_w^* = L^* \Lambda^{-1} L^{*\prime}$, where now Λ contains the r largest latent roots of $\hat{\Omega}_w$ and L^* the corresponding latent vectors. It follows as before that

$$\hat{w}'\Omega_w^*\hat{w}/s^2 \underset{a}{\sim} \chi_r^2.$$

3 THE CASE WHERE W INCLUDES ESTIMATED LAGGED ERRORS

We now consider the case where W contains u_{t-1}, or more generally some set of u_{t-s}. Denoting this by the vector u_s, we have

$$\frac{\hat{u}'\hat{u}_s}{\sqrt{T}} = \frac{u'u_s}{\sqrt{T}} + \left(\frac{u_s'X}{T}\right)\left(\frac{\partial a}{\partial \theta}\right)^* \Delta\theta\sqrt{T} + \left(\frac{u'X_s}{T}\right)\left(\frac{\partial a}{\partial \theta}\right)^* \Delta\theta\sqrt{T} + O\left(\frac{1}{\sqrt{T}}\right)$$

and we assume that $\text{plim}\left(\dfrac{u'X_s}{T}\right) = 0$. ($X_s$ has $x_{i(t-s)}$ as its t_ith element.) Thus the third term is $O(1\sqrt{T})$, and can therefore be neglected asymptotically. Thus we have the same asymptotic distribution as if we had included u_s (the exact lagged error) rather than $\hat{u}_s$ in W. Similarly we have that $\hat{\Omega}_w$ will be a consistent estimate of Ω_w whether we use $\hat{u}_s$ or u_s in defining $\hat{\Omega}_w$. Thus all our previous methods go through and the criterion $\hat{w}'\hat{\Omega}_w^-\hat{w}/s^2 \underset{a}{\sim} \chi_r^2$ as before. Note that the result allows us to consider a case where all columns of W are $\hat{u}_s$ for some set of s.

4 THE 2SLS ESTIMATOR

Suppose now that the equation can be considered as part of a model in which the errors are serially uncorrelated. This may be obtained by taking a simultaneous equation model of which the errors are generated by general rth order autoregressive processes as in [5]. By substituting the errors of the structural equations into the autoregressive equations generating them one obtains a set of equations involving the original variables with up to r lags, but with serially independent errors. Then the equation which we are estimating is of the same type and the two stage least squares estimates are obtained when Z, the set of instrumental variables, contains all the predetermined variables in this model, including the lagged values of all the variables in the original structural equations up to rth order lagged. Then we can summarise the serially uncorrelated version of the reduced form of the model by writing

$$X' = PZ' + V'$$

where

$$\text{plim}\frac{V'Z}{T} = \text{plim}\left(\frac{V'W}{T}\right) = 0.$$

Then the formula for Ω_w can be simplified. This is perhaps most easily seen by considering the plim of $\hat{\Omega}_w$ given by equation (3). Denote

$$\bar{D}=\operatorname{plim}\left(\frac{W'W}{T}\right)^{-1/2}\left(\frac{W'Z}{T}\right)\left(\frac{Z'Z}{T}\right)^{-1/2}$$

and

$$\bar{Q}_\theta=\operatorname{plim}Q_\theta$$

then we note that

$$\operatorname{plim}\left(\frac{W'X}{T}\frac{\partial\mathbf{a}}{\partial\theta}\right)=\operatorname{plim}\left(\frac{W'Z}{T}\right)P'\frac{\partial\mathbf{a}}{\partial\theta}+\operatorname{plim}\left(\frac{W'V}{T}\right)\frac{\partial\mathbf{a}}{\partial\theta}$$

$$=(M^*)^{1/2}\bar{D}M^{1/2}P'\frac{\partial\mathbf{a}}{\partial\theta}$$

and also that $\operatorname{plim}\left(\left(\frac{W'Z}{T}\right)\left(\frac{Z'Z}{T}\right)^{-1}(Z'X)\frac{\partial\mathbf{a}}{\partial\theta}\right)$ is the same. Thus the last two terms of the plim of $\hat{\Omega}_w$ from (7) cancel and the plim can be written $\Omega_w=M^*-M^{*1/2}\bar{D}\bar{Q}_\theta\bar{D}'M^{*1/2}$.

We can then consider a simpler consistent estimate of Ω_w

$$\hat{\Omega}_w=\frac{W'W}{T}-\left(\frac{W'Z}{T}\right)\left(\frac{Z'Z}{T}\right)^{-1}\frac{Z'X}{T}\frac{\partial\mathbf{a}}{\partial\hat{\theta}}\left[\frac{\partial\mathbf{a}}{\partial\hat{\theta}}\left(\frac{X'Z}{T}\right)\left(\frac{Z'Z}{T}\right)^{-1}\left(\frac{Z'X}{T}\right)\frac{\partial\mathbf{a}}{\partial\hat{\theta}}\right]$$

$$\times\frac{\partial\mathbf{a}'}{\partial\hat{\theta}}\frac{X'Z}{T}\left(\frac{Z'Z}{T}\right)^{-1}\left(\frac{Z'W}{T}\right). \tag{14}$$

There is no difficulty in giving a similar proof to that of Section (2) that $\hat{\Omega}_w$ is of rank less than or equal to $N+m_2-p$. More specifically if $m_2\geqslant p$, then $\hat{\Omega}_w$ is non-singular, but if $p>m_2$ then Ω_w and $\hat{\Omega}_w$ will generally be of rank $N+m_2-p$. In this case

$$\hat{\mathbf{w}}'\hat{\Omega}_w^{-1}\hat{\mathbf{w}}/s^2\underset{a}{\sim}\chi^2_{N+m_2-p}.$$

Now finally consider the case when W contains all the variables Z. It will then be possible to introduce a linear transformation so that

$$W^*=WH=(Z:Z^*)\qquad\text{and}\qquad\operatorname{plim}\frac{Z'Z^*}{T}=0$$

and we now consider

$$\hat{\mathbf{w}}'\left(\frac{W'W}{T}\right)^{-1}\hat{\mathbf{w}}=\hat{\mathbf{w}}^{*'}\left(\frac{W^{*'}W^*}{T}\right)^{-1}\hat{\mathbf{w}}^*$$

$$=\hat{\mathbf{w}}_1'\left(\frac{Z'Z}{T}\right)^{-1}\hat{\mathbf{w}}_1+\hat{\mathbf{w}}_2'\left(\frac{Z^{*'}Z^*}{T}\right)^{-1}\hat{\mathbf{w}}_2$$

where

$$\hat{\mathbf{w}}^* = H\hat{\mathbf{w}} = \begin{pmatrix} \mathbf{w}_1 \\ \mathbf{w}_2 \end{pmatrix}_{N-m}^{m}.$$

Now from (6)

$$\hat{\mathbf{w}}_1 = \frac{Z'u}{\sqrt{T}} + \frac{Z'X}{T}\left(\frac{\partial \mathbf{a}}{\partial \theta}\right)^* \sqrt{T}(\Delta\theta)$$

$$\hat{\mathbf{w}}_2 = \frac{Z^{*'}u}{\sqrt{T}} + \frac{Z^{*'}X}{T}\left(\frac{\partial \mathbf{a}}{\partial \theta}\right)^* \sqrt{T}(\Delta\theta).$$

Now note that

$$\text{plim}\left(\frac{Z^{*'}X}{T}\right) = \text{plim}\left(\frac{Z^{*'}Z}{T}\right)P' + \text{plim}\left(\frac{Z^{*'}u}{T}\right)$$

so that

$$\hat{\mathbf{w}}_2 = \frac{Z^{*'}u}{\sqrt{T}} + O\left(\frac{1}{\sqrt{T}}\right).$$

On the other hand

$$\hat{\mathbf{w}}_1 = \left(\frac{Z'Z}{T}\right)^{1/2}(I - Q_\theta)\left(\frac{Z'Z}{T}\right)^{-1/2}\frac{Z'u}{\sqrt{T}} + O\left(\frac{1}{\sqrt{T}}\right).$$

Thus it follows in the usual way that

$$\phi_1 = \hat{\mathbf{w}}_2'\left(\frac{Z^{*'}Z^*}{T}\right)^{-1}\hat{\mathbf{w}}_2/s^2 \underset{a}{\sim} \chi^2_{N-m}$$

and

$$\phi_2 = \hat{\mathbf{w}}_1'\left(\frac{Z'Z}{T}\right)^{-1}\hat{\mathbf{w}}_1/s^2 \underset{a}{\sim} \chi^2_{m-p}$$

but we also have easily that $\hat{\mathbf{w}}_1$ and $\hat{\mathbf{w}}_2$ are asymptotically independent so that

$$\hat{\mathbf{w}}'\left(\frac{W'W}{T}\right)^{-1}\hat{\mathbf{w}}/s^2 = \phi_1 + \phi_2 \underset{a}{\sim} \chi^2_{N-p}.$$

Note that in order to avoid explicitly computing the Z^* it might be convenient to consider

$$\left[\hat{\mathbf{w}}'\left(\frac{W'W}{T}\right)^{-1}\hat{\mathbf{w}} - \hat{\mathbf{w}}_1'\left(\frac{Z'Z}{T}\right)^{-1}\hat{\mathbf{w}}_1\right]/s^2 = \phi_1.$$

It would certainly seem reasonable to consider ϕ_1 and ϕ_2 independently.

As an example of this case consider a case where the Z are as before, and the ϕ_2 test can be regarded as a test of the assumption that an equation of the given form can be found with errors independent of the predetermined variables in the model; this is the same as the usual test for misspecification in the model. Suppose in particular now that the remaining instrumental variables in W are lagged values of $\hat{u}$. Then the ϕ_1 test might be regarded as particularly relevant to testing the specification of the autoregressive process generating the errors. Note that any misspecification of the equation will equally affect the distribution of ϕ_1, so that it cannot be regarded as particularly powerful against misspecification of the autoregressive side of the model without detailed analysis.

5 THE APPLICATION TO MULTIPLE REGRESSION

Suppose now that

$$u = X\mathbf{a}(\theta) = y - Z\beta(\theta)$$

where y is the only current endogenous variable in the equation, and its coefficient is constrained to be one. (14) is now replaced by

$$\tilde{\Omega}_w = \frac{W'W}{T} - \left(\frac{W'Z}{T}\right)\frac{\partial\beta}{\partial\theta}\left[\left(\frac{\partial\beta}{\partial\theta}\right)'\frac{Z'Z}{T}\frac{\partial\beta}{\partial\theta}\right]^{-1}\left(\frac{\partial\beta}{\partial\theta}\right)'\left(\frac{Z'W}{T}\right), \quad (15)$$

but the previous discussion of Section 4 is then immediately applicable.

Now returning to the model of equation (2) and (3) of Section 2, suppose that now y_t is a scalar, so that the equation contains only one endogenous variable both current and lagged but there may be any number of non-stochastic exogenous variables. Now Z is made up of $y_{t-i}, i = 1, \ldots, r+k$, and the $Z_{t-i}, i = 0, \ldots, r+j$. Our discussion of Section 4 is still valid and in particular if W contains all the Z and some set of $\hat{u}_{t-i}, i = 1, \ldots, m$, then we can consider the two criteria ϕ_1 and ϕ_2. Consider now the case where W contains only a set of $\hat{u}_{t-i}, i = 1, \ldots, m$ then if we write $Z = Z^0 + Z^*$, where Z^0 is non-stochastic, and Z^* is stochastic (i.e. that the part of y_{t-i} that is a linear combination of $u_{t-s}, s = i, \ldots, \infty$), then we have that $\text{plim}\,\dfrac{W'Z}{T} = \text{plim}\,\dfrac{W'Z^*}{T}$, but $\text{plim}\left(\dfrac{Z'Z}{T}\right) = \text{plim}\left(\dfrac{Z^{0'}Z^0}{T}\right) + \text{plim}\left(\dfrac{Z^{*'}Z^*}{T}\right)$. It follows in this case $M^{*-1/2}\Omega_w M^{*-1/2}$ is not an idempotent matrix and so

$$\hat{\mathbf{w}}'\left(\frac{W'W}{T}\right)^{-1}\hat{\mathbf{w}}/s^2 \text{ is not an asymptotic } \chi^2.$$

On the other hand if there are no exogenous variables so that Z contains only lagged endogenous variables then if W contains sufficient $\hat{u}_{t-i}$, we can express y_{t-i}, $i = 1, \ldots, r+k$ in the form

$$y_{t-i} = \sum_{s=0}^{m-r-k} \delta_s u_{t-i-s} + \text{remainder}.$$

The δ_s come from expressing the autoregressive equation as an infinite moving average. The remainder will be small if m is large. Thus appropriately we can carry out a linear transformation on the W which are the $\hat{u}_{t-i}, i = 1, \ldots, m$, to get an equivalent W^* whose instrumental variables are y_{t-i}, $i = 1, \ldots, r+k$, $\hat{u}_{t-i}$, $i = r+k+1, \ldots, m$. Also note that $\text{plim}\left(\dfrac{W'W}{T}\right) = s^2 I_m$. Thus we have that $\hat{w}'\hat{w}/s^4 \underset{a}{\sim} \chi^2_{m-r-k}$.

6 THE EXTENSION TO SETS OF EQUATIONS

Consider now the case where we have a set of q equations which can be written

$$X A'(\theta) = U \tag{16}$$

where now the errors in the tth period u_t are serially independent with $E(u_t u_t') = \Omega_u$, a positive definite $q \times q$ matrix. If $\hat{\Omega}_u$ is some preliminary consistent estimate of Ω_u, and Z is some suitable set of m instrumental variables one can define an improved instrumental variable estimator as the values of θ minimising

$$\text{tr}(\hat{\Omega}_u^{-1} A(\theta)(X'Z)(Z'Z)^{-1}Z'X A'(\theta))/T$$
$$= \mathbf{a}^{*\prime}(\theta)(\hat{\Omega}_u^{-1} \otimes \hat{R})\mathbf{a}^*(\theta)$$

where

$$\hat{R} = (X'Z)(Z'Z)^{-1}(Z'X)/T$$

and

$$\mathbf{a}^*(\theta) = \text{vec}(A(\theta)).$$

The first order conditions for a minimum are

$$\left(\frac{\partial \mathbf{a}^*}{\partial \hat{\theta}}\right)'(\hat{\Omega}_u^{-1} \otimes \hat{R})\mathbf{a}^*(\hat{\theta}) = 0 \tag{17}$$

where $\mathbf{a}^*(\theta)$ is $qn \times 1$, $\hat{R}$ is $n \times n$. Now we consider $\hat{w} = \text{vec}(\hat{U}'W/\sqrt{T})$ where $\hat{U} = X A'(\theta)$. Then

$$\hat{w} = \text{vec}(U'W/\sqrt{T}) + \text{vec}(\sqrt{T}(A(\hat{\theta}) - A(\theta))(X'W/T)$$

$$= \text{vec}(U'W/\sqrt{T}) + (I \otimes W'X/T)\left(\frac{\partial \mathbf{a}^{**}}{\partial \theta}\right)\sqrt{T}(\Delta\theta)$$

where $\dfrac{\partial \mathbf{a}^{**}}{\partial \theta}$ is evaluated at some point between $\hat{\theta}$ and θ.

Now

$$\sqrt{T}(\Delta\theta) = -\left(\frac{\partial \mathbf{a}^{*\prime}}{\partial \hat{\theta}}(\hat{\Omega}_u^{-1} \otimes \hat{R})\frac{\partial \mathbf{a}^{**}}{\partial \theta}\right)^{-1}$$

$$\times \left(\frac{\partial \mathbf{a}^{*\prime}}{\partial \hat{\theta}}\left(\hat{\Omega}_u^{-1} \otimes \left(\frac{X'Z}{T}\right)\left(\frac{Z'Z}{T}\right)^{-1}\right)\mathrm{vec}\left(\frac{U'Z}{T}\right)\right)$$

and following the same arguments as in Section 2 and writing

$$\Omega_\theta = \left(\frac{\partial \mathbf{a}^{*\prime}}{\partial \theta}(\Omega_u^{-1} \otimes R)\frac{\partial \mathbf{a}^*}{\partial \theta}\right)^{-1} \quad \text{where } R = \mathrm{plim}\,\hat{R} = KM^{-1}K'$$

we find that

$$\hat{\mathbf{w}}' \underset{a}{\sim} N(0, \Omega_w)$$

where

$$\Omega_w = \Omega_u \otimes M^* - (I \otimes K^{*\prime})\frac{\partial \mathbf{a}^*}{\partial \theta}\,\Omega_\theta\,\frac{\partial \mathbf{a}^{*\prime}}{\partial \theta}(I \otimes KM^{-1}\tilde{M}') - (I \otimes \tilde{M}M^{-1}K')$$

$$\times \frac{\partial \mathbf{a}^*}{\partial \theta}\,\Omega_\theta\,\frac{\partial \mathbf{a}^{*\prime}}{\partial \theta}(I \otimes K^*) + (I \otimes K^{*\prime})\frac{\partial \mathbf{a}^*}{\partial \theta}\,\Omega_\theta\left(\frac{\partial \mathbf{a}^*}{\partial \theta}\right)'(I \otimes K^*)$$

and where $\tilde{M} = \mathrm{plim}\left(\dfrac{W'Z}{T}\right)$ and writing

$$\hat{\Omega}_\theta = \left(\frac{\partial \mathbf{a}^{*\prime}}{\partial \hat{\theta}}(\hat{\Omega}_u^{-1} \otimes \hat{R})\frac{\partial \mathbf{a}^{*\prime}}{\partial \theta}\right)^{-1}$$

we obtain a non-negative definite estimate of Ω_w by taking

$$\hat{\Omega}_w = \hat{\Omega}_u \otimes (W'W/T) - \left[(I \otimes W'X/T)\frac{\partial \mathbf{a}^*}{\partial \hat{\theta}}\,\hat{\Omega}_\theta\,\frac{\partial \mathbf{a}^*}{\partial \hat{\theta}}\right.$$

$$\left.\times \left(I \otimes \left(\frac{X'Z}{T}\right)\left(\frac{Z'Z}{T}\right)^{-1}\left(\frac{Z'W}{T}\right)\right)\right] - \left(I \otimes \left(\frac{W'Z}{T}\right)\left(\frac{Z'Z}{T}\right)^{-1}\frac{Z'X}{T}\right)$$

$$\times \left(\frac{\partial \mathbf{a}^*}{\partial \hat{\theta}}\right)\hat{\Omega}_\theta\left(\frac{\partial \mathbf{a}^*}{\partial \hat{\theta}}\right)'\left(I \otimes \frac{X'W}{T}\right) + \left(I \otimes \frac{W'X}{T}\right)\frac{\partial \mathbf{a}^*}{\partial \hat{\theta}}\,\hat{\Omega}_\theta\,\frac{\partial \mathbf{a}^{*\prime}}{\partial \hat{\theta}}\left(I \otimes \frac{X'W}{T}\right)$$

$$\tag{18}$$

In the 3SLS case where the Z include all the predetermined variables in the model, we can use the alternative estimate,

$$\tilde{\Omega}_w = \hat{\Omega}_u \otimes W'W/T - \left(I \otimes \left(\frac{W'Z}{T}\right)\left(\frac{Z'Z}{T}\right)^{-1}\left(\frac{Z'X}{T}\right)\left(\frac{\partial \mathbf{a}^*}{\partial \tilde{\theta}}\right)\hat{\Omega}_\theta \left(\frac{\partial \mathbf{a}^*}{\partial \tilde{\theta}}\right)'\right.$$

$$\left. \times \left(I \otimes \left(\frac{X'Z}{T}\right)\left(\frac{Z'Z}{T}\right)^{-1}\left(\frac{Z'W}{T}\right)\right)\right)$$

as in Section 4.

In either case the estimated Ω_w will be non-singular in general if $qm_2 \geqslant p$; and is of rank $qN + qm_2 - p$ if $p > qm_2$. In either case $\hat{\mathbf{w}}'\tilde{\Omega}_w^- \hat{\mathbf{w}}$ or $\hat{\mathbf{w}}'\tilde{\Omega}_w^- \hat{\mathbf{w}}$ is asymptotically distributed as a χ^2 with degrees of freedom equal to the rank of the estimated Ω_w.

Considering now the case where the equations (16) are all the non-identities in a complete model and this is estimated by FIML, writing $\tilde{\theta}$ for the corresponding estimates, and

$$\tilde{Q} = \begin{pmatrix} P(\tilde{\theta}) \\ I \end{pmatrix}$$

where $P(\tilde{\theta})$ is the matrix of reduced form coefficients, and $\tilde{\Omega}_u = A(\tilde{\theta})((X'X)/T)A'(\tilde{\theta})$, the first order condition for the minimum can be written

$$\left(\frac{\partial \mathbf{a}^*}{\partial \tilde{\theta}}\right)'(\tilde{\Omega}_u^{-1} \otimes \tilde{Q}(Z'X)/T))\mathbf{a}^*(\tilde{\theta}) = 0$$

and defining

$$\tilde{u} = XA'(\tilde{\theta}),$$

$$\tilde{\mathbf{w}} = \text{vec}(\tilde{u}'W/\sqrt{T})$$

and noting that Z contains all the predetermined variables in the model, we have that $\tilde{\mathbf{w}}$ and $\hat{\mathbf{w}}$ have asymptotically equivalent distributions, and we can introduce a further estimate of Ω_w

$$\Omega_w^+ = \tilde{\Omega}_u \otimes W'W/T - (I \otimes (W'Z/T)\tilde{Q}')\left(\frac{\partial \mathbf{a}^*}{\partial \tilde{\theta}}\right)\tilde{\Omega}_\theta \left(\frac{\partial \mathbf{a}^*}{\partial \tilde{\theta}}\right)'(I \otimes \tilde{Q}(ZW)/T)$$

and the criterion $\tilde{\mathbf{w}}'\Omega_w^{+-}\tilde{\mathbf{w}}$ has the same asymptotic distribution as $\hat{\mathbf{w}}'\tilde{\Omega}_w^-\hat{\mathbf{w}}$.

Considering finally the case where W contains all the variables Z. As in Section 4 we can now consider

$$\hat{\mathbf{w}}'(\hat{\Omega}_u^{-1} \otimes (W'W/T)^{-1})\hat{\mathbf{w}}$$

or

$$\tilde{\mathbf{w}}'(\tilde{\Omega}_u^{-1} \otimes (W'W/T)^{-1})\tilde{\mathbf{w}}.$$

Both these criteria are distributed asymptotically as $\chi^2 s$ of degree of freedom $Nq - p$.

Of course it is possible to use lagged values of $\hat{U}$ as elements of W without changing the form of the criterion.

7 CHANGING THE ESTIMATE OF THE VARIANCE MATRIX

The various estimates of Ω_w which have been considered in the previous sections have all been chosen so that they are non-negative, definite; in practice they will be of the same rank as Ω_w with probability one, and the corresponding criteria will also be non-negative. However minor changes in the $\hat{\Omega}_w$, which take account of the known structure of the instrumental variables second moment matrix, and which should still be a consistent estimators of Ω_w, may lead to a negative value for the criterion. In fact it is well known that in Durbin's case, where W consists of a single variable equal to $\hat{u}_{t-1}$, the corresponding estimate of the scalar Ω_w may turn out to be negative. This is presumably because the first term of the formula corresponding to (15) is being estimated from $u_t, t = 1, \ldots, T$ and not from $u_{t-1}, t = 1, \ldots, T$ and that expected values of the $(W'Z/T)$ terms are also being used in the later terms. The use of the $\hat{\Omega}_w$, $\tilde{\Omega}_w$ and Ω_w^+ of this paper, without taking account of the implied simplifications that may follow from the knowledge of the model generating the endogenous variables and the lagged endogenous variables may be crude, but it has the advantage of producing criteria which are very general, and of sufficiently simple definition that general computing programs are easily written, and finally that the criteria are always non-negative. (Of course, if making use of a consistent estimate of Ω_w we produce a negative quantity which is on the null hypothesis asymptotically distributed as a χ^2, this may be regarded as a sign that the model is misspecified, i.e. that the null hypothesis is incorrect although not necessarily simply that the error is higher order autoregressive, or alternatively that the asymptotic approximation is poor.)

8 THE RELATIONSHIP TO OTHER χ^2 TESTS

The tests of this paper are an extension of the Durbin and Box–Jenkins tests. But for the instrumental variables and 3SLS estimators they are an extension of the usual χ^2 tests for misspecification. For the single equation the misspecification test is

$$(\hat{u}'Z)(Z'Z)^{-1}(Z'\hat{u}) \underset{a}{\sim} \chi^2_{m-p} \tag{19}$$

and for the set of equations case we have

$$\mathrm{tr}(\hat{\Omega}_u^{-1}\hat{U}'Z(Z'Z)^{-1}Z'\hat{U}) = \mathrm{vec}(\hat{U}'Z)'(\hat{\Omega}_u^{-1} \otimes (Z'Z)^{-1})\,\mathrm{vec}(U'Z) \underset{a}{\sim} \chi^2_{qm-p}. \tag{20}$$

Where we have a complete set of equations (except for identities) and the Zs include all the predetermined variables in the model, this can be shown to be asymptotically equivalent to the corresponding log likelihood test for the constrained model compared with the completely unconstrained reduced form.

Now in general asymptotic significance tests based on χ^2 criteria discriminate between nested hypotheses on the basis of the difference between criterion functions, e.g. differences in likelihood functions. This is true for the instrumental variable estimator.

To illustrate, suppose that in the equation of Section 2 we have $\mathbf{a}(\theta) = \mathbf{a}(\phi(\theta))$, i.e. $\mathbf{a}$ is a function of $p^* \times 1$ vector ϕ, which is in turn a function of a $p \times 1$ vector θ, and consider the estimates of $\mathbf{a}(\phi)$ obtained by minimising

$$\mathbf{a}(\phi)'(X'Z)(Z'Z)^{-1}(Z'X)\mathbf{a}(\phi).$$

Suppose we denote the estimates of ϕ obtained in this way by $\hat{\phi}$ and the corresponding estimates of u by u_1. Then asymptotically

$$(\hat{u}'Z)(Z'Z)^{-1}(Z'\hat{u}) - (\hat{u}_1'Z)(Z'Z)^{-1}(Z'\hat{u}_1)$$

is distributed as a χ^2 with $p^* - p$ degrees of freedom. On the other hand if we consider the original equation with $\mathbf{a} = \mathbf{a}(\theta)$, but with two sets of instrumental variables Z and W of which the latter set contains the former, and two corresponding estimates of θ, $\hat{\theta}$, $\hat{\theta}_2$ and corresponding estimates of u, $\hat{u}$ and $\hat{u}_2$ then we can show easily that

$$(\hat{u}'Z)(Z'Z)^{-1}(Z'\hat{u}) \underset{a}{\sim} \chi^2_{m-p} \tag{21}$$

and

$$(\hat{u}_2'W)(W'W)^{-1}(W'\hat{u}_2) \underset{a}{\sim} \chi^2_{N-p}.$$

We can also show directly that

$$(\hat{u}_2'W)(W'W)^{-1}(W'\hat{u}_2) - (\hat{u}'Z)(Z'Z)^{-1}(Z'\hat{u}) \tag{22}$$

is asymptotically a χ^2_{N-m} independent of (21). For (22) can obviously be written as a quadratic in $\mathbf{w} = (W'u/\sqrt{T})$ and we now show that (22) is always non-negative. As in Section 4 we can introduce a linear transformation H such that

$$W^* = WH = (Z:Z^*), \text{ where } Z'Z^* = 0.$$

Then

$$(\hat{u}_2'W)(W'W)^{-1}(W'\hat{u}_2) = (\hat{u}_2'Z)(Z'Z)^{-1}(Z'\hat{u}_2) + (\hat{u}_2'Z^*)(Z^{*'}Z^*)^{-1}(Z^{*'}\hat{u}_2)$$

and since $\hat{\theta}$ minimised $(\hat{u}'Z)(Z'Z)^{-1}(Z'\hat{u})$,

$$(\hat{u}_2'Z)(Z'Z)^{-1}(Z'\hat{u}_2) \geqslant (\hat{u}'Z)(Z'Z)^{-1}(Z'\hat{u}).$$

Thus

$$(\hat{u}_2'W)(W'W)^{-1}W'\hat{u}_2 \geqslant (\hat{u}'Z)(Z'Z)^{-1}(Z'\hat{u}).$$

It follows that the asymptotic quadratic form is non-negative, but since it can be expressed as the difference of two idempotent quadratic forms, we can use the well-known theorem that shows that the difference is also idempotent and independent of the idempotent matrix which is being subtracted. Thus the required result follows that (22) is asymptotically a χ^2_{N-m}.

Now specialising on the case where the Z contain all the predetermined variables in the model it is not difficult to prove that in this case

$$W'\hat{u}_2/\sqrt{T} - W'\hat{u}/\sqrt{T} = O\left(\frac{1}{\sqrt{T}}\right)$$

so that

$$(\hat{u}_2'W)(W'W)^{-1}W'\hat{u}_2$$

has the same distribution as

$$(\hat{u}'W)(W'W)^{-1}(W'\hat{u})$$

which is $\phi_1 + \phi_2$ of Section 4.

To compare the tests discussed at the beginning of this section with the tests discussed in Section 2 of this article we have to consider a somewhat arbitrary generalisation of the original equation. Consider the equation

$$X\mathbf{a}(\theta) + Z^*\gamma = u^* \tag{23}$$

where Z^* as defined in Section 4 satisfied $\text{plim}(Z^{*\prime}Z/T) = 0$, and $W = (Z:Z^*)$ is an extended set of instrumental variables. Then we estimate θ and γ by minimising

$$(u^{*\prime}W)(W'W)^{-1}(W'u^*) = (u'Z)(Z'Z)^{-1}(Z'u) + (u'Z^*)(Z^{*\prime}Z^*)^{-1}Z^{*\prime}u$$

$$+ 2(u'Z^*)\gamma + \gamma'(Z^{*\prime}Z)\gamma$$

where $u = X\mathbf{a}(\theta)$.

Minimising first w.r.t. γ we have

$$\gamma = -(Z^{*\prime}Z^*)^{-1}Z^{*\prime}u$$

and now we minimise the following function w.r.t. θ (this being the resulting minimum w.r.t. γ)

$$(u'Z)(Z'Z)^{-1}(Z'u) = \mathbf{a}(\theta)'(X'Z)(Z'Z)^{-1}(Z'X)\mathbf{a}(\theta).$$

Thus the equation (23) estimated using W as instrumental variables gives the same estimate of θ as is obtained by estimating $Xa(\theta) = u$, using Z as instrumental variables. Now as before writing $\hat{u}_2$ as the estimated residuals on the latter equation when W are used as instrumental variables the difference

$$(\hat{u}_2 W)(W'W)^{-1}(W'\hat{u}_2) - (\hat{u}'Z)(Z'Z)^{-1}(Z'\hat{u}) = \phi_1 \qquad (24)$$

is asymptotically a χ^2 of $N - m$ degrees of freedom which can be regarded as that appropriate for testing whether $\gamma = 0$.

Note in particular that if $\text{plim}(X'Z^*/T) = 0$ then (24) can be shown to be asymptotically equivalent to

$$(\hat{u}'W)(W'W)^{-1}(W'\hat{u}) - (\hat{u}'Z)(Z'Z)^{-1}(Z'\hat{u})$$

and as equivalent to ϕ_2 of Section 3.

However note that if $\text{plim}(Z^{*\prime}Z/T) \neq 0$ and/or $\text{plim}(X'Z^*/T) \neq 0$ then the asymptotic equivalence established here is not valid, and the two sets of significance tests although both asymptotic χ^2 with the same number of degrees of freedom are not asymptotically equivalent even on the null hypothesis, and can certainly be expected to differ in power against hypotheses. In particular criteria of the type (24) above, being asymptotically equivalent to LIML type likelihood ratio tests can be expected to be asymptotically more powerful than the tests discussed in Section 2. These results extend to the corresponding tests for sets of equations.

Considering two sets of instrumental variables Z and Z^* such that $\text{plim}(Z'Z^*)/T = 0$, and writing $W = (Z:Z^*)$ we consider the alternative hypothesis that

$$A(\theta)X' + \Gamma Z^{*\prime} = U^{*\prime} \qquad (25)$$

and the null hypothesis that $\Gamma = 0$. Now (25) is estimated using W as instrumental variables by minimising

$$\text{vec}(U^*W)'(\hat{\Omega}_u^{-1} \otimes (W'W)^{-1})\,\text{vec}(U^{*\prime}W) \qquad (26)$$

and differentiating w.r.t. Γ we find that

$$\Gamma = -A(\theta)(X'Z^*)(Z^{*\prime}Z^*)^{-1}$$

and that if we substitute this into (26) we obtain

$$\text{vec}(U'Z)'(\hat{\Omega}_u^{-1} \otimes (Z'Z)^{-1})\,\text{vec}(U'Z) \quad \text{where } U = XA'(\theta). \qquad (27)$$

Thus the corresponding estimates of θ are equal to those obtained by setting $\Gamma = 0$ and using Z as instrumental variables. Denote the corresponding residuals U by $\hat{U}$, and the residuals obtained by minimising (26) subject to $\Gamma = 0$ by $\hat{U}_2$. Then the usual χ^2 criterion for testing $\Gamma = 0$ is

$$\text{vec}(\hat{U}_2'W)'(\hat{\Omega}_u^{-1} \otimes (W'W)^{-1}) \, \text{vec}(\hat{U}_2'W)$$

$$-\text{vec}(\hat{U}'Z)'(\hat{\Omega}_u^{-1} \otimes (Z'Z)^{-1} \, \text{vec}(\hat{U}'Z) \quad (28)$$

which is asymptotically a χ^2 of $n(N-m)$ degrees of freedom.

Now finally if $\text{plim}(X'Z^*/T)=0$, which will certainly be true if the null hypothesis is true, and Z contains all the predetermined variables in the model as in Section 4, then we can show that

$$\text{vec}(\hat{U}_2'W)/\sqrt{T}-\text{vec}(\hat{U}'W)/\sqrt{T}=0(1\sqrt{T}).$$

Thus the last χ^2 criterion is asymptotically equivalent to

$$\text{vec}(\hat{U}'W)(\hat{\Omega}_u^{-1} \otimes (W'W)^{-1}) \, \text{vec}(\hat{U}'W)$$

$$-\text{vec}(\hat{U}'Z)'(\hat{\Omega}_u^{-1} \otimes (Z'Z)^{-1}) \, \text{vec}(\hat{U}'Z).$$

This is an extension of the criterion discussed at the end of Section 6.

Note that (28) is the usual 3SLS criterion for the restriction $\Gamma=0$, and can easily be shown to be asymptotically equivalent to the usual likelihood ratio test for the FIML estimates of the two models.

9 A SPECIAL TEST FOR AUTOREGRESSIVE STRUCTURE

Returning to the model of equation (2) and (3) we consider estimates of ρ_s, β_i and γ_i made by autoregressive 2SLS, using all the predetermined variables in the model, in particular y_{t-i}, $i=1,\ldots,k+r$ and z_{t-i}, $i=0,\ldots,j+r$. We refer to this set of variables as Z. We now wish to consider increasing r to $r+1$. The criterion analogous to that of Durbin would consider $\hat{u}'\hat{u}_1$, and the more general Box–Pierce procedure would consider $\hat{u}'\hat{u}_s$, $s=1,\ldots,q$.

Considering first the conventional test statistics it is convenient to look at the Wald criterion which follows from the consideration of the extra constraints which are being applied to the less constrained model. The only difference between the more and less constrained model is that in the less constrained model we estimate ρ_s, $s=1,\ldots,(r+1)$ and in the more constrained model we set $\rho_{(r+1)}=0$. However a better formulation from our point of view is obtained by defining X to be made up of the set of variables Z plus the y_t.

Then we can think of the null hypothesis as corresponding to the equation

$$X\mathbf{a}(\theta)=u. \quad (29)$$

Now the alternative model is obtained by considering an equation of the form

$$X\mathbf{a}(\theta)-\rho^*X_1\mathbf{a}(\theta)=e \quad (30)$$

where the suffix 1 denotes the same set of variables with a unit lag. If we write equation (2) in terms of the lag operator L as

$$\rho(L)\eta_t = u_t$$

then (30) is equivalent to assuming an autoregressive equation of the form

$$(1 - \rho^* L)\rho(L)\eta_t = u_t.$$

Thus (30) is equivalent to introducing an extra root ρ^* into the autoregressive characteristic polynomial. Clearly the Wald test criterion is equivalent to the t ratio testing that $\hat{\rho}$ (the unconstrained estimate of ρ^*) is not significantly different from zero.

Writing $\theta^* = \begin{pmatrix} \theta \\ \rho^* \end{pmatrix}$, and X^* for the set of variables $y_{t-r-k-1}, Z_{t-r-j-1}$, and $X^+ = (X:X^*)$, then we have

$$X^+ \mathbf{a}^*(\theta^*) = X\mathbf{a}(\theta) - \rho^* X_1 \mathbf{a}(\theta).$$

Then the unconstrained estimates of θ^* are obtained by minimising

$$\mathbf{a}^*(\theta^*)'(X^{+\prime}W)(W'W)^{-1}(W'X^*)\mathbf{a}^*(\theta^*)$$

where initially we consider any set of instrumental variables W. Then writing $\hat{X} = X - \beta X_1$, we can write the first order conditions for a minimum as follows:

$$\left(\frac{\partial \mathbf{a}}{\partial \hat{\theta}}\right)'(\hat{X}'W)(W'W)^{-1}(W'\hat{X})\mathbf{a}(\hat{\theta}) = 0,$$

$$\mathbf{a}(\hat{\theta})(X_1'W)(W'W)^{-1}(W'\hat{X})\mathbf{a}(\hat{\theta}) = 0.$$

Now choosing the smallest root $\hat{\rho}$ it will be a consistent estimate of zero so that $\hat{\rho} = O(1/\sqrt{T})$, and using the expansion, $\mathbf{a}(\hat{\theta}) = \mathbf{a}(\theta) + \left(\frac{\partial \mathbf{a}}{\partial \theta}\right)\Delta\theta$ and substituting $X\mathbf{a}(\theta) = u$, $X_1\mathbf{a}(\theta) = u_1$ we find

$$\sqrt{T}\left[\left(\frac{\partial \mathbf{a}}{\partial \theta}\right)'\left(\frac{X'W}{T}\right)\left(\frac{W'W}{T}\right)^{-1}\left(\frac{W'X}{T}\right)\frac{\partial \mathbf{a}}{\partial \theta}\right]\Delta\theta$$

$$-\left(\frac{\partial \mathbf{a}}{\partial \theta}\right)'\left(\frac{X'W}{T}\right)\left(\frac{W'W}{T}\right)^{-1}\frac{W'u}{T}(\sqrt{T}\hat{\rho})$$

$$= -\left(\frac{\partial \mathbf{a}}{\partial \theta}\right)'\left(\frac{X'W}{T}\right)\left(\frac{W'W}{T}\right)^{-1}\left(\frac{W'u}{\sqrt{T}}\right) + O\left(\frac{1}{\sqrt{T}}\right),$$

$$\sqrt{T}\left(\frac{u_1'W}{T}\right)\left(\frac{W'W}{T}\right)^{-1}\left(\frac{W'X}{T}\right)\frac{\partial \mathbf{a}}{\partial \theta}\Delta\theta - \sqrt{T}\left(\frac{u_1'W}{T}\right)\left(\frac{W'W}{T}\right)^{-1}\left(\frac{W'u}{T}\right)\hat{\rho}$$

$$= -\left(\frac{u_1'W}{T}\right)\left(\frac{W'W}{T}\right)^{-1}\left(\frac{W'u}{\sqrt{T}}\right) + O\left(\frac{1}{\sqrt{T}}\right).$$

Thus the asymptotic distribution of $\hat{\rho}$ is obtained by eliminating $\Delta\theta$ to get

$$
\sqrt{T}\hat{\rho}\left(\left(\frac{u_1'W}{T}\right)\left(\frac{W'W}{T}\right)^{-1}\left(\frac{W'u_1}{T}\right)-\left(\frac{u_1'W}{T}\right)\left(\frac{W'W}{T}\right)^{-1}\left(\frac{W'X}{T}\right)\left(\frac{\partial\mathbf{a}}{\partial\theta}\right)\right.
$$

$$
\times\left[\left(\frac{\partial\mathbf{a}}{\partial\theta}\right)'\left(\frac{X'W}{T}\right)\left(\frac{W'W}{T}\right)^{-1}\left(\frac{W'X}{T}\right)\left(\frac{\partial\mathbf{a}}{\partial\theta}\right)\right]^{-1}\left(\frac{\partial\mathbf{a}}{\partial\theta}\right)'\left(\frac{X'W}{T}\right)\left(\frac{W'W}{T}\right)^{-1}\frac{W'u_1}{T}\right)
$$

$$
=\left(\frac{u_1'W}{T}\right)\left(\frac{W'W}{T}\right)^{-1}\frac{W'u}{\sqrt{T}}-\frac{u_1'W}{T}\left(\frac{W'W}{T}\right)^{-1}\left(\frac{W'X}{T}\right)\frac{\partial\mathbf{a}}{\partial\theta}
$$

$$
\left[\left(\frac{\partial\mathbf{a}}{\partial\theta}\right)'\left(\frac{X'W}{T}\right)\left(\frac{W'W}{T}\right)^{-1}\left(\frac{W'X}{T}\right)\frac{\partial\mathbf{a}}{\partial\theta}\right]^{-1}\left(\frac{\partial\mathbf{a}}{\partial\theta}\right)'\left(\frac{X'W}{T}\right)\left(\frac{W'W}{T}\right)^{-1}\frac{W'u}{\sqrt{T}}
$$

$$
+O\left(\frac{1}{\sqrt{T}}\right). \tag{31}
$$

Note that in general if we denote the estimates of θ obtained by estimating (29) using W as instrumental variables by $\tilde{\theta}$, and $\tilde{u}$, $\tilde{u}_1$ as the corresonding estimates of u and u_1 respectively then the right hand side of (31) is asymptotically equivalent of

$$
\left(\frac{\tilde{u}_1'W}{T}\right)\left(\frac{W'W}{T}\right)^{-1}\left(\frac{W'\tilde{u}}{\sqrt{T}}\right)
$$

and it follows that

$$
\left(\left(\frac{\tilde{u}_1'W}{T}\right)\left(\frac{W'W}{T}\right)^{-1}\frac{W'\tilde{u}}{\sqrt{T}}\right)^2 \bigg/ s^2\left\{\frac{\tilde{u}_1'W}{T}\left(\frac{W'W}{T}\right)^{-1}\left(\frac{W'\tilde{u}_1}{T}\right)\right.
$$

$$
-\left(\frac{\tilde{u}_1'W}{T}\right)\left(\frac{W'W}{T}\right)^{-1}\left(\frac{W'X}{T}\right)\frac{\partial\mathbf{a}}{\partial\tilde{\theta}}\left[\left(\frac{\partial\mathbf{a}}{\partial\tilde{\theta}}\right)'\left(\frac{X'W}{T}\right)\left(\frac{W'W}{T}\right)^{-1}\left(\frac{W'X}{T}\right)\left(\frac{\partial\mathbf{a}}{\partial\tilde{\theta}}\right)\right]^{-1}
$$

$$
\times\left(\frac{\partial\mathbf{a}}{\partial\tilde{\theta}}\right)'\left(\frac{X'W}{T}\right)\left(\frac{W'W}{T}\right)^{-1}\frac{W'\tilde{u}_1}{T}\right\} \tag{32}
$$

where s^2 is the usual estimate of σ^2, is asymptotically a χ^2 of one degree of freedom which is asymptotically equivalent to the efficient χ^2 with this set of instrumental variables. Note that this differs from Durbin's criterion in the introduction of the $W(W'W)^{-1}W'$ between $(\tilde{u}_1'\tilde{u})$.

Now we return to consider the standard 2SLS case considered at the beginning of this section where $W=(Z:X^*)$. Since X_1 is a subset of the W variables $u_1=X_1\mathbf{a}(\theta)$ is a linear combination of the W variables and $(u_1'W)(W'W)^{-1}W'=u_1'$. Also using the transformation of Section 4

$$\left(\frac{X'W}{T}\right)\left(\frac{W'W}{T}\right)^{-1}\left(\frac{W'X}{T}\right)=\left(\frac{X'Z}{T}\right)\left(\frac{Z'Z}{T}\right)^{-1}\left(\frac{Z'X}{T}\right)$$

$$+\left(\frac{X'Z^*}{T}\right)\left(\frac{Z^{*\prime}Z^*}{T}\right)^{-1}\left(\frac{Z^{*\prime}X}{T}\right)$$

$$=\left(\frac{X'Z}{T}\right)\left(\frac{Z'Z}{T}\right)^{-1}\left(\frac{Z'X}{T}\right)+O\left(\frac{1}{T}\right)$$

and

$$\left(\frac{X'W}{T}\right)\left(\frac{W'W}{T}\right)\left(\frac{W'u}{\sqrt{T}}\right)=\left(\frac{X'Z}{T}\right)\left(\frac{Z'Z}{T}\right)^{-1}\frac{Z'u}{\sqrt{T}}+O\left(\frac{1}{\sqrt{T}}\right).$$

Thus

$$\sqrt{T}\hat{\rho}\left(\frac{u_1'u_1}{T}-\frac{(u_1'Z)(Z'Z)^{-1}(Z'X)}{T}\left(\frac{\partial\mathbf{a}}{\partial\theta}\right)\left[\left(\frac{\partial\mathbf{a}}{\partial\theta}\right)'\left(\frac{X'Z}{T}\right)\left(\frac{Z'Z}{T}\right)^{-1}\left(\frac{Z'X}{T}\right)\frac{\partial\mathbf{a}}{\partial\theta}\right]^{-1}\right.$$

$$\left.\left(\frac{\partial\mathbf{a}}{\partial\theta}\right)'\left(\frac{X'Z}{T}\right)\left(\frac{Z'Z}{T}\right)^{-1}\frac{Z'u_1}{T}\right)$$

$$=\frac{u_1'u}{\sqrt{T}}-\frac{(u_1'Z)(Z'Z)^{-1}Z'X}{T}\left(\frac{\partial\mathbf{a}}{\partial\theta}\right)\left[\left(\frac{\partial\mathbf{a}}{\partial\theta}\right)'\left(\frac{X'Z}{T}\right)\left(\frac{Z'Z}{T}\right)^{-1}\left(\frac{Z'X}{T}\right)'\left(\frac{\partial\mathbf{a}}{\partial\theta}\right)\right]^{-1}$$

$$\times\left(\frac{\partial\mathbf{a}}{\partial\theta}\right)'\left(\frac{X'Z}{T}\right)\left(\frac{Z'Z}{T}\right)^{-1}\frac{Z'u}{\sqrt{T}}+O\left(\frac{1}{\sqrt{T}}\right).$$

Thus the criterion corresponding to (32) in this case is

$$\left(\frac{\hat{u}_1^{\circ}\hat{u}}{T}\right)^2\bigg/s^2\left\{\frac{\hat{u}_1'\hat{u}_1}{T}-\left(\frac{\hat{u}_1'Z}{T}\right)\left(\frac{Z'Z}{T}\right)^{-1}\frac{\partial\mathbf{a}}{\partial\hat{\theta}}\left[\left(\frac{\partial\mathbf{a}}{\partial\hat{\theta}}\right)'\left(\frac{X'Z}{T}\right)\left(\frac{Z'Z}{T}\right)^{-1}\left(\frac{Z'X}{T}\right)\frac{\partial\mathbf{a}}{\partial\hat{\theta}}\right]^{-1}\right.$$

$$\left.\times\left(\frac{\partial\mathbf{a}}{\partial\hat{\theta}}\right)'\left(\frac{X'Z}{T}\right)\left(\frac{Z'Z}{T}\right)^{-1}\left(\frac{Z'\hat{u}_1}{T}\right)\right\} \qquad (33)$$

where $\hat{u}$, $\hat{u}_1$ are the estimates of the errors on (29) using Z as instrumental variables. This is then asymptotically a χ^2 of one degree of freedom. Note that this is precisely equivalent to the use of the Durbin criterion using the formula (14) for the variance of the $\hat{u}_1'\hat{u}/\sqrt{T}$. This could be deduced from Durbin's results [2] if we note that 2SLS estimators are equivalent to LIML estimators, and that Durbin's general results cover all types of maximum likelihood estimators. He proves that his test is asymptotically powerful in the general context of maximum likelihood estimators. Indeed we note that in the 2SLS case his results could be extended to show that a χ^2 criterion based on $\hat{u}'\hat{u}_s$, $s=1,\ldots,q$ would be asymptotically equivalent to a Wald or likelihood ratio test against the alternative that r should be replaced by $r+q$, and that these three types of tests are all asymptotically most powerful.

Note however that this does not extend to general instrumental variables estimators and the tests suggested in Section 3 of this paper are not in general asymptotically equivalent to Wald tests for the coefficients of higher order autoregressions.

10 GENERAL COMMENTS

In the context of 2SLS and 3SLS estimators the class of tests discussed here are asymptotically equivalent to the corresponding Wald tests that certain regression coefficients are all zero. On the other hand in the context of general instrumental variable estimates the different tests are not asymptotically equivalent.

It is not difficult to discuss the asymptotic theory of these tests but it is clear that the finite sample behaviour of these tests may be very difficult. It would seem worthwhile to investigate this in some cases by Monte Carlo studies.

REFERENCES

[1] Box, G. E. P. and Pierce, D. A., 'Distribution of residual autocorrelation in autoregressive–integrated moving average time series models', *J.A.S.A.*, **65**, 1509–26 (1970).

[2] Durbin, J., 'Testing for serial correlation in least squares regression when some of the regressors are lagged dependent variables', *Econometrica*, **38**, 410–21 (1970).

[3] Mann, H. B. and Wald, A., 'On the statistical treatment of linear stochastic difference equations', *Econometrica*, **11**, 173–220 (1943).

[4] Pierce, D. A., 'Residual correlation and diagnostic checking in dynamic-disturbance time series models', *J.A.S.A.*, **67**, 636–40 (1972).

[5] Sargan, J. D., 'Wages and prices in the United Kingdom', Colston Papers (1964); printed in this volume.

[6] Sargan, J. D., 'The estimation of relationships with autocorrelated residuals by the use of instrumental variables', *J.R.S.S.* series B, **21**, 91–105 (1959).

J. D. SARGAN

—— · ——

12 THE IDENTIFICATION AND ESTIMATION OF SETS OF SIMULTANEOUS STOCHASTIC EQUATIONS

Unpublished discussion paper No. A1, *LSE*, November 1975

1 INTRODUCTION

This paper was originally given to a meeting of the Royal Statistical Society Multivariate Study Group in response to a request for a general paper on identification. It is an attempt to consider particularly the type of lack of identification that often arises in estimating time series models, where there are a finite number of observationally equivalent models, each corresponding to a different parameter vector. It has been revised, and some of the estimation procedures of Section 6 have been applied with the assistance of programme grant SEPDEM from the SSRC.

2 NUMERICAL OPTIMISATION IN THE MULTI-EQUATION LINEAR MODEL

Y is a $T \times n$ matrix of dependent variables, and Z is a $T \times m$ matrix of predetermined variables (lagged or exogenous). The Y are explained by

$$Y = ZP'(\theta) + V \tag{1}$$

where V are a set of serially independent errors such that $\Omega_v = \mathrm{E}(v_t v_t')$. The elements of the coefficient matrix $P(\theta)$ are continuous functions of a set of parameters θ.

Generalised least squares estimates would be obtained with known Ω_v by minimising (1) $\mathrm{tr}(\Omega_v^{-1} V'V) = \mathrm{tr}(\Omega_v^{-1}(Y' - P(\theta)Z')(Y - ZP'(\theta)))$ with respect to θ. If Ω_v is unknown a possible procedure is, (i) with arbitrary Ω_v minimise (1) with respect to θ, (ii) estimate $\hat{\Omega}_v = \hat{V}'\hat{V}/T$, (iii) iterate (i) and (ii). An alternative procedure notes that if the iteration converges it will converge to a maximum of the log-likelihood function.

$$L_0(\Omega_v, \theta) = -\tfrac{1}{2}Tn \log (2\pi) - \tfrac{1}{2}T \log \det \Omega_v - \tfrac{1}{2}\mathrm{tr}(\Omega_v^{-1} V'V). \tag{2}$$

This maximum can be obtained immediately by using the concentrated likelihood function

$$L_0^*(\theta) = \max_{\Omega_v} L_0(\Omega_v, \theta) = \tfrac{1}{2}Tn \log (2\pi) - \tfrac{1}{2}Tn - \tfrac{1}{2}T \log \det \left(\frac{V'V}{T}\right), \quad (3)$$

which is (2) with $\Omega_v = V'V/T$. The maximum is therefore obtained by minimising the generalised variance, $\det ((Y' - P(\theta)Z')(Y - ZP'(\theta)))$ w.r.t. θ.

3 IDENTIFICATION

Rothenberg (1971) discusses the problem of identification for certain estimates of linear models. Generalising the problem consider a stochastic model where a set of p parameters θ are to be estimated, and the log-likelihood function can be written as a function $L(\theta, M)$ of the vector of parameters θ, and a vector of sufficient statistics M.* For generality it will be assumed that a set of q constraints on θ, $\phi(\theta) = 0$ are known to be satisfied by the true value $\bar\theta$. If there exists some θ^* such that $L(\bar\theta, M) = L(\theta^*, M)$ for all M in the sample space and $\phi(\theta^*) = 0$ then there is no way on empirical and *a priori* grounds of distinguishing θ^* from $\bar\theta$, and in particular no consistent estimates of $\bar\theta$ can be made. The set of values of θ^* satisfying these conditions will be called the set of θ observationally equivalent to $\bar\theta$. This section considers the relation between consistency and identification criteria of the above type, especially when this set of θ^* is finite. Again the problem is slightly generalised by considering a function $\lambda_T(\theta, M)$ with the following properties. It is assumed that $\text{plim}_{T \to \infty} M = \bar M$ exists, but M need no longer be a sufficient statistic.

(A) $\lambda(\theta, M) = \lim_{T \to \infty} \lambda_T(\theta, M)$ uniformly for all θ and M in some neighbourhood S_1 of $\bar M$.

(B) If $\lambda(\theta, \bar M)$ is maximised with respect to θ subject to $\phi(\theta) = 0$, the global maximum is $\bar\lambda$.

(C) $\lambda(\theta, M)$ is bounded below $\bar\lambda$ at infinity in the sense that for some neighbourhood S_2 of $\bar M$ and some hypersphere $H(0, R)$ in θ space $\lambda(\theta, M) < B < \bar\lambda$ if $M \in S_2$ and $\theta \notin H$.

(D) $\lambda(\theta, M)$ is a continuous function of (θ, M) if $\theta \in H$ and $M \in S_3$ where S_3 is a neighbourhood of $\bar M$.

(E) $\phi(\theta)$ is continuous on H.

It is clear that by considering the smallest of the neighbourhoods S_1, S_2, S_3 we can introduce a neighbourhood S_0 on which (A), (C) and (D) are all satisfied.

---

* The assumption that there is a set of sufficient statistics is limiting in view of B. O. Koopman (1936), but covers not only the linear models discussed in Sections 5 and 6 but binomial and Poisson models with probabilities depending in a general way on other sets of variables.

The set of points in θ space such that θ is a global maximum of $\lambda(\theta, \bar{M})$, will be called the set of asymptotic maxima and denoted by E. Denote by $E(\delta)$ those points in θ space which are within a distance less than δ of a point of E.

THEOREM 1. *The probability that all the global maxima of $\lambda_T(\theta, M)$ subject to $\phi(\theta) = 0$ are contained in $E(\delta)$ tends to one as $T \to \infty$.*

Proof. $E(\delta)$ is defined as an open set. H^* is the set of points in H but not in $E(\delta)$. The intersection of H^* and the set defined as $(\theta : \phi(\theta) = 0)$ is a compact set and $\lambda(\theta, \bar{M})$ has a maximum $\lambda^* < \bar{\lambda}$ on this set. Define $5h = \min(\bar{\lambda} - \lambda^*, \bar{\lambda} - B)$.

From the uniformity of continuity of $\lambda(\theta, M)$ on the compact set in (θ, M) space defined by $\theta \in H$, $M \in S_0$ there exists δ_2 such that $|\lambda(\theta, M) - \lambda(\theta, \bar{M})| < h$ if $\|M - \bar{M}\| < \delta_2$ and $\theta \in H$. From the uniformity of convergence of $\lambda_T(\theta, M)$ to $\lambda(\theta, M)$ there exists T_0 such that $|\lambda_T(\theta, M) - \lambda(\theta, M)| < h$ if $\|M - \bar{M}\| < \delta_0$ and $T > T_0$ where δ_0 is the radius of S_0. Define $\delta^* = \min(\delta_0, \delta_2)$. Suppose that θ^* is a global maximum of $\lambda_T(\theta, M)$ lying in H^* and $\|M - \bar{M}\| < \delta^*$. Take θ^+ as any global maximum of $\lambda(\theta, \bar{M})$ lying in H. Then

$$\lambda_T(\theta^*, M) - (\lambda_T(\theta^+, M)) = (\lambda(\theta^*, \bar{M}) - \lambda(\theta^+, \bar{M}))$$

$$+ (\lambda_T(\theta^*, M) - \lambda(\theta^*, M))$$

$$+ (\lambda(\theta^*, M) - \lambda(\theta^*, \bar{M})) - (\lambda_T(\theta^+, M) - \lambda(\theta^+, M))$$

$$- (\lambda(\theta^+, M) - \lambda(\theta^+, \bar{M}))$$

$$< \lambda^* - \bar{\lambda} + h + h + h + h \leqslant -h < 0, \text{ if } \phi(\theta^*) = 0.$$

Thus θ^* is not a global maximum, and therefore no global maximum of $\lambda_T(\theta, M)$ subject to $\phi(\theta) = 0$ can be in H^* if $\|M - \bar{M}\| < \delta^*$.

Suppose then that θ^* is a global maximum of $\lambda_T(\theta, M)$ subject to $\phi(\theta) = 0$, and $\theta^* \notin H$ and $\|M - \bar{M}\| < \delta^*$. Then

$$\lambda_T(\theta^*, M) - \lambda_T(\theta^+, M) = \lambda(\theta^*, M) - \lambda(\theta^+, \bar{M}) + (\lambda_T(\theta^*, M) - \lambda(\theta^*, M))$$

$$- (\lambda_T(\theta^+, M) - \lambda(\theta^+, M))$$

$$- (\lambda(\theta^+, M) - \lambda(\theta^+, \bar{M}))$$

$$< B - \bar{\lambda} + h + h + h \leqslant -2h < 0.$$

Thus θ^* cannot be a global maximum and so no global maximum lies outside H if $\|M - \bar{M}\| < \delta^*$.

There exists T_1 for arbitrary $\varepsilon > 0$ such that $P(\|M - \bar{M}\| < \delta^*) > 1 - \varepsilon$ if $T > T_1$. Define $T^* = \max(T_0, T_1)$. Then if $T > T^*$ the probability that every global maximum of $\lambda_T(\theta, M)$ lies in $E(\delta)$ is greater than $1 - \varepsilon$.   Q.E.D.

COROKLARY 1.1. *If E consists of a set of isolated maxima the probability that the global maximum of $\lambda_T(\theta, M)$ subject to $\phi(\theta)=0$ is within a distance δ of one of these points tends to one as $T \to \infty$.*

COROLLARY 1.2. *If there is a unique global maximum θ^+ of $\lambda(\theta, \bar{M})$ subject to $\phi(\theta)=0$ then the set of global maxima $\lambda_T(\theta, M)$ subject to $\phi(\theta)=0$ has probability limit θ^+ in the sense that if $\hat{\theta}_i$ is one of the latter maxima for some index set i then $\mathrm{plim}_{T \to \infty} \sup_i \|\hat{\theta}_i - \theta^+\| = 0$.*

THEOREM 2. *If θ^* is an isolated local maximum of $\lambda(\theta, \bar{M})$ subject to $\phi(\theta)=0$ and $\theta^* \in H$ then the probability that there is a local maximum of $\lambda_T(\theta, M)$ in any neighbourhood of θ^* tends to one as $T \to \infty$. Denoting any such local maximum by $\hat{\theta}$, $\mathrm{plim}_{T \to \infty} \hat{\theta} = \theta^*$.*

Proof. Define $\lambda^* = \lambda(\theta^*, \bar{M})$. Take a neighbourhood of θ^* to be defined by $\|\theta - \theta^*\| \leq \delta$, and choose δ sufficiently small that there is no other maximum of $\lambda(\theta, \bar{M})$ subject to $\phi(\theta)=0$ in the neighbourhood. Consider a further open neighbourhood of θ^*, $\|\theta - \theta^*\| < \delta_3 < \delta$, and define $\lambda^{**} = \max \lambda(\theta, \bar{M})$ subject to $\phi(\theta)=0$ and $\delta_3 \leq \|\theta - \theta^*\| \leq \delta$. Take $5h = \lambda^* - \lambda^{**}$. Consider now the maximum of $\lambda_T(\theta, M)$ subject to $\phi(\theta)=0$ and $\|\theta - \theta^*\| \leq \delta$. Suppose that a maximum occurs for θ^{**} such that $\|\theta^{**} - \theta^*\| \geq \delta_3$. Now define δ^* and T_0 as in Theorem 1. Then

$$\lambda_T(\theta^{**}, M) - \lambda_T(\theta^*, M) = \lambda(\theta^{**}, \bar{M}) - \lambda(\theta^*, \bar{M})$$

$$+ (\lambda_T(\theta^{**}, M) - \lambda(\theta^{**}, M))$$

$$+ (\lambda(\theta^{**}, M) - \lambda(\theta^{**}, \bar{M}))$$

$$- (\lambda_T(\theta^*, M) - \lambda(\theta^*, M))$$

$$- (\lambda(\theta^*, M) - \lambda(\theta^*, \bar{M}))$$

$$< \lambda^{**} - \lambda^* + h + h + h + h = -h < 0.$$

Thus if $\|M - \bar{M}\| < \delta^*$ and $T > T_0$ the maximum occurs in the open neighbourhood $\|\theta - \theta^*\| < \delta_3$. As in Theorem 1, if θ^{**} is any maximum of $\lambda_T(\theta, M)$ subject to $\phi(\theta)=0$ and $\|\theta - \theta^*\| < \delta$, then $\lim_{T \to \infty} P(\|\theta^{**} - \theta^*\| \geq \delta_3) = 0$. Q.E.D.

COROLLARY 2.1. *If θ^+ is any isolated global maximum of $\lambda(\theta, \bar{M})$ subject to $\phi(\theta)=0$ then the probability that there is a local maximum of $\lambda_T(\theta, M)$ subject to $\phi(\theta)=0$ within any neighbourhood of θ^+ tends to one as $T \to \infty$. If θ_i is one of the latter local maxima then $\mathrm{plim}_{T \to \infty} \sup_i \|\theta_i - \theta^+\| = 0$.*

A further result giving more information on the behaviour of the local maxima of $\lambda_T(\theta, M)$ subject to $\phi(\theta)=0$ requires the following assumptions.

(F) The Hessian matrix $(\partial^2 \lambda_T(\theta, M)/\partial\theta^2)$ is well defined for all θ and $M \in S_0$ and converges uniformly to $(\partial^2 \lambda(\theta, M)/\partial\theta^2)$ as $T \to \infty$.

(G) $(\partial^2 \lambda(\theta, M)/\partial\theta^2)$ is continuous in (θ, M) for $\theta \in H$ and $M \in S_0$.

(H) The stationary points of $\lambda(\theta, \bar{M})$ within $\theta \in H$ are isolated. If the second order conditions for a constrained maximum of $\lambda(\theta, \bar{M})$ are satisfied as weak inequalities at any stationary point then they are satisfied as strict inequalities at that point.

Define the set $E^*(\delta)$ as the set of points within a distance δ of a constrained local maximum of $\lambda(\theta, \bar{M})$.

THEOREM 3. *The probability that there is a local maximum inside H and outside $E^*(\delta)$ tends to zero as $T \to \infty$.*

The proof is omitted.

These general theorems can be applied to a wide range of estimation problems, for example, non-linear least squares models, minimum generalised variance estimators, stochastic models, generalised 2SLS and 3SLS, instrumental variables, weighted regression.

To illustrate, consider the application to maximum likelihood or quasi-maximum likelihood estimators. In this case we take $\lambda_T(\theta, M) = L(\theta, M)/T$ where $L(\theta, M)$ is the log-likelihood function. The requirement that conditions (A), (B), (C), (D), (E) be satisfied is often met for linear models where the errors are normally distributed, although there is often an implied restriction on the behaviour of the exogenous variables. The use of the previous theorems requires that $\lambda(\theta, \bar{M})$ should have $\bar{\theta}$ as global maximum subject to $\phi(\theta) = 0$.

THEOREM 4. *If $\lambda(\theta, M) = \lim_{T \to \infty}(L(\theta, M)/T)$ converges uniformly for all M in some neighbourhood of $\bar{M}$, and is a continuous function of M at $\bar{M}$ for all θ, and (i) $E(L(\theta, M)^2) = O(T^2)$ for all θ, then $\lambda(\theta, \bar{M}) \leqslant \lambda(\bar{\theta}, \bar{M})$ for all θ.*

Proof. The information inequality (see Kullback (1959)), shows that

$$E(\lambda_T(\theta, M)) \leqslant E(\lambda_T(\bar{\theta}, M)) \tag{4}$$

with equality only if $\lambda_T(\theta, M) = \lambda_T(\bar{\theta}, M)$ for almost all M. In the latter case clearly $\lambda(\theta, \bar{M}) = \lambda(\bar{\theta}, \bar{M})$. Assuming inequality in (4) for some θ the proof is by contradiction. Suppose that $\lambda(\theta, \bar{M}) - \lambda(\bar{\theta}, \bar{M}) = d > 0$ for some θ, and note that (i) implies that $E((\lambda_T(\theta, M) - \lambda_T(\bar{\theta}, M))^2) < B$ for some B (which may depend on θ). Then choose a neighbourhood $\|M - \bar{M}\| < \delta$, such that $|\lambda(\theta, M) - \lambda_T(\theta, M)| < \frac{1}{5}d$, if $T > T_0$, and $|\lambda(\theta, M) - \lambda(\theta, \bar{M})| < \frac{1}{5}d$, if M is in the neighbourhood.

We write

$$E(\lambda_T(\bar{\theta}, M) - \lambda_T(\theta, M)) = E_1(\lambda_T(\bar{\theta}, M) - \lambda_T(\theta, M))$$
$$+ E_2(\lambda_T(\bar{\theta}, M) - \lambda_T(\theta, M)) \quad (5)$$

where E_1 is the contribution to the expectation from points M such that $\|M - \bar{M}\| < \delta$ and E_2 is the contribution to the expectation from outside the neighbourhood.

Then for $\|M - \bar{M}\| < \delta$,

$$\lambda_T(\bar{\theta}, M) - \lambda_T(\theta, M) = \lambda(\bar{\theta}, \bar{M}) - \lambda(\theta, \bar{M}) + \lambda_T(\bar{\theta}, M) - \lambda(\bar{\theta}, M)$$
$$- (\lambda_T(\theta, M) - \lambda(\theta, M)) + \lambda(\bar{\theta}, M)$$
$$- \lambda(\bar{\theta}, \bar{M}) - (\lambda(\theta, M) - \lambda(\theta, \bar{M})) < -\tfrac{1}{5}d.$$

Thus

$$E_1(\lambda_T(\bar{\theta}, M) - \lambda_T(\theta, M) < -\tfrac{1}{10}d \quad (6)$$

provided the probability that $\|M - \bar{M}\| < \delta$ is greater than 0.5, which will be true for sufficiently large T. Now using the Schwarz inequality

$$[E_2(\lambda_T(\bar{\theta}, M) - \lambda_T(\theta, M))]^2 \leqslant E_2[(\lambda_T(\bar{\theta}, M) - \lambda_T(\theta, M))^2] P(\|M - \bar{M}\| > \delta) \quad (7)$$

and

$$E_2[(\lambda_T(\theta, M) - \lambda_T(\theta, M))^2] < B.$$

Choose T_1 such that $BP(\|M - \bar{M}\| > \delta) < d^2/100$ if $T > T_1$, and then we deduce from (5), (6) and (7) that

$$E(\lambda_T(\bar{\theta}, M) - \lambda_T(\theta, M)) < 0.$$

This contradicts the information inequality, and so completes the proof.

A sufficient condition that the maximum is unique is that there is no θ^* such that $\lambda(\theta^*, \bar{M}) = \lambda(\bar{\theta}, \bar{M})$ and $\phi(\theta^*) = 0$. I therefore propose that a model should be described as asymptotically identified if conditions (A), (B), (C), (D) and (E) are satisfied and if the only solution of $\lambda(\theta^*, \bar{M}) = \lambda(\bar{\theta}, \bar{M})$ and $\phi(\theta^*) = 0$ is $\theta^* = \bar{\theta}$. Theorem 1, Corollary 2 shows that the quasi-maximum likelihood estimator is then consistent.

A special case where there is lack of identification is that where the likelihood function can be written $L(\theta, M) = L^*(\mu(\theta), M)$ where $\mu(\theta)$ is a vector of functions of θ and where the solution of the equations $\mu(\theta) = \mu(\bar{\theta})$, $\phi(\theta) = 0$ is not unique. Similarly a special case where there is lack of asymptotic identification is when $\lambda(\theta, \bar{M}) = \lambda^*(\mu(\theta), \bar{M})$ and the solutions of the equations $\mu(\theta) = \mu(\bar{\theta})$, $\phi(\theta) = 0$ are not unique.

An example of a non-likelihood function is given at the end of Section 6.

4 APPLICATION TO LINEAR MODELS

Returning to the special case introduced in Section 2 the concentrated likelihood function apart from a constant can be written

$$\lambda_T(\theta, M) = -\tfrac{1}{2}\log \det\left[Y'Y/T - P(\theta)(Z'Y)/T \right.$$
$$\left. - (Y'Z)P'(\theta)/T + P(\theta)(Z'Z/T)P'(\theta)\right]$$

The matrix M can be taken as the second moment matrix of the variables

$$\begin{pmatrix} Y'Y/T & Y'Z/T \\ Z'Y/T & Z'Z/T \end{pmatrix}.$$

Alternatively assuming $\mathrm{plim}(Z'Z/T)$ exists and is non-singular with probability one we can define $\hat{P} = (Y'Z)(Z'Z)^{-1}$ and

$$W = \left(\frac{Y'Y - (Y'Z)(Z'Z)^{-1}Z'Y}{T} \right)$$

and $M_{zz} = Z'Z/T$, and regard M as made up of the elements of these matrices. Since $\mathrm{plim}\,\hat{P} = P(\bar{\theta})$, $\mathrm{plim}\,W = \Omega_v$ writing $\mathrm{plim}\,M_{zz} = \bar{M}_{zz}$ we have

$$\lambda(\theta, \bar{M}) = -\mathrm{plim}\,\tfrac{1}{2}\log \det\left(W + (P(\theta) - \hat{P})\left(\frac{Z'Z}{T}\right)(P(\theta) - \hat{P})' \right)$$

$$= -\tfrac{1}{2}\log \det\left[\Omega_v + (P(\theta) - P(\bar{\theta}))\bar{M}_{zz}(P(\theta) - P(\bar{\theta}))' \right]. \tag{8}$$

Assuming that both $\bar{M}_{zz}$ and Ω_v are positive definite it follows that θ is asymptotically identified if $P(\theta) = P(\bar{\theta})$ and $\phi(\theta) = 0$ implies that $\theta = \bar{\theta}$, which also ensures that the model is identified in the usual sense. Sufficient conditions for the existence of unique solutions to equations of completely general form are not readily available. Fisher (1966) discusses this problem and gives some general results. It may be possible to say more for special cases such as those discussed below. The preceding theorems give some indication of the behaviour of the maximum likelihood estimator when the equations above are identified.

As a special case, if for arbitrary θ^* satisfying $\phi(\theta^*) = 0$, the equations $P(\theta) = P(\theta^*)$, $\phi(\theta) = 0$ have a set of isolated solutions $\theta_r \neq \theta^*$, then the sample gives more than one global maximum of the likelihood function. For if θ^* maximises

$$\lambda_T(\theta, M) = -\log \det (W + (P(\theta) - \hat{P})M_{zz}(P(\theta) - \hat{P})')$$

subject to $\phi(\theta) = 0$, clearly θ_r gives the same $\lambda_T(\theta^*, M)$ and so is also a global maximum of the likelihood function.

The discussion up to this point has not considered the case of the non-isolated maximum $\lambda(\theta, \bar{M})$, or in this case a solution of $P(\theta^*) = P(\bar{\theta})$,

$\phi(\theta^*) = 0$, which is such that some sequence of solutions $\theta_j \to \theta^*$. Using an argument similar to that of Rothenberg (1971) and writing

$$f(\theta) = \begin{pmatrix} \text{vec } P(\theta) \\ \phi(\theta) \end{pmatrix}$$

so that we have $f(\theta_j) = f(\theta^*)$ as $j \to \infty$, a sufficient condition that θ^* is an isolated maximum is that $(\partial f/\partial \theta)_{\theta = \theta^*}$ is of rank p. If $(\partial f/\partial \theta)_{\theta = \bar{\theta}}$ is of rank less than p it is possible that there are solutions of $f(\theta) = f(\bar{\theta})$ in any neighbourhood of $\bar{\theta}$ so that the model is not identified, although the contrary is also possible.

As an example, if both $P(\theta)$ and $\phi(\theta)$ are linear in the parameters θ, then the matrix $\partial f/\partial \theta$ is a constant matrix, and a necessary and sufficient condition for identification is that this matrix is of rank p. If the model is unidentified the set of observationally equivalent θ is an affine linear subspace.

5 SIMULTANEOUS EQUATION MODELS

Using analogous notation to that of Section 2 consider a set of equations

$$YB'(\theta) + ZC'(\theta) = U.$$

These are called structural equations and are related to the previous reduced form equations (1) by the assumption that $B(\theta)$ is a non-singular square matrix such that

$$P(\theta) = -B(\theta)^{-1}C(\theta)$$

and

$$U = V(B'(\theta))^{-1}.$$

Neglecting the possibility of restrictions on the variance matrix of the U errors the criterion for identification is that $P(\theta) = P(\bar{\theta})$, $\phi(\theta) = 0$ has the unique solution $\theta = \bar{\theta}$.

The first set of equations can be written

$$B(\theta)^{-1}C(\theta) = B(\bar{\theta})^{-1}C(\theta)$$

or writing

$$H = B(\theta)B(\bar{\theta})^{-1}$$

we have

$$\left. \begin{array}{l} B(\theta) = HB(\bar{\theta}), \\ C(\theta) = HC(\bar{\theta}). \end{array} \right\} \tag{9}$$

The simplest case is that where the elements of the matrices B and C are the parameters that we are attempting to estimate and we can write

$$\theta = \text{vec}(B \vdots C)$$

where vec is the operation of forming an $n(n+m) \times 1$ vector which can be split in n sub-vectors each of which is a row of $(B \vdots C)$. Equations (9) can then be written

$$\theta = (H \otimes I)\bar{\theta}$$

where $H \otimes I$ is the Kronecker direct product of the $n \times n$ matrix H with the $(N+m)$th order unit matrix.

If θ satisfies $\phi(\theta) = 0$, we require $\phi((H \otimes I)\bar{\theta}) = 0$. The model is identified if $H = I$ is the only solution of these equations. If the restrictions are linear there is no difficulty in stating rank conditions for identification. Non-linear restrictions are difficult to analyse except for conditions for local identification.

As a more complex example, suppose we consider a model of the form

$$BY' + CY'_{-1} + DZ' = U' \tag{10}$$

where Y_{-1} is the data matrix of Y lagged one time period.

Suppose that with the same suffix convention

$$U' = RU'_{-1} + E' \tag{11}$$

where R is an arbitrary square matrix and E is a matrix of serially independent errors. (10) and (11) can be combined to give

$$BY' + (C - RB)Y'_{-1} - RCY'_{-2} + DZ' - RDZ'_{-1} = E'.$$

The reduced form of this equation can be written

$$Y' = P_1 Y'_{-1} + P_2 Y'_{-2} + P_3 Z' + P_4 Z'_{-1} + V' \tag{1)2}$$

where

$$P_1 = -B^{-1}C + B^{-1}RB, \quad P_2 = B^{-1}RC, \quad P_3 = -B^{-1}D, \quad P_4 = B^{-1}RD$$

and

$$V' = B^{-1}E'.$$

Suppose that the parameters to be estimated are B, C, D and R, but there are no restrictions on R. Define $P_1^* = -B^{-1}C$, $P_2^* = -B^{-1}D$, $S = B^{-1}RB$, and note that we can assume that S has no restrictions but P_1^* and P_2^* are restricted. The problem can then be posed in the form: 'Is there more than one solution to

$$\bar{P}_1 = P_1^* + S, \tag{13}$$

$$\bar{P}_2 = -SP_1^*, \tag{14}$$

$$\bar{P}_3 = P_2^*, \tag{15}$$

$$\bar{P}_4 = -SP_2^*, \tag{16}$$

subject to $B P_1^* + C = 0$, $B P_2^* + D = 0$, $\phi(B, C, D) = 0$, where $\bar{P}_1$, $\bar{P}_2$, $\bar{P}_3$, $\bar{P}_4$ are the true values of these reduced form coefficients and $\phi(B, C, D) = 0$ represent the restrictions?' A simple special case is that where $\bar{P}_3$ is of rank n. Then we have from (15) and (16)

$$S\bar{P}_3 + \bar{P}_4 = 0. \tag{17}$$

If $\bar{P}_3$ is of rank n, S is uniquely determined as the solution of this equation and P_2^* is uniquely determined by (15). Then (13) gives $P_1^* = \bar{P}_1 - S$, so that P_1^* and P_2^* are both uniquely determined, and (14) must be satisfied. The unique solutions can be written

$$P_1^* = -\bar{B}^{-1}\bar{C},$$

$$P_2^* = -\bar{B}^{-1}\bar{D}.$$

The model is therefore identified provided that the equations $B\bar{P}_1^* + C = 0$, $B\bar{P}_2^* + D = 0$, $\phi(B, C, D) = 0$ have a unique solution. The problem is formally identical with that for the serially independent error case already discussed and the solution is well known if the $\phi(B, C, D) = 0$ are linear restrictions.

Suppose now that $\bar{P}_3$ is of rank less than n. From equations (13) and (14) we have

$$S^2 - S\bar{P}_1 - \bar{P}_2 = 0. \tag{18}$$

Considering these as equations to determine S it is well-known that in general there may be up to C_n^{2n} solutions. Considering each of this finite set of solutions in turn it might be the case that only one of the S satisfy $S\bar{P}_3 + \bar{P}_4 = 0$. Thus S would be uniquely determined and the discussion of the determination of B, C proceeds as before. However it is also possible that more than one of the solutions of equations (18) satisfy (17). Suppose that (18) and (17) have $k > 1$ solutions, S_i, $i = 1, \ldots, k$. For each i (15) gives $P_2^* = \bar{P}_3$ and (13) gives $P_{1i}^* = \bar{P}_1 - S_i$. Of course for some i, say $i = 1$, we have $P_{11}^* = -\bar{B}^{-1}\bar{C}$, and $P_2^* = -\bar{B}^{-1}\bar{D}$, and $S_1 = -\bar{B}^{-1}\bar{R}\bar{B}$. Considering then the solution of the equation $B P_{11}^* + C = 0$, $B P_2^* + D = 0$, $\phi(B, C, D) = 0$ leads to the usual conditions for identification. But even if these conditions are satisfied we must still consider the cases $i \neq 1$.

Consider the solutions of the equations

$$B P_{1i}^* + C = 0, \qquad B P_2^* + D = 0, \qquad \phi(B, C, D) = 0. \tag{19}$$

The only difference from the case $i = 1$ is that it is no longer true that there is at least the solution $B = \bar{B}, C = \bar{C}, D = \bar{D}$. There may be no solution in which case the conditions for identification are the same as in the serially independent case. If the equations have a finite number of solutions for each i then the set of asymptotic maxima may be finite and isolated. Alternatively there may be an infinite set of maxima for $i \neq 1$, even though the conditions for a unique solution are satisfied for $i = 1$.

Considering the case where the restrictions $\phi(B, C, D) = 0$ are linear, for $i = 1$ the usual conditions for identification must be satisfied. For $i \neq 1$ there are three cases. One is that no further solution is obtained. The second is that a unique solution is obtained. The third is that an infinite set of solutions to (19) is obtained. Which of these cases occurs depends upon the rank of the matrix of coefficients of the elements of B, C, D in (19). In the second case a finite set of asymptotic maxima is found. In the third case an infinite set of maxima is found. Only in the first case is the model identified.

As an example of the application of the theorems of this paper to a non-maximum likelihood estimator, consider the general instrumental variable estimator obtained by minimising

$$\lambda_T(\theta, M) = \operatorname{tr}[\hat{\Omega}_u^{-1}(U'Q/T)(Q'Q/T)^{-1}(Q'U)/T)]$$
$$= \operatorname{tr}(\hat{\Omega}_u^{-1}(B(\theta)Y' + C(\theta)Z')Q(Q'Q)^{-1}Q'(YB'(\theta) + ZC'(\theta)))/T$$

where Q is $T \times N$ data matrix of instrumental variables with the assumed properties that $\operatorname{plim}(Q'Q)/T = \bar{M}_{11}$ exists and is non-singular, and that $\operatorname{plim}(Q'Z)/T = \bar{M}_{12}$ is of rank m, and that $\operatorname{plim}(Q'U)/T = 0$. Also we assume that $\hat{\Omega}_u$ is some consistent estimator of Ω_u, but for identification it will be sufficient to assume that $\operatorname{plim} \hat{\Omega}_u$ exists and is positive definite. Then

$$\operatorname{plim}(Q'Y/T) = \operatorname{plim}(Q'Z/T)P(\bar{\theta})' + \operatorname{plim}(Q'U/T)B(\bar{\theta})'^{-1}$$
$$= \bar{M}_{12}P(\bar{\theta})'.$$

We take the matrix M to be made up of $Q'Q/T, Q'Z/T, Q'Y/T, \hat{\Omega}_u$ and then

$$\lambda(\theta, \bar{M}) = \operatorname{tr}(\Omega_u^{-1}(B(\theta)P(\bar{\theta}) + C(\theta))(\bar{M}'_{12}\bar{M}_{22}^{-1}\bar{M}_{21})(B(\theta)P(\bar{\theta}) + C(\theta))).$$

Clearly $\lambda(\theta)$ achieves its global minimum zero, if and only if $B(\theta)P(\bar{\theta}) + C(\theta) = 0$. And it follows that the model estimators of this type are identified if $\bar{\theta}$ is the unique solution of the equations $B(\theta)^{-1}C(\theta) = B(\bar{\theta})^{-1}C(\bar{\theta})$.

The discussion proceeds as in equation (6), so that the conditions for identification are as before.

6 ESTIMATION PROBLEMS

Although it is useful in discussing the statistical theory to use a more general formulation which includes constraints it is simpler and saves computer space to parameterise the constraints when calculating the solutions. The problem is therefore reformulated so that (4) is to be maximised subject to no constraints. It may in simple models be possible to obtain consistent estimates of θ, in which case a simple approximation leads to estimates asymptotically equivalent to maximum likelihood estimates. The first order maximum lielihood conditions for the concentrated likelihood function can be written

$$\frac{1}{T} \operatorname{tr}(\Omega_v^{-1}(\hat{\theta})(Y' - P(\hat{\theta})Z') \frac{\partial P'}{\partial \theta_i} = 0, \qquad i = 1, \ldots, p \qquad (20)$$

where $\Omega_v(\theta) = (Y' - P(\theta)Z')(Y - ZP'(\theta))/T$. If θ^* is a consistent estimate of θ and $\Omega_v^* = \Omega_v(\theta^*)$ we can approximate (20) using

$$P(\theta) = P(\theta^*) + \sum_{j=1}^{p} \left(\frac{\partial P}{\partial \theta_j}\right)_{\theta^*} \Delta \theta_j + O(1/T)$$

where $\Delta \theta_j = \hat{\theta}_j - \theta_j^*$, since $\hat{\theta}_j$ and θ_j^* will differ by $O(1/\sqrt{T})$ if $\hat{\theta}_j$ the maximum likelihood estimator is consistent. We replace (20) by

$$\sum_{j=1}^{p} \Delta \theta_j \operatorname{tr}\left(\Omega_v^{*-1} \frac{\partial P}{\partial \theta_j} \left(\frac{Z'Z}{T}\right) \frac{\partial P'}{\partial \theta_i}\right)\Bigg|_{\theta = \theta^*}$$

$$+ \operatorname{tr}\left(\Omega_v^{*-1}(Y' - P(\theta^*)Z')Z \frac{\partial P'}{\partial \theta_i}\right)/T = 0, \qquad i = 1, \ldots, p. \quad (21)$$

If $\operatorname{plim}(Z'Z/T) = M_{zz}$ exists and the matrix whose elements are

$$\operatorname{tr}\left(\Omega_v^{-1} \frac{\partial P}{\partial \theta_i} M_{zz} \frac{\partial P'}{\partial \theta_j}\right)\Bigg|_{\theta = \bar{\theta}}$$

is positive definite then there is no difficulty in showing that the solutions of (21) have the same asymptotic error variance as (20). A similar procedure can be used for the serially independent simultaneous equation if we write $A(\theta) = (B(\theta) : C(\theta))$ and $X = (Y : Z)$, so that the equation can be written,

$$A(\theta)X' = B(\theta)Y' + C(\theta)Z' = U'.$$

Writing

$$Q(\theta) = \begin{pmatrix} -B(\theta)^{-1}C(\theta) \\ I \end{pmatrix}$$

an approximation similar to (20) can be written

$$\sum_{j=1}^{p} \Delta \theta_j \operatorname{tr}\left(\Omega_u^{*-1} \frac{\partial A}{\partial \theta_j} Q(\theta^*)\left(\frac{Z'Z}{T}\right)Q'(\theta^*) \frac{\partial A'}{\partial \theta_i}\right)\Bigg|_{\theta = \theta^*}$$

$$+ \operatorname{tr}\left(\Omega_u^{*-1} A(\theta^*)\left(\frac{X'Z}{T}\right)Q'(\theta^*) \frac{\partial A'}{\partial \theta_i}\right)\Bigg|_{\theta^*} = 0, \qquad i = 1, \ldots, p \quad (22)$$

where $\Omega_u^* = A(\theta^*)X'XA'(\theta^*)/T$.

However, it is usually impossible to find a consistent estimator and then it is necessary to iterate. A gradient method which has been found to work well in practice uses equations similar to (22). Writing θ_r for value of θ at the rth iteration and $\Delta\theta_{jr} = \theta_{j(r+1)} - \theta_{jr}$,

$$\Omega_r = A(\theta_r)X'XA'(\theta_r)/T, \qquad Q_r = \begin{pmatrix} -B(\theta_r)^{-1}C(\theta_r) \\ I \end{pmatrix}$$

the iteration is

$$\sum_{j=1}^{p} \Delta\theta_{jr} \, \mathrm{tr}\left(\Omega_r^{-1} \frac{\partial A}{\partial \theta_j} Q_r \left(\frac{Z'Z}{T}\right) Q_r' \frac{\partial A}{\partial \theta_i}\right)_{\theta_r}$$
$$+ c\left(\mathrm{tr}\left(\Omega_r^{-1} A(\theta_r)\left(\frac{X'Z}{T}\right) Q_r' \frac{\partial A}{\partial \theta_i}\right)_{\theta_r}\right) = 0.$$

c is a scalar factor chosen at each iteration to maximise the likelihood. The advantage of this version of gradient maximisation will be greatest in large samples when it is a close approximation to a Newton–Raphson iteration. It has been found to work well with $p \simeq 20$, $T \simeq 60$. A program has been written using a sub-routine which differentiates analytically rational functions of any order in a set of parameters. This has worked well on models with autoregressive errors and on models or complete sets of consumer demand equations.

A problem that remains is to ensure that iterative procedures converge to global maxima rather than local maxima. In the linear model it is theoretically possible to reject a non-global maximum by using the result that

$$T \log\left(\det\left(\frac{(Y'-P(\hat{\theta})Z')(Y-ZP(\hat{\theta}'))}{T}\right)\Big/\det W\right) \tag{23}$$

is twice a log-likelihood-ratio and so is asymptotically distributed as a χ^2 of degrees of freedom $nm - p + q$ where q is the number of restrictions. However the χ^2 also tests for misspecification of the model. If the model is correctly specified the significance of (23) may be taken as showing that the maximum which has been attained is not a global maximum.* However, it gives no basis for choosing a better starting point for iteration. In practise the economist has some *a priori* ideas on acceptable values for his parameters and if having started iterations from several points within the

---

* In a similar way it can be shown that for the instrumental variable estimator $T\lambda_T$ is asymptotically distributed as a χ^2 of $Nn - p + q$ degrees of freedom. Both results depend on the matrices of first derivatives being continuous at $\bar{\theta}$ and $\partial f/\partial \theta$ of full rank, and also on $Z'U/\sqrt{T}$ or $Q'U/\sqrt{T}$ being asymptotically normal, which follows if the assumptions of Mann and Wald (1943) are satisfied.

range of acceptable values and he finds only unacceptable maxima he will conclude that his model is misspecified.

REFERENCES

Fisher, F. M. (1966), *The Identification Problem in Econometrics*, McGraw-Hill.

Koopman, B. O. (1936), 'On distributions admitting a sufficient statistic', *Trans. Am. Math. Soc.*, **39**, 399–412.

Kullback, S. (1959), *Information Theory and Statistics*, Wiley.

Malinvaud, E. (1970), 'The consistency of nonlinear regressions', *Annals of Maths. Stats.*, **41**, 956–69.

Mann, H. B. and A. Wald (1943), 'On the statistical treatment of linear stochastic difference equations', *Econometrica*, **11**, 173–220.

Rothenberg, T. J. (1971), 'Identification in parametric models', *Econometrica*, **39**, 577–92.

Sargan, J. D. (1961), 'The maximum likelihood estimation of economic relationships with autoregressive residuals', *Econometrica*, **29**, 414–26.

J. D. SARGAN

——— . ———

13 IDENTIFICATION AND LACK OF
IDENTIFICATION*

(First published in *Econometrica* (1983), *Vol.* 51, *pp.* 1605–33.)

The paper discusses cases where an econometric model linear in the variables is identified, but where the estimators are not asymptotically normally distributed. Maximum likelihood estimators and instrumental variable estimators are considered in some detail and the results are illustrated by means of a Monte Carlo simulation of a particularly simple case.

1 INTRODUCTION

This paper is intended to stress the distinction between the conditions for lack of identification in models linear with respect to the variables but non-linear in the parameters in the sense originally defined by Fisher [2], and the less numerous set of conditions required for first order lack of identification. The latter set of conditions involve only the first derivatives of the coefficients as functions of the parameters. It is argued that if the model suffers from first order lack of identification, it will generally be the case that the usual estimators are consistent, although not asymptotically normally distributed. In a leading special case the asymptotic distribution is discussed, and the simulation of a simple model illustrates the extent to which this asymptotic distribution approximates the actual finite sample distribution.

2 MODELS NON-LINEAR IN PARAMETERS BUT LINEAR IN VARIABLES

Suppose that we have a set of n endogenous variables y_t, $t = 1, \ldots, T$, determined by a set of m predetermined variables z_t; the set of z_t may include lagged values of the y_t, and so the equations below may be

---

* This paper was presented as the Presidential Address at the Econometric Society World Congress held in Aix-en-Provence, France, August 28–September 2, 1980.

dynamic, or they may be completely static if the z_t include only exogenous variables. The reduced form equations determining the y_t can be written

$$y_t = \bar{P}z_t + v_t \qquad (1)$$

where v_t is a vector of serially independent errors, with $E(v_t)=0$, and $E(v_t v_t')=\Omega$, and the general model of which this is an example can be written either in the form

$$y_t = P(\theta)z_t + v_t, \qquad (2)$$

or

$$B(\theta)y_t + C(\theta)z_t = u_t, \qquad (3)$$

where θ is a vector of parameters and $P(\theta)$, $B(\theta)$, $C(\theta)$ are general functions of θ. Thus we assume that for model (2) for some $\bar{\theta}$, $P(\bar{\theta})=\bar{P}$, or for model (3) for some $\bar{\theta}$, $B(\bar{\theta})\bar{P}+C(\bar{\theta})=0$. An observationally equivalent model will be obtained if, for some $\theta \neq \bar{\theta}$,

$$P(\theta) = \bar{P} \qquad (4)$$

or

$$B(\theta)\bar{P}+C(\theta)=0. \qquad (5)$$

It is convenient to write either (4) or (5) in the form $\phi(\theta)=0$. Then $\phi(\bar{\theta})=0$, and we define the model as being locally unidentifiable following Fisher [2] if for some sequence of θ_i, such that $\lim_{i \to \infty} \theta_i = \bar{\theta}$, $\phi(\theta_i)=0$.

A generalisation of this concept in the context of instrumental variables estimation which I discussed first in my 1959 article [6] considers a single equation which can be written

$$a'(\theta)x_t = u_t \qquad (6)$$

where x_t is a set of n variables generated by a dynamic simultaneous equation model, including both endogenous and predetermined variables, and where $a(\theta)$ is an $n \times 1$ vector function of the p parameters which are the components of the vector θ. Then taking an arbitrary set of m instrumental variables z_t, and defining X and Z as the $T \times n$ and $T \times m$ data matrices whose rows are x_t' and z_t', we define the corresponding instrumental variable estimators of θ as the vector minimising

$$a'(\theta)(X'Z)(Z'Z)^{-1}Z'Xa(\theta). \qquad (7)$$

Assuming that $\text{plim}(Z'Z/T)=M$ exists and is non-singular, that $\text{plim}(X'Z/T)=K$ exists, that $\text{plim}(u'Z/T)=0$, and that $a(\theta)$ is a continuous function of θ for all θ under consideration, it was shown in [7] that a sufficient condition that the IV estimators are consistent is that the equation

$$K'a(\theta)=0 \tag{8}$$

has the unique solution $\theta = \bar{\theta}$. By analogy with the previous theory I find it convenient to say that when this condition is satisfied the set of instrumental variables Z are adequate to identify the equation, and then assuming that $a(\theta)$ is continuous at $\theta = \bar{\theta}$, to describe the equation as locally unidentifiable by the set of IV given by Z, if there is a sequence of $\theta_i \neq \bar{\theta}$ such that $\lim_{i < \infty} \theta_i = \bar{\theta}$, and $K'a(\theta_i)=0$.

If the model is locally identifiable, as in [7], it can be shown that the minimum of (7) on a sufficiently small closed set surrounding $\bar{\theta}$ is a consistent estimator of $\bar{\theta}$, or alternatively that as the sample size $T \to \infty$ the probability that there is a minimum of (7) in the interior of the set tends to one. Again we can write (8) in the form

$$\phi(\theta)=0, \tag{9}$$

noting that as before

$$\phi(\bar{\theta})=0,$$

and we are considering the possibility that for a sequence of θ_i such that $\lim \theta_i = \bar{\theta}$, $\phi(\theta_i)=0$.

The basic discussion of this type of problem in the literature is due to Fisher [2] and Rothenberg [5]. They point out that a necessary condition for local unidentifiability is that the first derivative matrix $\partial\phi/\partial\theta$, if it is a continuous function of θ, should be of less than full rank, i.e.

$$\mathrm{rank}\left(\frac{\partial\phi}{\partial\theta}\right) < p. \tag{10}$$

I shall refer to this later as the first order condition for lack of identification.

One of the general points that I wish to make is that this is by no means sufficient for lack of local identifiability, and that rather generally if this condition is satisfied, the model is still locally identified. Now in a sense what we are arguing about is the prior probability of a given type of model satisfying the conditions (10) or the full conditions for lack of identifiability. By a given type of model we must have in mind a set of models, and these can be indexed by using a further set of parameters. Thus we can think of our basic mathematical specification for the models as depending upon a further vector of parameters θ^*, and then assume that θ^* has been chosen on *a priori* grounds leaving θ to be estimated from the data. Thus as an example in the model of type (1) (the multi-equation regression model) we now suppose the matrix P depends both on θ and θ^*, and in general we can discuss the probability of obtaining a model which is (a) locally unidentifiable, or (b) satisfies the first order conditions for unidentifiability, by considering corresponding prior probabilities in (θ, θ^*) space. Now since the conditions for (a) and (b) require exact equations to be satisfied by (θ, θ^*), if the prior distributions are absolutely continuous then the probabilities to be attached to (a) or (b) are both zero. But instead we consider the concepts of almost local unidentifiability and the first derivative matrix ill-conditioned, with the usual interpretation that any equation equating some function of (θ, θ^*) to zero is replaced by an approximation equation requiring this function to have absolute value less than ε. For ε sufficiently small a set of ε-approximation equations of this form define a volume in (θ, θ^*) space proportional to ε^r, where r is the number of equations under consideration. And in this sense we can say that the prior probability of almost (a) is less than the prior probability of almost (b), if (a) requires more equations to be satisfied than (b). Now the importance of the concept of almost unidentifiability is that almost all the models we discuss in econometrics are only approximate. We have no particular reason for believing that our equations are linear, or are non-linear in a particular fashion. We use convenient formulations which behave in a general way that corresponds to our economic theories and intuitions, and which cannot be rejected from the available data. With this background, identification is a property of the model, but not necessarily of the real world. The question that I am currently exploring is 'If the data were generated by this model, what would be the properties of the estimators?' But we can conjecture that if the model is almost unidentifiable then in finite samples it behaves in a way which is difficult to distinguish from the behaviour of an exactly unidentifiable model. This seems a natural consequence of a continuity argument, and can be discussed analytically in very simple models. I will not discuss these rather over-simple models here, but I have some Monte Carlo simulation results for case (b) to present which I hope at least illustrates the idea.

I label the Fisher–Rothenberg conditions first order conditions since I intend to discuss order conditions next. In this paper I am limiting my attention to a rather special case of (10). In fact if

$$\operatorname{rank}\left(\frac{\partial \phi}{\partial \theta}\right)_{\theta = \bar{\theta}} = p - 1 \tag{11}$$

all the results are much simpler and I will discuss this case only.

Suppose now that ϕ has continuous derivatives up to the rth order at the origin. Then by rearranging the order of the elements of the vectors ϕ and θ, we can write

$$\phi = \begin{pmatrix} \phi_1 \\ \phi_2 \end{pmatrix}, \qquad \theta = \begin{pmatrix} \theta_1 \\ \theta_0 \end{pmatrix}$$

where both ϕ_1 and θ_1 are of dimension $p - 1$, θ_0 is a scalar, and ϕ_2 is of dimension $N-p+1$, where N is the dimension of ϕ, and we assume that

$$\frac{\partial \phi_1}{\partial \theta_1}$$

is a non-singular square matrix at $\theta = \bar{\theta}$.

Then using the implicit function theorem in some neighbourhood of $\bar{\theta}$, we can solve

$$\phi_1(\theta) = 0$$

for θ_1 in terms of θ_0, to give

$$\theta_1 = \psi(\theta_0)$$

and define $\eta(\theta_0) = \phi_2(\psi(\theta_0), \theta_0)$. It is convenient to shift the origin of θ so that $\bar{\theta} = 0$.

Now supposing the model is locally unidentifiable we have a sequence $\theta_i \to 0$ as $i \to \infty$, such that $\phi(\theta_i) = 0$, and correspondingly $\theta_{0i} \to 0$, such that $\eta(\theta_{0i}) = 0$ for all i. Also both $\psi(\theta_0)$ and $\eta(\theta_0)$ have continuous derivatives up to the rth order at $\theta_0 = 0$. Consider the Taylor series expansion at the origin for $\eta(\theta_0)$:

$$0 = \eta(\theta_{0i}) = \sum_{j=1}^{r} \frac{1}{j!} \theta_{0i}^j \left(\frac{\partial^j \eta}{\partial \theta_0^j} \right) + O(\theta_{0i}^r).$$

Note that $\eta(0) = 0$, and the first term is $O(\theta_{0i})$ as $\theta_{0i} \to 0$, and all other terms are of lower order of magnitude. Thus dividing by θ_{0i} and allowing $i \to \infty$ we see that

$$\frac{\partial \eta}{\partial \theta_0} = 0 \qquad \text{at } \theta_0 = 0.$$

But now the first term is zero, and the second term is of $O(\theta_{0i}^2)$ as $i \to \infty$, and all further terms are of lower order. Thus dividing by θ_{0i}^2 and allowing $i \to \infty$, we find that

$$\frac{\partial^2 \eta}{\partial \theta_0^2} = 0$$

and repeating this argument $r-2$ times we obtain

$$\frac{\partial^k \eta}{\partial \theta_0^k} = 0 \qquad \text{at } \theta_0 = 0 \qquad (k = 1, \ldots, r). \tag{12}$$

Now more generally, we can take an arbitrary differentiable scalar function and arbitrary parameter s, and write $\theta_0 = \kappa_0(s)$, $\theta_1 = \psi(\kappa_0(s)) = \kappa_1(s)$, $\theta = \kappa(s)$, and noting that from the definition of the implicit function ψ,

$\theta_1(\kappa(s)) = 0$ for all relevant s, so that

$$\frac{\partial^k \phi_1}{\partial s^k} = 0 \qquad (k = 1, \ldots, r),$$

and from (12)

$$\frac{\partial^k \phi_2}{\partial s^k} = \left(\frac{\partial^k \eta}{\partial \theta_0^k}\right)\left(\frac{\partial \theta_0}{\partial s}\right)^k = 0 \qquad (k = 1, \ldots, r).$$

So we can write the conditions (12) in the form

$$\left(\frac{\partial^k \phi}{\partial s^k}\right) = 0 \qquad (k = 1, \ldots, r). \tag{13}$$

In fact we can write these as implicit conditions on the derivatives of ϕ with respect to θ by writing

$$\kappa(s) = \kappa_1 s + \frac{\kappa_2 s^2}{2!} + \cdots + \frac{\kappa_r s^r}{r!}$$

where κ_k is the vector of derivatives with respect to s of the kth order and then differentiating $\phi(\kappa(s))$ with respect to s up to r times. Thus specifically we have to the first order

$$\left(\frac{\partial \phi_i}{\partial \theta_j}\right)\kappa_{1j} = 0$$

with the suffix convention that a repeated suffix should lead to summation of the term with respect to this suffix. These give $N - p + 1$ implicit constraints on the first derivatives. But now the $k = 2$ version of (13) gives

$$\frac{\partial \phi_i}{\partial \alpha_j}\kappa_{2j} + \frac{\partial^2 \phi_i}{\partial \theta_j \partial \theta_k}\kappa_{1j}\kappa_{1k} = 0$$

which combined with the first order conditions gives $2(N - p + 1)$ implicit conditions on the first and second derivatives of ϕ. Similarly the third order conditions are given by

$$\frac{\partial \phi_i}{\partial \theta_j}\kappa_{3j} + 3\frac{\partial^2 \phi}{\partial \theta_j \partial \theta_k}\kappa_{1i}\kappa_{2j} + \frac{\partial^3 \phi_i}{\partial \theta_j \partial \theta_k \partial \theta_q}\kappa_{1j}\kappa_{1k}\kappa_{1q} = 0$$

and so on. Thus considering conditions up to the rth order one obtains $r(N - p + 1)$ conditions in all. Note that if the functions ϕ are analytic at the origin then we obtain an infinity of conditions which must be satisfied if the model is to be locally unidentifiable. However, if we have a simple type of model where for example the coefficients are rational functions of the parameters or are rational except for certain one variable transformations, e.g. logarithmic or exponential functions, then the lower order conditions may imply the higher order conditions. An example of this is now considered where the $\phi(\theta)$ are quadratic in θ. In this case if we directly consider that $\phi(\kappa(s)) = 0$ for some curve with parameterisation $\kappa(s)$ we find that various solutions can be found, but that the type of curve which involves the lowest number of constraints on the coefficients of $\phi(\theta)$ is the case where the curve is a straight line through $\bar{\theta}$. By linearly transforming both θ and the ϕ one can write the constraints in the canonical form

$$\left.\begin{array}{ll} \theta_i = \alpha_i \theta_0^2 + \theta_0(\beta_i'\theta) + \theta'\Gamma_i\theta' & (i = 1, \ldots, p-1), \\ 0 = \alpha_i \theta_0^2 + \theta_0(\beta_i'\theta) + \theta'\Gamma_i\theta' & (i = p, \ldots, N), \end{array}\right\} \tag{14}$$

where θ is the $(p-1) \times 1$ vector which was previously denoted θ_1 when partioning our previous $p \times 1$ vector θ, and θ_i is the ith component of θ; α_i is a scalar, β_i is a $(p-1) \times 1$ vector, and Γ_i a $(p-1) \times (p-1)$ symmetric matrix of coefficients which together mean that the model has $\frac{1}{2}Np(p+1)$ *a priori* known parameters (previously denoted by θ^*). Note, however, that we have already eliminated some known parameters in linearly transforming the equatons to their canonical form. It follows easily that $\theta_i = \alpha_i \theta_0^2 + O(\theta_0^3)$ on any curve satisfying the first block of equations (14), so then the second block of equations leads to $\alpha_i = 0$, $i = p, \ldots, N$. Then the smallest set of additional constraints which are sufficient conditions for a path from the origin to exist is: $\alpha_i = 0$, $i = 1, \ldots, p-1$. The corresponding path is the straight line $\theta_i = 0$, $i = 1, \ldots, p-1$. Note that these are N constraints in addition to the $(N-p+1)$ first order constraints.

3 ASYMPTOTIC DISTRIBUTIONS FOR LOCALLY IDENTIFIABLE ESTIMATORS WHERE THE FIRST ORDER CONDITIONS ARE NOT SATISFIED

In the cases discussed in the previous section, we can take our estimator as obtained by minimising a criterion function which is a continuous function of θ and q, where q is a vector with elements made up of the second moments of the observed variables, i.e. for the FIML estimators of the previous section a vectorised version of the second moments $Y'Y/T$, $Y'Z/T$, and $Z'Z/T$ and similarly for the instrumental variable estimators. Writing the criterion function for either the FIML or IV case (the details are discussed in the Appendix) as

$$f(\theta, q)$$

if $\text{plim}_{T \to \infty} q = \bar{q}$, we assume that for q in some neighbourhood of radius δ of $\bar{q}$, f has the two properties: (i) for some $R > 0$ and all θ such that $\|\theta\| \leqslant R$, $f(\theta, q)$ is a continuous function of θ and q, and (ii) for $\|\theta\| \geqslant R$, $f(\theta, q) < f(\bar{\theta}, \bar{q}) - h$ for some $h > 0$. If $\bar{\theta}$ is a global minimum of $f(\theta, \bar{q})$, it can be shown that a local minimum of $f(\theta, q)$ occurs in any neighbourhood of $\bar{\theta}$

with a probability which tends to one as the sample size $T \to \infty$, and that if $\bar{\theta}$ is the unique global minimum of $f(\theta, q)$ then the global minimum of $f(\theta)$ is a consistent estimator of $\bar{\theta}$. (For the proof of these statements see [7].) These conditions are satisfied by the FIML criterion function provided the model is identified (i.e. $\bar{\theta}$ is the unique solution of $\phi(\bar{\theta}) = 0$), and the condition for a local maximum of the likelihood function in a neighbourhood of $\bar{\theta}$ is satisfied if the model is locally identified. Similarly if we consider the $f(\theta, q)$ which corresponds to the criterion function (7) for the instrumental variable estimator the conditions are satisfied if the set of instrumental variables are adequate to identify or locally identify the equation respectively. Thus if the model is locally identified the error in the estimator has probability limit zero even if the first order conditions for identification are not satisfied. It is known that if the first order conditions for identification are satisfied the errors in these estimators are asymptotically normally distributed. As a partial converse to this in the case where the rank of $(\partial \phi / \partial \theta)$ is $p - 1$, the asymptotic distribution of the error is not difficult to describe and it is distinctly non-normal. To discuss this distribution it is convenient to make a linear transformation to θ. We assume that this has been carried out so that we can write

$$\theta = \begin{pmatrix} \theta_1 \\ \theta_0 \end{pmatrix}$$

where θ_1 is a $(p - 1)$ vector, and θ_0 is a scalar. Then the linear transformation can be chosen so that the equivalent of

$$\left(\frac{\partial \phi}{\partial \theta} \right) \kappa_1 = 0$$

is

$$\frac{\partial \phi}{\partial \theta_0} = 0,$$

where the linear transformation on θ converts the arbitrary vector κ_1 to a vector all of whose elements are zero except the last. Now given that $\partial \phi / \partial \theta_1$ is of full rank in some neighbourhood of $\bar{\theta}$, it follows that $\partial f / \partial \phi_1$ is full of rank q in some neighbourhood of $\bar{q}$. In considering the asymptotic distribution of θ we can ignore values of q outside this neighbourhood. Define a concentrated criterion function by

$$f^*(\theta_0, q) = \min_{\theta_1} f(\theta, q).$$

Provided that the original coefficient functions (i.e. $P(\theta)$ or $(B(\theta) : C(\theta))$ or $a(\theta)$ depending on which set of estimators are considered) have continuous fourth derivatives in the neighbourhood of $\bar{\theta}$, then $f^*(\theta_0, q)$ is well defined and has continuous derivatives up to the fourth order with respect to θ_0, for

θ_0 in some interval surrounding $\bar{\theta}_0$, and q in some neighbourhood of $\bar{q}$. Note that since $\hat{\theta}$, the estimated θ, is a consistent estimator of $\bar{\theta}$, in determining the asymptotic distribution we need only consider θ within a neighbourhood of $\bar{\theta}$.

It is convenient from now on to assume that $\bar{\theta}_0 = 0$, which requires only a shift in the origin of θ_0. Then we write

$$f^*(\theta_0, q) = f_0 + f_1\theta_0 + f_2\theta_0^2/2 + f_3\theta_0^3/6 + f_4^*\theta_0^4/24. \tag{15}$$

From the definition in terms of a Taylor series expansion f_0, f_1, f_2, f_3 are the derivatives of $f^*(\theta_0)$ at the origin, and f_4^* is the fourth derivative at a point intermediate between θ_0 and the origin. But further, as shown in the Appendix, f_4^* is non-negative for all values of θ_0 and q under consideration.

Considering q as a stochastic variable it is shown in the Appendix that the f_i have the following orders of magnitude:

$$f_4^* = O(1),$$

and indeed that

$$0 < \operatorname*{plim}_{T \to \infty} f_4^* < \infty,$$

$$f_0 = O(1/T),$$

$$f_1 = O(1/T),$$

$$f_2 = O(T^{-1/2}),$$

$$f_3 = O(T^{-1/2}).$$

Both $\sqrt{T}f_2$ and $\sqrt{T}f_3$ are asymptotically normally distributed variables with zero means and finite variance matrices. Tf_0 is asymptotically distributed as a χ^2 of $(nm - p + 1)$ d.f. for the maximum likelihood case, and of $(m - p - 1)$ d.f. for the instrumental variable case. Tf_1 on the other hand is asymptotically distributed like a homogeneous quadratic form in a set of normally distributed variables, but not a quadratic form which gives a χ^2 distribution.

Now writing $z_T = T^{1/4}\hat{\theta}_0$, note that

$$0 \leqslant f^*(\hat{\theta}_0, q) \leqslant f^*(0, q)$$

from the non-negativity of $f(\theta, q)$ and the definition of $\hat{\theta}_0$ as a minimum. Thus

$$-Tf_0 \leqslant T^{3/4}f_1 z_T + T^{1/2}f_2 z_T^2/2 + T^{1/4}f_3 z_T^3/6 + f_4^* z_T^4/24 \leqslant 0. \tag{16}$$

Denote now

$$f^* = T^{3/4}f_1 z_T + T^{1/2}f_2 z_T^2/2 + T^{1/4}f_3 z_T^3/6 + f_4^* z_T^4/24,$$

and then from the previous inequality $f^* = O(1)$ asymptotically. In order to discuss the asymptotic order of magnitude of z_T, we must consider the sign of f_2. Introduce an arbitrary positive bound b_z and consider

$$\Pr(|z_T| > b_z | f_2 > 0).$$

If $f_2 > 0$ and $|z_T| > b_z$, from (16)

$$f_4^* z_T^4/24 \leqslant -T^{3/4} f_1 z_T - T^{1/4} f_3 z_T^3/6$$

$$\leqslant |z_T|^3 [T^{1/4}|f_3|/6 + T^{3/4}|f_1|/b_z^2]$$

so that

$$\Pr(|z_T| > b_z | f_2 > 0) \leqslant \Pr(|z_T| < f^+ | f_2 > 0)$$

where

$$f_4^* f^+ = 4T^{1/4}|f_3| + 24T^{3/4}|f_1|/b_z^2.$$

But from the orders of magnitude of f_3 and f_1, $\text{plim}_{T \to \infty} f^+ = 0$, so that both probabilities tend to 0 as $T \to \infty$, i.e. $\text{plim}_{T \to \infty}(|z_T||f_2 > 0) = 0$.

Now to discuss the unconditional order of magnitude of z_T, if we take any δ and $\varepsilon > 0$, we can then find T_0 such that

$$\Pr\left(4\left|\frac{T^{1/4} f_3}{f_4^* b_z}\right| + 24\left|\frac{T^{3/4} f_1}{f_4^* b_z^3}\right| > \delta\right) < \varepsilon$$

if $T > T_0$, and so from the definition of f^*, if $|z_T| > b_z$,

$$\left(z_T^2 + 6\frac{T^{1/2}}{(1-\delta)}\frac{f_2}{f_4^*}\right)^2 < \left(\frac{24f^*}{f_4^*(1-\delta)} + \frac{36T}{(1-\delta)^2}\frac{f_2^2}{f_4^{*2}}\right)$$

with probability greater than $(1-\varepsilon)$. Now either $z_T^2 \leqslant b_z^2$ or

$$z_T^2 \leqslant \left(\frac{24f^*}{f_4^*(1-\delta)} + T\frac{36f_2^2}{f^*(1-\delta)}\right)^{1/2} - 6\frac{T^{1/2}}{(1-\delta)}\frac{f_2}{f_4^*}$$

with probability $1 - \varepsilon$, where ε can be taken arbitrarily small. Thus $z_T = O(1)$, and $\hat{\theta}_0 = O(T^{-1/4})$ as $T \to \infty$.

Now given $\hat{\theta}_0 = O(T^{-1/4})$, we can explore its asymptotic distribution more directly by considering the first order condition

$$\frac{\partial f^*}{\partial \theta_0} = 0,$$

again taking a Tayor series expansion but retaining one more term (i.e. taking a fourth order expansion for the first derivative of f^*). The corresponding equation now takes the form

$$\frac{\partial f^*}{\partial \theta_0} = f_1 + f_2\theta_0 + f_3\theta_0^2/2 + f_4\theta_0^3/6 + f_5^*\theta_0^4/24 = 0. \tag{17}$$

Note that all these f_i are defined to be as before in equation (15) but now f_4 is the derivative at the origin of f^*, and f_5^* is defined as the fifth derivative of $f^*(\theta_0)$ at some point between θ_0 and the origin. We now assume that f_5^* is bounded if θ_0 and q lie in appropriate neighbourhoods and we need only consider such values for the asymptotic distribution.

Now consider the two cases $f_2 > 0$ and $f_2 \leqslant 0$ separately. If $f_2 > 0$, by substituting $\theta_0 = -f_1/f_2(1 \pm \delta)$, for some $\delta > 0$, into (17) we find that there is a root of (17) in this neighbourhood of $(-f_1/f_2)$ with probability tending to one as $T \to \infty$. This corresponds to a local minimum of $f^*(\theta_0, q)$, and by considering the order of magnitude of the different terms in (17) we have easily that $\partial f^*/\partial \theta$ is increasing in z_T so long as $z_T = O(1)$ with probability tending to one as $T \to \infty$. Thus the corresponding solution is unique and for this solution we also have that $\hat{\theta}_0 = O(T^{-1/2})$. Then revising the orders of magnitude of the terms in (17) in this way, we then find we can write

$$\hat{\theta}_0 = -\left[\frac{f_1}{f_2} + \frac{f_3}{f_2}\frac{\theta_0^2}{2} + \frac{f_4}{f_2}\frac{\theta_0^3}{6} + \frac{f_5^*}{24}\theta_0^4\right]$$

$$= -\frac{f_1}{f_2} + O(T^{-1}).$$

Since we can deduce the asymptotic distribution of $\hat{\theta}_0$ from the joint asymptotic distribution of f_1 and f_2 we can deduce that the asymptotic distribution of $\sqrt{T}\hat{\theta}_0$ is of a generalised Cauchy type, *and* depends upon a large number of parameters and has no integral finite moments. Now taking the samples where f_2 is negative by similar arguments we can show that $\partial f^*/\partial \theta_0$ is negative for small $|z_T|$ and positive for large $|z_T|$. The corresponding root can then be approximated by

$$\hat{\theta}_0^2 = -\frac{6f_2}{f_4} + O(T^{-3/4}).$$

There are in fact two roots here, one positive and one negative. If we write $\theta_0^* = +\sqrt{(-6f_2/f_4)}$, then further expansion gives

$$\hat{\theta}_0^{(1)} = \theta_0^* + d_0 + O(T^{-3/4}),$$

where d_0 is $O(T^{-1/2})$,

$$\hat{\theta}_0^{(2)} = -\theta_0^* + d_0 + O(T^{-3/4}),$$

for the two roots. Now in order to see which of these gives a global maximum we can consider

$$f^*(\hat{\theta}_0^{(1)}, q) - f^*(\hat{\theta}_0^{(2)}, q)$$

using the Taylor series expansion. We find

$$f^*(\hat{\theta}_0^{(1)}, q) - f^*(\hat{\theta}_0^{(2)}, q) = d_f + O(T^{-3/2})$$

where Td_f/θ_0^* is asymptotically distributed as a homogeneous quadratic in a set of normally distributed variables. Not all the latent roots of the quadratic form are positive, so that there will be an asymptotic limit probability that $f^*(\hat{\theta}_0^{(1)}, q) < f^*(\hat{\theta}_0^{(2)}, q)$. It follows that if $\hat{\theta}_0$ is taken as the global minimum it can be expected to have a bimodal distribution, obtained by mixing the distributions of $\hat{\theta}_0^{(1)}$ and $\hat{\theta}_0^{(2)}$.

Now which of these two cases, the single minimum or the double minimum of $f^*(\theta_0, q)$, occurs depends on the sign of f_2, and f_2 is asymptotically distributed normally with mean zero. It follows that the asymptotic probability that the first case occurs is one half, and the unconditional distribution of $\hat{\theta}_0$ is a half and half mixture of the two conditional distributions.

Note that one further intriguing possibility exists for improving the estimator of $\hat{\theta}_0$. Consider $\hat{\theta}_0^{(3)} = \frac{1}{2}(\hat{\theta}_0^{(1)} + \hat{\theta}_0^{(2)}) = d_0 + O(T^{-3/4})$. Since $d_0 = O(T^{-1/2})$, $\hat{\theta}_0^{(3)}$ has errors asymptotically of order $T^{-1/2}$, and so in large samples would be expected to be a considerably better estimator of θ_0 than the global minimum of $f^*(\theta_0, q)$. The suggestion is that if in estimating in large samples a unique minimum is found within the set of θ which correspond to reasonable values for the parameters, then $\hat{\theta}$ is equated to the minimum; but if on the other hand two minima are found in this set, and that the inverse of the estimated asymptotic variance matrices at both are close to singularity, then $\hat{\theta} = \frac{1}{2}(\hat{\theta}^{(1)} + \hat{\theta}^{(2)})$ is used. Note that the order of magnitude of the error in this estimator is $O(T^{-1/2})$, but the asymptotic distribution of the estimator is very non-normal (no moments are finite) so that even in large samples there is a relatively strong probability of large errors.

Now considering the joint distribution of $\hat{\theta}_1$ and $\hat{\theta}_0$, a more precise discussion in the Appendix leads to results which can be summarised as follows. We can find a vector γ such that $\theta_1^* = \hat{\theta}_1 - \gamma\hat{\theta}_0^2$ is asymptotically normally distributed independently of $\hat{\theta}_0$. Thus when $f_2 > 0$, $\hat{\theta}_0 = O(T^{-1/2})$ and $\hat{\theta}_1$ is asymptotically normally distributed. When $f_2 < 0$, $\hat{\theta}_0^2$ is asymptotically distributed in the positive half of a normal distribution and $\hat{\theta}_1$ is distributed as the sum of the linear combination of $\hat{\theta}_0^2$ and a set of normal variables independent of $\hat{\theta}_0$. Note that by a linear transformation of θ_1 we can make

$$\gamma = \begin{bmatrix} 1 \\ 0 \\ 0 \\ 0 \\ 0 \end{bmatrix}$$

in which case all except the first variable would have the same asymptotic normal distribution for $f_2 \lessgtr 0$, and the first component of $\hat{\theta}_1$ would have the mixed distribution. The asymptotic distribution can be specified as follows. In a $(p-2)$ dimensional subspace the distribution is asymptotic normal with standard errors of order $T^{-1/2}$. For the remaining transformed $\hat{\theta}_1$ the distribution is a mixture of two different asymptotic normal distributions with standard errors of order $T^{-1/2}$. Finally $\hat{\theta}_0$ is asymptotically distributed with probability one half as the square root of the modulus of a normally distributed variable with errors of order $T^{-1/4}$, or with probability one half as a non-normally distributed variable with errors of order $T^{-1/2}$. However, if we now revert to a non-transformed θ vector, and consider the marginal distribution of one component, then generically its asymptotic distribution must be considered to be a mixture of a normal distribution for samples where $f_2 > 0$, and a non-normal distribution for samples where $f_2 < 0$ ($f_2 = 0$ occurs with probability zero).

Perhaps before leaving the contemplation of these asymptotic distributions it should be stressed that it seems likely that even larger sample sizes are required for these asymptotic approximations to be valid than usual since the errors in the approximation will be $O(T^{-1/4})$ whereas the errors in the approximations for a regular model are $O(T^{-1/2})$, where regular is intended to mean satisfying the first order conditions for identification.

4 SPECIAL CASE SIMULATIONS

It seemed appropriate to illustrate all this with an example drawn from my old field of interest, the estimation of a single equation by instrumental variables when the error is generated by a first order autoregressive equation. However, to make it very simple to simulate and to understand the results of the simulation it was decided to take a static model, preserving only the basic feature of the non-linearity for the autoregressive model, which is that the coefficients in the final form of the equation are bilinear in two sets of parameters: the structural coefficients, and the autoregressive coefficients. In order to reduce the dimensions of the problem, and avoid time-consuming iterative minimisation, it was decided to consider a case where there are only two parameters θ_1 and θ_2. Then we simplify by assuming that the number of endogenous variables is four, and that no exogenous variables occur in the equation. Then it is first possible to change the origin of θ so that $\bar{\theta}$, the true value, equals zero, and then to linearly transform the y variables so that $a(\theta)$ takes the form

$$a(\theta) = \begin{bmatrix} -1 \\ \theta_1 \\ \theta_2 \\ \theta_1\theta_2 \end{bmatrix}.$$

If we take the reduced form equations in the form

$$y_t = Pz_t + v_t, \tag{18}$$

and assume that the number of variables y_t is four, we note that we have transformed the variables so that the equation to be estimated takes the form

$$y_{1t} = u_t,$$

so that if we write

$$P = \begin{bmatrix} p'_1 \\ p'_2 \\ p'_3 \\ p'_4 \end{bmatrix},$$

$$p'_1 = 0,$$

$$u_t = v_{1t}.$$

Now

$$P' \left(\frac{\partial a}{\partial \theta} \right)_{\theta=0} = P' \begin{bmatrix} 0 & 0 \\ 1 & 0 \\ 0 & 1 \\ 0 & 0 \end{bmatrix}$$

and the first order condition for local unidentifiability, which is

$$P' \frac{\partial a}{\partial \theta} \lambda = 0,$$

will be assumed satisfied with

$$\lambda = \begin{pmatrix} 1 \\ 1 \end{pmatrix}.$$

This requires $p_3 = -p_2$.

In order to linearly transform θ so that this is equivalent to

$$P' \frac{\partial a}{\partial \theta_0} = 0$$

we can define

$$\theta_1 = \theta_0,$$

$$\theta_2 = \theta_0 + \theta^*.$$

Then we can write

$$a(\theta) = \begin{bmatrix} -1 \\ \theta_0 \\ \theta_0 + \theta^* \\ \theta_0(\theta_0 + \theta^*) \end{bmatrix}.$$

Then

$$\frac{\partial^2 a}{\partial \theta_0^2} = \begin{bmatrix} 0 \\ 0 \\ 0 \\ 2 \end{bmatrix}$$

so that the condition that

$$\text{rank}\left[P'\left(\frac{\partial a}{\partial \theta} : \frac{\partial^2 a}{\partial \theta_0^2} \right) \right] = 2$$

is that p_4 is not proportional to p_2. For simulation purposes we take

$$P = \begin{bmatrix} 0 & 0 & 0 & 0 \\ 1 & 0 & -1 & 0 \\ -1 & 0 & 1 & 0 \\ 0 & 1 & 0 & 1 \end{bmatrix}$$

and

$$E(v_t v_t') = \sigma^2 \begin{bmatrix} 1 & 0.6 & 0.36 & 0.216 \\ 0.6 & 1 & 0.6 & 0.36 \\ 0.36 & 0.6 & 1 & 0.6 \\ 0.216 & 0.36 & 0.6 & 1 \end{bmatrix} = \sigma^2 \Omega_V.$$

If we write

$$\hat{P} = (Y'Z)(Z'Z)^{-1}$$

and choose

$$Z'Z/T = I_4,$$

then we simulate by generating $\hat{P}$ noting that $\text{vec}(\hat{P} - P) \sim N(0, I \otimes \Omega_v/T)$. Then define

$$R = \hat{P} \frac{(Z'Z)}{T} \hat{P}'$$

and write

$$f(\theta) = r_{11} - 2r_{12}\theta_1 - 2r_{13}\theta_2 - 2r_{14}\theta_1\theta_2 + r_{22}\theta_1^2 + 2r_{23}\theta_1\theta_2$$
$$+ r_{33}\theta_2^2 + 2r_{24}\theta_1^2\theta_2 + 2r_{34}\theta_1\theta_2^2 + r_{44}\theta_1^2\theta_2^2.$$

Differentiating with respect to θ_2 (which will be equivalent to differentiating with respect to θ^*), we obtain

$$\hat{\theta}_2 = \frac{r_{13} + r_{14}\hat{\theta}_1 - r_{23}\hat{\theta}_1 - r_{24}\hat{\theta}_1^2}{r_{33} + 2r_{34}\hat{\theta}_1 + r_{44}\hat{\theta}_1^2}$$

so that

$$f^*(\theta_0) = r_{11} - 2r_{12}\theta_0 + r_{22}\theta_0^2 - \frac{(r_{13} + r_{14}\theta_0 - r_{23}\theta_0 - r_{24}\theta_0^2)^2}{(r_{33} + 2r_{34}\theta_0 + r_{44}\theta_0^2)}$$

$$= \frac{g_0 + g_1\theta_0 + g_2\theta_0^2 + g_3\theta_0^3 + g_4\theta_0^4}{r_{33} + 2r_{34}\theta_0 + r_{44}\theta_0^2},$$

say, where

$$g_0 = r_{11}r_{33} - r_{13}^2,$$

$$g_1 = -2(r_{12}r_{33} - r_{11}r_{34} + r_{13}(r_{14} - r_{23})),$$

$$g_2 = r_{11}r_{44} + r_{33}r_{22} - 4r_{12}r_{34} - (r_{14} - r_{23})^2 + 2r_{13}r_{24},$$

$$g_3 = -2(r_{12}r_{44} - r_{22}r_{34} - (r_{14} - r_{23})r_{24}),$$

$$g_4 = r_{22}r_{44} - r_{24}^2.$$

Making use of the stochastic properties of the r_{ij} which follow from (18) and the assumed value of P, that is, $r_{11}, r_{12} + r_{13}$, are of order $T^{-1}, r_{12}, r_{13}, r_{14}, r_{22} + r_{32}, r_{32} + r_{33}, r_{42} + r_{43}$, of order $T^{-1/2}$, and all the r_{ij} are of order one, except for those already considered, it can be shown that g_0 and g_1 are $O(T^{-1}), g_2$ and g_3 are $O(T^{-1/2}), g_4, r_{33}, r_{34}, r_{44}$ are of $O(1)$. Thus taking the Taylor series expansion at the origin, we need only retain one term in the expansion of $1/(r_{33} + 2r_{34}\theta_0 + r_{44}\theta_0^2)$ to obtain coefficients f_i of appropriate accuracy. In fact we can write

$$f_0 = g_0/r_{33},$$

$$f_1 = g_1/r_{33} - 2r_{34}g_0/r_{33}^2,$$

$$f_2 = 2(g_2/r_{33} - 2g_1 r_{34}/r_{33}^2),$$

$$f_3 = 6(g_3/r_{33} - g_2 r_{34}/r_{33}^2),$$

$$f_4 = 24(g_4/r_{33} - g_3 r_{34}/r_{33}^2).$$

For each sample the sign of f_2 was used to predict whether one or two minima would occur, and to set a wide grid to compute an initial set of values of $f^*(\theta_0)$. The interval was taken to be $|f_1/f_2|$ if $f_2>0$, or $(\sqrt{(-f_2/3f_4)})/4$ if $f_2<0$. When one or two minima had been found using this wide grid, a better value was obtained by using an interval for a finer grid equal to one tenth the original interval. The model was simulated using the fact that

$$\text{vec } \hat{P} - \text{vec } P \sim N(0, \sigma^2/T(I \otimes \Omega_v))$$

with $\sigma/\sqrt{T}=0.10, 0.03, 0.01$ *and* 0.005. *It was also simulated for*

$$P_2 = \begin{bmatrix} 0 & 0 & 0 & 0 \\ 1 & 0 & -1 & 0 \\ -0.95 & 0 & 1.05 & 0 \\ 0 & 1 & 0 & 1 \end{bmatrix}.$$

For this matrix P_2 the equation is first order identified, but for $\sigma/\sqrt{T}$ within some range it is to be expected that the distribution of $\hat{\theta}_0$ will approximate that for the first order unidentified case. When P is used the equation is first order unidentified and as $\sigma/\sqrt{T} \to 0$ the distribution would be expected to tend to the asymptotic distribution of the last section. On the other hand when P_2 is used as $\sigma/\sqrt{T} \to 0$ the distribution tends to an asymptotic normal distribution, but it is to be expected that only for very small $\sigma/\sqrt{T}$ would the distribution tend to this limit (and consequently would a large proportion of samples have a single minimum) but that for some intermediate values of $\sigma/\sqrt{T}$ the distribution would be similar to the asymptotic distribution of the last section.

Table I summarises the results of 1000 simulations for each of four values of $\sigma/\sqrt{T}$. The top of the table gives the number of cases for which $f_2 \geqslant 0$ and $f_2<0$. The former are divided into those where a single minimum and no minimum occurred. The latter are very few in number, and simply show a failure of the computer procedure to find a minimum within a given wide range of zero. The cases where $f_2<0$ were divided into those with two, one, and no minimum. The latter again must be regarded as a residual category, indicative of a failure of the computer procedure to locate a minimum. Unfortunately the proportion of these cases is not negligible, and it can be guessed that there is in these cases a single minimum outside the grid of values for which the computer calculated $f^*(\theta_0)$. The second half of the table gives the arithmetic mean and mean square error of the $\hat{\theta}_0$ for each case previously distinguished. The positive and negative minima are separately distinguished (since in practice in all cases where there were two minima the errors had opposite signs). The $\hat{\theta}_0$ corresponding to the smallest of the two minima is given in the row labelled global. Finally the mean of the θ_0 for the two minima is given in the last line.

The results are reasonably consistent with expectations. The proportion

Table I. *Simulation for almost first order unidentified case* $N = 1000$

$\sigma/\sqrt{T}$	0.1	0.03	0.01	0.005
	No. of cases	No. of cases	No. of cases	No. of cases
$f_2 \geqslant 0$				
single min.	681	606	626	704
no min.	4	0	0	0
	Total = 685	Total = 606	Total = 626	Total = 704
$f_2 < 0$				
no min.	48	55	50	64
single min.	120	102	148	149
double min.	147	237	176	83
	Total = 315	Total = 394	Total = 374	Total = 296

Arithmetic mean and mean square errors

$f_2 \geqslant 0$	0.1058 (0.0345)	0.0351 (0.0053)	0.0125 (0.0017)	0.0070 (0.0010)
$f_2 < 0$				
θ_1^*	−0.3391 (0.1279)	−0.1853 (0.0375)	−0.1040 (0.0118)	−0.0730 (0.0057)
θ_2^*	0.3037 (0.1000)	0.1605 (0.0278)	0.0876 (0.0084)	0.0653 (0.0047)
global	0.1254 (0.1116)	0.0217 (0.0337)	−0.0254 (0.0118)	−0.0043 (0.0063)
mean of				
2 min.	−0.0177 (0.0038)	−0.0124 (0.0009)	−0.0082 (0.0003)	−0.0037 (0.0001)

Note: The mean square error is given in brackets for each case in the lower half of the table.

of cases with $f_2 < 0$ tends to one half as $\sigma/\sqrt{T} \to 0$. When $f_2 \geqslant 0$ there are no double minima. When $f_2 < 0$, but close to zero, there is often a single minimum. Clearly this produces a bias in the total sample such that the proportion of double minima is less than half and rather slowly tending to one half as $T \to \infty$. The order of magnitude of the biases and mean square errors in relation to $\sigma/\sqrt{T}$ is as expected. Note that in considering the separate minima for the double minima the bias contributes the majority of the mean square error (the standard deviation of the error is roughly one third of the bias in all cases). The mean of the two minima does give a distribution which has a notably lower mean square error than the global minimum.

Turning to Table II, again the results are as expected. The proportion of double minima varies as expected with $\sigma/\sqrt{T}$ achieving a minimum for 0.03, and the distribution is rather close to that for the previous first order unidentified case for this value of $\sigma/\sqrt{T}$.

London School of Economics

Manuscript received March, 1982; revision received February, 1983.

Table II. *Simulation for first order unidentified case $N = 1000$*

$\sigma/\sqrt{T}$	0.1	0.03	0.01	0.005
	No. of cases	No. of cases	No. of cases	No. of cases
$f_2 > 0$				
single min.	671	570	520	509
no min.	3	2	0	0
	Total = 674	Total = 572	Total = 520	Total = 509
$f_2 < 0$				
no min.	50	45	37	29
single min.	128	109	116	91
double min.	148	274	327	371
	Total = 326	Total = 428	Total = 480	Total = 491
	Arithmetic mean and mean squares			
$f_2 \geqslant 0$				
single min.	0.1087 (0.0370)	0.0452 (0.0049)	0.0176 (0.0008)	0.0095 (0.0002)
$f_2 < 0$	−0.3407 (0.1293)	−0.1810 (0.0363)	−0.0950 (0.0101)	−0.0655 (0.0048)
double min.	0.2965 (0.0967)	0.1612 (0.0282)	0.0899 (0.0088)	0.0652 (0.0046)
global	0.0904 (0.1105)	0.0807 (0.0314)	0.0419 (0.0094)	0.0365 (0.0048)
mean of				
2 min.	−0.0221 (0.0041)	−0.0099 (0.0008)	−0.0026 (0.0001)	−0.0002 (<0.0001)

Note: The mean square error is given in brackets for each case in the lower half of the table.

APPENDIX: CRITERION FUNCTIONS FOR ECONOMETRIC ESTIMATORS

C1 *Maximum likelihood estimators*

If the model of Section 2 of this paper is written

$$y_t = P(\theta)z_t + v_t \qquad (t = 1, \ldots, T),$$

the maximum likelihood estimator is obtained by minimising

$$f(\theta, q) = \log \det (W + (\hat{P} - P(\theta))M(\hat{P} - P(\theta))') - \log \det W$$

where $M = Z'Z/T$, $\hat{P} = (Y'Z)(Z'Z)^{-1}$, $W = Y'Y/T - \hat{P}M\hat{P}'$, Y and Z are the data matrices whose rth rows are y_t and z_t respectively, and q is a vector whose elements are made up of the elements of M, $\hat{P}$ and W.

It is convenient to introduce a linear transformation of the θ vector, so that $\theta' = (\theta'_1, \theta_0)$ where θ_0 is a scalar parameter, such that $\partial P/\partial \theta_0 = 0$ at $\theta = \bar{\theta}$, and also to choose the origin of θ so that $\bar{\theta} = 0$. From the identification theorem of [7] quoted in the body of the report we assume that $\text{plim}_{T \to \infty} q = \bar{q}$, and subject to satisfaction of the identification condition plim $\hat{\theta} = \bar{\theta}$. To determine the asymptotic distribution it is only necessary to consider the properties of the estimator for $\|\hat{\theta} - \bar{\theta}\| < \delta$, and $\|q - \bar{q}\| < \delta_2$. We assume that $\Omega_v = E(v_t v_t')$ is non-singular, and that $\text{plim}_{T \to \infty} M$ is non-singular. We ensure that for points satisfying these inequalities θ_1 can be determined as an implicit function of θ_0 by requiring that for given θ_0, θ_1 minimises $f(\theta, q)$, from our assumption that $\partial(\text{vec } P(\theta))/\partial\theta_1$ is continuous in the neighbourhood of $\theta = 0$, and that this matrix is of rank $p - 1$. Provided all derivatives up to the fourth order of P with respect to θ are continuous at the origin, we can show that the fourth order derivatives of

$$f^*(\theta_0, q) = \max_{\theta_1}(f(\theta, q))$$

are also continuous for θ_0 in some neighbourhood of zero so that we can write a Taylor series expansion

$$f^*(\theta_0, q) = f_0 + f_1\theta_0 + f_2\theta_0^2/2 + f_3\theta_0^3/6 + f_4^*\theta_0^4/24.$$

The f_i, $i = 0, \ldots, 3$, are the derivatives of order i at the origin; f_4^* is the fourth derivative at some point between θ_0 and the origin. (Note that if higher order derivatives were assumed to be continuous, a higher order Taylor series expansion would be possible, but from the discussion of the fourth order case it can be deduced that the higher order terms in the expansion are of lower order in T (and so negligible in large samples) than the terms which are retained in the fourth order expansion.) The asymptotic properties of the f_i, and f_4^* can be deduced by approximating the derivatives as follows. Each f_i, $i = 0, 1, 2, 3$, is a function of q and so we can consider a Taylor series expansion for the f_i about $q = \bar{q}$. In fact it is somewhat simpler to consider the Taylor series expansion with respect to $\hat{P} - P(\bar{\theta})$ only. Each f_i is then expanded as a quadratic in $\hat{P} - P(\bar{\theta})$ with remainder of order $T^{-3/2}$. f_4^* depends both on q and θ_0 and in considering its probability limit using Slutsky's theorem and the continuity of the fourth derivative it is only necessary to set $q = \bar{q}$, and $\theta_0 = 0$. We can then use the following mathematically crude procedures, knowing that the results must coincide with the required Taylor series expansions since they are equivalent to omitting remainders from various approximations, and where the validity of the approximations can be proved retrospectively by noting that the terms retained must coincide with the corresponding terms of the Taylor series expansion. The procedure is the following. First expand $P(\theta)$ in a Taylor series expansion of the fourth order in $(\theta - \bar{\theta})$ (note that we have taken $\bar{\theta} = 0$, so that the expansion is a polynomial in θ). Then expand $f(\theta, q)$ as a Taylor series expansion in $\Delta P = \hat{P} - P(\bar{\theta})$ up to the second order, and substitute the expansion for $P(\theta)$ as a quartic in θ. Denote the corresponding approximation to $f(\theta, q)$ by $\tilde{f}(\theta, q)$.

Now approximate the first order conditions

$$\frac{\partial f}{\partial\theta_1} = 0 \qquad \text{by} \qquad \frac{\partial \tilde{f}}{\partial\theta_1} = 0.$$

Solve the latter equations for θ_1, using a repeated substitution procedure to derive a power series expansion for the solution in powers of θ_0 and ΔP. It is clear that $\partial\tilde{f}/\partial\theta_1$ gives a Taylor series expansion for $\partial f/\partial\theta_1$ up to the order of the terms retained, and that the expansion for the solution (using the formulae for the derivatives of the implicit function) then gives a Taylor series expansion for the implicit function to the same order provided that the Jacobian matrix is non-singular at the origin. Finally substituting the approximate solution into $f(\theta, q)$ one obtains the required Taylor series expansion for $f^*(\theta_0, q)$ where the required approximations to the f_i are obtained by gathering together terms which contain $\theta_0^i, i \sim 0, 1, 2, 3$, as factors. Retrospectively it was found sufficient to retain terms in expansion of $P(\theta)$ which are of order greater than or equal to $(T^{-3/4})$, if θ_1 is taken $O(T^{-1/2})$ and θ_0 is taken $O(T^{-1/4})$, and similarly in the expansion of the solution for the minimum θ_1.

We use the convention

$$vec(P) = \begin{bmatrix} p_1 \\ p_2 \\ \vdots \\ p_n \end{bmatrix} \quad \text{if} \quad P = \begin{bmatrix} p_1' \\ p_2' \\ \vdots \\ p_n' \end{bmatrix}$$

Then

$$vec\, P(\theta) = vec\, \bar{P} + \frac{\partial\, vec\, P}{\partial \theta_1} \theta_1 + \frac{1}{2}\frac{\partial^2\, vec\, P}{\partial \theta_0^2} \theta_0^2 + \theta_0 \frac{\partial^2\, vec\, P}{\partial \theta_0 \partial \theta_1} \theta_1 + \frac{1}{6}\frac{\partial^3\, vec\, P}{\partial \theta_0^3} \theta_0^3,$$

and writing

$$\bar{vec}(\hat{P} - P(\theta)) = vec\, \Delta\hat{P} - vec(P(\theta) - \bar{P}),$$

and

$$\log\det[W + (\Delta\hat{P} - (P(\theta) - \bar{P}))M(\Delta\hat{P} - (P(\theta) - \bar{P}))'] - \log\det\, W$$

$$= tr[W^{-1}(\Delta\hat{P} - (P(\theta) - \bar{P}))M(\Delta\hat{P} - (P(\theta) - \bar{P}))']$$

$$+ O((\Delta\hat{P} - (P(\theta) - \bar{P}))^3)$$

$$\simeq (vec\, \Delta P)'(W^{-1} \otimes M)\, vec\, \Delta P - 2(vec\, \Delta P)'(W^{-1} \otimes M)\, vec(P(\theta) - \bar{P})$$

$$+ vec(P(\theta) - \bar{P})'(W^{-1} \otimes M)\, vec(P(\theta) - \bar{P})$$

where we now write $\Delta P = \Delta\hat{P} = \hat{P} - \bar{P}$, so that

$$\tilde{f}(\theta, p) = (vec\, \Delta P)'(W^{-1} \otimes M)\, vec\, \Delta P - \theta_0^2 (vec\, \Delta P)'(W^{-1} \otimes M)\frac{\partial^2(vec\, P)}{\partial \theta_0^2}$$

$$+ \frac{1}{4}\theta_0^4 \frac{\partial^2(vec\, P)'}{\partial \theta_0^2}(W^{-1} \otimes M)\frac{\partial^2(vec\, P)}{\partial \theta_0^2}$$

$$- 2(vec\, \Delta P)'(W^{-1} \otimes M)\frac{\partial(vec\, P)}{\partial \theta_1}\theta_1$$

$$+ \theta_1' \frac{\partial(vec\, P)'}{\partial \theta_1}(W^{-1} \otimes M)\frac{\partial(vec\, P)}{\partial \theta_1}\theta_1$$

$$+ \theta_0^2 \frac{\partial^2(vec\, P)'}{\partial \theta_0^2}(W^{-1} \otimes M)\frac{\partial(vec\, P)}{\partial \theta_1}\theta_1$$

$$-2\theta_0(\text{vec }\Delta P)'(W^{-1}\otimes M)\frac{\partial^2(\text{vec }P)}{\partial\theta_1\partial\theta_0}\theta_1$$

$$-\frac{1}{3}\theta_0^3(\text{vec }\Delta P)'(W^{-1}\otimes M)\frac{\partial^3(\text{vec }P)}{\partial\theta_0^3}$$

$$+2\theta_0\left(\theta_1'\frac{\partial(\text{vec }P)}{\partial\theta_1}(W^{-1}\otimes M)\frac{\partial^2(\text{vec }P)}{\partial\theta_0\partial\theta_1}\theta_1\right)$$

$$+\frac{1}{3}\theta_0^3\left(\theta_1'\frac{\partial(\text{vec }P)'}{\partial\theta_1}(W^{-1}\otimes M)\frac{\partial^3(\text{vec }P)}{\partial\theta_0^3}\right)$$

$$+\theta_0^3\left(\frac{\partial^2(\text{vec }P)'}{\partial\theta_0^2}(W^{-1}\otimes M)\frac{\partial^2(\text{vec }P)}{\partial\theta_0\partial\theta_1}\theta_1\right),\tag{C1}$$

where terms including θ_0^5 or $O(T^{-3/2})$ have been omitted. Now writing

$$C=\left[\frac{\partial(\text{vec }P)'}{\partial\theta_1}(W^{-1}\otimes M)\frac{\partial(\text{vec }P)}{\partial\theta_1}\right]^{-1}$$

and

$$D=\frac{\partial(\text{vec }P)'}{\partial\theta_1}(W^{-1}\otimes M)\frac{\partial^2(\text{vec }P)}{\partial\theta_1\partial\theta_0}+\frac{\partial^2(\text{vec }P)'}{\partial\theta_1\partial\theta_0}(W^{-1}\otimes M)\frac{\partial(\text{vec }P)}{\partial\theta_1},$$

differentiation with respect to θ_1 gives the equation

$$\theta_1=C\frac{\partial(\text{vec }P)'}{\partial\theta_1}(W^{-1}\otimes M)\text{ vec }\Delta P-\frac{1}{2}\theta_0^2 C\frac{\partial(\text{vec }P)'}{\partial\theta_1}(W^{-1}\otimes M)\frac{\partial^2(\text{vec }P)}{\partial\theta_0^2}$$

$$+\theta_0 C\frac{\partial^2(\text{vec }P)'}{\partial\theta_1\partial\theta_0}(W^{-1}\otimes M)\text{ vec }\Delta P-\theta_0 CD\theta_1$$

$$-\frac{1}{6}\theta_0^3 C\frac{\partial(\text{vec }P)'}{\partial\theta_1}(W^{-1}\otimes M)\frac{\partial^3(\text{vec }P)}{\partial\theta_0^3}$$

$$-\frac{1}{2}\theta_0^3 C\frac{\partial^2(\text{vec }P)'}{\partial\theta_0\partial\theta_1}(W^{-1}\otimes M)\frac{\partial^2(\text{vec }P)}{\partial\theta_0^2}.\tag{C2}$$

Now approximating θ_1 by the first two terms on the right hand side of (C2), and substituting this approximation into the fourth term on the right hand side of (C2) one obtains an approximation with errors of $O(T^{-3/2})$, and this expansion for the minimum θ_1 can be inverted in (C1) to give a corresponding expansion of $f^*(\theta_0,q)$ as follows:

$$f^*(\theta_0,q)=(\text{vec }\Delta P)'(W^{-1}\otimes M)\text{ vec }\Delta P-\theta_0^2(\text{vec }\Delta P)'(W^{-1}\otimes M)\frac{\partial^2(\text{vec }P)}{\partial\theta_0^2}$$

$$+\frac{1}{4}\theta_0^4\frac{\partial^2(\text{vec }P)'}{\partial\theta_0^2}(W^{-1}\otimes M)\frac{\partial^2(\text{vec }P)}{\partial\theta_0^2}$$

$$-\frac{1}{3}\theta_0^3(\text{vec }\Delta P)'(W^{-1}\otimes M)\frac{\partial^3(\text{vec }P)}{\partial\theta_0^3}$$

$$-\left[(\text{vec }\Delta P)'(W^{-1}\otimes M)\frac{\partial\text{ vec }P}{\partial\theta_1}-\frac{1}{2}\theta_0^2\frac{\partial^2(\text{vec }P)'}{\partial\theta_0^2}(W^{-1}\otimes M)\frac{\partial\text{ vec }P}{\partial\theta_1}\right.$$

$$+\theta_0(\text{vec }\Delta P)'(W^{-1}\otimes M)\frac{\partial^2(\text{vec }P)}{\partial\theta_0\partial\theta_1}$$

$$-\frac{1}{6}\theta_0^3\left(\frac{\partial^3(\text{vec }P)'}{\partial\theta_0^3}(W^{-1}\otimes M)\frac{\partial\text{ vec }P}{\partial\theta_1}\right)$$

$$\left.-\frac{1}{2}\theta_0^3\left(\frac{\partial^2(\text{vec }P)'}{\partial\theta_0^2}(W^{-1}\otimes M)\frac{\partial^2(\text{vec }P)}{\partial\theta_0\partial\theta_1}\right)\right]\theta_1 \qquad (C3)$$

(since the remaining terms vanish in minimising a quadratic in θ_1).

Defining

$$Q=(W^{-1}\otimes M)-(W^{-1}\otimes M)\frac{\partial\text{ vec }P}{\partial\theta_1}C\frac{\partial(\text{vec }P)'}{\partial\theta_1}(W^{-1}\otimes M),$$

we can then write

$$f^*(\theta_0,q)=(\text{vec }\Delta P)'Q\text{ vec }\Delta P$$

$$-2\theta_0(\text{vec }\Delta P)'Q\frac{\partial^2(\text{vec }P)}{\partial\theta_0\partial\theta_1}C\frac{\partial(\text{vec }P)'}{\partial\theta_1}(W^{-1}\otimes M)(\text{vec }\Delta P)$$

$$-\theta_0^2(\text{vec }\Delta P)'Q\frac{\partial^2(\text{vec }P)}{\partial\theta_0^2}$$

$$-\theta_0^3\left[\frac{1}{3}(\text{vec }\Delta P)'Q\frac{\partial^3(\text{vec }P)}{\partial\theta_0^3}\right.$$

$$-(\text{vec }\Delta P)'Q\frac{\partial^2(\text{vec }P)}{\partial\theta_0\partial\theta_1}C\frac{\partial(\text{vec }P)}{\partial\theta_1}(W^{-1}\otimes M)\frac{\partial^2(\text{vec }P)}{\partial\theta_0^2}$$

$$\left.-(\text{vec }\Delta P)'(W^{-1}\otimes M)\frac{\partial(\text{vec }P)}{\partial\theta_1}C\frac{\partial^2(\text{vec }P)'}{\partial\theta_1\partial\theta_0}Q\frac{\partial^2(\text{vec }P)}{\partial\theta_0^2}\right]$$

$$+\frac{1}{2}\theta_0^4\frac{\partial^2(\text{vec }P)'}{\partial\theta_0^2}Q\frac{\partial^2(\text{vec }P)}{\partial\theta_0^2}.$$

Now for f_i, $i=0,1,2,3$, if we take the next term in the expansion, it will be a homogeneous polynomial in ΔP of the next highest order to the one retained. Thus

$$f_0=(\text{vec }\Delta P)'Q\text{ vec }\Delta P+O(T^{-3/2}),$$

and since

$$\sqrt{T}\text{ vec }\Delta P\underset{a}{\sim}N(0,\Omega_v\otimes\bar{M}^{-1}) \qquad (C4)$$

and $\text{plim}_{T\to\infty}((\Omega_v\otimes\bar{M}^{-1})Q)$ is an idempotent matrix of rank $(nm-p+1)$, Tf_0 is asymptotically distributed as a χ^2 with $(nm-p+1)$ degrees of freedom. Similarly

$$Tf_1=-\sqrt{T}(\text{vec }\Delta P)'F_1\sqrt{T}(\text{vec }\Delta P)+O(T^{-1/2})$$

where

$$F_1 = \left[Q \frac{\partial^2 (\text{vec } P)}{\partial \theta_0 \partial \theta_1} C \frac{\partial (\text{vec } P)'}{\partial \theta_1} (W^{-1} \otimes M) + (W^{-1} \otimes M) \frac{\partial (\text{vec } P)}{\partial \theta_1} C \frac{\partial^2 (\text{vec } P)'}{\partial \theta_0 \partial \theta_1} Q \right],$$

but although F_1 has a finite probability limit, this does not correspond to a χ^2 distribution and Tf_1 is distributed asymptotically as a quadratic form in a set of normally distributed variables, which may be indefinite, so that Tf_1 is distributed asymptotically taking all values between $-\infty$ and $+\infty$.

Similarly

$$f_2 = -2 \frac{\partial^2 (\text{vec } P)'}{\partial \theta_0^2} Q \text{ vec } \Delta P + O(T^{-1}),$$

and

$$\operatorname*{plim}_{T \to \infty} \left(\frac{\partial^2 (\text{vec } P)'}{\partial \theta_0^2} Q \right) = \frac{\partial^2 (\text{vec } P)'}{\partial \theta_0^2} \bar{Q}$$

where

$$\bar{Q} = (\Omega_v^{-1} \otimes \bar{M}) - (\Omega_v^{-1} \otimes \bar{M}) \frac{\partial (\text{vec } P)}{\partial \theta_1}$$
$$\times \left[\frac{\partial (\text{vec } P)'}{\partial \theta_1} (\Omega_v^{-1} \otimes \bar{M}) \frac{\partial (\text{vec } P)}{\partial \theta_1} \right]^{-1} \frac{\partial (\text{vec } P)'}{\partial \theta_1} (\Omega_v^{-1} \otimes M).$$

Using (C4) and the Cramer linear transformation theorem it follows that

$$\sqrt{T} f_2 \underset{a}{\sim} N(0, \Omega_{f_2})$$

where

$$\Omega_{f_2} = \frac{\partial^2 (\text{vec } P)'}{\partial \theta_0^2} \bar{Q} \frac{\partial^2 (\text{vec } P)}{\partial \theta_0^2},$$

and $\underset{a}{\sim}$ denotes 'is asymptotically distributed'. In a similar fashion we have that

$$f_3 = F_3' \text{ vec } \Delta P + O(T^{-1})$$

where F_3 is a vector such that plim $F_3 = \bar{F}_3$ is finite. Thus

$$\sqrt{T} f_3 \underset{a}{\sim} N(0, \bar{F}_3'(\Omega_v \otimes \bar{M}^{-1}) \bar{F}_3).$$

Finally

$$f_4^* = 6 \frac{\partial^2 (\text{vec } P)'}{\partial \theta_0^2} Q \frac{\partial^2 (\text{vec } P)}{\partial \theta_0^2} + O(T^{-1/4}), \tag{C5}$$

noting that the remainder term on the expansion depends on θ_0, and that initially the argument that $\operatorname{plim}_{T \to \infty} (f_4^*)$ is finite and positive is required to establish that $\theta_0 = O(T^{-1/4})$, and only then can the order of magnitude of the remainder in (C5) be established as $T^{-1/4}$. In fact

$$\operatorname*{plim}_{T \to \infty} f_4^* = 6\Omega_{f_2},$$

and it is only if this is strictly positive that the asymptotic distributions are as stated in this article.

The criterion for f_4^* to have a positive probability limit is equivalent to requiring that

$$\left[\begin{array}{c} \dfrac{\partial(\operatorname{vec} P)'}{\partial\theta_1} (\Omega_v^{-1} \otimes \bar{M}) \dfrac{\partial(\operatorname{vec} P)}{\partial\theta_1} : \dfrac{\partial(\operatorname{vec} P)'}{\partial\theta_1} (\Omega_v^{-1} \otimes \bar{M}) \dfrac{\partial^2(\operatorname{vec} P)}{\partial\theta_0^2} \\[4mm] \dfrac{\partial^2(\operatorname{vec} P)'}{\partial\theta_0^2} (\Omega^{-1} \otimes \bar{M}) \dfrac{\partial(\operatorname{vec} P)}{\partial\theta_1} : \dfrac{\partial^2(\operatorname{vec} P)'}{\partial\theta_0^2} (\Omega_v^{-1} \otimes \bar{M}) \dfrac{\partial^2(\operatorname{vec} P)}{\partial\theta_0^2} \end{array} \right]$$

be non-singular. But given that $\Omega_v^{-1} \otimes \bar{M}$ is positive definite, this is equivalent to the requirement that the matrix

$$\left(\frac{\partial(\operatorname{vec} P)}{\partial\theta_1} : \frac{\partial^2(\operatorname{vec} P)}{\partial\theta_0^2} \right) \tag{C6}$$

be of rank p.

Thus the necessary and sufficient conditions that there should be a set of maxima of the likelihood function in some neighbourhood of $\bar{\theta}$, with asymptotic distribution as in the body of the paper are:

(I) Plim $M = \bar{M}$ is non-singular.
(II) $P(\theta) = P(\bar{\theta})$ has its only solution in some neighbourhood of $\bar{\theta}$, at $\theta = \bar{\theta}$.
(III) Rank $((\partial(\operatorname{vec} P))/\partial\theta) = p - 1$.
(IV) $P(\theta)$ has continuous fourth order derivatives at $\theta = \bar{\theta}$.
(V) Matrix (C6) above is of rank p.

In the special case where

$$P(\theta) = -B(\theta)^{-1} C(\theta)$$

where

$$A(\theta) = (B(\theta) : C(\theta))$$

and $B(\bar{\theta})$ is the square non-singular endogenous variable coefficient matrix, then in the neighbourhood of $\bar{\theta}$

$$\frac{\partial(\operatorname{vec} P)}{\partial\theta_1} = -(B(\theta)^{-1} \otimes \Pi'(\theta)) \frac{\partial(\operatorname{vec} A)}{\partial\theta_1}$$

where

$$\Pi(\theta) = \begin{pmatrix} P(\theta) \\ I \end{pmatrix},$$

and

$$\frac{\partial^2(\operatorname{vec} P)}{\partial \theta_0^2} = 2\left[(B(\theta))^{-1}\frac{\partial B}{\partial \theta_0}(B(\theta))^{-1}\otimes \Pi'(\theta)\right]\frac{\partial \operatorname{vec} A}{\partial \theta_0}$$
$$-(B(\theta)^{-1}\otimes \Pi'(\theta))\frac{\partial^2(\operatorname{vec} A)}{\partial \theta_0^2}.$$

But the choice of the linear transformation of θ is such that

$$\frac{\partial(\operatorname{vec} P)}{\partial \theta_0}=0 \qquad \text{at} \quad \theta=\bar{\theta}$$

which is equivalent to

$$(I\otimes \Pi'(\bar{\theta}))\frac{\partial(\operatorname{vec} A)}{\partial \theta_0}=0.$$

Thus the condition that matrix (C6) is of rank p is equivalent to the condition that

$$\operatorname{rank}\left(I\otimes \Pi'(\bar{\theta})\left[\frac{\partial(\operatorname{vec} A)}{\partial \theta_0}:\frac{\partial^2(\operatorname{vec} A)}{\partial \theta_0^2}\right]\right)=p.$$

Also for this case

$$\Omega_{f_2}=\frac{\partial^2(\operatorname{vec} A)'}{\partial \theta_0^2}(\bar{Q}^*)\frac{\partial^2(\operatorname{vec} A)}{\partial \theta_0^2}$$

where

$$\bar{Q}^*=(\Omega_v^{-1}\otimes \bar{R})-(\Omega_u^{-1}\otimes \bar{R})\frac{\partial(\operatorname{vec} A)}{\partial \theta_1}$$
$$\times\left[\frac{\partial(\operatorname{vec} A)'}{\partial \theta_1}(\Omega_u^{-1}\otimes \bar{R})\frac{\partial(\operatorname{vec} A)}{\partial \theta_1}\right]^{-1}\frac{\partial(\operatorname{vec} A')}{\partial \theta_1}(\Omega_u^{-1}\otimes \bar{R})$$

and

$$\Omega_u=B(\bar{\theta})\Omega_v B(\bar{\theta})', \qquad \bar{R}=\Pi(\bar{\theta})\bar{M}\Pi'(\bar{\theta}).$$

C2 *The instrumental variable estimator*

In this case

$$f(\theta,q)=(1/T)[a'(\theta)(X'Z)(Z'Z)^{-1}(Z'X)a(\theta)],$$

and writing

$$a(\theta)\simeq \bar{a}+\left(\frac{\partial a}{\partial \theta_1}\right)\theta_1+\frac{1}{2}\left(\frac{\partial^2 a}{\partial \theta_0^2}\right)\theta_0^2+\theta_0\left(\frac{\partial^2 a}{\partial \theta_0\partial \theta_1}\right)\theta_1+\frac{1}{2}\frac{\partial^2 a}{\partial \theta_1^2}\theta_1\Theta\theta_1+\frac{1}{6}\frac{\partial^3 a}{\partial \theta_0^3}\theta_0^3,$$

$$u=X\bar{a}, \qquad R=\frac{(X'Z)(Z'Z)^{-1}(Z'X)}{T}, \qquad r=R\bar{a},$$

we can expand

$$f(\theta, q) = (u'Z)(Z'Z)^{-1}Z'u/T + 2r'\frac{\partial a}{\partial \theta_1}\theta_1 + r'\frac{\partial^2 a}{\partial \theta_0^2}\theta_0^2 + 2r'\frac{\partial^2 a}{\partial \theta_0 \partial \theta_1}\theta_1\theta_0$$

$$+ \frac{1}{3}r'\frac{\partial^3 a}{\partial \theta_0^3}\theta_0^3 + \theta_1'\left(\frac{\partial a'}{\partial \theta_1} R \frac{\partial a}{\partial \theta_1}\right)\theta_1 + \theta_0^2\left(\frac{\partial^2 a}{\partial \theta_0^2} R \frac{\partial a}{\partial \theta_1}\right)\theta_1 + \frac{\theta_0^4}{4}\left(\frac{\partial^2 a'}{\partial \theta_0^2} R \frac{\partial^2 a}{\partial \theta_0^2}\right)$$

$$+ 2\theta_0\left(\theta_1'\frac{\partial a'}{\partial \theta_1} R \frac{\partial^2 a}{\partial \theta_0 \partial \theta_1}\theta_1\right) + \frac{1}{3}\theta_0^3\left(\theta_1'\frac{\partial a'}{\partial \theta_1} R \frac{\partial^3 a}{\partial \theta_0^3}\right) + \theta_0^3\left(\theta_1'\frac{\partial^2 a'}{\partial \theta_1 \partial \theta_0} R \frac{\partial^2 a}{\partial \theta_0^2}\right)$$

$$+ \frac{1}{6}\theta_0^5\left(\frac{\partial^2 a'}{\partial \theta_0^2} R \frac{\partial^3 a}{\partial \theta_0^3}\right) + O(T^{-3/2}).$$

Now writing $E^{-1} = (\partial a'/\partial \theta_1)R(\partial a/\partial \theta_1)$, and writing the similar expansion for $\partial f/\partial \theta_1$, we have

$$\theta_1 = -E\left(\frac{\partial a'}{\partial \theta_1} r\right) - \frac{1}{2}E\left(\frac{\partial a'}{\partial \theta_1} R \frac{\partial^2 a}{\partial \theta_0^2}\right)\theta_0^2 - E\left(\frac{\partial^2 a}{\partial \theta_0 \partial \theta_1} r\right)\theta_0$$

$$- \theta_0 E D^* \theta_1 - \frac{1}{3}E\left(\frac{\partial a'}{\partial \theta_1} R \frac{\partial^3 a}{\partial \theta_0^3}\right)\theta_0^3$$

where

$$D^* = \frac{\partial^2 a'}{\partial \theta_0 \partial \theta_1} R \frac{\partial a}{\partial \theta_1} + \frac{\partial a'}{\partial \theta_1} R \frac{\partial^2 a}{\partial \theta_0 \partial \theta_1}.$$

Now substituting in the $\tilde{f}(\theta, q)$ as in the previous section, and writing

$$Q^* = \left(I - \frac{\partial a}{\partial \theta_1} E \frac{\partial a'}{\partial \theta_1} R\right),$$

we obtain

$$f^*(\theta_0, q) \simeq \frac{(u'Z)(Z'Z)^{-1}Z'u}{T} - r'\frac{\partial a}{\partial \theta_1} E \frac{\partial a'}{\partial \theta_1} r$$

$$- 2\theta_0\left(r'Q^*\frac{\partial^2 a}{\partial \theta_0 \partial \theta_1} E \frac{\partial a'}{\partial \theta_1} r\right) + \frac{1}{2}\theta_0^2\left(r'Q^*\frac{\partial^2 a}{\partial \theta_0^2}\right)$$

$$+ \theta_0^3\left(\frac{1}{3}r'Q^*\frac{\partial^3 a}{\partial \theta_0^3} - r'Q^*\frac{\partial^2 a}{\partial \theta_0 \partial \theta_1} E \frac{\partial a'}{\partial \theta_1} R \frac{\partial^2 a}{\partial \theta_0^2} - r'\frac{\partial a}{\partial \theta_1} E \frac{\partial^2 a'}{\partial \theta_0 \partial \theta_1} RQ^*\frac{\partial^2 a}{\partial \theta_0^2}\right)$$

$$+ \frac{1}{4}\theta_0^4\left(\frac{\partial^2 a'}{\partial \theta_0^2} RQ^*\frac{\partial^2 a}{\partial \theta_0^2}\right).$$

Now since $\sqrt{T}r \underset{a}{\sim} N(0, \sigma^2\bar{R})$ where $\sigma^2 = E(u_t^2)$, and $\bar{R} = \text{plim } R$, it follows that $\sqrt{T}f_2 \underset{a}{\sim} N(0, \Omega_{f_2})$ where now

$$\Omega_{f_2} = \text{plim}\frac{\partial^2 a'}{\partial \theta_0^2}\bar{R}\bar{Q}\frac{\partial^2 a}{\partial \theta_0^2}$$

and that $\text{plim } f_4 = 6\Omega_{f_2}$, where $\bar{Q} = \text{plim } Q^*$.

The condition that Ω_{f_2} is non-zero is that

$$\text{rank}\left(K\left[\frac{\partial a}{\partial \theta_1}, \frac{\partial^2 a}{\partial \theta_0^2}\right]\right) = p,$$

where

$$K = \text{plim}\left(\frac{Z'X}{T}\right).$$

Note that, defining $\phi(\theta)$ as in the body of the paper, the condition for each case is equivalent to

$$\text{rank}\left(\frac{\partial \phi}{\partial \theta_1} : \frac{\partial^2 \phi}{\partial \theta_0^2}\right) = p.$$

C3 *The mixture distribution of θ_0 and θ_1*

In the text of the paper it is shown that the asymptotic distribution of $\hat{\theta}_0$ can be regarded as a mixture of two distributions, and clearly the asymptotic distribution of $\hat{\theta}_1$ must be a similar mixture. The description of the resulting distribution is simplified by introducing a change of variables. We consider the details for the instrumental variable estimator but the maximum likelihood estimator distribution can be described in the same way (and the notation is designed to facilitate the extension).

Define

$$V = \left(\frac{\partial a'}{\partial \theta_1} R \frac{\partial a}{\partial \theta_1}\right),$$

$$v = \frac{\partial a'}{\partial \theta_1} R \frac{\partial^2 a}{\partial \theta_0^2},$$

$$v_0 = \left(\frac{\partial^2 a'}{\partial \theta_0^2} R \frac{\partial^2 a}{\partial \theta_0^2}\right),$$

where all the derivatives are taken at $\hat{\theta}_0$ and $\hat{\theta}_1$. Now define plim $V = \bar{V}$, plim $v = \bar{v}$, plim $v_0 = \bar{v}_0$, and $\gamma = \frac{1}{2}\bar{V}^{-1}\bar{v}$, and then $\theta_1^* = \theta_1 + \gamma\theta_0^2$, as a revised set of parameters (note that we have already changed the origin so that the true value of θ_1 is $\bar{\theta}_1 = 0$). Then if

$$a^*(\theta_1^*, \theta_0) = a(\theta_1^* - \gamma\theta_0^2, \theta_0),$$

$$\frac{\partial a^*}{\partial \theta_1^*} = \frac{\partial a}{\partial \theta_1},$$

$$\frac{\partial a^*}{\partial \theta_0} = \frac{\partial a}{\partial \theta_0} - 2\gamma'\theta_0 \frac{\partial a}{\partial \theta_1},$$

$$\frac{\partial^2 a^*}{\partial \theta_0^2} = \frac{\partial^2 a}{\partial \theta_0^2} - 2\gamma' \frac{\partial a}{\partial \theta_1} + O(\theta_0^2).$$

It follows that if

$$V^* = \left(\frac{\partial a^{*\prime}}{\partial \theta_1^*} \, R \, \frac{\partial a^*}{\partial \theta_1^*} \right),$$

$$v^* = \left(\frac{\partial a^{*\prime}}{\partial \theta_1^*} \, R \, \frac{\partial^2 a^*}{\partial \theta_0^2} \right),$$

$$v_{00}^* = \left(\frac{\partial^2 a^{*\prime}}{\partial \theta_0^2} \, R \, \frac{\partial^2 a^*}{\partial \theta_0^2} \right), \qquad \text{all at} \quad \theta = 0,$$

then $\operatorname{plim} v^* = 0$. Now considering the minimisation of $f(\theta_1^* - \gamma\theta_0^2, \theta_0, p)$ with respect to θ_1^*, θ_0, and writing $\hat\theta_1^*, \hat\theta_0$ for the minimum value, the first order condition with respect to θ_1^*, $(\partial f/\partial \theta_1^*) = 0$, can be expanded by the mean value theorem:

$$\left(\frac{\partial^2 f}{\partial \theta_1^* \partial \theta_0} \right) \hat\theta_0 + \left(\frac{\partial^2 f}{\partial \theta_1^* \partial \theta_1^*} \right) \hat\theta_1^* = - \left(\frac{\partial f}{\partial \theta_1^*} \right)_{\theta=0}. \qquad \text{(C5)}$$

In fact the two terms on the left hand side of this equation are obtained by considering first a change from $\theta = 0$ to

$$\theta^+ = \begin{pmatrix} 0 \\ \hat\theta_0 \end{pmatrix},$$

and then a second change from θ^+ to $\hat\theta$. Thus the derivative in the first term on the left hand side is evaluated at a point

$$\theta = \begin{pmatrix} 0 \\ k_1 \hat\theta_0 \end{pmatrix},$$

and in the second term at

$$\theta = \begin{pmatrix} k_2 \hat\theta_1 \\ \hat\theta_0 \end{pmatrix}$$

where k_1 and k_2 are positive scalars $k_1 \leqslant 1$, $k_2 \leqslant 1$. Now in the first term

$$\frac{\partial^2 f}{\partial \theta_1^* \partial \theta_0} = 2\left(\frac{\partial a^{*\prime}}{\partial \theta_1^*} \, \bar{R} \, \frac{\partial a^*}{\partial \theta_0} \right) + 2\left(a^{*\prime} \bar{R} \, \frac{\partial^2 a^*}{\partial \theta_1^* \partial \theta_0} \right) + O(T^{-1/2})$$

where $\bar{R} = \operatorname{plim} R$.

Using Taylor series expansions for a^* and $\partial a^*/\partial \theta_0$ we have $a^* = O(T^{-1/2})$, and

$$\frac{\partial a^*}{\partial \theta_0} = k_1 \hat\theta_0 \, \frac{\partial^2 a^*}{\partial \theta_0^2},$$

and finally from $\bar{v}^* = 0$, we have

$$\frac{\partial a^{*\prime}}{\partial \theta_1^*} \, \bar{R} \, \frac{\partial^2 a^*}{\partial \theta_0^2} = O(T^{-1/4})$$

provided both

$$\frac{\partial^2 a^*}{\partial \theta_1 \partial \theta_0} \qquad \text{and} \qquad \frac{\partial^2 a^*}{\partial \theta_0^3}$$

are finite in some neighbourhood of the origin.

Thus

$$\frac{\partial^2 f}{\partial \theta_1^* \partial \theta_0} = O(T^{-1/2}),$$

and so (C5) can be written as

$$\left(\frac{\partial^2 f^*}{\partial \theta_1^* \partial \theta_1^*}\right)\sqrt{T}\hat{\theta}_1^* = \sqrt{T}\frac{\partial f^*}{\partial \theta_1^*} + O(T^{-1/4}). \tag{C6}$$

It follows using the Cramer linear transformation theorem that

$$\sqrt{T}\hat{\theta}_1^* \underset{a}{\sim} N(0, \sigma^2 \bar{V}^{*-1}) \tag{C7}$$

where $\sigma^2 = E(u_t^2)$, and $\bar{V}^* = \text{plim } V^*$.

Now writing the equation $\partial f^* / \partial \theta_0 = 0$ at $\theta = \hat{\theta}$, as

$$\left(\frac{\partial f^*}{\partial \theta_0}\right)\theta^+ + \left(\frac{\partial^2 f^*}{\partial \theta_1^* \partial \theta_0}\right)\hat{\theta}_1^* = 0 \tag{C8}$$

where

$$\theta^+ = \begin{pmatrix} 0 \\ \hat{\theta}_0 \end{pmatrix}$$

and the latter derivative is taken at

$$\begin{pmatrix} k_3\hat{\theta}_1 \\ \hat{\theta}_0 \end{pmatrix}.$$

Now since $\hat{\theta}_1 = O(T^{-1/2})$, this derivative can be shown to be of the same order, and so the last term in (C7) is $O(T^{-1})$. Now as in the body of the paper we distinguish the two cases where $\hat{\theta}_0 = O(T^{-1/2})$ and where $\hat{\theta}_0 = O(T^{-1/4})$. In the latter case from the asymptotic distribution of $\hat{\theta}_0$, we can deduce that $\hat{\theta}_0 T^{1/4}$ has a non-trivial distribution, and substituting

$$a(\theta^+) = \bar{a} + \frac{1}{2}\left(\frac{\partial^2 a}{\partial \theta_0}\right)\hat{\theta}_0^2 + O(T^{-3/4})$$

we find that

$$\sqrt{T}\hat{\theta}_0^2 \underset{a}{\sim} N_+(0, \bar{v}_{00}^{**}\sigma^2)$$

asymptotically independent of $\sqrt{T}\hat{\theta}_1^*$, where $\bar{v}_0^* = \text{plim } v_{00}^*$, and N_+ represents the positive half of the normal distribution. On the other hand if $\hat{\theta}_0 = O(T^{-1/2})$, then $\hat{\theta} - \theta_1^* = O(T^{-1})$, so that in either case we can summarise the asymptotic distribution of $\hat{\theta}_1^*$ by stating that $\hat{\theta}_1^*$ has the asymptotic distribution given by equation (C7) independent of the asymptotic distribution of $\hat{\theta}_0$.

Considering now the case where there are two minima, we can make a second order expansion

$$\hat{\theta}_0^{(1)} = \theta_0^* + 8d_0$$

where $\theta_0^* = +\sqrt{(-6f_2/f_4)}$.

Substituting this into equation (17) we have

$$d_0 = (f_1 f_4 - 3 f_2 f_3)/2 f_2 f_4.$$

d_0 is $O(T^{-1/2})$ and is asymptotically distributed as the ratio of a quadratic form in normally distributed variables divided by a normally distributed variable. Now to the same order of magnitude

$$\hat{\theta}_0^{(2)} = -\theta_0^* + d_0.$$

Substituting this into $f^*(\theta_0)$ we have

$$f^*(\hat{\theta}_0^{(1)}) - f^*(\hat{\theta}_0^{(2)}) = 2\theta_0^* \left(f_1 + f_2 d_0 + \frac{f_3 \theta_0^{*2}}{6} + \frac{f_4 d_0 \theta_0^{*2}}{6} \right) + O(T^{-3/2})$$

$$= 2\theta_0^* \left(f_1 - \frac{f_2 f_3}{f_4} \right) + O(T^{-3/2}).$$

$f_1 - f_2 f_3 / f_4$ is asymptotically distributed as a quadratic form in normally distributed variables and f_1 itself is asymptotically distributed as a quadratic form which is indefinite, so that the difference has a distribution which includes both negative and positive values. Thus it is to be expected that in the distribution of the global minimum both positive and negative values of $\hat{\theta}_0$ will be combined and so the dispersion of the distribution of the global minimum will be greater than that of the distribution of either $\hat{\theta}_0^{(1)}$ or $\hat{\theta}_0^{(2)}$.

REFERENCES

[1] Dieudonne, J.: *Foundations of Modern Analysis.* New York: Academic Press, 1969.

[2] Fisher, F. M.: *The Identification Problem in Econometrics.* New York: McGraw-Hill, 1966.

[3] ———: 'Identifiability criteria in non-linear systems. A further note', *Econometrica*, **33** (1965), 197–205.

[4] Lang, S.: *Introductin to Algebraic Geometry.* New York: Wiley, 1964.

[5] Rothenberg, T. J.: 'Identification in parametric models', *Econometrica*, **39** (1971), 577–92.

[6] Sargan, J. D.: 'The estimation of relationships with autocorrelated residuals by the use of instrumental variables', *Journal of the Royal Statistical Society, Series B*, **21** (1959), 91–105.

[7] ———: 'The identification and estimation of sets of simultaneous stochastic equations', London School of Economics Econometrics Programme Discussion Paper A1, 1975.

[8] ———: 'Identification in models with autoregressive errors', London School of Economics Econometrics Programme Discussion Paper A16, 1977.

J. D. SARGAN

—— · ——

14 IDENTIFICATION IN MODELS WITH AUTOREGRESSIVE ERRORS

London School of Economics and Political Science

(First published in *Studies in Econometrics, Time Series and Multivariate Statistics* (1983), Academic Press.)

1 INTRODUCTION

Consider the model

$$A(L)x_t = B(L)y_t + C(L)z_t = u_t, \qquad t = 1, \ldots, T$$

where $A(L) = (B(L) : C(L))$ is a matrix of polynomials in the lag operator so that $L^r x_t = x_{t-r}$, and y_t is a vector of n endogenous variables, $B(L) = \sum_{s=0}^{k} B_s L^s$ and $B_0 = I_n$, and the remaining B_s are $n \times n$ square matrices, $C(L) = \sum_{s=0}^{k} C_s L^s$, and C_s is $n \times m$.

Suppose that u_t satisfies $R(L)u_t = e_t$, where $R(L) = \sum_{s=0}^{r} R_s L^s$, $R_0 = I_n$, R_s is a $n \times n$ square matrix. e_t may be white noise, or generated by a vector moving average stochastic process. Now write

$$\Psi(L) = R(L)A(L), \tag{1}$$

it is assumed that ignoring the implicit restrictions which follow from equation (1), $\Psi(L)$ can be consistently estimated, so that if the equation

$$\Psi(L)x_t = e_t$$

has a moving average error stochastic process, suitable conditions, see Hannan (1971, 1975), for the identification of the unconstrained model are satisfied, and that the appropriate conditions (lack of multicollinearity) on the data second moment matrices discussed by Hannan are also satisfied. Then the essential conditions for identification of the $A(L)$ and $R(L)$ can be considered by requiring that for the true $\Psi(L)$ equations (1) have a unique solution for $A(L)$ and $R(L)$. There are three cases to be considered. The first is the possibility that equations (1) have a finite number of solutions, if the true $\Psi(L)$ is on the left hand side, so that observations of data cannot discriminate between this finite number of observationally equivalent models. Now writing equations (1) in the form

$$\theta = g(\xi) \tag{2}$$

where θ is a $p \times 1$ vector of the $n(n+m)(r+k+1) - n^2$ unknown coefficients of $\Psi(L)$ in some order, and $\xi' = (\alpha', \rho')$ where α' is a similar vector of coefficients of $A(L)$, and ρ' a vector of coefficients of $R(L)$. Then there is the possibility that for a given θ an infinity of ξ satisfy the conditions. Typically if $g(\xi)$ has continuous derivatives almost everywhere the solutions determine a differential manifold in ξ space. A necessary condition for this is that $\partial g / \partial \xi'$ is not of full rank. Note that ξ as specified has $Q = kn(n+m) + nm + rn^2$ unconstrained elements, so that this is the case where the rank of $\partial g / \partial \xi'$ is less than Q. A model where this latter occurs will be referred to as a model failing to satisfy the full rank conditions, or a singular model, whereas the case where the solutions of (2) form a differential manifold in the neighbourhood of the true value ξ will be called a case where the model is locally unidentified.

The discussion by Fisher (1967) of this point is correct but seems to have a wrong emphasis. In models non-linear in the parameters, failure of Jacobian or rank conditions are not important in the sense that the failure is likely to be exact for the parameters of a correct model of the real world. (The *a priori* probability is zero that the restrictions, which lead to a failure of the full rank conditions, are satisfied.) The restrictions corresponding to the rank conditions can be represented by taking some suitable set of $(P - Q + 1)$ determinants, selected from $\partial g / \partial \xi'$, and equating them to zero. Denoting these $(P - Q + 1)$ restrictions by the vector $h(\xi) = 0$, we consider the probability that a model occurs where the restrictions are almost satisfied in the sense that $\|h(\bar{\xi})\| < \varepsilon$ for some suitable norm. It is possible that there is no ξ such that $h(\xi) = 0$, or such that $\|h(\xi)\| < \varepsilon$. But if for some ξ, $h(\xi) = 0$, and if we consider a proper prior probability density, the prior probability that a model with $\|h(\bar{\xi})\| < \varepsilon$ will occur will generally be $O(\varepsilon^{P-Q+1})$. If we take $(P - Q)$ as an index of overidentification in this context, the greater the degree of overidentification the smaller the probability for small ε. But the importance of the ε being small is that in finite samples the distributions of estimators derived from models which are almost singular tend to approximate those from models which are exactly singular. This is not easy to prove rigorously, but we can approach it indirectly by noting that the sample size required for asymptotic approximation to be good depends particularly on the parameters associated with rank conditions. In very large samples an almost singular model will have the usual asymptotic normal distribution with a relatively large asymptotic variance. But an unpublished study by the author of the asymptotic distribution in the singular case shows that, unless the model is locally unidentified, the usual estimators are consistent, but not usually of order $(T^{-1/2})$ or asymptotically normal distributed. The conjecture that for an almost singular model the behaviour, when the sample size is smaller than that required for the true asymptotic distribution to be well approximated, is similar to the asymptotic behaviour of an exactly singular model, is based partly on proximity or continuity arguments, partly on an analytical study of some particularly simple cases, and partly on some very suggestive Monte Carlo studies.

The conditions that $\bar{\theta} = g(\xi)$ has an infinite set of solutions in the neighbourhood of $\bar{\xi}$ are in fact much more limiting and numerous (within a given class of functional forms) than those required to ensure that the model is singular. This will be illustrated for the particular model considered in this paper in Section 3. Fisher considers a case which corresponds to $\partial g/\partial \xi'$ being of rank $r^* < Q$ throughout some neighbourhood of $\bar{\xi}$. Use of the implicit function theorem then shows that we can write

$$\bar{\theta} = g_1(g_2(\xi)) \qquad \text{where} \quad \xi_1 = g_2(\xi)$$

is a vector of r^* functions of ξ, and $g_1(\xi_1)$ is a $p \times 1$ vector function of the $r^* \times 1$ vector ξ_1. This can be labelled a case of overparametrisation, since clearly all possible models which we are prepared to consider can be labelled in terms of the r^* dimension ξ_1 parameter space. However, this is by no means the only case where the model is locally unidentified. Suppose that all solutions of

$$\bar{\theta} = g(\xi)$$

in the neighbourhood of $\bar{\xi}$ form a differential manifold of dimension p, which can locally be parameterised in the form

$$\xi = \xi(\phi)$$

where ϕ is a $p \times 1$ parameter vector. Then clearly at any point of the differential manifold we must have

$$\frac{\partial g}{\partial \xi'} \frac{\partial \xi}{\partial \phi'} = 0$$

so that $\partial g/\partial \xi'$ is at most of rank $Q - p$ (given that for a valid parameterisation $\partial \xi/\partial \phi'$ must be of rank p almost everywhere). Note, however, that it will usually be the case that $\partial g/\partial \xi'$ is of full rank for points not on the differential manifold.

As a general conclusion to this general discussion of singular and unidentified models, we only need to conclude that singularity is a much more frequent problem than lack of local identifiability; that the establishment that a model is singular does not give a high probability that it is not locally identifiable, and that the only way to establish that a model is locally unidentified is by way of a direct consideration of the solution of the equations $\bar{\theta} = g(\xi)$.

2 ALGEBRAIC PREREQUISITES

In discussing identification it is assumed that the maximal lag in the variables x_{it} are specified for each i, and that it is then required to discuss the stochastic properties of the estimators of the $A(L)$ matrices, when given maximum lags are assumed, and similarly that r, the degree of $R(L)$, is prespecified. Within this specification it is possible to consider cases where the true coefficients are zero, in such a way that the maximum lags are lower than those specified. A discussion which turns on $A(L)$ being left prime does not adequately discuss the case where alternative factorisations exist, but only such that the specified maximum lags are exceeded either on $A(L)$ or $R(L)$. This paper is therefore concerned to develop conditions for alternative factorisations with specified lags, where an approach making use of the Jordan canonical form is used (see MacDuffee, 1971; Perlis, 1952; or Turnbull and Aitken, 1932).

We start by considering the possibility of factorising

$$U(x) = V(x)W(x) \tag{3}$$

when $U(x)$, $V(x)$, $W(x)$ are all square $n \times n$ matrices whose elements are polynomials is a scalar real variable x. We write

$$U(x) = \sum_{i=0}^{f} U_i x^{f-i}, \qquad V(x) = \sum_{i=0}^{r} V_i x^{r-i}, \qquad W(x) = \sum_{i=0}^{k} W_i x^{k-i}$$

where $U_0 = V_0 = W_0 = I$, and $f = r + k$.

Note that for comparison with the equation (1) of the previous section we are replacing L by $1/x$. Then, from (3), writing $W_i = 0, i > k$, and $i < 0$, we can write

$$U_s = \sum_{j=0}^{r} V_j W_{s-j}, \qquad s = 0, \ldots, f. \tag{4}$$

In Sargan (1978) a direct approach to the solution of these equations was given, and was shown to be equivalent to the following:
Define a companion matrix to $U(x)$ by

$$U^+ = \begin{bmatrix} 0 & I & 0 & \cdots & 0 & 0 \\ 0 & 0 & I & & 0 & 0 \\ \vdots & & & & & \\ 0 & 0 & 0 & & 0 & I \\ -U'_f & -U'_{f-1} & -U'_{f-2} & & -U'_2 & -U'_1 \end{bmatrix}$$

and denote by Λ the Jordan canonical form of U^+, so that the latent roots λ_j of U^+ occur on the diagonal of Λ, and we can write $U^+H^+ = H^+\Lambda$, where H^+ is the square matrix whose columns are the latent vectors of U^+.

If λ is a latent root of $V(x)$ then det $V(\lambda) = 0$, and if h' is a corresponding left hand latent vector

$$h'V(\lambda) = 0 \tag{5}$$

and also

$$h'U(\lambda) = h'V(\lambda)W(\lambda) = 0. \tag{6}$$

Now write $h^{*\prime} = (h', \lambda h', \lambda^2 h', \dots, \lambda^{r-1} h')$ and $h^{+\prime} = (h', \lambda h', \lambda^2 h', \dots, \lambda^{f-1} h')$.

Define

$$V^{+\prime} = \begin{bmatrix} 0 & 0 & \cdots & 0 & -V_r \\ I & 0 & 0 & 0 & -V_{r-1} \\ \vdots & & & & \\ 0 & 0 & & I & -V_1^2 \end{bmatrix}.$$

We note that

$$h^{*\prime}V^{+\prime} = \lambda h^{*\prime}, \tag{7}$$

$$h^{+\prime}U^{+\prime} = \lambda h^{+\prime}. \tag{8}$$

Denote the Jordan canonical form of V^+ by Λ_1. Considering now the case where λ is a multiple root of det $(V(x)) = 0$, any latent vector h' satisfying (10) will be called a basic latent vector, and the corresponding vectors h^* and h^+ will also be called 'basic'. The number of such basic latent vectors associated with $V(x)$ will depend on the rank of $V(\lambda)$, and will be equal to the nullity of $V(\lambda)$, denoted by N. Clearly $(V^+ - \lambda I)$ has the same nullity. If M is the multipicity of the latent root λ, then it may be that $N < M$. Whereas corresponding to a single root λ of $V(x)$, (or of V^+) there is a column of Λ_1 containing all zero elements except for a diagonal element equal to λ, corresponding to a multiple root λ, Λ_1 contains an $M \times M$ diagonal block. This diagonal block is made up of a set of square diagonal submatrices (the simple classical submatrices of Turnbull and Aitken (1932)) of the form

$$\begin{bmatrix} \lambda & 1 & 0 & \cdots & 0 \\ 0 & \lambda & 1 & & 0 \\ \vdots & & & & \\ 0 & 0 & 0 & & 1 \\ 0 & 0 & 0 & & \lambda \end{bmatrix}. \tag{9}$$

Such a classical submatrix with all its diagonal elements λ, and all its superdiagonal elements 1, will be referred to as a classical λ submatrix. The ith classical λ submatrix will have its dimension denoted by s_i, where $s_i \geqslant s_{i+1}$. The s_i, enclosed in a bracket, are referred to as the Segre characteristic for λ. Thus (3 3 2 1 1 1) means that $M = 11$, that there are two classical λ submatrices of dimension 3, one of dimension 2, and 3 diagonal elements (equal to λ) in Λ_1. We refer to the largest dimension, s_1, as the largest exponent, and find it convenient later to also denote it by S (i.e., $S = s_1$). Note that the number of classical submatrices is N, and $\sum_{i=1}^{N} s_i = M$.

Corresponding to a given classical submatrix of the form (9) from $V^+ H^* = H^* \Lambda_1$ we deduce that there are a set of s latent vectors satisfying (i) for the basic latent vector

$$V^+ h_1^* = \lambda h_1^*, \tag{10}$$

and (ii) for the remaining latent vectors

$$(V^+ - \lambda I) h_j^* = h_{j-1}^*, \qquad j = 1, \ldots, s. \tag{11}$$

Writing

$$h_1^{*\prime} = (h_1', h_1', \lambda^2 h_1', \ldots, \lambda^{r-1} h_1')$$

and

$$h_2^{*\prime} = (h_{21}', h_{22}', h_{23}', \ldots, h_{2r}')$$

(11) gives

$$h_{2(j+1)} - \lambda h_{2j} = \lambda^{j-1} h_1, \qquad j = 1, \ldots, r-1,$$

or

$$h_{2(j+1)}/\lambda^{j+1} - h_{2j}/\lambda^j = h_1/\lambda^2.$$

Thus

$$h_{2j} = h_{21} \lambda^{j-1} + (j-1) h_1 \lambda^{j-2}.$$

Now writing $h_2 = h_{21}$ and substituting into the last block of equations (11) we get

$$V(\lambda)' h_2 + \left(\sum_{j=1}^{r} j \lambda^{j-1} V_{(r-j)}' \right) h_1 = 0.$$

Now writing $V_i(\lambda) = \partial^i V(\lambda)/(\partial \lambda)^i$, this can be written $h_1' V_1(\lambda) + h_2' V(\lambda) = 0$.

Then considering h_j^*, $j > 2$, in the same way, we obtain the sets of equations

$$\sum_{i=0}^{j} h_{(j-i+1)}' V_i(\lambda)/i! = 0, \qquad j = 0, \ldots, s-1. \tag{12}$$

We will refer to h_1, h_1^* below as basic latent vectors, and the $h_i, h_i^*, i > 1$, as the succeeding latent vectors. We can now summarise these equations by writing

$$V_s^*(\lambda) = \begin{bmatrix} V(\lambda) & V_1(\lambda) & V_2(\lambda)/2 & \cdots & V_{s-1}(\lambda)/(s-1)! \\ 0 & V(\lambda) & V_1(\lambda) & & V_{s-2}(\lambda)/(s-2)! \\ 0 & 0 & V(\lambda) & & V_{s-3}(\lambda)/(s-3)! \\ \vdots & & & & \\ 0 & 0 & 0 & & V(\lambda) \end{bmatrix}.$$

Clearly (12) is equivalent to

$$(h_1', h_2', \ldots, h_s') V_s^*(\lambda) = 0.$$

Given the correspondence between the vectors h_j and h_j^*, it is clear that the nullity of $V_s^*(\lambda)$ is equal to the nullity of $(V^+ - \lambda I)^s$. If we consider the left hand annihilator of $V_s^*(\lambda)$, it has a block triangular form which we write

$$\Phi^{(s)} = \begin{bmatrix} 0 & 0 & \cdots & 0 & \Phi_{11} \\ 0 & 0 & & \Phi_{21} & \Phi_{22} \\ \vdots & & & & \\ \Phi_{s1} & \Phi_{s2} & & \Phi_{s(s-1)} & \Phi_{ss} \end{bmatrix}.$$

The rows of Φ_{11} are the set of basic latent λ vectors. The rows of Φ_{ji}, $i = 1, \ldots, j$, satisfy the system of equations (12) for each j. Note that Φ_{j1} does not depend on s. The number of rows, N_j say, in Φ_{ji} is equal to the number of classical λ submatrices of dimension greater than or equal to j in Λ_1. Or alternatively N_p equals the number of latent vectors satisfying equations of the form (12) with $h_p \neq 0$. N_j is the jth Weyr characteristic number for V^+ (MacDuffee, 1946). Note that S, the largest exponent, is defined as the smallest integer such that nullity $(V_{S+1}^*(\lambda)) =$ nullity $V_S^*(\lambda)$.

We also need to consider the right hand annihilator of $V_s^*(\lambda)$. This has clearly similar properties to $\Phi^{(s)}$, and if we denote it by $\Psi^{(s)}$, so $V_s^*(\lambda)\Psi^{(s)} = 0$, we can partition

$$\Psi^{(s)} = \begin{bmatrix} \Psi_{11} & \Psi_{12} & \cdots & \Psi_{1s} \\ 0 & \Psi_{22} & & \Psi_{2s} \\ 0 & 0 & & \Psi_{3s} \\ \vdots & & & \\ 0 & 0 & & \Psi_{ss} \end{bmatrix}$$

where Ψ_{ij} is independent of s. By comparing the ranks of $V_s^*(\lambda)$ for different s, it must be the case that the number of columns of Ψ_{ij} is equal to N_j.

Furthermore, both Ψ_{jj} and Φ_{jj} must be of rank N_j, otherwise the annihilators would not be of full rank when $s=j$. The number of rows in $\Phi^{(s)}$ is equal to the number of columns in $\Psi^{(s)}$, and, when $s=S$, is equal to M, the multiplicity of the root λ.

Now from $U(\lambda)=V(\lambda)W(\lambda)$ by differentiation we have $U_j(\lambda)=\sum_{i=0}^{j} V_i(\lambda)W_{(j-i)}(\lambda)C_i^j$, where $U_j(x)$ and $W_j(x)$ are the jth derivatives of $U(x)$ and $W(x)$, respectively.

By substitution it follows that

$$\sum_{i=0}^{j} h'_{(j-i+1)}U_i(\lambda)/i!=0, \qquad j=0,\dots,s-1, \tag{1)3}$$

for the same vectors h_j satisfying (12).

Considering now all the latent vectors of V^+, corresponding to the single latent roots of V^+ there is a corresponding latent vector h^+ of U^+; and corresponding to any $s\times s$ classical λ submatrix in Λ_1 (the canonical form of V^+), there is a corresponding set of s latent vectors of U^+, and a corresponding classical λ submatrix of Λ. Thus writing H^* for all the latent vectors of V^+ we have

$$V^+H^*=H^*\Lambda_1. \tag{14}$$

Writing H_1^+ for the corresponding latent vectors of U^+, it follows from the equations of the form (13) that

$$U^{+\prime}H_1^+=H_1^+\Lambda_1. \tag{15}$$

Clearly we must be able to partition Λ, so that

$$\Lambda=\begin{bmatrix}\Lambda_1 & \Lambda_2\\ 0 & \Lambda_3\end{bmatrix}. \tag{16}$$

Also, if

$$H^*=\begin{bmatrix}H_{11}^*\\ H_{12}^*\\ \vdots\\ H_{1r}^*\end{bmatrix} \qquad H_1^+=\begin{bmatrix}H_{11}^+\\ H_{12}^+\\ \vdots\\ H_{1f}^+\end{bmatrix}$$

where both H_{1j}^* and H_{1j}^+ are $n\times(nr)$ matrices for all j, clearly the columns of H_{11}^* and H_{11}^+ are the latent vectors satisfying both (5) for single roots and (12) for multiple roots. Thus we can identify $H_{11}^*=H_{11}^+$. From (14) and (25) we have $H_{1j}^+=H_{11}^+\Lambda_1^{j-1}=H_{11}^*\Lambda_1^{j-1}=H_{1j}^*$.

Now defining

$$H_1^+=\begin{bmatrix}\tilde{H}_1\\ \tilde{H}_2\end{bmatrix},$$

where $\tilde{H}_1$ is a square $(nr \times nr)$ matrix we have $H^* = \tilde{H}_1$. Thus provided $\tilde{H}_1$ is non-singular, we deduce that $V^+ = \tilde{H}_1 \Lambda_1 \tilde{H}_1^{-1}$. Again the proof requires that a partitioning of the form (16) is used, and that $\tilde{H}_1$ is non-singular. Note that if Λ contains multiple roots, then the form of the partitioning requires that any set of latent vectors in $\tilde{H}_1$, corresponding to a classical λ submatrix of Λ_1, should correspond to a set of latent vectors selected from those columns of H^+ corresponding to a single classical λ submatrix of Λ. The selection should include the basic latent vectors, followed in order by its succeeding latent vectors. If the Λ classical submatrix is of dimension s, not all h_j^+, $j = 0, \ldots, s-1$, need be included in H_1^+, but if h_i^+ is excluded, then h_j^+ for all $j > i$ must also be excluded. This selection omitting the later latent vectors in the set will be referred to as 'trimming Λ, or H^{+}' in the subsequent section of this article.

Clearly if we start with an arbitrary $U(x)$ such that Λ is diagonal, at least one factorisation is possible for any $r < f$, since at least one non-singular $\tilde{H}_1$ can be found in the first nr rows of H^+. Generally there will be more than one possible factorisation, corresponding to all permutations of the rows and columns of Λ yielding a partition of the form (16) with a corresponding non-singular $\tilde{H}_1$. The corresponding $\tilde{V}$ will be real provided that whenever a complex root λ is included in Λ_1, so is the conjugate complex root, and whenever a complex classical submatrix is included in Λ_1, so is its conjugate complex. This will automatically ensure corresponding conditions on the columns of H_1. If only real factorisations are considered this may considerably reduce the number of alternative factorisations. Similar restrictions on the possibility of alternative real factorisations need to be considered later, but these are judged to be sufficiently obvious not to be made explicit.

3 MULTIPLE SOLUTIONS

We apply these results to the model of Section 1, noting that we wish to consider a case where it is known that there are different maximum lags in the variables, so that if we take the ith column of $A(L)$ to be $a_i(L)$, then $a_i(L)$ has degree (maximum lag) k_i, and we write $f_i = k_i + r$, and $\psi_i(L) = R(L)a_i(L)$.

Then define $\bar{u}_i(x) = x^{f_i}\psi_i(1/x)$, $\bar{V}(x) = x^r R(1/x)$, $\bar{w}_i(x) = x^{k_i}a_i(1/x)$, where the bars are intended to refer to the true values for the model. Then defining $\bar{U}(x)$ to be the $n \times (n+m)$ matrix whose columns are equal to $u_i(x)$, $i = 1, \ldots, n+m$, and similarly $\bar{W}(x)$ to be $n \times (n+m)$ matrix whose columns are equal to $w_i(x)$, $i = 1, \ldots, n+m$, we can write

$$\bar{U}(x) = V(x)W(x). \tag{17}$$

We assume $\bar{U}(x)$ is known, and that Ψ_0 is of rank n. We also assume that no column of Ψ_0 is a zero vector. Indeed if this occurs for column j, signifying that the jth variable occurs only in lagged form in the equations, if the smallest lag were d, we would redefine x_{jt} as equal to the previous $x_{j(t-d)}$. At the same time we redefine f_j as equal to the previous $f_j - d$. We then consider the possibility of factorising (17) so that $V(x)$ is of degree r, and the ith column of $W(x)$ is of degree k_i in x. Clearly one possible factorisation is $\bar{U}(x) = \bar{V}(x)\bar{W}(x)$, where these correspond to the true model. We wish to establish conditions under which alternative factorisations are possible.

THEOREM 1. *If $\bar{U}(x)$ has more than one factorisation with the given specification then there is a root λ and a corresponding vector β such that $\beta' \bar{W}(\lambda) = 0$.*

If, conversely, there exist λ and β such that $\beta' \bar{W}(\lambda) = 0$, and the relevant factorisation condition (A1) stated below is satisfied, then more than one factorisation of the specified form is possible.

Proof. Consider the first proposition stated and assume that $\bar{U}(x) = \bar{V}(x)\bar{W}(x) = V(x)W(x)$, where $V(x) \neq \bar{V}(x)$. Suppose first that $V(x)$ has some latent root λ, not belonging to $\bar{V}(x)$, and that $\alpha'V(\lambda) = 0$, $\alpha'\bar{V}(\lambda) = \beta' \neq 0$. Then $\alpha'\bar{U}(x) = \alpha'V(\lambda)W(\lambda) = \alpha'\bar{V}(\lambda)\bar{W}(\lambda) = \beta'\bar{W}(\lambda) = 0$, i.e., β' is the required latent vector of $\bar{W}(\lambda)$.

Suppose now that $V(x)$ and $\bar{V}(x)$ have the latent root λ in common but $V(x)$ has a latent vector α corresponding to λ, which is not also the corresponding latent vector for $\bar{V}(x)$. Then the same argument can be used. Finally suppose more generally that λ is a multiple latent root for $V(x)$, that satisfies for some sets of latent vectors α_i, $i = 1, \ldots, s$

$$\sum_{i=0}^{j} \alpha_{(j-i+1)} V_i(\lambda)/i! \quad \text{for} \quad j = 0, \ldots, s-1, \tag{18}$$

and

$$\sum_{i=0}^{j} \alpha_{(j-i+1)} \bar{V}_i(\lambda)/i! = 0 \quad \text{for} \quad j = 0, \ldots, s-2,$$

but

$$\sum_{i=0}^{s} \alpha_{(s-i+1)} \bar{V}_i(\lambda)/i! = \beta \neq 0.$$

Now using the same sets of identities as those used to deduce equation (13), we can deduce from (18) that

$$\sum_{i=0}^{j} \alpha_{(j-i+1)} \bar{U}_i(\lambda)/i! = 0, \quad j = 0, \ldots, s-1. \tag{19}$$

But now using $\bar{U}_j(\lambda) = \sum_{i=0}^{j} C_i^j \bar{V}_{j-i} W_i$,

$$0 = \sum_{j=0}^{s-1} \alpha'_{(s-j+1)} \bar{U}_j(\lambda)/j! = \sum_{j=0}^{s-1} \sum_{i=0}^{j} \alpha'_{(s-j+1)} C_i^j \bar{V}_{(j-i)} W_i/j!$$

$$= \sum_{i=0}^{s-1} \left(\sum_{q=0}^{s-i} \alpha'_{s-i-q+1} \bar{V}_q/q! \right) W_i/i!, \quad \text{where } q = j - i,$$

$$= \left(\sum_{q=0}^{s-1} \alpha'_{s+1-q} \bar{V}_q/q! \right) \bar{W}_0,$$

since all the terms for $i \neq 0$ are zero.

Now $\bar{W}_0 = \bar{W}(\lambda)$, and so $\beta' \bar{W}(\lambda) = 0$, which again shows that β is the required latent vector.

Turning now to the second proposition in the statement of the theorem, we now show that if we define

$$U_s^*(\lambda) = \begin{bmatrix} \bar{U}(\lambda) & \bar{U}_1(\lambda) & \dots & \bar{U}_{s-1}(\lambda)/(s-1)! \\ 0 & \bar{U}(\lambda) & & \bar{U}_{s-2}(\lambda)/(s-2)! \\ \vdots & & & \\ 0 & 0 & & \bar{U}(\lambda) \end{bmatrix}$$

by analogy with $V_s^*(\lambda)$, then clearly any row in its left hand annihilator satisfies a set of equations of the form (19). If the maximum nullity of $U_s^*(\lambda)$ for all s is M, then M can be called the multiplicity of root λ in $\bar{U}(x)$, and we call a value of λ such that $M > 0$ a latent root of $\bar{U}(x)$. The sum of the multiplicities for all latent roots we call the total multiplicity of $\bar{U}(x)$.

We now prove the following lemma.

LEMMA. *If the total multiplicity of $\bar{U}(x)$ is greater than nr, and condition (A1) below is satisfied, then $\bar{U}(x)$ has more than one facotrisation.*

Proof. We consider the possibility of setting up a one-to-one correspondence between sets of equations of the form (19), and solutions of equation (20) below. We write $\bar{U}(x) = \sum_{i=0}^{f} \bar{U}_i x^{f-i}$, and

$$U_a^+ = \begin{bmatrix} 0 & I & 0 & \dots & 0 \\ 0 & 0 & I & & 0 \\ \vdots & & & & \\ 0 & 0 & 0 & & I \\ -\bar{U}'_f & -\bar{U}'_{f-1} & -\bar{U}'_{f-2} & & -\bar{U}'_1 \end{bmatrix},$$

$$U_b^+ = \begin{bmatrix} I & 0 & \cdots & 0 & 0 \\ 0 & I & & 0 & 0 \\ \vdots & & & & \\ 0 & 0 & & I & 0 \\ 0 & 0 & & 0 & \bar{U}_0' \end{bmatrix},$$

and note that all the zero and unit submatrices except those in the last row of U_b^+ are $n \times n$ square submatrices. U_a^+ and U_b^+ are $(fn+m) \times fn$ matrices. Then suppose H^+ and Λ satisfy

$$U_a^+ H^+ = U_b^+ H^+ \Lambda, \tag{20}$$

where Λ is a canonical form matrix and the columns of H^+ are generalised latent vectors with respect to (U_a^+, U_b^+).

Now pursuing the same kind of arguments as those used in deriving equation (12) of Section 2, we deduce that if Λ contains a classical submatrix of dimension s, and

$$H^+ = \begin{bmatrix} H_a \\ H_b \end{bmatrix},$$

where H_a has n rows, and if the columns of H_a, which correspond to the $s \times s$ classical submatrix are denoted by h_p, $p = 1, \ldots, s$, then

$$(h_1', h_2', \ldots, h_s')U_s^*(\lambda) = 0. \tag{21}$$

Thus the total multiplicity of $\bar{U}(x)$ is $\bar{M}$ if and only if Λ is an $\bar{M} \times \bar{M}$ square matrix. Suppose now that $\bar{M} > nr$, and that the $(nr) \times (nr)$ matrix Λ_1 is obtained from Λ by appropriately trimming its classical submatrices, and H_1^+ is defined so that it contains the same set of columns of H^+ as corresponds to the rows and columns of Λ which occur in Λ_1, so that

$$U_a^+ H_1^+ = U_b^+ H_1^+ \Lambda_1. \tag{22}$$

We consider first the case where $f = f_i$ for all i. Then in this case $\bar{U}_0 = \Psi_0$, and by assumption this is of rank n. Thus if we take any column of $\bar{U}_0$, and we take $n-1$ other columns and denote the resulting $n \times n$ matrix by $U^{(s)}$, we can choose the columns so that $U^{(s)}$ is non-singular. Now denote the corresponding submatrix of $\bar{U}(x)$ by $\bar{U}^{(s)}(x)$, and denote

$$\bar{U}^{(s)}(x)(U^{(s)})^{-1} = \sum_{i=0}^{f} U_i x^{f-i}. \tag{23}$$

Now by considering only those rows of the last block of rows in equations (22) which correspond to the columns of $U^{(s)}$, we see that we can write $U^+ H_1^+ = H_1^+ \Lambda_1$, where U^+ is defined as in the last section from the U_i

defined by (23). Now, using the results of the last section, if the following factorisation condition is satisfied:

$$H_1^+ = \begin{bmatrix} \tilde{H}_1 \\ \tilde{H}_2 \end{bmatrix} \tag{A1}$$

and $\tilde{H}_1$ is a square $(nr \times nr)$ non-singular matrix; then $V^+ = H_1 \Lambda_1 \tilde{H}_1^{-1}$ is well defined, and a corresponding factorisation can be found $\bar{U}^{(s)}(x)(U^{(s)})^{-1} = V(x)\bar{W}^{(s)}(x)$.

Note that $V(x)$ depends only on H_1^+ and Λ_1, but not upon the particular set of columns of $\bar{U}(x)$ selected to define $U^{(s)}$. Also, note that the condition (A1) does not depend on this selection.

Thus $\bar{U}^{(s)}(x) = V(x)\bar{W}^s(x)U^{(s)}$. Now taking any column of $\bar{U}^{(s)}(x)$, we can write $\bar{u}_i(x) = V(x)\bar{w}_i(x)$ and clearly the $\bar{w}_i(x)$ does not depend upon the selection defining $U^{(s)}$. So finally providing condition (A1) is satisfied, we must be able to find a factorisation $\bar{U}(x) = V(x)W(x)$, corresponding to Λ_1. Of course, by assumption $\bar{U}(x) = \bar{V}(x)\bar{W}(x)$, and so there is always at least one submatrix Λ_1, such that the factorisation condition is satisfied.

Now considering again the more general case where $f_i < f$ for some f. Consider a new $\bar{U}_e(x)$ matrix, derived from $\bar{U}(x)$ as follows. If $\bar{u}_i(x)$ is of degree $f_i < f$ then $\bar{U}_e(x)$ contains two columns defined as $\bar{u}_i(x)(x^{f-f_i}-1)$ and $\bar{u}_i(x)(x^{f-f_i}+1)$. If $f = f_i$, $\bar{U}_e(x)$ contains $\bar{u}_i(x)$. Note that every column of $\bar{U}_e(x)$ is of degree f. Also if we define

$$U_{se}^*(\lambda) = \begin{bmatrix} \bar{U}(\lambda) & \bar{U}_{1e}(\lambda) & \cdots & \bar{U}_{(s-1)e}(\lambda) \\ 0 & \bar{U}_e(\lambda) & & \bar{U}_{(s-2)e}(\lambda) \\ \vdots & & & \\ 0 & 0 & & \bar{U}_e(\lambda) \end{bmatrix}$$

by considering the separate columns of equations of the form

$$\sum_{i=0}^{j} h'_{(j-i+1)}\bar{U}_{ie}(\lambda)/i! = 0, \qquad j = 0, \ldots, s-1$$

we can show that

$$(h'_1, h'_2, \ldots, h'_s)U_{se}^*(\lambda) = 0$$

if and only if

$$(h'_1, h'_2, \ldots, h'_s)U_s^*(\lambda) = 0.$$

Thus $\bar{U}_e(x)$ has total nullity greater than nr, if and only if $\bar{U}(x)$ has total nullity greater than nr. It also follows that if $H, \Lambda, H_1, \Lambda_1$ are all defined with respect to $\bar{U}(x)$, then if condition (A2) is satisfied we can factorise

$$\bar{U}_e(x) = V(x)\bar{W}_e(x).$$

Now considering the separate columns of $\bar{U}_e(x)$, we must have

$$\bar{u}_i(x) = V(x)w_i(x) \qquad \text{if} \quad f_i = f$$

and

$$\bar{u}_i(x)(x^{f-f_i} - 1) = V(x)w_{ia}(x)$$
$$\bar{u}_i(x)(x^{f-f_i} + 1) = V(x)w_{ib}(x),$$

if

$$f_i < f.$$

Thus if $f_i < f$,

$$V(x)[w_{ia}(x) + w_{ib}(x) - x^{f-f_i}(w_{ib}(x) - w_{ia}(x))] = 0.$$

Now $V_0 = I$, so that for sufficiently large x $V(x)$ is non-singular. So for sufficiently large x

$$w_{ia}(x) + w_{ib}(x) = x^{f-f_i}(w_{ib}(x) - w_{ia}(x)).$$

Clearly since $w_{ia}(x) + w_{ib}(x)$ is of degree k in x, $w_{ib}(x) - w_{ia}(x) = w_{ic}(x)$ say is of degree $f_i - r$ and then $\bar{u}_i(x) = V(x)w_{ic}(x)$, and we have a factorisation with $w_{ic}(x)$ of the specified degree. An exception to the stated result occurs with one special form for Λ, which gives no multiple factorisation. This is where there is only one latent root of multiplicity Q, and Λ is a $Q \times Q$ classical submatrix. In this case there is only one possible way of trimming to form Λ_1.

To prove the second half of Theorem 1 we must now prove that, if $\bar{W}(x)$ has a latent root, $\bar{U}(x)$ is of total nullity greater than nr. Suppose that $\beta'\bar{W}(\lambda) = 0$. A simple case to dispose of first is where λ is not a latent root of $\bar{V}(x)$, for then $\bar{V}(\lambda)$ is non-singular, and $\alpha' = \beta'(\bar{V}(\lambda))^{-1}$, is a latent vector of $\bar{U}(x)$ corresponding to a latent root λ. This together with the nr latent vectors of $\bar{V}(x)$ ensures that total nullity of $\bar{U}(x)$ is greater than nr.

Now suppose that λ is a latent root of $\bar{V}(x)$, and that $S = s_1$ is the largest λ exponent. From the definition of $V_s^*(\lambda)$ from the previous section it follows that

$$(\alpha_0', \alpha_1', \ldots, \alpha_S')V_{(S+1)}^*(\lambda) = 0 \tag{24}$$

has no solutions for which $\alpha_S \neq 0$.

We consider the possibility of solving equations of the form

$$(\alpha_0', \alpha_1', \ldots, \alpha_S')V_{(S+1)}^*(\lambda) = (0, 0, \ldots, \beta'). \tag{25}$$

Note that if we consider the right hand annihilator of $V_{(S+1)}^*(\lambda)$, denoted in the previous section by $\Psi^{(S+1)}$, the fact that $V_{(S+1)}^*(\lambda)$ has the same nullity as

$V_S^*(\lambda)$ ensures that we can write

$$\Psi^{(S+1)} = \begin{bmatrix} \Psi^{(S)} \\ 0 \end{bmatrix}$$

where the zero matrix has n rows.

But a necessary and sufficient condition that a set of linear equations $x'A = y'$ has a solution is that if B is the right hand annihilator of A then $y'B = 0$.

Applying this to the equations (25) we see that a vector satisfying (25) exists since

$$(0, 0, \ldots, 0, \beta')\Psi^{(S+1)} = 0.$$

Furthermore, any such solution gives a unique α_S, since if two different solutions had different values for α_S, then the difference would satisfy (24) with $\alpha_S \neq 0$, which would contradict the condition that S is the largest λ exponent.

Then from

$$\sum_{j=0}^{p} \alpha'_{(p-j)} \bar{U}_j(\lambda)/j! = \sum_{i=0}^{p} \left(\sum_{q=0}^{p-i} \alpha'_{(p-i-q)} \bar{V}_q(\lambda)/q! \right) \bar{W}_i(\lambda)/i! = 0, \qquad (26)$$

for $0 \leqslant p \leqslant S$, we deduce that $\bar{U}(x)$ has a largest λ exponenent equal to $S+1$, unless $\alpha_0 = 0$, for the solution of equation (25). If, however, $\alpha_0 = 0$, if we write $\alpha_i^* = \alpha_{(i-1)}$, we have a set of solutions of the equations (26) for $0 \leqslant p \leqslant S-1$. But from

$$\sum_{j=1}^{S} \alpha_{j-1}^{*'} V_{S-j}(\lambda)/(S-j)! = \beta'$$

it is clear that α_i^* is not a latent vector corresponding to an $S \times S$ classical Λ submatrix of V^+. It is also possible that $\alpha_i = 0$, $1 \leqslant i < j$, for the solutions of (25), and a similar argument shows a latent vector $\bar{U}(x)$ has then been found corresponding to a classical λ submatrix of order $S-j+1$. This can occur only if $j = S - s_i$, for some i, as will be established in Section 5. But in any case the existence of an extra latent vector of $\bar{U}(x)$ has been discovered, corresponding to the latent vector, β, of $\bar{W}(x)$, or correspondingly that equations of the form (20) are satisfied with Λ of order $Q > nr$. This completes the proof.

4 FAILURE OF THE RANK CONDITIONS ON THE FIRST DERIVATIVE MATRIX

Suppose in the notation of Section 1 that $\partial g/\partial \xi$ is not of full rank, so that

$$\frac{\partial g}{\partial \xi'} \xi^* = 0 \qquad (27)$$

for some non-zero vector ξ^*. In the particular model of this paper, the relation between the coefficients $\Psi(L)$ (corresponding to $g(\xi)$), and the coefficients of $R(L)$ and $A(L)$ (corresponding to ξ), or equivalently the coefficients of $U(x)$, and of $V(x)$ and $W(x)$ can be represented by equations of the form (4), but a more powerful approach is to use the relationship in the generator form $\bar{U}(x) = V(x)W(x)$, where the $U(x)$, $V(x)$, and $W(x)$ are assumed to be of standard form specified in Section 3, i.e., $V_0 = I$, some set of coefficients in U_0 may also be fixed *a priori*, and the ith column of $W(x)$ is of degree $k_i = f_i - r$.

Then (26) can be written in the form

$$V(x)W^*(x) + V^*(x)W(x) = 0 \qquad (28)$$

where $V^*(x)$ and $W^*(x)$ have non-zero coefficients corresponding to ξ^* wherever $V(x)$ and $W(x)$ have non-standardised coefficients. Since $V_0 = I$, it follows that $V^*(x)$ is of degree $(r-1)$. Now again using $V_0 = I$ we see that the ith column of $W^*(x)$ is of degree $k_i - 1$. Clearly $V^*(x) \neq 0$ identically since then $W^*(x) = 0$ identically and so $\xi^* = 0$.

Now define

$$\tilde{V}(x) = V(x) - V^*(x), \qquad \tilde{W}(x) = W^*(x) + W(x)$$

and note that $\tilde{V}(x)$ and $\tilde{W}(x)$ satisfy the restrictions originally applied to $V(x)$ and $W(x)$ and $V(x)\tilde{W}(x) = \tilde{V}(x)W(x)$.

THEOREM 2. *A necessary and sufficient condition that $\partial g/\partial \xi'$ is of less than full rank is that $V(x)$ and $W(x)$ have latent root in common.*

Proof. Suppose that $V(x)$ and $W(x)$ have a common root λ, and $V(\lambda)\delta = 0$, $\beta'W(\lambda) = 0$. Then $V(x)\delta = (V(x) - V(\lambda))\delta$ is a vector which is not identically zero, with elements each of which is a polynomial in x, and each polynomial is zero when $x = \lambda$. Thus we can write $V(x)\delta = (x - \lambda)\gamma_1(x)$, where $\gamma_1(x)$ is a vector of degree $(r-1)$ in x.

Similarly, $\beta'W(x) = (x - \lambda)\gamma_2(x)'$ and $\gamma_2(x)$ is a vector of polynomials whose ith element is of degree $k_i - 1$ in x. Write $W^*(x) = \delta\gamma_2'(x)$, and $V^*(x) = -\gamma_1(x)\beta'$, and note that these satisfy equations (28), and have the correct non-zero form. If λ is complex it is easy to show that either Real$(-\gamma_1(x)\beta')$ or Imag$(-\gamma_1(x)\beta')$ provides a suitable $V^*(x)$.

Conversely, suppose that $V(x)\tilde{W}(x) = \tilde{V}(x)W(x)$ and $V(x) \neq \tilde{V}(x)$.

Suppose first that $V(x)$ has a latent root λ which does not belong to $\tilde{V}(x)$, and $\alpha'V(\lambda) = 0$. Then write $\alpha'\tilde{V}(\lambda) = \beta' \neq 0$, and it follows that $\alpha'V(\lambda)\tilde{W}(\lambda) = \beta'W(\lambda) = 0$. Thus β' is a latent vector of $W(\lambda)$, and λ is a common latent root of $V(x)$ and $W(x)$. Now suppose that $V(x)$ and $\tilde{V}(x)$ have a latent root λ in common, and have a set of latent vectors, h_i, $i = 1, \ldots, s$, in common satisfying equations of the form (12) for both $V(x)$ and $\tilde{V}(x)$, but $V(x)$ has a succeeding latent vector $h_{(s+1)}$, which does not belong to $\tilde{V}'(x)$. Then if $\beta' = \sum_{i=0}^{s} h'_{(s-i+1)} \tilde{V}_i(\lambda)/i!$ we can use an argument similar to those of the last section to show that $\beta' W(\lambda) = 0$. This completes the proof.

5 LOCAL UNIDENTIFIABILITY

The model is locally unidentifiable if in any neighbourhood of the true value there is a solution of $\bar{U}(x) = V(x)W(x)$, different from $\bar{V}(x)$, $\bar{W}(x)$. It follows from the discussion of Fisher (1967) and Rothenberg (1971) that a necessary condition for this is that $\partial g/\partial \xi'$ is of less than full rank, at $\xi = \bar{\xi}$, and so that $\bar{V}(x)$ and $\bar{W}(x)$ have a latent root in common. However this is not a sufficient condition for local unidentifiability. To consider this we find conditions for the uniqueness of the factorisation corresponding to a given choice of Λ_1 in Section 3. Consider the equation $V^+ \tilde{H}_1 = \tilde{H}_1 \Lambda_1$. Given the choice of Λ_1, V^+ will not be uniquely determined by this, if a linear transformation of $\tilde{H}_1$ can be introduced which changes V^+. (Note that in discussing local identifiability we are only interested in small changes in H_1; so that we are not interested in alternative choices of canonical matrices Λ_1 which correpond to discontinuous changes in V^+.) Now from $U_a^+ H_1^+ = U_b^+ H_1^+ \Lambda_1$, general scalar multiplications of the set of latent vectors corresponding to a given classical submatrix are permissible, but this does not affect V^+. However, if Λ_1 contains multiple roots then more general linear transformations of H_1^+ are permissible. If $U_a^+ - \lambda U_b^+$ has nullity greater than one, then the equations $(U_a^+ - \lambda U_b^+)h^+ = 0$ define a linear subspace of dimension equal to the nullity. Also if we consider a set of equations of the form

$$(U_a^+ - \lambda U_b^+)h_1^+ = 0,$$

$$(U_a^+ - \lambda B_b^+)h_j^+ = h_{j-1}^+, \qquad j = 2, \ldots, s,$$

corresponding to an $s \times s$ classical λ submatrix of Λ_1, then

$$\alpha_j = \sum_{i=1}^{j} k_i h_{j+1-i}^+, \qquad j = 1, \ldots, s, \tag{29}$$

satisfies the set of equations, for any vector of scalars $k_i, i = 1, \ldots, s$. Also if a set of β_i satisfy a set of equations,

$$(U_a^+ - \lambda U_b^+)\beta_1 = 0, \tag{30}$$

$$(U_a^+ - \lambda U_b^+)\beta_j = \beta_{j-1}, \qquad j = 2, \ldots, p,$$

$$\alpha_j = k_1 \beta_j + k_2 h_{j-q}^+, \qquad j = 1, \ldots, p, \tag{31}$$

satisfies equations (24) if $q \geq p - s$, provided that we define $h_i^+ = 0$, if $i \leq 0$. Now suppose that there are $Q > nr$ latent vectors for $\bar{U}(x)$, so that we can write $U_a^+ H^+ = U_b^+ H^+ \Lambda$, where Λ is $Q \times Q$, and subject to factorisation conditions, there is more than one factorisation of $\bar{U}(x)$.

Then if there are multiple roots, all the preceding linear transformations can be summarised by noting that if the $Q \times Q$ non-singular matrix K has the property that

$$K^{-1} \Lambda K = \Lambda, \tag{32}$$

then we also have $U_a^+ H^+ K = U_b^+ H^+ K(K^{-1}\Lambda K) = U_b^+ H^+ K\Lambda$.

Thus if $H_e^+ = H^+ K$, $U_a^+ H_e^+ = U_b^+ H_e^+ \Lambda$. Thus any K satisfying

$$\Lambda K = K\Lambda, \tag{33}$$

gives a linear transformation of H^+, which corresponds to the same $\bar{U}(x)$. Any K satisfying (33) will be called a compatible transformation.

Now assuming that the rows of Λ are ordered so that it is block diagonal, with each block corresponding to a single root, it is easily seen by writing (33) in suffix notation that K is block diagonal in the same way. If we write

$$K = \begin{bmatrix} K_{11} & 0 & \cdots & 0 \\ 0 & K_{22} & & 0 \\ \vdots & & & \\ 0 & 0 & & K_{dd} \end{bmatrix}$$

and we consider the detail structure of K_{ii}, assuming that this is the block which corresponds to the latent root λ, we write

$$K_{ii} = \begin{bmatrix} E_{11} & E_{12} & \cdots & E_{1N} \\ E_{21} & E_{22} & & E_{2N} \\ \vdots & & & \\ E_{N1} & E_{N2} & & E_{NN} \end{bmatrix}$$

where N is the nullity of $(\Lambda - \lambda I)$, i.e., N is equal to the total number of classical λ submatrices. The diagonal E_{ii} is $s_i \times s_i$ where s_i is the Segre characteristic number defined in Section 2, equal to the dimension of the ith classical submatrix. Note that $s_i \geqslant s_j$ if $i < j$, and $s_1 = S$. Then it can be shown by considering the equation $(\Lambda - \lambda I)K = K(\Lambda - \lambda I)$ that each E_{ij} is a Toeplitz matrix such that if the (p, q) element of E_{ij} is E_{ij}^{pq} then $E_{ij}^{pq} = e(p - q)$, and that $e(s) = 0$ if either $s > s_i - s_j$ or $s > 0$. From this we deduce that if we define a selection matrix P, which is $Q \times (Q - h)$ and obtained by deleting h successive columns from I_Q; in fact, the columns $S - h + 1$ to S, where $h \leqslant S - s_2$, then KP has zero rows for rows $S - h + 1$ to S. It follows that we can write

$$KP = PK^*. \tag{34}$$

Note that P can be regarded as trimming the columns of K which correspond to the last latent vectors of the set corresponding to an $S \times S$ classical λ submatrix.

K^* is a square matrix derived from K by omitting this same set of rows and columns.

More generally, if we take a selection matrix P, satisfying an equation of the form (34), we will prove that when applied to Λ to produce Λ_1, it leads to a unique V^+, provided that K^* has the same structure as K. If we write $\Lambda_1 = P'\Lambda P$, we can check that such a P has the property of trimming the last columns of classical submatrices referred to at the end of Section 2. But if we consider (34) applied to each block K_{ii} of K, taking account of the form of the E_{ij}, a necessary and sufficient condition for (34) is that each trimmed classical λ submatrix in Λ_1 has a dimension equal to the maximal λ exponent in Λ_1, i.e., if S^* is the maximal λ exponent in Λ_1, then all the trimmed classical λ submatrices should have dimension equal to S^*. Note that S^* need not be the same for all latent roots.

From $\Lambda_1 = P'\Lambda P$, and $H_1^+ = H^+ P$ where P has nr columns, following a compatible linear transformation of H^+, we would have a new $H_e^+ = H^+ K$, and applying the same selection matrix to derive H_{e1}^+, we have $H_{e1}^+ = H^+ KP = H^+ PK^*$, from $(34) = H_1^+ K^*$.

Now writing $\tilde{H}_{e1}$ for the first nr rows of H_{e1}^+, we have $\tilde{H}_{e1} = \tilde{H}_1 K^*$, but by assumption K^* is a compatible transformation of Λ_1 so that $\Lambda_1 = K^{*1}\Lambda_1 K^*$, and $V^+ = \tilde{H}_{e1}\Lambda_1\tilde{H}_{e1}^{-1}$, and so $V(x)$ remains unchanged by the transformation K of H^+. On the other hand, if P^* is an arbitrary $Q \times (nr)$ selection matrix not satisfying (36); then we would have had $H_{e1}^+ = H^+ KP^*$, and denoting the first nr rows of H^+ by $\tilde{H}$, we have $\tilde{H}_{e1} = \tilde{H}KP^*$, and $V_e^+ = \tilde{H}_{e1}\Lambda_1\tilde{H}_{e1}^{-1}$, but now as K varies in the neighbourhood of I, the values of V_e^+ vary, so that the factorisation is non-unique, and so $V(x)$ and $W(x)$ are not locally identified.

THEOREM 3. *The model is locally unidentified only if $\bar{W}(x)$ and $\bar{V}(x)$ have a common root λ and either (i) the nullity of $\bar{W}(\lambda)$, p, say, is greater than N_S, the number of classical λ submatrices of maximal dimension S, or (ii) a set of conditions of number $(N_S - p + 1)$ are satisfied.*

Proof. For simplicity we now drop the bars in referring to the true model coefficients. Suppose that λ is a common latent root of $W(x)$ and $V(x)$, and that in V^+ we have a maximal exponent S associated with λ, and that the nullity of $W(\lambda)$ is p, i.e., the rank of $W(\lambda)$ is $n - p$. Suppose β is any corresponding latent vector, so that

$$\beta' W(\lambda) = 0. \tag{35}$$

Considering now as at the end of Section 3 the solution of equation (25), we note that Λ has a classical λ submatrix of dimension $(S+1)$ unless $\alpha_0 = 0$ is the solution of (25). A necessary and sufficient condition that $\alpha_0 = 0$, is that there should be a solution of

$$(\alpha_1', \alpha_2', \ldots, \alpha_S')V_S^*(\lambda) = (0, \ldots, 0, \beta'), \tag{36}$$

and applying the right hand annihilator of $V_S^*(\lambda)$ a necessary and sufficient condition for this is

$$\beta'\Psi_{SS} = 0. \tag{37}$$

Since Ψ_{SS} is of rank N_S

$$(\Psi_{SS} : W(\lambda)) \tag{38}$$

is at most of rank $N_S + n - p$, so that if $p > N_S$, then at least one non-zero β can be found satisfying (37) and $\beta'W(\lambda) = 0$. If on the other hand $p \leqslant N_S$, the rank of (38) will be less than n, if $(N_S - p + 1)$ conditions are satisfied referred to in the statement of the theorem. However from (35) and (36) we have

$$\sum_{j=0}^{q} \alpha_{(q-j+1)}' U_j(\lambda)/j! = 0, \qquad q = 0, \ldots, S-1 \tag{39}$$

and also that

$$\sum_{j=0}^{q} \alpha_{(q-j+1)}' V_j(\lambda)/j! = 0, \qquad q = 0, \ldots, S-2. \tag{40}$$

Equation (40) shows that the α_s are a linear combination of the rows of $\Phi^{(S-1)}$. However, equation (36) shows that these latent vectors cannot be associated with a classical submatrix of Λ_1 of dimension S. If $N_{(S-1)} > N_S$, clearly corresponding to β, we may have a classical λ submatrix of Λ of dimension S. On the other hand, if $N_{(S-1)} = N_S$, then the only solutions of (40) correspond to solutions of (36) with $\beta = 0$, or have $\alpha_1 = 0$. That is, they correspond to a classical λ submatrix of Λ_1 of dimension $S-2$ or less, with a corresponding classical submatrix of Λ of one extra dimension. We can then say that this submatrix of Λ is being trimmed back to a dimension which is less than S, the largest λ exponent of $V(x)$. If the dimension of the classical λ submatrix of Λ_1 is s, then clearly $s = s_i$ for some i.

In a similar way it can be shown that if $W(x)$ has multiple roots in the sense that for some set of β_j

$$\sum_{i=0}^{j} \beta_{(j-i+1)} W_i(\lambda) = 0, \qquad j = 0, \ldots, q,$$

then $U(x)$ will have a classical λ submatrix of dimension $S+q$, unless certain rank conditions are satisfied by the $V(x)$ and $W(x)$ coefficients.

Now returning to the earlier discussion of uniqueness it is clear that if a comparison is made between Λ and Λ_1, Λ_1 is obtained by trimming all classical λ submatrices of $U(x)$ of dimension greater than S to dimension S, where S is the largest λ exponent in V^+, provided that the stated conditions (i) and (ii) of Theorem 3 are unsatisfied, i.e., provided $N_S \geqslant p$ and (38) is of full rank for each λ. Thus unless conditions (i) or (ii) are satisfied the solution is locally unique.

6 SOME SPECIAL CASES AND PRIOR PROBABILITIES

If we pursue the idea put forward in Section 1 that conditions for lack of identifiability are unlikely to be exactly satisfied, we should consider the case where the constraints are satisfied up to an ε, since in practice in finite samples with ε sufficiently small, the asymptotic behaviour in the unidentified model is a good approximation to the finite sample behaviour. Considering first in this way the case of multiple optima, we note that if $\beta' W(\lambda) = 0$, we must have $W(\lambda)$ of rank $\leqslant j-1$, which requires $(m+1)$ determinants to be zero. Since we choose λ so that one of these is zero, we have m implicit constraints giving *a priori* probability of $O(\varepsilon^m)$ for multiple solutions. Clearly unidentifiability is more probable for small m. Consider now the probability of multiple roots. We now require that for every square $n \times n$ submatrix of $W(\lambda)$, $W_i(\lambda)$ say, det $W_i(\lambda) = 0$ has multiple roots. This requires two conditions for every such matrix, and it is sufficient to consider $(m+1)$ such matrices. Subtracting one constraint for the choice of λ, we have $(2m+1)$ constraints *or* $(m+1)$ in addition to those required to give a single root. On the other hand if $W(\lambda)$ is of rank $(n-2)$, taking some basic square matrix of dimension $(n-2) \times (n-2)$, and requiring every $(n-1) \times (n-1)$ matrix containing it to have determinant zero, we have $2(m+2)$ constraints. This gives three extra constraints for the Segre characteristic to be $(1, 1)$ rather than (2). It is clear that the most likely unidentified case will be that where $W(x)$ has a single root, and only this will be considered from now on.

Consider now the probability of failure of the full rank condition for the derivative matrix. This requires that a root λ of $V(x)$ is equal to a root λ of $W(x)$. This is one extra constraint in addition to the m constraints required for multiple solutions. Considering now local unidentifiability, noting that we only consider the case where $p = 1$, we see that the most likely form of Λ_1 is the diagonal form, where all the roots of V^+ are single. In this case $N_S = N_1 = 1$, and only one extra constraint is required for local unidentifiability.

Thus in these simple cases, where $p = N_S = 1$ only one extra constraint is required to move from failure of full rank condition to local unidentifiability. Note however, that in a sense this is a difference of a whole order of magnitude, meaning that for small ε the great majority of cases of type (iii) are locally identified.

There is one rather special case of some interest. This is where r the degree of $R(L)$ has been underspecified, so that the true model has an $R^*(L)$ which is of degree $r^* > r$. Thus

$$\Psi(L) = R^*(L)A^*(L).$$

Suppose we first consider factorising $R^*(L) = R_1(L)R_2(L)$, where $R_1(L)$ is of degree r, and $R_2(L)$ of degree $r^* - r$. Using the factorising discussion of Section 2 there will usually be several ways of making this factorisation. Then $\Psi(L) = R_1(L)R_2(L)A^*(L) = R_1(L)A_1(L)$ if $A_1(L) = R_2(L)A^*(L)$.

There are clearly as many ways of stating a valid factorisation of $\Psi(L)$ into $R(L)$ and $A(L)$ of the stated degrees as there are ways of factorising $R^*(L)$ into $R_1(L)$ and $R_2(L)$ of degrees r and $r^* - r$, quite apart from the possibility that $A^*(L)$ has a latent root. Ignoring the question of reality of the roots and the satisfaction of the basic factorisation condition, if all the latent roots of $R(L)$ are single, the number of alternative factorisations is $C_{rn}^{r^*n}$, so that in estimation it may require considerable computer time to locate all corresponding multiple estimates (for example, local optima of the likelihood function).

The condition that the full rank condition fails (assuming that $A^*(L)$ has no latent root) is that $R_1(L)$ and $R_2(L)$ have a latent root in common. Thus $R^*(L)$ has a multiple latent root. (The same conclusion was reached in the single equation case in Sargan and Mehta (1983).) Note that the same problem of using likelihood ratio tests to test the degree of r arises here as in Sargan and Mehta (1983), because of the presence of multiple solutions, and that a test similar to the three part division test of that paper can be used to solve this problem.

7   ZERO ROOTS AND IDENTIFICATION

Although common roots appear unlikely *a priori* for general values of the roots, the special case where the roots are zero requires further consideration. Given that the econometrician has no *a priori* certainty of the maximum lags in his model, it appears very possible that at least for testing purposes he might specify models with maximum lags which are too large in the sense that k_i is such that $a_{ik_i} = 0$ for some i. Let us write $\tilde{W} = W(0)$; the ith column of $\tilde{W}$ is a_{ik_i}. From $\beta' W(0) = \beta' \tilde{W}$, if $\tilde{W}$ has rank less than n then there is a zero latent root of $W(x)$. Similarly there is a zero latent root to $V(x)$ if R_r is of less than full rank. If both R_r is singular and $\tilde{W}$ is of less than full rank then the first derivative matrix is not of full rank, but the model is still locally identifiable unless $R_r\tilde{W}$ is of rank less than $n-1$. The model has multiple solutions if $\tilde{W}$ is not of full rank.

Writing $\tilde{U} = U(0) = R_r \tilde{W}$ a sufficient condition (Hannan, 1975) that the set of equations $\Psi(L)x_t = S(L)e_t$ is identified without taking account of the factorisation condition, is that $(\tilde{U}:S_s)$ is of full rank.

Thus a sequence of sufficient conditions for identification is obtained by requiring (i) that $(\tilde{U}:S_s)$ is of rank n, (ii) that $W(x)$ has no latent root, (iii) the normal simultaneous equations identification conditions that the only matrix lag polynomial of the form $HA(L)$, where H is a square matrix, which satisfies a set of linear or non-linear *a priori* constraints, is given by $H = I$, where $A(L)$ has B_0 non-singular but not now restricted to unit matrix. These conditions are by no means necessary, but this paper will not attempt to discuss the problem of identification where either (i) or (ii) fails, but the model is identified by overidentifying constraints on the coefficients of $A(L)$.

Finally, if (i) and (ii) are satisfied it might be possible to identify the model by using Hatanaka conditions specifying that some variables do not appear in some equations in either current or lagged form, and that the overall lags in each equation are the minimum consistent with the preceding. Again we can achieve sufficient conditions which are similar to those of Hatanaka (1975) but these are by no means necessary.

8 ALTERNATIVE APPROACHES AND GENERAL CONCLUSION

The algebra presented here is different from that presented in much of the control theory literature (for example, Rosenbrock, 1970), in particular in relying upon the canonical form of the matrix polynomials for its results. An alternative approach using the concepts of left divisor (MacDuffee, 1946) gives some of the results of this paper easily. In particular it is clear that $\bar{V}(x)$ is the unique greatest left divisor of $\bar{U}(x)$ if $\bar{W}(x)$ is left prime, which in turn follows from the condition that $\bar{W}(x)$ has no left hand latent vector. However, the possibility of refactoring with polynomials of the specified degrees does depend upon a factorisation condition equivalent to that (Condition A1) of Theorem 1. The discussions of Section 4 and 5 do not seem easily proved by direct methods.

The result on failure of Jacobian conditions of Theorem 2, is, in a sense, the most important, since if this fails the resulting estimates of the model will not possess the usual asymptotic normality properties. But clearly any failure of identification is of importance to the econometrician.

REFERENCES

Deistler, M. (1976). *International Economic Review*, **17**, 26.

Deistler, M. and Shrader, J. (1977). Paper presented at Vienna European Econometric Society Meeting.

Fisher, F. M. (1967). *The Identification Problem in Econometrics*. McGraw-Hill, New York.

Hannan, E. J. (1971). *Econometrica*, **39**, 751.

Hannan, E. J. (1975). *Annals of Statistics*, **3**, 975.

Hatanaka, M. (1975). *International Economic Review*, **16**, 545.

MacDuffee, C. C. (1946). *The Theory of Matrices*. Chelsea Publishing Company, New York.

Perlis, S. (1952). *Theory of Matrices*. Addison-Wesley, Cambridge.

Rosenbrock, H. H. (1970). *State Space and Multivariable Theory*. Nelson, London.

Rothenberg, T. J. (1971). *Econometrica*, **39**, 577.

Sargan, J. D. (1961). *Econometrica*, **29**, 414.

Sargan, J. D. (1975a). *L.S.E. Econometrics Programme Discussion Paper A1*.

Sargan, J. D. (1975b). *L.S.E. Econometrics Programme Discussion Paper A2*.

Sargan, J. D. (1978). *L.S.E. Econometrics Programme Discussion Paper A17*.

Sargan, J. D. and Mehta, F. (1983). *Econometrica*, **51**.

Turnbull, H. W. and Aitken, A. C. (1932). *An Introduction to the Theory of Canonical Matrices*. Blackie, London.